hungry ghosts

Mao's Secret Famine

JASPER BECKER

THE FREE PRESS

New York   London   Toronto   Sydney   Singapore

THE FREE PRESS
A Division of Simon & Schuster Inc.
1230 Avenue of the Americas
New York, NY 10020

First Published in Great Britain by John Murray (Publishers) Ltd.

The Free Press and colophon are trademarks
of Simon & Schuster Inc.

Manufactured in the United States of America

10 9 8 7 6 5 4 3 2 1

Library of Congress Cataloging-in-Publication Data

Becker, Jasper.
    Hungry ghosts: Mao's secret famine / Jasper Becker.
       p.   cm.
    Includes bibliographical references and index.
    ISBN 0–684–83457–X
    1. Famines—China. 2. Food supply—China. 3. Mao, Tse-Tung,
1893–1976. I. Title.
    HC430.F3B33 1997
    363.8'0951'09045—dc20

                                        96–32803
                                             CIP

ISBN 0–684–83457–X

For Ru who supplied me with
tea and sympathy

Contents

Illustrations

The author and publisher would like to thank David King for
permission to reproduce Plates 1 and 16.

Foreword

ONE OF THE most remarkable things about the famine which occurred in China between 1958 and 1962 was that for over twenty years, no one was sure whether it had even taken place. Whatever else the Communists in China might have done, it was widely assumed that they had at least fed their vast population and had ended China's seemingly perennial famines. Then, in the mid-1980s, American demographers were able to examine the population statistics which had been released when China launched her open-door policy in 1979. Their conclusion was startling: at least 30 million people had starved to death, far more than anyone, including the most militant critics of the Chinese Communist Party, had ever imagined.

Why, and how, did such a cataclysm take place? Who was to blame? How was it kept secret for so long? And what was life like in the countryside? How did people behave and how did they survive?

This book is an attempt to seek answers to these questions. Inside China, the famine is rarely mentioned or discussed, and much of the story remains shrouded in secrecy. In the official view, there were merely three years of natural disasters: the real disaster took place later, during the Cultural Revolution, when senior Communist leaders were persecuted. Yet in the last few years, a growing number of Chinese living abroad have written memoirs that shed more light on the subject. It has become clear that the greatest trauma suffered by the Chinese people was indeed the famine, not the Cultural Revolution. However, most of these memoirs are by intellectuals who, during the famine, were either in the cities or in prison camps and so knew little about the fate of the vast majority of the Chinese population – the peasants. It was the peasants who were the chief victims of the famine but peasants do not write books, or make films, and rarely have a chance to talk to outsiders. Even those who obtain official permission to carry out research in China's countryside are rarely, if ever, allowed to speak freely to peasants. Invariably, local officials have coached the peasant beforehand on what to say and insist on being present at the interview. Often, too, they interrupt to talk on behalf of the peasants who, in any case, may well speak a dialect unintelligible to outsiders.

For those who were in the countryside at the time, the horror of the famine is indelibly imprinted on their memories. As the dissident Wei Jingsheng has written, peasants talk of those days as if they had lived through an apocalypse. Even after three decades, memories are still fresh, as became clear when I started to find people who had then been in the countryside but who were now living outside China. Advertisements placed in the overseas Chinese press in 1994 brought hundreds of responses, ranging from a few scribbled lines to accounts twenty or thirty pages long. I visited some of those who replied, at first in Britain and later in the United States, Hong Kong and eventually Dharamsala in India where I met Tibetans who had fled to the Dalai Lama's place of exile. Then, armed with a clearer picture of what had happened, I travelled around rural areas of Henan, Anhui and Sichuan and talked to older peasants who had survived the famine.

The background to the famine is drawn from the growing body of academic work on Chinese agriculture. I was also fortunate in being able to find written sources to substantiate the cruelties that eyewitnesses had described. The relative freedom allowed to obscure publishing houses in the provinces in recent years has meant that a surprising amount of material about the famine has become available. In addition, Chinese intellectuals who went into exile after 1989 were able to provide a number of official documents about events in Henan and Anhui which offered detailed facts and figures.

Even so, many pieces of the jigsaw puzzle are still missing. Knowledge of events at the highest levels of the Communist Party at key moments is often sketchy, making it difficult to understand clearly why things happened as they did. Much data about death totals is also absent and it is hard to be sure of the reliability of what has come to light. Even today Chinese statistics are rarely coherent, and the central government frequently complains about the regularity with which the lower levels of the administration falsify figures. As Walter Mallory wrote in 1926 of a request for the 'bottom facts' about an earlier famine in China, 'There is no bottom in China, and no facts.' A fuller account of the famine may have to wait until the Party's own archives are open to researchers but this is unlikely to occur so long as those who share responsibility for the famine remain in power. Lord Acton once spoke of the 'undying penalty which history has the power to inflict on the wrong': it is no surprise that the Communist Party believes its control over the past is the key to its future.

Acknowledgements

I WOULD LIKE to thank the following for their help: John Ackerly; Alex and Moira; Robbie Barnett; Dr Alfred Chan, Huron College, Canada; Jung Chang; Madhusudan Chaubey; Chen Yizi, Center for Modern China, Princeton University; Nien Cheng; Chi Chunghuang; Robert Delfs; Ding Shu; Guy Dinmore, Reuters; Professor Edward Friedman, University of Wisconsin; Fu Hua; Ge Yang; The Great Britain-China Centre; John Halliday; Dr Jeya Henry, Oxford Brookes University, Oxford; Martha Higgins; Hong Zhen; Peter and Kathleen Hopkirk; Dr Jayewardene; Stanley Karnow; Dr Benjamin Y. Lee; Lee Yee; Li Yikai; Liu Binyan; Tim and Alison Luard; Clare McDermott, Reuters; Colina McDougall; Jonathan Mirsky, *The Times*; Robin Munro, Human Rights Watch Asia, Hong Kong; Pu Ning; Andrew Roche; Tsering Shakyu; Shu Cassen; Si Liqun; Daniel Southerland, *Washington Post*; Mrs M. Sykes; T. C. and Nancy Tang; Sander Tideman; Buchung Tsering and Tsering Tashi, Dharamsala; Jimmy Wang; Mary Wang; Wang Ruowang; Sechun Wangchuk; Dick Wilson; Sophia Woodman; Wu Hongda; Professor Wu Ningkun; Zheng Haiyu; Zheng Yi; and the many people inside and outside China who would prefer not to be named. In particular I would like to thank Gail Pirkis at John Murray both for her initial enthusiasm for the project and for the considerable effort and skill she applied to editing the manuscript.

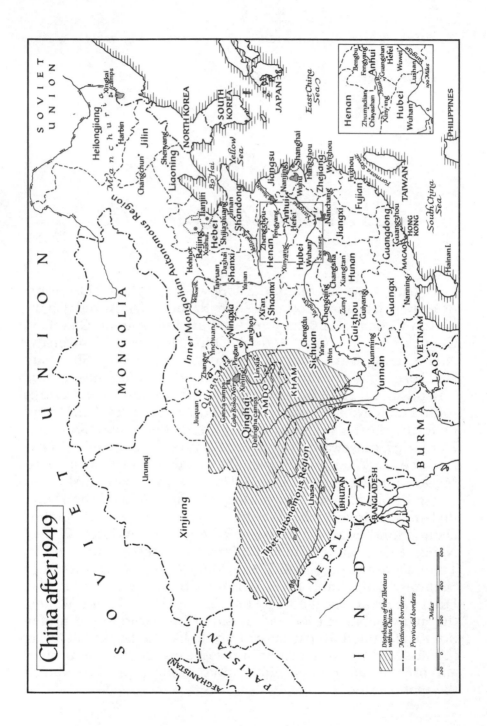

China after 1949

The Year Zero

THE YEAR 1960 was the darkest moment in the long, long history of China. Two thousand years before, a massive peasant uprising brought about the collapse of the Qin empire, the first great dictatorship to unify and control all the disparate peoples of ancient China. Now the nation had been unified once again under one great leader, Mao Zedong; and the fertile fields of Henan, where the first known Chinese dynasty, the Shang, was founded, were littered with the bodies of peasants who had starved to death.

In a small village in Guangshan county in Henan, Mrs Liu Xiaohua, now aged 65, still vividly remembers the events of thirty-six years ago. One afternoon in 1994, perched on a small footstool, dressed in faded blue cotton trousers and smock, and occasionally smoking a cigarette, she recalled what had happened. On the muddy path leading from her village, dozens of corpses lay unburied. In the barren fields there were others; and amongst the dead, the survivors crawled slowly on their hands and knees searching for wild grass seeds to eat. In the ponds and ditches people squatted in the mud hunting for frogs and trying to gather weeds.

It was winter, and bitterly cold, but she said that everyone was dressed only in thin and filthy rags tied together with bits of grass and stuffed with straw. Some of the survivors looked healthy, their faces puffed up and their limbs swollen by oedema, but the rest were as thin as skeletons. Sometimes she saw her neighbours and relatives simply fall down as they shuffled through the village and die without a sound. Others were dead on their earthen *kang* beds when she awoke in the morning. The dead were left where they died because she said that no one had the strength to bury them.

She remembered, too, the unnatural silence. The village oxen had died, the dogs had been eaten and the chickens and ducks had long ago been confiscated by the Communist Party in lieu of grain taxes. There were no birds left in the trees, and the trees themselves had been stripped of their leaves and bark. At night there was no longer even the scratching of rats and mice, for they too had been eaten or had starved to death. Lucky villagers would sometimes find their corpses curled up in a hole but it was better still to find an old burrow from another season which might contain a winter store of grain or berries. Most of all she missed the cries of young babies, for no one had been able to give birth for some time. The youngest children had all perished, the girls first. Mrs Liu had lost a daughter. The milk in her breasts had dried up and she had been forced to watch her child die. Her aunt, her mother and two brothers had also died.

The village is now a collection of mud huts surrounded by bamboo and trees, and the most prosperous villagers are building fine brick houses with tiled roofs and walled courtyards. Thirty-six years ago, all the villagers lived in houses made of mud bricks with thatched straw roofs, each divided into two or three rooms. In February 1960, Mrs Liu remembered, most of the huts were deserted. The straw roofs had fallen in and weeds grew in the courtyards. The wood from the doors and windows had been taken away and often the lintels too, all to be burnt in furnaces to make steel. At night the family slept together on the *kang* which could be heated from underneath. That winter, however, without even a cotton eiderdown to keep them warm, they froze. The best eiderdowns had been given to the commune and in many households the last shreds of cotton had been eaten. There was no fire in the clay hearth under the *kang* because the cadres, the officials of the Communist Party, had forbidden the peasants to cook food at home and all fires had been outlawed. Their iron griddles and nearly all the woks and pans had been taken away to be melted down into steel. Sometimes the peasants used an earthenware pot to try and boil some soup or bake a kind of pancake of leaves but they were usually caught and a savage beating would follow. There was only one place in the village from which smoke was allowed to rise. This was the collective kitchen, set up when the commune was founded two years earlier. It was established in the house of the Wang family. They had once been the richest peasants in the village but they had been dispossessed of their land and killed before the commune was created. On the wall outside, the cadres had painted a slogan: 'Long live the people's communes.'

The collective kitchen was, said Mrs Liu, the most terrible aspect of the commune. The grain from the autumn harvest had been taken from the villagers and delivered up to the state. Now the only source of food was the kitchen. Twice a day, at 11 a.m. and 4 p.m., the cook would bang a piece of metal hanging from a rope and the villagers would queue up with their bowls to receive their ration of soup. The soup was a thin gruel into which the cooks had thrown the leaves of sweet potatoes and turnips, ground corn stalks, wild grasses and anything else the peasants could gather. In queuing for the soup the villagers fought with each other, the younger and stronger ones pushing the elderly aside. The first to be served risked getting nothing but water, and those who came late might find it had all gone. She remembered one incident when a cadre tried to restore discipline and punched a woman so hard that she fell down and never got up. Those who worked in the kitchen survived the longest but the best off were the family of the village Party secretary. At night he was able to steal food to feed his family, and although this was only dried pea powder, it kept Mrs Liu, his sister-in-law, alive.

The first to die, she said, were the families of those who had been labelled rich peasants, for they were given the lowest rations. The next group were those who became too weak to work, for they were given nothing. Families tried to pool their rations and often the husband would rule that any female children should be allowed to die first since if they lived they would later be given in marriage to another family. Their food was given to the elderly. Then these too began to die. Often the villagers hid the corpses in their huts so that they could claim an extra ration. A few villagers had tried to hide some food by burying it underground. She remembered in particular the constant searches for hidden grain. Teams of cadres looking for secret cavities would go round the huts with iron rods, poking at the roofs and walls and prodding the ground. They searched through the courtyards and the piles of dung and straw, determined to find the grain that they said the peasants were hiding. By that time the peasants had nothing, but a few months earlier they had collected some grain which they had gathered from the fields at night before the harvest was taken in. During the harvest season, the cadres had searched the peasants as they left the fields and had beaten anyone they caught trying to eat the wheat kernels. Mrs Liu had been forced to spit out some kernels when she was spotted chewing while labouring in a field. She was not severely punished but others were. One man was tied with his hands behind his back and suspended from a tree. Another, the widow of a rich peasant, was buried alive with her children. Still others were dragged by their hair through the village while the rest were ordered to beat and kick them.

She knew, too, that at night some of her neighbours went into the fields to cut the flesh from the corpses and eat it. She pointed to a neighbouring village, another collection of huts across the fields, where a woman had killed her own baby. She and her husband had eaten it. Afterwards she went mad and the secret came out. That winter, said Mrs Liu, human beings turned into wolves. There were stories that some of the villagers who fled were killed and eaten. Too weak to walk far, they often collapsed and died where they had fallen on the road. Some of those who fled were caught by the militia, villagers wearing red armbands and armed with sticks and knives, who were ordered to patrol the main roads. She thought they were put in prison and died there. In other places, she heard that the villagers, led by the Party secretary, had tried to storm the granary at the commune headquarters but had been shot by members of the militia armed with guns.

When the villagers were too feeble to go out into the fields, the cadres came and beat them, trying to force them to go out and forage for food. And throughout that winter they were made to gather for frequent political meetings and to receive instructions on work quotas. There were health inspections, too, and she remembered how difficult it was trying to keep her hut clean. Many villagers suffered bouts of diarrhoea and vomiting from the strange diet. Others became constipated and had to use their fingers to pull out the hardened waste from their rectums. A few tried to eat earth mixed with grass but it solidified in their stomachs and they died.

Above all, Mrs Liu recalled the end when the soldiers came in trucks and began throwing sacks of wheat on to the road. She managed to walk the six miles to the road and ate the grain raw. Out of the 300 people that had been in her village at the start of the famine, only 80 survived. Mrs Liu still believes it was Chairman Mao who saved them by sending troops to rescue them and that otherwise all would have perished.

This book is the story of what happened not just in this one village in Guangshan county but in a million others throughout China.

Part One

China:

Land of Famine

1

China: Land of Famine

'What is important after all? Everyone must
eat – that is important.'
Chen Duxiu, founder of the
Chinese Communist Party

'In the wake of mighty armies, bad harvests
follow without fail.'
Lao Tzu

ON A TOMB in the capital of the Shang dynasty (c.1480–
1050 BC), the first in Chinese history, is an inscription: 'Why
are there disasters? It is because the Emperor wants to punish
mankind.' Historical records show that China has always been
the land of famine and the Chinese a people who have pros-
trated themselves before the wayward power of the Emperor,
the Son of Heaven. The records of succeeding dynasties reveal
that every year floods and droughts brought famine to some
part or other of the empire. Indeed, researchers in the 1930s
discovered documentary evidence that from the year 108 BC
until AD 1911, China suffered no fewer than 1,828 major
famines.[1]

It was the greatest task of the Emperor and his ministers to
control the floods and to intercede with Heaven to bring rain
in times of drought. In the Zhou dynasty (c.1122–221 BC), the
Emperor held ceremonies in which young girls were cast into
the rivers to prevent floods, and on altars and in temples he
presided over sacrifices and ritual dances to placate Heaven.
Five hundred years ago, in the Ming dynasty, the Emperor

would walk barefoot to pray at the Temple of Heaven and sleep on the altar in his clothes to beg for rain. During the last dynasty, the Qing (1644–1911), each year the Emperor would order local officials to build temples and pray. Even in modern times little changed. Newspapers in the late 1930s reported how, as in many primitive societies, people still slaughtered animals to bring rain. The Nationalist Governor of Hunan province would go into temples to pray, throwing tiger bones into ponds to please the dragon in the waters and forbidding the slaughter of livestock for three days. Even the Panchen Lama was summoned from Tibet by the Nationalist government to recite scriptures and to pray for rain.[2]

It was also the responsibility of the Emperor to levy taxes on the peasantry and to store surplus grain in state granaries. If in times of famine his officials failed in their responsibility or sold the grain for profit, the people starved or tried to flee to other parts of the empire. And when they had sold all that they possessed, they sold their children. Cannibalism was common and at times people even ate their own children. During the terrible famine of 1877 the Roman Catholic Bishop of Shanxi, Monsignor Louis Monagata, reported that 'now they kill the living to have them for food. Husbands eat their wives. Parents eat their sons and daughters and children eat their parents.'[3]

The terrible famines which devastated China in the nineteenth century convinced Europeans who witnessed them that Thomas Malthus had been right: in China the population was growing faster than the food supply. Chinese scholars have attributed this growth to imperial policies. When the Manchu tribes of Manchuria established the Qing dynasty, they abolished the poll tax and instead preferred to rely on land taxes. Thus people were not penalized for having more children and land ownership became more important than ever. The population grew at the formidable annual rate of more than 2.5 per cent: by 1762 it had passed the 200 million mark, by 1790 it had reached 300 million, and by 1834 it stood at well over 400 million.[4]

The crisis created by the population explosion almost brought down the Qing dynasty. In 1851, a massive peasant rebellion erupted. Led by Hong Xiuquan, a peasant who believed himself to be the brother of Christ, the leaders of what became known as the Taiping sought to establish a 'heavenly kingdom' through social reform, the sharing of property in common and the equal distribution of land. Though the Manchus, with the help of the Western powers, eventually defeated the Taipings and restored order, they could find no way of ending the food shortages which steadily worsened. In 1876, three years of drought in northern China carried off some 13 million people. A decade later a further 2 million died when the Yellow River burst its banks, drowning many and inundating fields.

Some Westerners saw famine as a necessary evil, nature's check on overpopulation. The American A. K. Norton wrote in *China and the Powers* that 'The numbers of the people must be cut down and if disease, war and plague are not sufficient, famine may be depended upon to fill up the toll. Herein lies the paramount reality of the China problem.'

The Manchus tried to cope with the crisis by allowing their subjects to emigrate abroad and to migrate into Manchu and Mongolian lands. Until then they and their Inner Mongolian allies had forbidden Chinese to settle in the thinly populated steppes of their homeland. From the end of the nineteenth century millions of Chinese peasants crossed the Great Wall and settled in Manchuria, Inner Mongolia and elsewhere. This 'colonization' policy met with the approval of some Westerners and was facilitated by the building of railways linking these regions to central China.

The introduction of new crops from the Americas also helped an internal colonization of hitherto neglected parts of China. Maize, peanuts and sweet potatoes could grow in poor hilly regions and provide a living where before there had been none. Such gains, however, were short-lived. Intensive cultivation all too often resulted in environmental degradation and diminishing returns. A Western traveller, Graham Peck, wrote of what he saw in Shaanxi province in north-west China in 1941:

The land was dying and its people with it. The first Westerners who travelled through Shuangshipu and wrote about it in the early nineteenth century had reported that this was wild empty country, heavily wooded with pines, holding only a few farmhouses along the torrential mountain stream. Now there were wretched little farms right up to the summit of the mountains. Except for the cherished domestic trees around the farmhouses, only a scruff of secondary domestic growth was left on the most inaccessible steps. Already the thin red and yellow soil of the hilly fields was clutched on every flank by jagged erosion gullies . . .

The few acres of good farmland in the flatter valleys were slowly being covered by dry deltas of gravel and boulder, tumbled out of the ravines by the fierce, brief rains which came in the summer when they could also harm the mountain fields, washing out the new crops.[5]

The thoughtless felling of trees was, he recorded, part of the 'slow murder of the country', accelerating both the erosion of the soil and the speed with which rainwater ran off the land. Today the same process is still underway, filling the main rivers with silt and increasing the risk of sudden floods.

Chinese and foreigners like Peck observed, too, that over-population by the dead as well as the living was reducing the amount of arable land available for cultivation. Even in this region, Peck wrote, 'on the mountains the homes of the living were outnumbered by the mounds which housed the dead and the shrines to appease local spirits. Each new grave, always placed in a good field, took more farmland from the survivors.' Others noticed that many peasants were reluctant to leave their ancestral lands and seek a better life elsewhere because, as Walter H. Mallory, the Secretary of the China International Famine Relief Commission, complained, they felt impelled to stay and care for the graves of their ancestors.

From the turn of the century Westerners in China became increasingly concerned with famine relief. When a major famine struck Gansu and Shaanxi provinces in 1920, mission-aries helped launch an International Famine Relief Commission which raised money in China and abroad. At the same time the US President, Woodrow Wilson, appointed an Ameri-can famine relief committee. Its chairman, a prominent banker called Thomas Lamont, collected US $4.6 million in America alone.[6] Altogether 37 million Mexican dollars (the currency of China's foreign trade) were raised, much of it from Western sources. The International Famine Relief Commission thought that its efforts were so successful that, of the nine and half million who might have died, only half a million perished.

Even so the famines continued. M. H. Hutton wrote of his journey in 1924 from Sichuan to Guizhou province: 'The famine conditions in this province are heartrending ... Dogs feasting on human flesh. Skeletons in thousands to be seen everywhere. As we journeyed over the road, over and over again our chairbearers had to carry us over dead bodies of people who had died on the road. One very sad sight was a poor victim kneeling before an idol shrine – dead.'[7] For many of those who became involved with China in the first half of this century, witnessing famine became the defining experience. One such was Edgar Snow, the American journalist who first interviewed Mao Zedong in his guerrilla base in Yanan, a famine-stricken region in Shaanxi province. (Ironically, Snow would return to China during the Great Leap Forward in 1960 and deny that a real famine was then taking place.) During the great famine which struck north-west China in 1927 and affected 60 million people, he travelled with a New Zealander, Rewi Alley, who would stay on in China and become an acolyte of Mao. At the time Edgar Snow wrote this moving description of what he witnessed:

Have you ever seen a man – a good honest man who has worked hard, a 'law-abiding citizen', doing no serious harm to anyone – when he has had no food for more than a month? It is a most agonising sight. His dying flesh hangs from him in wrinkled folds; you can clearly see every bone in his body: his eyes stare out unseeing; and even if he is a youth of twenty he moves like an ancient crone, dragging himself from spot to spot. If he has been lucky he has long ago sold his wife and daughters. He has sold everything he owns, the timber of his house itself, and most of his clothes. Sometimes he has, indeed, even sold the last rag of decency, and he sways there in the scorching sun, his testicles dangling from him like withered olive seeds – the last grim jest to remind you that this was once a man.

Children are even more pitiable, with their little skeletons bent over and misshapen, their crooked bones, their little arms like twigs, and their purpling bellies, filled with bark and sawdust, protruding like tumours. Women lie slumped in corners, waiting for death, their black blade-like buttocks protruding, their breasts hanging like collapsed sacks. But there are, after all, not many women and girls. Most of them died or had been sold.

The shocking thing was that in many of those towns there were still rich men, rice hoarders, wheat hoarders, money-lenders, and landlords, with armed guards to defend them, while they profiteered enormously. The shocking thing was that in the cities – where officials danced or played with sing-song girls – there was grain and food, and had been for months.[8]

Snow estimated that between 3 and 6 million perished in this famine. The sight of the starving was one horror but there were others. Human flesh was traded. Boys were sold as adopted sons. Girls were sold as wives, concubines, slave-girls or prostitutes. The 1927 report of the Peking United International Famine Relief Committee stated that 'in many districts, the children sold during the famine were reckoned by the thousands . . . Shijiazhuang [a city south-west of Beijing] was found to be one of the largest centres of the traffic. One of the workers in the famine field speaks of the contrast seen on the same day between a train of cars loaded with grain going out to relieve the people and a car filled with girls, who had been bought out in the country and were being brought to the railway station.'[9] Another report by Walter H. Mallory described what the starving peasants ate: 'flour made with ground leaves, fuller's earth, flower seed, poplar buds, corncobs, *hongqing cha* [steamed balls of wild herbs], sawdust, thistles, leaf dust, poisonous tree beans, sorghum husks, cotton seed, elm bark, beancakes, sweet potato vines, roots, pumice stone ground into flour . . .'[10] Both Chinese and foreign experts argued that if in the long term famines were to be prevented then communications must be improved. In India the British had been able to end endemic famine. As the *Imperial Gazetteer of India* stated: 'the greatest administrative achievement of the last 20 years has been the extension of communications. Railways have revolutionised relief. The final horror of famine, an absolute dearth of food, is not known.' China's tragedy was that it had far fewer railways than India. If there was a surplus in one part of the country and a famine in another, it was impossible to transport grain from the one to the other. Yet, as the 1925 annual report of the China International Famine Relief Commission noted, 'in such a vast country there is such a range of climate that a crop failure in all the provinces simultaneously is almost impossible. Even though four or five provinces are without a harvest there are still seventeen or eighteen where there is a yield and some of them are almost sure to have a bumper crop.'

Past dynasties had tried to solve the problem by digging the Grand Canal to ship grain by barge from the south to the north. Grain could travel, too, along the major rivers. But in large parts of the country the only mode of transporting grain was on a man's back. Animals were too valuable to use. In the 1920s China, with an area as big as the United States, had less than 2,000 miles of roads. Both men and goods were carried by coolies up and down hills and along narrow tracks for days on end. One reporter in China recorded that even if farmers in the interior of China gave their grain to mill owners in Shanghai for nothing, it would still be cheaper for the millers to buy American grain and ship it across the Pacific than to transport it across China.[11]

The Qing dynasty had been reluctant to allow foreigners to build many railways, and after its downfall the new republic was too unstable and too short of resources to fund major roadbuilding or railway schemes. Aside from the main river valleys and the coastal belt, the vast interior of China is mountainous, making it costly to construct roads. Yet without good communications it was impossible to create a commercial grain market. Even successful farmers found that the cards were always stacked against them. Prices fluctuated wildly and since most peasants were smallholders, they possessed little capital and were unable to borrow cheaply. The peasant had to sell immediately after the harvest when prices were low while the trader could hold stocks until prices were high. To finance the period between sowing and harvest, the peasant often borrowed money. Local landlords and dealers would charge 60 per cent interest on mortgaged land, 30 per cent on money loans and 50 per cent on grain. Many farmers were perennially in debt as John Ridley, correspondent of the *Daily Telegraph*, observed: 'The average Chinese farmer has a holding of one or two acres. Half of everything he grows is turned over to the landlord. Bad communications make production for a wide market impossible. The farmer has no incentive to put more land under the plough and increase the yield when he is unable to sell the additional produce. Primitive transport by oxen, mules or human beings is so slow that it is expensive as compared with railway charges.'

The famines also prompted the first research into peasant life. Professor John Lossing Buck, an American academic, established a team at Nanjing University which produced detailed surveys of Chinese agriculture, while his wife Pearl S. Buck won the Nobel Prize for Literature for *The Good Earth*, the story of an Anhui peasant who is driven from his land by drought and famine. Researchers began to realize that famine was not just a periodic crisis but a permanent state for tens of millions. In *Land and Labour in China*, published in 1932, R. H. Tawney wrote that 'there are in China districts in which the position of the rural population is that of a man standing permanently up to his neck in water, so that even a ripple is sufficient to drown him.' Another writer, A. K. Norton, tried to calculate the numbers involved:

> It is estimated that thirty million Chinese are continually attempting to sustain life on less than the minimum required for subsistence. Thousands of these die daily; yet it is only when some great catastrophe such as a flood or a drought concentrates millions of starving in one area that we hear of a famine. Of the famine that is present every day we hear little: and the three million or more that die each year of starvation, due to lack of adjustment to changing conditions, are accepted as representing the normal mortality of the Chinese people.[12]

Westerners argued that peasant agriculture must be modernized if China was to feed herself. A thousand years earlier China had been at the forefront of farming technology; now she was regarded as primitive. Many peasants were too poor to use draught animals and pulled a plough themselves. The ploughs were made of wood, not metal, and they barely scratched the surface of the soil. In places the peasants did not even use a plough but broke up the soil by hitting it with a wooden instrument shaped like a hoe. The Chinese peasant, observed one writer, was 'twin brother to the ox'.

The land itself was easily exhausted because there was not enough fertilizer, and land was too scarce and too highly taxed for it to be left fallow. After the harvest, the peasants would strip their land of every piece of straw to burn as fuel because there was no coal or wood, and instead used human waste to fertilize the soil. Englishmen travelling up the Grand Canal in the mid-nineteenth century had been astonished to see peasants running after them to take their faeces: 'Whenever servants and soldiers left the junks, they would be pursued to their places of retirement with receptacles to collect manure for their fields.'

Before 1949 it was reckoned that in Britain one person could grow enough food for himself and four urban dwellers but in China it took four farmers to produce enough for themselves and one city-dweller. If only China could reach the same rate of productivity as Britain, she could easily feed herself. Yet plans to modernize Chinese agricultural methods, rationalize ownership, provide cheap credit through co-operatives and build roads, railways, irrigation canals and dykes, were frustrated by the greatest problem of all – political instability.

At the end of the nineteenth century the Empress Dowager Ci Xi crushed efforts to modernize the country, fearing that it would open the door to foreign influences that would undermine the remaining authority of the imperial court. In 1911 the Qing dynasty was overthrown and China became a republic. Yet the opportunity to modernize foundered once more when power was seized by one of her generals, Yuan Shikai, who tried to establish a new dynasty. After his death in 1916, the empire disintegrated into a mass of fiefdoms run by warlords, and the central government was reduced to impotence. By 1928, however, a new ruling party had risen to power, the Nationalists or Kuomintang (KMT).

The KMT had been founded as a revolutionary party by Sun Yat-sen with the support of Marxists sent from Moscow who also nurtured the birth of the Chinese Communist Party (CCP). Strongly nationalist and anti-imperialist, the KMT attempted to unite China and to import Western scientific ideas and methods of government. In 1925 Sun died and the KMT fell under the control of Generalissimo Chiang Kai-shek. The following year he launched the Northern expedition to suppress the warlords. However, he was soon faced with another threat to his power in the shape of the growing Communist Party. Initially, it had functioned as a branch of the KMT but it soon began to establish itself as a rival.

Lenin himself believed that to become Communist, China must first pass through a stage of bourgeois revolution, but after his death the Chinese Communists took a different tack. In 1927 they launched a series of agrarian and urban uprisings against the KMT. In response Chiang Kai-shek turned on the Communists and destroyed their urban organizations, especially in Shanghai. Thereafter the Communists became a largely agrarian movement controlling small areas, or soviets, in the mountains, often on the intersection of provincial borders. In 1930 Chiang Kai-shek launched the first of several campaigns to eradicate these soviets and, in 1934, encircled the largest stronghold, finally forcing the Communists to break out in what has since become known as the Long March. On this epic journey Mao Zedong seized control and led his dwindling band to a new base in Yanan on the borders of Shanxi and Shaanxi provinces.

The Nationalists were never able to establish proper control of China. The most important coastal cities such as Shanghai were run by the foreign powers. In Manchuria, the Japanese imperial army set up a puppet state, Manchukuo, and from 1937 invaded China south of the Great Wall, forcing the Nationalists to retreat. The capital was moved from Nanjing inland to Chongqing in Sichuan province and the Nationalists steadily lost control over most of China. During the Second World War, the Communists infiltrated behind Japanese lines and established their grip over the rural hinterlands in the north. After Japan's defeat, civil war between the Nationalists and the Communists broke out once more and the Nationalists were finally defeated in 1949, retreating to the island of Taiwan.

Between 1912 and 1949, the shifting alliances of the warlords and, later, the constant movement of armies, whether Communist, Nationalist or Japanese, reduced many parts of China to near anarchy and starvation. Millions of landless or impoverished peasants enlisted in the armies of local bandits and warlords or in the forces established by the Communists and Nationalists. A study of Shandong province in 1930 estimated that there were 192,000 regular troops and an additional 310,000 militia and bandits living off the countryside.[13] An earlier report, produced in 1929 by the International Famine Relief Commission in western China, concluded that famine was less the result of natural disasters than of man-made events. The millions of armed men in China fed themselves by seizing food from the peasants, taking their sons and animals, and demanding taxes years or even generations in advance. If the peasants refused to pay, then the troops would seize their entire belongings, creating more desperate men whose only recourse was banditry. Wherever the troops went there was starvation: 'the famine areas corresponded almost exactly to the main billet areas and lines of march of the armies retreating from, and advancing to, the civil wars in the East'.

The American Red Cross drew the same conclusions about a famine in north-west China which began in 1929. It started with a severe drought but the ensuing destitution was caused by the 'crushing exactions of the warlords, the depredations of bandits and the enforced payment of confiscatory taxation'. The solution, it said, lay in the establishment of a strong, stable central government which could 'command the power and resources and continuity of policy necessary to lead China out of her condition of disorder into a new era of peace, security and prosperity'. It predicted that 'disastrous conditions leading to continued suffering will constantly recur until such a government comes into being'.

In the spring of 1943, an American reporter for *Time* magazine, Theodore White, was covering the war between the Japanese and Nationalist armies in Henan province, central China. Millions were fleeing the Japanese advance but White discovered to his horror that it was not the fighting itself which was killing most people but hunger. 'The blood was not my chief distress – it was my inability to make sense of what I was seeing. In a famine where no one kills but nature, there are no marks on the body where people die: nature itself is the enemy – and only government can save from nature. I could not understand this at the beginning.'

White, who later became the doyen of political reporters in America, was convinced that it would be the Communists, not the Nationalists, who would eventually provide this stable government. In his book, *In Search of History*, he described how the Nationalists dealt with the famine in Henan. At the time he was staying with a Catholic bishop and missionary in Luoyang, the province's capital.

Missionaries left their compound only when necessary for a white man walking in the street was the only agent of hope and was assailed by wasted men, frail women, children, people head-knocking on the ground, grovelling, kneeling, begging for food, wailing 'K'o lien, k'o lien' ('Mercy, mercy') but pleading really only for food. The handful of missionaries who staked out the Christian underground in the area of famine were the only thread of sense – the sense that life is precious.

What we saw, I now no longer believe . . . There were the bodies: the first, no more than an hour out of Luoyang, lying in the snow, a day or two dead, her face shrivelled about her skull: she must have been young; and the snow fell on her eyes; and she would lie unburied until the birds or the dogs cleansed her bones. The dogs were also there along the road, slipping back to their wolf kinship, and they were sleek, well fed. We stopped to take a picture of dogs digging bodies from sand piles; some were half-eaten, but the dogs had already picked clean one visible skull. Half the villages were deserted; some simply abandoned, others already looted. To hear a sound or see a person in such a village was startling; an old man tottering through the street all by himself; or in another village, two women shrieking at each other with no one else in sight, where normally there would be a crowd to watch them scold – and what were they arguing about in death?

White found, too, that hunger had driven the peasants to break the ultimate taboo.

So I saw these things, but the worst was what I heard, which was about cannibalism. I never saw any man kill another person for meat, and never tasted human flesh. But it seemed irrefutably true that people were eating people meat. The usual defence was that the people meat was taken from the dead. Case after case which we tried to report presented this defence. In one village a mother was discovered boiling her two-year-old to eat its meat. In another case a father was charged with strangling his two boys to eat them;

his defence was that they were already dead. A serious case in one village; the army had insisted that the peasants take in destitute children and an eight-year-old had been imposed on a peasant family. Then he disappeared. And on investigating, his bones were discovered by the peasant's shack, in a big crock. The question was only whether the boy had been eaten after he died or had been killed to be eaten later. In two hours in the village, we could not determine the justice of the matter; anyone might have been lying; so we rode on.[14]

White believed that this misery was caused not by war but by poor government. The Nationalists were relentless in collecting taxes to finance the war and since they did not trust the paper money that they issued as currency, the armies in the field were instructed to gather taxes in kind, mostly by seizing grain. White discovered that in Henan the Nationalist army had tried to collect more grain than the land produced. The troops had emptied the countryside of food, leaving the populace with nothing to eat. Peasants were forced to sell their animals, tools and homes. At the same time the civilian administration was trying to levy its own taxes.

He also noticed that where army units were under strength, the army storehouses bulged with surplus grain which the officers sold for their own profit. This was the grain which the missionaries and honest officials bought to feed the starving. In Chongqing, Chiang Kai-shek's administration responded to reports of famine by declaring that it would remit the tax on next year's grain harvest. Since this did not exist the gesture was meaningless; and the funds that it sent were equally useless because the paper currency had no value.

White returned to Chongqing and found that Chiang had little knowledge of, or interest in, the famine. The various layers of bureaucracy had effectively shielded him from the facts. White finally managed to force an audience with the General-issimo and showed him photographs of the starving and of wild dogs standing over corpses. Only then did Chiang believe him and take measures to end the famine. Trainloads of grain arrived from neighbouring Shaanxi province, the army opened its stores in Henan and the provincial government set up soup kitchens. The famine abated, although cholera and typhus still claimed many. In all at least 5 million are thought to have perished although even today no one knows the precise figure.

The devastation caused by the Japanese invaders, the callousness of the Nationalists and endemic famine were, White believed, destroying traditional Chinese society:

> What was left was not a society, but a spongelike mass, a honeycomb of mashed cells in most of which some sting was left. Some villages supported the Nationalists, others the provincial government, and yet others supported the Communists – but they supported whoever could serve their need of protection best, who could save their women from rape by the Japanese, their men from impressment as coolies. The Japanese had come to kill; the Communists were the most efficient counterkillers.[15]

After the Japanese surrender in 1945, the Nationalists became the official government of China, yet the terrible famines continued. In 1946 famine gripped nineteen provinces and at least 20 million were starving. The British journalist John Ridley recorded what he saw in the same province, Henan: 'It was a ghastly experience walking through those towns and villages. All around was the dreadful apathy of people slowly dying of hunger and disease who watched you, dull as cattle, their eyes large, luminous and sad in putty coloured skeletal faces. As you wandered among the ruined mud-brick houses there was always the stench of death.'

While he was walking through one village a boy fell down in front of him: 'lying on the road he was a pathetic little figure, his stomach hideously distended, his face gaunt and pallid, his limbs thin and fragile as a bird's skeleton'. Ridley picked him up and carried him to a nearby hospital. Half an hour later the boy died without recovering consciousness. 'He died of starvation. We get dozens like him brought here every week,' a hospital doctor told Ridley. Throughout the province, people were subsisting on grass, roots, leaves and even human flesh, and children were abandoned or sold for a handful of grain.[16]

A mere twelve years later Henan province would embrace Mao's Great Leap Forward and his promise to end starvation for ever with more enthusiasm than any other part of China.

Yet the famine which followed the Great Leap Forward would be the greatest that the world had ever witnessed. To understand why one must first look at how the Chinese themselves proposed to banish hunger in the land of famine.

2

Arise, Ye Prisoners of Starvation

'In China what is called inequality between
poor and rich is only a distinction between
the very poor and the less poor.'

Sun Yat-sen

'Arise, ye prisoners of starvation, Arise, ye
wretched of the earth'

The 'Internationale'

REVOLUTION, DEMOCRACY, FREEDOM, Communism – all
meant one thing to the peasants: the redistribution of the land.
From earliest times, peasants had joined rebellions confident
that the victors would divide up all the land and reallocate it.
At the start of a new dynasty, the Emperor would invariably
annul all debts, taxes, land leases and contracts. Even the graves
of the old era would be ploughed under. The soldiers of the
new emperor would be rewarded with a choice of the best land
and the supporters of the old regime would lose theirs. The
population explosion that occurred under the Qing dynasty,
and the increasing shortage of land that it created, fuelled the
peasants' age-old desire for change. Their opportunity came
with the rise of the Taipings who, in rebelling against the Qing,
promised to establish the 'land system of the Heavenly Kingdom'. Land would be given to those who tilled it and would
be shared out equitably among all the families of the Taiping

supporters according to family size.[1] The founders of the Heavenly Kingdom also envisaged a proto-Communist state in which all food surplus to daily requirements would be kept in great common granaries while social order would be ensured by a 'sergeant' appointed to oversee the doings of units made up of twenty-five families.

The Taipings were crushed in 1864 but when the Qing dynasty was finally overthrown in the 1911 Republican Revolution, the peasants still hoped that there would be a great redistribution of land. They were disappointed and gained little from the dynasty's downfall, but the new rulers of China continued to promise that soon the land would be redistributed. Sun Yat-sen declared that 'those who till the land should have the land' and called his programme the 'equalization of land ownership'. Before his death the Nationalists made the land question a central plank in their political programme. In 1924 the Declaration of the First National Congress of the KMT stated:

> China is an agricultural country and the peasants are the class that has suffered most. The Kuomintang stands for the policy that those peasants who have no land and consequently have fallen into the status of mere tenants should be given land by the State for their cultivation. The State shall also undertake the work of irrigation and of opening up the waste land so as to increase the power of production of the land. Those peasants who have no capital and are compelled to borrow at high rates of interest and are in debt for life should be supplied by the State with credit by the establishment of rural banks. Only then will the peasants be able to enjoy the happiness of life.

While they were still in partnership with the Communists, the Nationalists set up a Peasant Movement Training Institute in which Mao Zedong, the son of a peasant landlord from Hunan, soon became heavily involved. In 1924 he was elected an alternate member of the KMT's Central Executive Committee and appointed Principal of the Institute. Perhaps more than anyone else in the Chinese Communist Party he argued that 'the peasant question is the central question in the national revolution'. The founders of the Chinese Communist Party were largely urban intellectuals with access to Western ideas who had studied events in Europe, especially in Russia. When they set up the Party they gave it a name in Chinese which would appeal to the peasants – the Gong Chan Dang, the 'share property party'. However, the orthodox Marxist view was that the workers – the urban proletariat – would be the advance guard of the revolution. Mao, on the other hand, believed that in China it would be the peasants who would bring the Party to power. As he later told the American journalist Edgar Snow, 'Whoever wins the peasants will win China. Whoever solves the land question will win the peasants.'

So in the countryside the Communists promised land reform, the equitable redistribution of land, the abolition of taxes and the cancellation of debts. And unlike the Nationalists, they not only promised this but also put it into effect in the areas that fell under their control. As Dean Acheson, US Secretary of State, observed in 1948 when the Nationalists were facing defeat, 'Much of the propaganda of the Chinese Communists is built on the promise that they will solve the land question . . . the KMT has attempted to solve the problem by formulating land reform decrees but some of these have failed and others have been neglected.'[2] The promise to provide equal shares of land to all brought the popular support which allowed the Communists to operate in rural areas and to enlist landless peasants in their armies. In a famous report on the peasants in his home province, written in 1927, Mao predicted that 'in a very short time, several hundred million peasants in China's central, southern and northern provinces will rise like a tornado or tempest – a force so extraordinarily swift that no power, however great, will be able to suppress it. They will break through all the trammels that now bind them and push forward along the road to liberation.'[3]

In implementing their own land reform decrees, the Nationalists were hamstrung by their dependency on warlords who controlled many parts of the country and who in turn drew their support from the local landlords and gentry. Yet those with property, even if they were nothing more than peasant smallholders, were horrified by the violent redistribution of wealth that the Communists enforced. In the Red soviets that the Party established, landlords and their families were brutally murdered and all that they owned was distributed among the have-nots.

Most rural Chinese were neither rich nor landless but subsisted in a series of subtle gradations of poverty. However, Marxist theory held that there were three distinct classes of peasants: rich, middle and poor. For the Chinese Communists operating in the countryside, the key question was what to do about the middle peasants. They might be led to think they would gain from a redistribution of property. Or, since they possessed some property, they might support the Nationalists if they feared it would be taken away, and if they believed that the Nationalists would provide stable government. On this issue the Communists were fortunate because the Republic's authorities manifestly failed to carry out the duties expected in a society with an intensely paternalistic tradition of government. After the fall of the Manchus, the state granaries were neglected or closed and the grain sold for money which was pocketed by the warlords. So there were no reserves in times of famine. The authorities also failed to remit taxes when harvests failed, as tradition dictated, and the taxes raised were not spent on maintaining dykes and embankments. The Nationalists thus broke a social contract between the peasants and their rulers that dated back to the earliest dynasties, thereby sowing the seeds of their eventual defeat.

Yet the Communists had no intention of re-establishing a feudal dynasty: they wanted to create something new. The Chinese Communist Party was controlled by leaders and advisers who were largely trained in Moscow and who wanted to implement the ideas of Marx, Lenin and Stalin.[4] In the *Communist Manifesto*, Marx had not envisaged a country of peasant smallholders but rather an agricultural system modelled on factories. He wrote of 'the abolition of property in land ... the improvement of the soil generally in accordance with a common plan. The establishment of industrial armies, especially for agriculture. The combination of agriculture with manufacturing industries: the gradual abolition of the distinction between town and country.'

When the Bolsheviks seized power in Russia after 1917, they divided up the land but then soon set about taking it away again to create the giant factory-farms which Marx had proposed. Some were state farms and some were huge collectives called *kolkhozi*. Knowing that the peasants wanted their own land and had no desire to be part of some Utopian scheme, the Russian revolutionaries despised them. The founder of Russian Marxism, Georgi Plekhanov, described the Russian peasants as 'barbarian tillers of the soil, cruel and merciless, beasts of burden whose life provided no opportunity for the luxury of thought', and Maxim Gorky, a writer much favoured by the Bolsheviks, accused the peasants of an 'animal-like individualism' and an 'almost total lack of social consciousness'. Lenin himself liked to quote Marx on the 'idiocy of rural life' and said that the peasant, 'far from being an instinctive or traditional collectivist, is in fact meanly and fiercely individualistic'. Indeed, he believed the peasant smallholder was inherently and irredeemably capitalist, that 'day by day, hour by hour, small scale [agricultural] production is engendering capitalism'. The peasants might be useful at an initial stage – after all Marx had said that a proletarian revolution might be supported by a new version of the sixteenth-century German peasant wars – but their interests were different. In 1905, Lenin wrote in *Two Tactics for Democracy* that though initially there would be a 'democratic dictatorship of the proletariat and the peasantry' this was no more than a tactical move. Later it would be 'ridiculous to speak of unity of will of the proletariat and peasantry, of democratic rule; then we shall have to think of the socialist, of the proletarian dictatorship.'

The theories that the Chinese Communists learned in Moscow and from advisers such as Borodin and Otto Braun were based on an analysis of feudalism which existed in Europe and Russia in the last century. When the future leaders of China, men such as Deng Xiaoping or Liu Shaoqi, studied at the 'University of the Toilers of the East', their textbooks referred to the liberation of the serfs, the overthrow of the landed aristocracy and the break-up of vast feudal estates in Germany, France or Russia. China was quite different, as both eighteenth-century Jesuit missionaries and scholars such as R. H. Tawney, writing in the 1920s, pointed out.[5] There was no landed aristocracy, no dominant clan of Junkers or squires, no feudal land law, no great estates worked by corvée labour. And, unlike in Europe, there were no commons, pastures or forests in public hands. Ministry of Agriculture statistics produced in 1918 showed that in China there was a higher percentage of peasant proprietors in the farming population than in Germany, Japan or the United States. In China, 51.6 per cent were owner-occupiers and a further 22.8 per cent owned part of their farmland while renting the remainder.

Again and again observers stressed the attachment of the Chinese peasantry to the land they owned. A German count travelling in China in the last century wrote: 'There is no other peasantry in the world which gives such an impression of absolute genuineness and of belonging so much to the soil. Here the whole of life and the whole of death takes place on the inherited ground. Man belongs to the soil, not the soil to man; it will never let its children go.'[6] The Chinese sociologist Fei Xiaotong, writing in the late 1930s, further observed: 'Honour, ambition, devotion, social approval are all thus linked up with the land. The villagers judge a person as good or bad according to his industry in working the land. A badly weeded farm, for instance, will give a bad reputation to the owner. The incentive to work is thus deeper than hunger.' As long as a peasant owned his land he felt secure: 'The relative inexhaustibility of the land gives people a relative security. Although there are bad years, the land never disillusions the people completely, since hope for plenty in the future remains and is not infrequently realised.'[7]

In Pearl S. Buck's *The Good Earth*, the central figure Wang Lung finds it incomprehensible that anyone, however destitute, should think of leaving the land. ' "Sell their land!" repeated Wang Lung, convinced. "Then indeed are they growing poor. Land is one's flesh and blood." '

Yet Lenin and Stalin had developed a theory of rural class struggle which the Chinese Communists were also to adopt and which ignored this relationship to the land in China. The rich and successful Russian peasants, the *kulaks*, were accused of exploiting the labour of others and of lending money at extortionate rates. The Russian Communists tried to enlist the poor peasants to overcome the *kulaks* who were the most influential group in the countryside and whose opposition to collectivization was the strongest. In May 1918 the Central Executive Committee in Russia considered that 'We must place before ourselves most seriously the problem of dividing the village by classes. Of creating in it two opposite hostile camps, setting the poorest layers of the population against the *kulak* elements. Only if we are able to split the village into two camps, to arouse there the same class war as in the cities, only then will we achieve in the villages what we have achieved in the cities.'

The Russian Communists launched a 'merciless war' against the *kulaks* that culminated in their eradication during Stalin's first five-year plan (1928–33) when the entire peasantry was collectivized. In December 1929 Stalin ordered the liquidation of the *kulaks* as a class and millions were killed or sent to labour camps. Such a policy was difficult to implement in China and was the subject of furious arguments among the Chinese Communist leadership. It was easy enough to enlist the most desperate and impoverished peasantry but who exactly were the middle peasants and the rich peasants? Did the Party need the support of the rich peasants or should they be dealt with later?

The Russians had found it hard enough to make clear distinctions and in China the issue was even more problematic during the 1930s. First, the Chinese Communists only controlled small regions and wanted the support of the entire rural population. Second, as Sun Yat-sen had said, all the peasants were poor and there was barely a distinction to be made between them. Before 1949, absentee landlords and landless peasants accounted for less than 10 per cent of the rural population, and tenants and hired labour accounted for only a small part of the rural labour force.[8] Moreover, in many villages everyone belonged to the same one or two extended families or clans. Often the whole village shared the same family name. The clan patriarch usually had the most land and helped his relatives with credit or hired their sons when extra help was needed at harvest time. So an attack on the village clan chief risked turning the entire village against the Communists.

In Communist-controlled regions, Party officials set about categorizing each peasant household, designating them poor, middle or rich depending on how they were faring that year. The Party defined 'landlords' as the largest landowners, who rented out a significant proportion of their land and might also hire labourers to work the fields. A rich peasant worked part of his land himself but also hired labour. These two classes were labelled as members of the exploiting classes whose ill-gotten wealth was taken from the labour of tenants and hired labourers. A middle peasant had some land but also worked on the land of others. Poor peasants included those who owned and cultivated very small holdings as well as tenant farmers and part tenants.[9] Once fixed, these labels could not be changed and were passed down to the next generation. In 1931, while Mao and other Communist leaders were based in the mountains of Jiangxi province, they issued a land reform law which was ruthless though not quite as tough as that in the Soviet Union. Middle peasants could keep their own land but rich peasants would have theirs taken away and substituted with inferior land. Later, in drought-stricken and impoverished Yanan where under Mao's leadership the Communists established a new base after 1935, Mao also insisted that Stalin's ideas on class warfare should be embraced. Over the next fourteen years as the Party extended its power and influence to more and more areas, it enforced the same policies. The peasants were classified and often the clan chief or largest landowner was humiliated or murdered in a rally organized by Party cadres.

What is unclear from many historical accounts of the Party in these decades is whether class warfare was pursued in the villages with the same fanaticism and brutality as in the Soviet Union. Writers such as Edgar Snow, who visited Mao in Yanan, were sympathetic to the Party's efforts to help the poor peasants. Others, such as William Hinton who wrote the history of a village in Shanxi province and Han Suyin, also tended to present a largely positive picture of land reform under the Communists. They convey the impression that any excesses in land reform were spontaneous episodes that were regrettable but understandable given the justified anger of the peasants.

However, a number of Chinese histories of early land reform have appeared in recent years which claim that it was always designed to be a brutal campaign of terror targeting anyone with property.[10] In his 1927 report on the Hunan peasant movement, Mao explicitly said: 'We must create a short reign of terror in all parts of the countryside. A revolution is not like a dinner party, or composing an article, or doing embroidery, a revolution is an uprising.' Even in this early period, Party

leaders ordered cadres to murder landlords and their supporters and to encourage looting and burning. And in a recent
publication, *History of Land Reform in China, 1921–1949* by Zhao
Xiaomin, it is claimed that 'some cadres who failed to carry
out this policy resolutely were also killed'. According to the
author, the policies of the Chinese Communists in 1931 were
as brutal as those of Stalin in the Soviet Union, if not more so:

> From 1931 they obeyed the instructions of the Comintern that
> landlords should not be allowed any land but should just sit and
> wait for death. In China some were sent to do hard labour, some
> expelled from the area under Party control and some were killed.
> Just as in the USSR, *kulaks* were killed and all their property confis-
> cated. The slogan was 'Kill all the rich peasants'.

Another recent book, *Land Revolution Report, 1927–1937* by
Tong Yingming, argues that the Chinese Communists had from
the start tried to go further than the Russians. The author
writes that after 1929 'when carrying out the collective farming
system, the Chinese Communist Party tried to be more pro-
gressive than the Soviet Union. They opposed all private ownership of land, banned the sale of land and the hiring of labour,
and opposed peasants and soldiers who wanted to own land.'
He and others claim that even in the 1930s the land of the
middle peasant was also redistributed but that the policies were
softened when the Communists joined the war against the
Japanese after 1937 and tried to form a united front with the
Nationalists against the invaders. Landlords' property was no
longer confiscated although money-lending rates were
reduced.

After 1946, it was official policy to protect the rich and middle
peasants when an area came under Communist control. A provisional law on land reform which was passed that year was
moderate in theory but not in practice. Even those who worked
their own land were often labelled as landlords. Those whose
parents or grandparents were considered to have been landlords were killed, their ancestors' tombs dug up and their relatives tortured to discover if the family had hidden gold or silver.
The Land Law formally adopted in 1948 appeared to protect
the interests of middle peasants but in practice priority was

given to satisfying the demands of poor peasants for more land as well as for possessions such as donkeys and carts.

Those who were to form the nucleus around Mao during the Great Leap Forward and the Cultural Revolution had always been prominent in waging class warfare. Chen Boda, one of Mao's key advisers in both periods, carried out a study of land rent in 1945 entitled *Chinese Agriculture and the Classes in the Chinese Countryside*. It set out to justify the harsh measures employed by proving that exploitation of peasants by landlords and *kulaks* was rife.

Another key figure, Kang Sheng, who in the Cultural Revolution during the late 1960s would mastermind Mao's destruction of his opponents in the Party, took the lead in trying to exterminate the rich peasants. A biography of Kang, *Claws of the Dragon*, based on an internal Party document, describes a visit he paid to Gansu province in 1946 to inspect its land reform. He accused the provincial leadership there of 'right deviation' and on his return to Yanan gave a series of speeches at the central Party school decrying the tendency to be lenient towards landlords. The authors of the biography claim that 'Kang's formula translated into countless acts of revenge at village level. Instead of merely confiscating the landlords' houses and goods and dividing their land among the peasants and retainers, in the name of social justice, he encouraged the peasants to settle scores by killing landlords and rich peasants.'[11]

Kang then spent four months in a county in Shaanxi province where he also reviewed land reform and insisted that landlords be murdered as part of the programme. Such ruthlessness extended to Party supporters and Party cadres. In Lin county two wealthy landowners who had supported the Communists in the fight against the Japanese were subjected to brutal struggle sessions. Kang ordered that one of them called Niu (meaning cow) should have an iron ring put through his nose and be led on a rope through the streets by his son. At the same time, local Party members were investigated and those not of peasant or proletarian birth were abused and beaten in mass struggle sessions. Kang even insisted that any cadre of slightly better social origins than the rest must be made to eat at a separate table.

Official policy was to judge a landowner according to his record in exploiting hired labourers or poor peasants but Kang thought that this was too moderate. He declared that three other factors should be taken into consideration – 'history, life and political attitudes'. So broad were these criteria that they could be used to target anyone. In one village in this county, of the 552 households, 124 were classified as those of rich peasants. The victims had their land taken away and were publicly humiliated and beaten. Some were shot, beheaded or buried alive.

Although in public Mao argued against Kang's excesses, elsewhere he singled him out for praise for having overcome the 'right deviations' in this district. At a high-level Party conference on land reform held just before the Communist victory of 1949, Kang delivered a report urging a policy of 'thoroughly equal land distribution' that would reduce the land holdings of middle-class peasants. The conference approved a much tougher line than that taken during the partnership with the Nationalists against the Japanese and during the civil war. Kang was then assigned to inspect land reform in his native Shandong province and there too he discovered that the local Party represented a 'landlord and rich peasant Party'. The leading cadres were imprisoned and the Party secretary Li Yu was accused of following the 'rich peasant line' and detained for six months before being transferred to another, lowlier job.

In many places, rural reform consisted of gangs drawn from the dregs of village society who were organized to incite the peasants at mass meetings which ended with the land reform team leading shouts of 'Shoot him! Shoot him!' or 'Kill! Kill! Kill!' The brutality of the campaign was described in an American report drawn up by the Consul-General in Hong Kong which recounted what had happened in villages in Henan province in 1949. Those categorized as landlords were shot, hanged, beheaded, battered to death, nailed to the walls of buildings or buried alive. Sometimes, in winter, the victim was dressed in a thin cotton garment and water was poured over him while he stood outside in sub-zero temperatures. This method of death was called 'wearing glass clothes'. Burying victims alive in the snow was called 'refrigeration'. A third method was dubbed 'opening the flower'. The victim was buried in a pit with only his head exposed which was then smashed, laying open his brains.[12]

There are no figures on how many died in the land reform movement prior to 1949 but subsequently, when the Party controlled all of China, between 2 and 5 million landlords are thought to have been killed.[13] This 'red terror' enabled the Party to establish its control over the villages but it was not followed by a real collectivization programme. On the contrary, the redistribution of land pleased many peasants and the Party found it difficult to stop its peasant recruits from deserting their army units and returning to their villages after the process had begun.

Yet collectivization was always one of the goals of the Party once it had established power and it was always clear that the land being given to the peasants would be taken away again. Before 1949, the Party had distributed leaflets and pamphlets describing in glowing terms the success of the collective farms in the Soviet Union. Woodcuts showed tractors and combine-harvesters, which peasants in China had never seen, criss-crossing fields and bringing in bumper harvests. One interviewee described how Party officials showed the peasants Soviet propaganda films:

We always heard lots of propaganda about the communes in the USSR. There were always films about the fantastic combine-harvesters with people singing on the back on their way to work. In the films there were always mountains and mountains of food. So many films showed how happy life was on the collective farms. I remember scenes of happy, healthy schoolchildren in uniform. In the shots of the homes of the peasants on the collectives there was always lots of food.

After 1949, delegations of peasants were sent on lengthy tours of the Ukraine and Kazakhstan to see model collectives with their own cinemas, bath houses and day-care centres. They ate in peasant homes from tables groaning with food and saw the ease with which fields were ploughed by tractors and harvests gathered in and threshed by modern machinery. Groups of village cadres returned from these study tours of Soviet collective farms filled with a desire to emulate the Russians. Yet the truth, as many in the Chinese Communist Party knew, was that collectivization had been a disaster in the Soviet Union. In attempting it, Stalin had created the worst famine in Russian history in which millions had perished, and the country was still not able to feed itself. The Ukraine famine of the early 1930s was in many ways the forerunner of what was to happen in China. Mao and his followers must have had some knowledge of the events described in the next chapter.

3

The Soviet Famine

'Hundreds of thousands of lives were lost –
maybe even millions. I can't give an exact
figure because no one was keeping count.
All we knew was that people were dying in
enormous numbers.'

Nikita Khrushchev

'The Soviet Union's today is China's to-
morrow.'

Mao Zedong

THE ORIGINS OF Mao's great famine lie as much in Russian
as in Chinese history. Towards the end of the nineteenth century, the Russian empire was racked by such severe famines
that Lenin was encouraged to think that a revolution was inevi-
table. He and his followers believed that peasant demands for
land would help destroy the social order. However, the crisis
in the countryside was partly defused by the reforms of an
energetic minister of the Tsar, P. A. Stolypin, who from
1906 introduced agricultural reforms that met some of the
demands for more land, thereby creating a class of prosperous
peasants.[1]

As a result, the disappointed Bolshevik faction under Lenin
redirected their activities towards exploiting the revolutionary
potential of the growing urban proletariat. Nonetheless, when
finally military defeat in the First World War led to the collapse
of the Tsarist regime in 1917, Russia's Marxist revolutionaries
still needed the support of the peasantry, who constituted
the great majority of the recruits in the Tsarist armies. The

revolutionaries promised these peasant soldiers that the land would be divided up. In consequence many deserted their units and returned to their villages in order to obtain their share.

However, once Lenin and his followers had consolidated their grip over the cities, it soon became clear that they did not have the interests of the peasants at heart. Within a few months of seizing power, they introduced measures that would bring about the first famine in the new state. In May 1918 a decree was issued empowering the Commissariat of Food to extract from the peasants any grain held in excess of the quotas that it set. In the name of 'War Communism', teams of politically reliable workers arrived in the countryside to seize the surplus grain. The peasants refused to hand it over and staged uprisings that were only put down with much bloodshed. The Communist Party then resorted to waging class warfare in the countryside, trying to enlist the poorest peasants in its struggle against the rich *kulaks* and grain hoarders. Millions perished or fled their homes while grain production fell steeply to half what it had been before 1914. Within three years the entire country was starving and in 1921 the Communist government was forced to appeal for international aid. A massive relief effort was undertaken and, at one stage, the American Relief Administration and other foreign aid organizations were feeding over 10 million mouths. Even so some believe that one-tenth of the population perished from hunger in the midst of a brutal civil war. Finally, a rebellion by sailors at Kronstadt forced Lenin to make a tactical retreat. He introduced his New Economic Policy to create a 'breathing space' for the Party, replacing grain requisitioning with taxes and reopening food markets as part of a massive retreat from the moneyless and propertyless Utopia that he had tried to create after 1918.

In a famous speech in 1923, one of Lenin's colleagues Nikolay Bukharin promised a new deal for the peasantry: 'To the peasants, we must say "Enrich yourselves, develop your farms, and do not fear that restrictions will be placed on you." However paradoxical it may appear, we must develop the well-to-do farm in order to help the poor peasant and the middle peasant.' Nearly sixty years later Deng Xiaoping was to use almost the same words when he abolished Mao's communes and told the Chinese peasants that 'to get rich is glorious'. As a result of the New Economic Policy, agricultural production in the Soviet Union returned to pre-1914 levels.

After Lenin's death in 1924, however, Stalin made a second attempt to realize Marx's schemes for giant factory-farms. In 1928 he repealed the New Economic Policy and launched the first five-year plan, which was to be the model for Mao's Great Leap Forward. This was a gigantic crash industrialization campaign in which Stalin wanted to double steel output and triple both pig-iron and tractor production within five years. The investment for industrialization was to come from squeezing the peasants, and this could only be done if they were brought under control in collective farms.

In the Kremlin, a bitter power struggle ensued as Stalin ousted his rivals and silenced opposition to his plan. He attacked Bukharin for restoring capitalism in the countryside and later had him put on trial and shot. Those who had voiced support for Bukharin's view that collectivization should be a gradual process of persuasion were also silenced. Stalin's collectivization campaign, which began in 1929, was violent, brutal and sudden. Overnight, small peasant holdings were merged into collectives – giant farms covering as much as 247,000 acres (100,000 hectares). Stalin claimed that these collective farms would create a new world of plenty: 'In some three years' time, our country will have become one of the richest granaries, if not the richest, in the whole world.' Tractors operating in immense fields of grain were supposed to double grain yields, while on the new factory-farms the output of milk, butter, cheese and meat would quadruple. A new life would begin for the peasants, too. They would move out of their medieval villages into modern 'socialist agro-towns' in each of which 44,000 people would inhabit skyscrapers with 'flats, libraries, restaurants, reading rooms and gymnasiums'. In the collectives, money was not altogether abolished but wages were, because the peasant now earned work points. The local Party secretary would calculate the value of these accumulated points and then pay the peasant a share of the collective's output. In an effort to abolish private property peasants were in many places incited to destroy their own possessions, including their eating utensils, and were encouraged to eat in collective dining-rooms and to live in dormitories. As Marx had foreseen in his *Manifesto*, the peasants were also organized in industrial-type armies or at least their activities were described using military jargon. So they worked in 'brigades' or were dispatched to 'agricultural fronts'; in emergencies they acted as 'shock troops' or 'shock workers'.

Inevitably, the peasants violently resisted these edicts and from 1929 onwards there were armed rebellions in the country-side. To justify his harsh counter-measures, Stalin alleged that the cities were short of food because the peasants were hoarding grain, speculating with it and resisting procurement as an act of sabotage. In fact, they were merely reluctant to sell to the state because procurement prices were set too low. The forcible seizure of grain was resumed as was the war against the *kulaks*, who were expelled from their villages and killed or deported to labour camps. To whip up mass hysteria against the rich peasants, the Party used the 'Committees of Poor Peasants' which it had organized in the villages after 1918. Just who was a *kulak* and who was not, was left deliberately vague. Technically, the term applied to anyone who used hired labour or gave credit to his neighbours, and it extended to wives and children, but anyone could be labelled a *kulak* at the discretion of the local Party.

The peasants responded by defending themselves with whatever weapons they had or by destroying their own property, burning their grain and slaughtering their animals. Much of the country's livestock died during the collectivization and for a while peasants gorged themselves on meat, eating until they could eat no more. The Kazakhs and other nomadic tribes with herds of livestock were forcibly settled and in the process most of the herds died. As a result a quarter of the Kazakh population starved to death.

To stop the peasants destroying their animals and farms, Stalin decreed that all collective property including cattle, standing crops and other agricultural produce as well as agricultural implements now belonged to the state. Anyone damaging such state property was 'a saboteur', 'a wrecker' and 'an enemy of the people' to whom no mercy could be shown. As millions tried to flee their villages, Stalin introduced what was called the internal passport. At entrance points to all cities, police set up checkpoints to inspect these registration documents. Those who were not registered as city-dwellers were turned back and only those with an urban registration could obtain grain ration cards. The peasants were forbidden to leave their villages without permission, just as they had been when they were serfs.

Collectivization was also the signal for a massive assault on all aspects of peasant life, and Stalin and others talked of launching a cultural revolution. Religion was outlawed, the clergy arrested, the churches closed and turned into store-rooms or barns. The state also set about erasing all aspects of ethnic identity among the Ukrainians and other subject peoples of the former Russian empire.

In 1930 there was a pause during which Stalin condemned the excesses of collectivization, accusing some cadres of 'left deviation' in abandoning the 'Leninist principle of voluntarianism' and of being 'dizzy with success'. For a brief period peasants could leave the collective farms, but it was not long before they were forced to rejoin them. At the same time, the Soviet Union doubled its grain exports to raise hard currency to buy equipment needed for industrialization. As Nikita Khrushchev later said of Stalin and his colleagues: 'Their method was like this. They sold grain abroad, while in some regions people were swollen with hunger and even dying for lack of bread.'

Just as in China thirty years later, the forced seizure of grain by the state was the greatest cause of the famine that now followed collectivization. In the Soviet Union this took place from 1931 to 1933 when the Party deliberately and consciously took all the grain it could from the peasants. Cadres suppressed accurate figures on the harvest and replaced them with inflated and spurious calculations based on the 'biological yield': in other words they guessed at the size of the harvest by looking at the grain growing in the fields. Even those farms that met their initial quotas were merely assigned supplementary quotas until there was no grain left. To stiffen the resolve of the rural cadres, Moscow dispatched 25,000 urban workers to the countryside. Later, more workers were brought from factories to harvest the grain and till the soil. On average, the peasants were left with a third less grain than they had had between 1926 and 1930 but the food shortages were at their most acute in the Soviet Union's richest grain-growing areas – the Ukraine, the lower reaches of the Volga and the northern Caucasus. It is also now clear that Stalin used the ensuing famine to extinguish Ukrainian nationalism and to crush the rebellious Cossacks, dismissing as 'right opportunist capitulators' those officials who truthfully reported the existence of famine in these regions. Any cadre who refused to participate in the grain seizures was arrested and found guilty of 'right opportunism' and a campaign against rightists was elevated to the 'main struggle' in the country.

In 1931, Stalin allowed relief grain to be delivered to drought-stricken areas and took other steps to alleviate the suffering caused by famine in all regions except the Ukraine. Instead, officials there went from house to house, ripping up the walls and floors and testing the ground for hidden reserves to find grain to meet procurement quotas. As one participant, Lev Kopolev, wrote in *The Education of a True Believer*: 'I took part in this myself, scouring the countryside, searching for hidden grain, testing the earth with an iron rod for loose spots that might lead to hidden grain. With the others I emptied out the old folks' storage chests, stopping my ears to the children's crying and the women's wails. For I was convinced that I was accomplishing the transformation of the countryside.' A peasant victim of the campaign later testified at a US Congressional investigation in 1988 that officials 'would walk all over our fields, probing the latter with sharp pikes. The pike was jammed into the ground and pulled up. If any grains of wheat were picked up, the conclusion was that grain was being hidden from the state. The men with pikes went everywhere.'

When the Ukrainian peasants became desperate in their search for food, militia were deployed to guard the grain stores and protect shipments of grain. Then Stalin issued a new law, 'On Safeguarding Socialist Property'. It authorized the death penalty for anyone stealing even an ear of wheat and in the first year of its enactment, 1932, 20 per cent of all persons sentenced in Soviet courts were convicted under it. Eyewitnesses said that in the midst of the famine peasants knew that their grain was being transported through the starving countryside and shipped out of Ukrainian ports.

Lev Kopolev described what he saw in the Ukraine and how he, a faithful Party member, felt:

In the terrible spring of 1932 I saw people dying from hunger. I saw women and children with distended bellies, turning blue, still breathing but with vacant, lifeless eyes. And corpses – corpses in ragged sheepskin coats and cheap felt boots, corpses in peasant huts, in the melting snow of the Vologda, under the bridges of Kharkov . . . I saw all this and did not go out of my mind or commit suicide. Nor did I curse those who had sent me to take away the peasant's grain in the winter, and in the spring to persuade the barely walking skeleton-thin or sickly-swollen people to go into the fields in order to 'fulfil the Bolshevik sowing plan in shock-worker style'. Nor did I lose my faith. As before I believed because I wanted to believe.

That year was followed by an even more terrible spring as the Soviet writer, Vasily Grossman, recorded:

When the snow melted true starvation began. People had swollen faces and legs and stomachs. They could not contain their urine . . . And now they ate anything at all. They caught mice, rats, sparrows, ants, earthworms. They ground up bones into flour, and did the same thing with leather and shoe soles; they cut up old skins and furs to make noodles of a kind and they cooked glue. And when the grass came up, they began to dig up the roots and ate the leaves and the buds, they used everything there was; dandelions, and burdocks and bluebells and willowroot, and sedums and nettles . . .

Another eyewitness testified at the US Congressional investigation that 'In the spring of 1933 the fertile Ukrainian soil was covered with human corpses. Corpses could be seen everywhere – on the roads, in the fields, at the railway station. Sometimes I went to visit my village (for I still had family there) and I saw how special brigades gathered the corpses from the streets and houses, and carted them to common graves, or simply threw them in ravines. Even the undertakers themselves were half dead.'

In the then Ukrainian capital of Kharkov, the Italian Consul noted that there was 'a growing commerce in human meat' and that people in the countryside were killing and eating their own children. The authorities distributed public information posters that said 'Eating dead children is barbarism', and the Ukrainian chief procurator issued a decree to the effect that since no civil law against cannibalism existed, all cases must be transferred to the local branch of the secret police, the OGPU. As the famine deepened, people tried desperately to flee. Viktor Serge recalled in *Memoirs of a Revolutionary*: 'Filthy crowds fill the stations; men, women and children in heaps, waiting for God knows what trains. They are chased out, they return without money or tickets. They board any train they can and stay on it until they are put off. They are silent and passive. Where are they going? Just in search of bread, of potatoes . . .'

People knew there was bread in the cities and left their babies in railway stations, hoping they would be taken to orphanages and cared for. It was a forlorn hope. In Kharkov in 1932, the police removed 250 corpses every morning from the railway station. They also collected the living, including children, who would be put in cells and then taken in trucks or freight trains back to the countryside. There they would throw the dead and the dying into large pits or down gullies.

Peasants hoped that if they got to the cities they would be able to buy bread using gold or foreign currency at the special foreign exchange shops called *torgsin* that the government had opened. These shops stocked goods and foodstuffs otherwise unobtainable and the government used them to obtain gold and foreign exchange cheaply. Relatives living abroad were also encouraged to send money through the *torgsin* in answer to desperate appeals. Those with no relatives abroad broke open graves to borrow gold from the dead.

At the same time the authorities organized a deliberate conspiracy of silence. Doctors were forbidden to disclose on death certificates that the deceased had starved to death, as one eyewitness reported to the US Congressional investigation: 'The Soviet government told officials on the *oblast* [region] and *raion* [district] levels that they must never write on a death certificate that someone had died of starvation. Since the authorities had to account for every single death, even the people who died on the roads and streets, they would make up all sorts of illnesses – intestinal disorders, heart attacks – as causes of death.'

At the height of the famine in 1933, the Party even invited the former French prime minister Edouard Herriot to make a state visit to Kiev. Before he arrived, mounted police dispersed people queuing for food, killing some. Other influential figures added their weight to Moscow's vehement denials that a famine was taking place. The Moscow correspondent of *The New York Times*, Walter Duranty, the American journalist Anna Louise Strong (who would later deny the Chinese famine) and the British social reformers Beatrice and Sidney Webb were among those who joined organized visits to collective farms and then poured scorn on those who said there was mass starvation. The few who did go and report the truth, like the *Guardian*'s Moscow correspondent Malcolm Muggeridge, were ignored.

The Ukrainian famine finally ended in 1934 after Stalin ordered a stop to the forced seizure of grain. Within three years, he was to launch the Great Terror, purging the old Party apparatus, executing his colleagues after show trials and sending huge numbers of other Party members, military officers and intellectuals to labour camps. One of those who made a direct link between the famine and the purges was the writer Boris Pasternak. In *Dr Zhivago* he wrote: 'Collectivization was an erroneous and unsuccessful measure and it was impossible to admit the error. To conceal the failure, people had to be cured, by every means of terrorism, of the habit of thinking and judging for themselves, and forced to see what didn't exist, to assert the very opposite of what their eyes told them.'

The existence of the famine and the extent of the man-made disaster remained a closely guarded secret until after Stalin's death in 1953, a silence only partly broken in 1956 by Nikita Khrushchev in his speech denouncing Stalin's crimes, and in his memoirs *Khrushchev Remembers*, published long after he had lost power. After 1956 a few writers in the Soviet Union such as Pasternak were permitted to allude to it in novels, but it was only in the late 1980s that detailed accounts were published. Until the Gorbachev era, the official Soviet line remained that the Soviet state was blameless but that local officials had committed crimes by exceeding their authority.

In *Harvest of Sorrow*, the historian Robert Conquest estimated that between 1930 and 1937, 11 million peasants died in the Soviet Union and a further 3.5 million died in labour camps. In the Ukraine he believed that out of a farm population of between 20 and 25 million about 5 million perished in the famine. More recently, fresh statistics have come to light with the release of the 1937 census. One expert, Michael Ellman, has recalculated the death toll from the famine and has concluded that perhaps 7.2 to 8.1 million died of starvation in 1933; and the investigation by the US Congress in 1988 judged that Stalin knew that people were starving to death and that he and those around him were guilty of genocide against the Ukrainian nation.[2]

In 1946, when Khrushchev became First Secretary of the Ukraine, the area was again experiencing famine and he later recounted that at the time people were suffering from oedema and had once more resorted to cannibalism. Soviet agriculture and the collectives were never a success. Not once during the 1930s did per capita grain yields regain the levels seen before 1914, and after the Second World War food supplies never matched those available in Western countries, despite the fact that the Soviet Union imported grain. Most of the food that was grown came from private plots. After 1934, Stalin had staged a retreat from his policy by allowing each household a small plot of land on which to grow vegetables and raise a cow, a pig and up to ten sheep. For the next fifty years, these private plots would provide most of the food consumed in the Soviet Union.

How much of all this the Chinese Communists knew in 1949 when they established the People's Republic of China it is hard to say. Many of them had studied and worked in the Soviet Union during the previous three decades and could scarcely have avoided hearing something of the famine or have failed to notice the food shortages. Even if they had not done so, they would have known what had happened once Khrushchev and Soviet writers began to expose the terrible deeds of Stalin, and some must have counselled against rashly copying Stalin's policies. Yet, astonishingly, Mao proceeded to do just this, though not without considerable opposition from within the Chinese Communist Party.

4

The First Collectivization, 1949–1958

'The people are hungry. It is because those above devour too much in taxes.'

Lao Tzu

AFTER THE PEOPLE'S Republic of China was formally proclaimed in October 1949, Mao Zedong wanted to press ahead as quickly as possible with the creation of collectives. Some of his colleagues advocated a gradualist approach, however, and a major debate opened up within the Party as to how, and at what pace, the peasants should be collectivized. Many felt China had other priorities – to heal the wounds inflicted by civil war, to establish a new civilian administration and to end the food shortages still plaguing some provinces. Officials in the countryside already had their hands full supervising land reform and persecuting landlords. On the periphery of China, the Party was still establishing its control over Tibet, Xinjiang, Manchuria and Hainan Island. Furthermore, China's leaders were still preoccupied with the threat posed by the Nationalists, who had retreated to Taiwan, and before long were committed to a war in Korea where a million troops fought the American-led United Nations forces.

The issue of collectivization divided the Party into two groups. The moderates argued that collectivization should be a distant goal and that it should be preceded by industrialization to provide the tractors and other machinery needed to

modernize China's backward agriculture, and they quoted
Lenin in support of their view: 'If we had 100,000 tractors . . .
then the peasants would say: we are for Communism.' At the
time not only did China lack a single plant to produce tractors
but hardly anyone had seen one. Some estimated that, given
China's size, 1.5 million tractors would be needed to mechanize
farming; and to make effective use of such tractors, the tiny
peasant plots would first have to be amalgamated into large
fields.[1] China's first tractor factory only went into operation
in 1958. In addition to tractors mechanics, spare parts and
deliveries of fuel would all be needed, involving innumerable
logistical problems. Unless the peasants could plainly see the
advantages of this modern technology, it would be hard to
persuade them to give up their land. The moderates talked in
terms of fifteen to twenty years to achieve their aim.

Ranged on the other side were those who believed that the
only way to finance industrialization was to squeeze the
peasants. Stalin had done this, and Soviet economists had
pointed out that when Japan had industrialized, 60 per cent of
the necessary capital had been raised by taxing the peasants.
To squeeze the peasants, the agricultural economy had to be
brought under government control which meant establishing
a monopoly over grain purchase and distribution. This would
allow the state to buy grain cheaply and sell it dear, and with
these funds China could make the steel and build the tractors
that she wanted. It also soon became apparent that China's
'big brother', the Soviet Union, was not willing or able to provide loans, grants or gifts of tractors in any quantity. Perhaps,
too, Mao hoped to catch up with the Soviet Union and to
emulate what Stalin was doing. For Khrushchev, then in charge
of agriculture, was implementing Stalin's plans to create still
larger collectives – giant farms, as big as provinces, that were
organized around agro-cities.

It was clear, though, that establishing a state monopoly of
food and depressing prices would provoke considerable opposition from the peasants and cause grain production to fall.
Inevitably, the more productive peasants with the most to lose
would put up the toughest resistance. These could only be
brought under Party control if they were amalgamated into
collectives. This was, in any case, considered a desirable objec-

tive since by sharing tools and draft animals the weaker farmers would be helped.

Those Party leaders who had studied in Russia during the period of War Communism were aware of the catastrophic famine which Lenin had created by hastily establishing a state grain monopoly. They did not want China to follow the Soviet Union's path and see civil war renewed by large-scale peasant resistance to grain seizures. In China this would be an even greater folly since the Chinese Communist Party owed its victory over the Nationalists to peasant support.

One of the moderates was Liu Shaoqi, who had joined the Party in 1921, and had been a member of the first group of Chinese to go to Moscow and study at the Sun Yat-sen University of the Working Chinese. There he may have witnessed the horrors of War Communism at first hand. On his return to China he began to play a major role in the Party and by 1949 was a member of the Politburo's Standing Committee. In 1959 he would become President of China and Mao's second-in-command but he would end his life as the chief victim of the Cultural Revolution. Although he was no liberal, materials published during the Cultural Revolution claim that already in 1950 he was arguing in favour of protecting the property of rich peasants and against requisitioning surplus land: 'This is a long-term policy . . . Only when conditions are mature for the extensive application of mechanised farming, for the organisation of collective farming and for the socialist reform of the rural areas, will the need for a rich peasant economy cease, and this will take a long time to achieve.'[2] Mao, however, stated that 'co-operatives must come first and only then can we use large machines'. A year later Liu went further and attacked Mao's plans to set up large collectives overnight as 'false, dangerous and Utopian agrarian socialism'. In a lecture to the Marx-Lenin Institute of Higher Cadres, he said that the peasants' desire to own their land 'cannot be checked . . . hiring labour and individual farming should be unrestricted . . . no collectivization before mechanization . . . production and financial reconstruction are top priorities'.[3] He was backed by other senior leaders such as the head of the North China Bureau, Bo Yibo, who said it was sheer 'fantasy' and 'Utopianism' to imagine that the peasants' desire to own their land would be erased by fostering co-operative peasant organizations.[4]

Mao, however, could not be dissuaded and the moderates were defeated. The government soon began to establish a state monopoly of grain on the grounds that it was necessary in order to curb inflation and guarantee supplies. Chen Yun, who drafted the Party's first five-year plan (1953–7), opposed these arguments and proposed that instead of closing rural markets, procurement prices should be raised. But he was ignored, the grain markets were closed, state procurement prices were kept low and state purchases began to account for a larger and larger share of the harvest. The peasants were now paying more in grain taxes than before 1949 but state investment in agriculture was pegged at only 7 per cent of government spending under the five-year plan. By the mid-1950s the Party was able to control the distribution of grain sufficiently to establish a grain rationing system for the cities. Cadres were dispatched to the villages to extract state procurement quotas by force and to push the peasants into signing promises to deliver still more grain. Such was the pressure exerted that local officials or peasants who failed to meet their quotas were beaten in struggle sessions. Some even committed suicide when they could no longer feed their families.[5]

Determined to press ahead with collectivization, in 1955 Mao impatiently castigated the doubters as behaving 'like old women with bound feet' and launched what has been termed the 'little leap forward' in which the peasants were forced to join higher or advanced co-operatives. After 1949, the peasants had been pushed into joining 'mutual aid teams' which grouped 5–15 households together. Then, in 1953, the pace was stepped up and they joined 'elementary agricultural co-operatives' of 20–40 households. In October 1955, Mao ordered that peasants must be grouped in higher or advanced co-operatives which brought together 100–300 families. These were as big as or even bigger than the average Soviet collective farm of 245 families. Mao repeated Stalin's condemnation of the small peasant holder as 'inherently capitalistic' and some 400 million of China's peasants were dragooned into joining 752,000 of these collectives.

The land had not been formally appropriated from the

peasants but they were forced to pool their draft animals, tools, seed grain and harvest grain, and to work in teams under the authority of the Party secretary. The methods used were the same as in the Soviet Union – the peasants were summoned to a meeting and made to stay there for days, or weeks if necessary, until they 'voluntarily' agreed to join the collective. Mao claimed that only by abolishing the small peasant holder could China escape from its constant food shortages: 'For thousands of years a system of individual production has prevailed among the peasant masses under which a household or family makes a productive unit: this scattered individual form of production was the economic foundation of feudal rule and has plunged the peasants into perpetual poverty.'[6]

Mao's ambitious plans for the peasantry also extended well beyond the economic sphere and, in the early 1950s, under what were termed 'democratic reforms', the whole world of the peasant was torn apart. The Party launched an assault on every aspect of peasant life in a bid to create a new society. On the positive side, there were renewed efforts to increase literacy, raise the status of women, improve public health and sanitation, and end foot-binding, child marriage and opium addiction. Yet other changes diminished the life of the peasant.

In the first eight years after 1949, the peasant's spiritual life came to an end as the Party closed temples, shrines and monasteries. The gallery of shamans, astrologers and *fengshui* (geomancy) experts, and the priests from various organized faiths – Daoism, Buddhism, Catholicism and Protestantism – who provided solace and guidance were all banished, disrobed or arrested. The ceremonies, rites and rituals that gave meaning to each phase of the agricultural cycle, and which marked the peasant's life from cradle to grave, were discouraged or forbidden. In place of traditional culture and festivals, the Party organized endless political meetings and agit-prop performances. The folk culture of the peasants had included songs that people sang while they worked, or operas that they performed at market festivals.[7] In Jiangsu province, peasants had performed different songs for weeding, hoeing or washing and, when they laboured in the paddy fields, would listen to long epics that went on for days. Now, even their love songs and operas were banned. The markets were closed. The holding of weddings and other feasts was also discouraged in order to avoid waste and extravagance at a time of national reconstruction.

From 1956 Mao introduced to China Stalin's internal passport. The peasant could no longer travel without permission to attend fairs, or to seek work outside the village in slack seasons. News from the outside world was no longer brought by pedlars, strolling beggars, wandering musicians and mendicant priests. The emphasis on grain production in the collectives and the travel restrictions discouraged handicrafts like embroidery or woodcarving that had been a part of peasant culture. All the small-scale private enterprises of village China withered and died, leaving the peasants dependent on what the state could supply from its factories. Yet the peasants were at the very bottom of the state's distribution chain, and many goods became unobtainable. Highest priority was now given to the urban proletariat for whom a fully fledged welfare state was created.[8] So while, for example, the Party outlawed traditional medicine and its practitioners, it was hard for peasants to obtain modern medicines or find an approved doctor to treat their ailments. 'The Party treated popular mores and peasant norms as enemy forces,' concluded the American authors of a study of one Hebei village, *Chinese Village, Socialist State.*[9] Even the tombs of the peasants' revered ancestors were not left alone but were dug up, or ploughed over, because they occupied valuable farming land.

Yet despite all these changes, or indeed because of them, agricultural output plummeted and there was widespread famine. In 1956, grain yields alone fell by as much as 40 per cent. The authors of *Chinese Village, Socialist State* recorded that in one part of Hebei province: 'Some villagers recalled 1956, the first year of collectivisation, as the low point of their economic fortunes. The data is fragmentary but it seems that Wugong [village], as with many Hebei communities, suffered a catastrophe exceeded in living memory in its toll of human life only by the great famine of 1943.' Reliable figures on the scale of the disaster are hard to obtain but some interviewees reported hearing of large-scale famine deaths in the provinces of Yunnan, Gansu, Guangxi and Sichuan. In Fujian province peasants were reported to be eating the bark off the trees. In

Shunyi county, not far from Beijing, one source said peasants were reduced to living off nothing but 'cakes' made of chaff and bark. Peasants in different parts of the country began to flee their homes in search of food and among the Tibetans in Sichuan and Qinghai provinces a full-scale rebellion erupted.

The collectivization of farm animals led peasants to kill them and sell their meat before the collective appropriated the animals. In Fengyang county in Anhui, records show why: the collective paid a peasant only 5.5 yuan for an ox but by selling it for meat he could earn 30 or 40 yuan. And since those animals that survived collectivization were now publicly owned, no one felt responsible for them. Peasants worked the animals to death and fed the fodder to their own pigs. In the autumn of 1956, 2,100 draught animals in Fengyang died: a further 440 died after the first big snow. Peasants sang a song which went: 'In the past when a cow died we cried because it was our own, but when a cow dies now, we are very happy because we have meat to eat.' In Hebei province, the number of draught animals fell from 4.3 million to 3.3 million in 1956.[10] By the following year the First Secretary of Henan, Pan Fusheng, was complaining that women were forced to yoke themselves to the plough with their wombs hanging down, such was the shortage of draught animals.

Though the Party's propaganda machinery continued to trumpet great successes in agriculture, especially in grain production, John Lossing Buck, who had surveyed and studied Chinese agriculture before 1949, later cast doubt on these claims. Now in America, he looked at the figures and concluded that the Communists had manipulated their statistics.[11] By using too low a figure for grain yields before 1949, they had produced a 'series of production data which record increases that are primarily statistical'. Even so, they could not disguise the fact that average grain harvests between 1949 and 1958 were below those of 1931–7 and that the peasants had been better off between 1929 and 1933 (years of great famine in northern China) when annual per capita grain production was higher.

The moderates in the Party leadership, including Zhou Enlai, wanted to retreat from collectivization. It was clear not only that Mao's 'little leap forward' had been an economic failure but also that it was causing political unrest.[12] They pointed to internal reports that in some places the peasants had beaten up cadres and withdrawn from the collectives, taking both grain and animals with them.[13] Their hand was further strengthened by Khrushchev's 1956 secret speech in which he exposed Stalin's crimes and criticized his agricultural policies. Collectivization under Stalin was no longer described as 'the greatest success'. Indeed Khrushchev believed that it had created a wasteland in the villages, the like of which had not been seen since the onslaught of the Tartar armies: 'One would go through a village and look around and have the impression that Mamai and his hordes had passed that way. Not only was there no new construction, but the old structures were not repaired.'[14]

Under Khrushchev's leadership, the Soviet Union retreated from Stalinism by raising procurement prices, rescinding taxes on private orchards and vegetable patches, and abolishing the system of forced deliveries from the produce grown on private plots. In China, little was said publicly about Khrushchev's secret speech, although Mao began to fear that the anti-Stalinism sweeping the Soviet Union would affect China.

In 1957 Mao responded to these different pressures by launching another political purge, the Anti-Rightist movement. Generally, this is portrayed as an attack against intellectuals who gave voice to their criticisms during a brief period of free speech which Mao orchestrated for a few weeks in 1957 under the banner of the 'Hundred Flowers campaign'. Reviving an old phrase, 'Let a hundred flowers and a hundred schools of thought contend', Mao apparently set a trap for intellectuals, because those who did speak out were soon arrested as 'right-ists'. Some believe that he was taken aback by the degree of criticism and feared a Hungarian-style uprising. Whatever the case, at least half a million were seized in the Anti-Rightist campaign which Deng Xiaoping, then General Secretary of the Communist Party, organized.

However, the origins of this purge may also lie in the failure of the first round of collectivization. The targets of the Anti-Rightist campaign were not just intellectuals but also large numbers of high- and low-ranking officials who had complained about Mao's agricultural policies. Among those who fell at the centre was Deng Zihui, the leader in charge of the Party's rural work department, who was declared a rightist for his opposition to overnight collectivization. He was replaced by the Stalinist Chen Boda. In the provinces, numerous deputy secretaries and governors lost their posts as well. In Henan, even the First Secretary, Pan Fusheng, was toppled for saying that the co-operatives were a mess and too large to be efficient. He had decided to break up some of the collectives and had allowed the peasants to leave if they wished. For this he was accused of being a follower of Bukharin and a patron of the peasant smallholder.[15] Mao replaced him with Wu Zhifu, an enthusiastic supporter of the collectives, whose efforts were highlighted in Mao's book devoted to such achievements, entitled *The High Tide of Socialism in the Countryside*. In Anhui province, the First Secretary Zeng Xisheng arrested not only large numbers of leading officials and intellectuals, including his deputy Li Shinong, but also any official who was critical of, or was even suspected of being opposed to, the collectives.[16] In one county alone, Fengyang, 4,362 Party cadres were investigated, 22 died under interrogation and 160 were sent to labour camps.

The Anti-Rightist campaign silenced any conceivable opposition within the Party, or from experts in the agricultural sciences, and paved the way for the Great Leap Forward. Mao began planning it in 1957. A year later he was ready to imitate Stalin with a crash industrialization campaign. Mao was no longer – if he ever had been – the first among equals but a semi-divine being who could ignore not only the advice of his colleagues but even that from his 'big brother' in Moscow. The Russians counselled him to avoid repeating Stalin's mistakes, pointing out that China was much poorer than Russia had been in 1928. In China, per capita grain output was still half that of the Russians in the 1920s and so the margin for error was much smaller. Khrushchev even told Mao that those who set up the collectives in the 1920s had 'a poor understanding of what Communism is and how it is to be built'. Yet, as he sarcastically remarked, 'Mao thought of himself as a man brought by God to do God's bidding. In fact, Mao probably thought God did Mao's own bidding.' He believed Mao wanted to show that the Chinese were capable of building socialism and to 'impress the world – especially the socialist world – with his genius and his leadership'.[17]

Mao's bid for the leadership of the Communist world inspired him not merely to match the Russians but to attempt to outdo them in reaching Communism first. His communes and his 'agro-cities' would be larger than those in the Soviet Union and more Communistic because they would abolish all private plots and private possessions – something not even Stalin had dared attempt. Khrushchev, who was himself far from modest when it came to devising grandiose goals and plans, announced in 1958 that in three or four years the Soviet Union would catch up with America in the per capita production of meat, milk and butter. At the same time he launched the massive 'virgin lands' scheme to bring 30 million acres of steppe in Kazakhstan and Siberia under the plough. Mao responded by proclaiming that China would overtake Britain; first he said this would be achieved within fifteen years, but he later shortened the time to three and then two years. Such rivalry was expressed even on relatively small issues. When the Soviets said in January 1958 that they would put their tractors in the hands of the collectives instead of machine tractor stations, a separate administration, Beijing delayed reporting this until China announced, quite independently, that she would do the same.[18]

In 1958, the Chinese Communists declared that the attainment of Communism and the withering away of the state 'is no longer a remote future event'. Chinese leaders talked as if it were only three or four years away. According to his doctor, Mao boasted to his circle that 'for decades the Soviet Union tried to establish an advanced form of social development but always they have failed. We have succeeded in less than ten years.' In 1961, Khrushchev was to take up the challenge and announce that the Soviet Union would enter the final stage of Communism in fifteen years.[19]

The two countries were to fall out over many other issues, such as Moscow's détente with the West and its unwillingness to help China build a nuclear bomb. The final split came in July 1960 when, in the space of a few weeks, the Soviets withdrew all the thousands of experts they had sent to help China after 1949, and widened still further after a series of vitriolic

exchanges. Yet Mao remained an avid believer in the achievements of Stalin, including his agricultural policies and the
miracles of Soviet agricultural science. He wanted China to
copy and then outdo the methods used by Russian scientists
such as Trofim Lysenko which had allegedly raised output to
record levels. Khrushchev had at first criticized Lysenko as a
fraud but later changed his mind when he launched his virgin
lands scheme. Lysenko convinced Khrushchev that he had discovered a way of making the steppe lands fertile without the
expense of manufacturing chemical fertilizers and herbicides.
This misplaced faith in the wonders of Soviet science betrayed
both Khrushchev and Mao into thinking they held the secret
to creating a bonanza of food. Khrushchev's ambitious agricultural schemes ended in disaster, the virgin lands turned to dust
and Soviet meat production figures proved to be fraudulent.
In 1964, Khrushchev was toppled from power, partly because
of this failure. No such fate awaited Mao, although in 1958 he
too was convinced that he had a formula for boosting agricultural production which would guarantee the success of his
Utopian plans. There would be so much food that, as Marx
had prophesied, the time would be reached when the principle
of each according to his needs would be realized. There was
no need to wait for gradual change because, as Hegel said,
progress, like evolution, comes in sudden leaps and bounds.
So Mao called his programme 'The Great Leap Forward'.

5

False Science,
False Promises

'Practical success in agriculture is the
ultimate criterion of truth'

Stalin

'Seeing all men behaving like drunkards,
how can I alone remain sober?'

Tang dynasty poem

TO LAUNCH THE Great Leap Forward, Mao whipped up a
fever of expectation all over China that amounted to mass
hysteria. Mao the infallible, the 'great leader', the 'brilliant
Marxist', the outstanding thinker and genius, promised that
he would create a heaven on earth. Even in the 1940s, the Party
had encouraged a personality cult around Mao but now this
reached new and grotesque heights: Mao was an infallible semi-
divine being. The nation's poets, writers, journalists and scientists, and the entire Communist Party, joined him in
proclaiming that Utopia was at hand. Out of China, the land
of famine, he would make China, the land of abundance. The
Chinese would have so much food they would not know what
to do with it, and people would lead a life of leisure, working
only a few hours a day. Under his gifted leadership, China
would enter the final stage of Communism, ahead of every
other country on earth. If the Soviets said they would reach

Communism in ten or twenty years, Mao said the Chinese could get there in a year or two. In fact, he promised that within a year food production would double or treble. Even Liu Shaoqi entered into the spirit of things by coining the slogan 'Hard work for a few years, happiness for a thousand.'[1]

The Great Leap Forward was preceded by a new campaign to raise Mao's personality cult to a level rivalling that of Stalin. From the end of 1957, his portraits, large and small, began appearing everywhere. Mao was compared to the sun and people declared that the era of Mao was already like heaven on earth. The *China Youth Daily* wrote that 'the dearest people in the world are our parents, yet they cannot be compared with Chairman Mao'. In songs, too, Mao was eulogized:

> Chairman Mao is infinitely kind,
> Ten thousand songs are not enough to praise him.
> With trees as pens, the sky as paper
> And an ocean of ink,
> Much would be left unwritten.[2]

Officials toured the country in 1958 describing what happiness and bliss were at hand. Tan Chen Lin, the Minister of Agriculture, painted a fantasy of peasants jumping in one leap from mud huts to skyscrapers, travelling not on donkeys but in aeroplanes.

> After all, what does Communism mean? . . . First, taking good food and not merely eating one's fill. At each meal one enjoys a meat diet, eating chicken, pork, fish or eggs . . . delicacies like monkey brains, swallows' nests, white fungi are served to each according to his needs . . .
>
> Second, clothing. Everything required is available. Clothing of various designs and styles, not a mass of black garments or a mass of blue outfits. After working hours, people will wear silk, satin and woollen suits . . . Foxes will multiply. When all people's communes raise foxes, there will be overcoats lined with fox furs . . .
>
> Third, housing. Housing is brought up to the standard of modern cities. What should be modernised? People's communes. Central heating is provided in the north and air-conditioning in the south. All will live in high buildings. Needless to say, there are

electric lights, telephones, piped water, receiving sets and TV . . .

Fourth, communications. Except for those who take part in races, all travellers and commuters will use transport. Air services are opened in all directions and every *xian* [county] has an airport . . . The time is not remote when each will have an aeroplane.

Fifth, higher education for everyone and education is popularised. Communism means this: food, clothing, housing, transportation, cultural entertainment, science institutes, and physical culture. The sum total of these means Communism.[3]

This fantasy of American life was repeated even to peasants in faraway Tibet where people had never even seen an aeroplane or heard of a skyscraper: 'Everyone would live in one big family . . . We would have no worries about food, clothing and housing as everyone would wear the same clothes, eat the same food and live in the same houses . . . practically everything would be done by machines. In fact a time would come when our meals would be brought by machines right up to our mouths.'[4]

Such fairy-tales of overnight prosperity had been spread as early as 1956. One interviewee, a former journalist from Shaanxi, recalled going to a meeting of propaganda chiefs in 1956 and hearing Mao say that after three years of hard work, China would enjoy such prosperity that no one would need to work hard, or grow much, yet all would live in great luxury.

Writers, too, were busy painting pictures of this happiness. A character in Qin Chaoyang's *Village Sketches* described what would happen:

Socialism means that our mountain district will be clothed with trees, that our peach blossom and pear blossom will cover the hillsides. Lumber mills will spring up in our district, and a railway too, and our trees will be sprayed by insecticide from aeroplanes, and we will have a big reservoir . . .

Can we cover more and more of the mountains in the whole district with green trees, and make the streams clearer each year? Can we make the soil more fertile and make the faces of the people in every village glow with health? Can we make this mountain district of ours advance steadily on the path to socialism? If you ask me, I tell you it can be done! We have the heart, and we have the hands! It can be done!

Another novel, *Great Changes in a Mountain Village* by Zhou Libo, describes how the secretary of a village youth league envisages a future with all modern conveniences:

> It'll be soon, we won't have to wait for ten or even five years. Then we'll use some of the co-operative's accumulated funds to buy a lorry and when you women go to the theatre in the town, you can ride a lorry. With electric light, telephones, lorries and tractors we shall live more comfortably than they do in the city, because we have the beautiful landscape and the fresh air. There'll be flowers all the year round and wild fruit, more than we can eat: chinquapins [dwarf chestnuts] and chestnuts all over the hills.[5]

Naturally enough, peasants all over China began to ask when they would get to Communism and were told soon, very soon. Such fantastic optimism was based on Mao's fundamental ignorance of modern science. Although he had barely ventured outside China and had never studied Western science, Mao believed that science could make his dreams come true. While in the remote hills of Yanan, Mao and his colleagues carefully studied Moscow's propaganda works eulogizing the great achievements of such Soviet scientists as Pavlov, Lysenko and others, and became convinced that they were genuine.

Marxism claims, above all, to be a 'scientific' philosophy, one which applies the principles of science to politics and society. In like manner, Mao believed, modern science could transform the lives of those millions of ignorant peasants sunk in the mire of centuries of feudal superstition. There was no time to wait for them to become convinced, they would have to be forcibly dragged into the twentieth century. Everything connected with traditional beliefs was smashed in the Great Leap Forward (although many observers tend to assume that this happened later, in the Cultural Revolution) but, ironically, what Mao put in place of these beliefs was a pseudo-science, a fantasy that could not be validated by science, or stand up to rational examination, any more than could the peasant superstitions which the Party ridiculed.

Kang Sheng, Mao's loyal henchman, exemplified this casual approach to facts: 'We should be like Marx, entitled to talk nonsense,' he told everyone, and he toured the country lecturing about the need to add imagination to science. 'What is science?' he asked teachers in Zhengzhou, Henan province, in 1958. 'Science is simply acting daringly. There is nothing mysterious about it.' In Hefei, Anhui province, he continued on the same theme: 'There is nothing special about making nuclear reactors, cyclotrons or rockets. You shouldn't be frightened by these things: as long as you act daringly you will be able to succeed very quickly . . . You need to have spirit to feel superior to everyone, as if there was no one beside you . . . You shouldn't care about any First Machine Building Ministry, Second Machine Building Ministry, or Qinghua University, but just act recklessly and it will be all right.'[6]

In Shanghai that year he told cadres that 'if by national day next year, Shanghai's schools are able to launch a third-grade rocket to an altitude of 300 kilometres, they should get three marks . . . A third-grade rocket with a satellite should get five marks. This is very easy. At New Year, the [ordinary] Shanghainese fire rockets, so surely the schools can launch [real] rockets!'[7]

Trained scientists such as Professor Qian Xusen, the American nuclear physicist who returned to serve Mao and help build China's nuclear bomb, gave credibility to this optimism. He wrote articles and gave lectures to agricultural experts stating that it was quite realistic to increase crop yields ten or a hundred times. Qian said that one small plot of land could yield over a dozen tonnes of grain if just a small percentage of the energy from sunlight were properly utilized.[8]

Such carelessness with the truth shocked even visiting Soviet scientists like Mikhail Klochko. He discovered first-year chemistry students at a teacher training school rewriting their organic chemistry textbooks as they went along. For example, the students had decided they would only learn about copper, because they lived in Yunnan province which is rich in copper ore, so there was no need to bother with the other metals and elements.[9] This approach to science mirrored that in Soviet Russia when Stalin launched his first five-year plan. Then, the message of countless books and articles was the same: the impossible could only be achieved by ignoring the advice of timid experts, the 'bourgeois specialists' who lived in ivory towers, pedantically inching their way forward. True scientists were peasants filled with intuitive knowledge and led by Party members driven by revolutionary fervour – that was how miracles were achieved. The Soviet novel *Izbrannoe* (*The Select*) by I. Babel, for example, contains a discussion in which a noted oil expert is reprimanded by a young Party member who says: 'We do not doubt the knowledge or goodwill of the professor . . . but we reject the fetishism of figures which hold us in thrall . . . We reject the multiplication table as the basis for policy.'

In the Great Leap Forward, much the same happened in China, only in real life. The *People's Daily* reported how students in one faculty of science and mathematics showed their disdain for basic theory by putting decimal points in the wrong place while others deliberately made mistakes when calculating square roots.[10] Still worse, the message was put out that science was so simple, even a child could excel at it. A propaganda book, *They Are Creating Miracles*, described how children at a primary school 'developed ten more new crops on its experimental plot', a feat presented as hard fact: 'It's a story out of a science-fiction book! But, no, my young friends, it is not! This is a true story. There are no fairy-tale magicians, no white-bearded wizards of never-never land. The heroes of our story are a group of Young Pioneers studying in an ordinary village primary school.'[11]

All over China in 1958, the Party created thousands of new colleges, universities and research institutes, while real scientists were imprisoned or sent to do manual labour. In their place, thousands of untrained peasants carried out 'scientific research'. Many kinds of miracles were announced but the Great Leap Forward was above all about creating huge increases in grain and steel production. These were the 'two generals' that Mao said would modernize China.

Just as Stalin saw a huge increase in steel production as the cornerstone of his crash industrialization programme, Mao envisaged a doubling or trebling of steel output within a year. The entire country, from peasants in remote villages on the Tibetan plateau to top Party officials in Zhongnanhai in Beijing, set up smelters in 1958 and 1959 to create 'steel' in backyard furnaces. Everyone had to meet a quota by handing over their metal possessions. People handed in bicycles, railings, iron bedsteads, door knobs, their pots and pans and cooking grates. And to fire the furnaces, huge numbers of trees were cut down. In the countryside people worked day and night fuelling these furnaces. While they did so, they could eat as much as they wanted out of the communes' collective food stores. The lumps of useless metal that emerged were supposed to be used in the mechanization of agriculture. Had China really produced a lot more steel then it could have been used to make the necessary tractors, ploughs, threshing machines, trucks, diesel engines and pumps. Instead the peasants relied on *tu fa* – literally 'earth methods' – to mechanize their work by inventing hundreds of Heath Robinson-type contraptions of pulleys, ropes and cogs, all made out of wood, not steel. Propaganda photographs showed wooden conveyor belts, wooden threshing machines, wooden automatic compost-appliers – a sort of wheelbarrow with a box on top – wooden rail tracks, wooden railcars, wooden rice-planting machines, wooden wheat harvesters, wooden jute harvesters and, in Shandong, a whole truck made of wood. They were all a great credit to the considerable ingenuity of the Chinese peasant but, in the end, perfectly worthless. Not one has survived in use. Yet, for all the waste and folly of the backyard furnace campaign, it was never more than a minor contributory factor to the starvation that was to result from the Great Leap Forward.

Rather, it was the half-baked ideas on growing more grain, Mao's second 'general', which he insisted the nation should follow, that led to a substantial decline in grain yields. Many Chinese believe his ideas were rooted in traditional Chinese peasant lore, but though this may explain their appeal to a peasant's son like Mao, in fact he merely adopted them from the Soviet Union. To understand what happened in China, therefore, one must first step back in time to the Stalin years and examine the theories of such pseudo-scientists as Lysenko, Michurin and Williams.

For twenty-five years Trofim Denisovitch Lysenko ruled over Soviet agricultural scientists as a dictator. Those who opposed him were shot or perished in labour camps, and his victims were not rehabilitated until 1986 when Mikhail Gorbachev came to power.[12] Until then, Lysenko's portrait hung in all scientific institutions. At the height of his personality cult, art stores sold busts and bas-reliefs of him, and cities erected statues in his honour. When he gave a lecture, he was preceded by a brass band and people sang songs in his honour:

> Merrily play one, accordion,
> With my girlfriend let me sing
> Of the eternal glory of Academician Lysenko.

Lysenko dismissed the developing science of genetics as an 'expression of the senile decay and degradation of bourgeois culture'. Instead, he advocated a mumbo-jumbo of his own which muddled up Darwin's theories on evolution and the competition in nature between different species and among members of the same species. His school rejected the 'fascist' theories that plants and animals have inherited characteristics which selective breeding can develop. Lysenkoists believed that, on the contrary, environmental factors determine the characteristics of plants and animals. Just as Communists thought that people could be changed by altering their surroundings, so Lysenko held that plants acquire new characteristics when their environment is changed and that these changes are transmitted to the next generation. As one observer pointed out, this was tantamount to saying that lambs would be born without tails just because you cut off their mother's tail. Yet Lysenko asserted that he could make orange trees flourish in Siberia, or change them into apple trees, not by selective breeding but by following Stalin's unintelligible teachings on evolution. As the Lysenkoist journal *Agrobiologiya* put it: 'Stalin's teachings about gradual, concealed, unnoticeable quantitative changes leading to rapid, radical qualitative changes permitted Soviet biologists to discover in plants the realisation of such qualitative transitions that one species could be transformed into another.'

Lysenko was a semi-literate peasant from Azerbaijan whom *Pravda* praised in 1927 as a 'barefoot scientist' after he claimed to have found a way of growing peas in winter. These peas, he said, would green the mountains of the Caucasus in winter and solve the problem of winter forage. His next, and equally bogus, achievement went under the name of 'vernalization' (from the Latin, *vernalis*, for spring). Most Russian wheat is sown in winter but the seeds are sometimes damaged by severe weather. The yield from spring wheat is higher so when Lysenko claimed he could turn winter wheat seeds into spring seeds, he was promising to raise yields in many parts of the Soviet Union. His method was simple: change the environment of the seeds by soaking them in very cold water and they themselves would change.

The second verse of the Lysenko song, quoted above, also commemorates another Soviet hero, Michurin:

> He walks the Michurin path
> With firm tread.
> He protects us from being duped
> By Mendelist-Morganists.

If the Austrian monk Gregor Mendel and the American scientist Thomas Morgan are the fathers of genetics, then I. V. Michurin, an impoverished nobleman turned tree-grafter, is the true founder of Lysenkoism. He first rose to fame in the early 1920s when a Soviet leader praised his hybrid creations, including a part melon, part squash vegetable, on show at the First All Russian Agricultural Exhibition. Michurin claimed to have created hundreds of hybrid fruit trees, and because he had received only primary education, he qualified as a genuine peasant hero. The whole nation had to follow his methods, although he insisted that 'intuition' was as vital an element in matching his success as his theories. Michurin dismissed real scientists as 'the caste priests of jabberology', especially those who espoused the theories of Mendel.

Although Michurin was later conclusively shown to be a fraud, he was hailed during Stalin's first five-year plan as an example of what could be done with the correct attitude to science. The daring, untrammelled spirit of his thinking was evoked in this call to arms published in the magazine *October*: 'Knock out sleepiness with punches, with demands, with insistence, with daring. With daring to master and transform the earth, nature, fruit. Is it not daring to drive the grape into the tundra? Drive! Drive! Drive! Into the furrows, into the gardens, into the orchards, into the machines of jelly factories . . . Faster, faster, faster, comrade agronomists!'

Another hero of the Lysenko school was the son of an American engineer, Vasily Williams, who became a professor at the Moscow Agricultural Academy. Williams thought that capitalism and American-style commercial farming based on the application of chemical fertilizers were taking the world to the brink of catastrophe. This was in the early 1930s when American farmers in Oklahoma saw their fields turn to dust. Williams believed that the answer was to rotate fields as medieval peasants had done, growing grain only every third year. The rest of the time the fields would be left fallow, allowing nitrogen to accumulate in the roots of clover and other grasses which would enrich the soil. He was opposed by other experts, among them Pryanishnikov, who stressed the importance of mineral fertilizers and shallow ploughing, but Williams dubbed them 'wreckers of socialist agriculture'. Khrushchev later explained: 'The debate was essentially decided on the basis of capital investments. Pryanishnikov's theory of mineral fertilizers would have required enormous capital investments in order to build fertilizer plants and new machinery. We were short of capital at that time and so Williams' theory was more attractive. That is how Williams' grasslands theory came to reign supreme.'[13]

Khrushchev was one of those who supported Williams, but he admits in his memoirs that 'the fact of the matter is that Williams' system didn't work. Even after it had been consistently implemented throughout the Ukraine, there was no improvement in our agricultural production.'

Stalin also turned to the ideas of Terenty Maltsev, a pupil of Williams, who recommended ploughing furrows four or five feet deep as a way of improving the soil texture and obtaining higher yields. New ploughs to do this were designed and manufactured and Stalin gave Maltsev the Lenin prize for science.

All these ideas helped transform a rich farming nation into one beset by permanent food shortages. On the collectives, farmers could use neither chemical fertilizers nor the hybrid corn that America was using to boost yields by 30 per cent. Furthermore, their fields were left fallow most of the time, and when the crops were sown, the 'vernalized' wheat did not sprout; nor did Lysenko's frost-resistant wheat and rye seeds, or the potatoes grown in summer and the sugar beet planted in the hot plains of Central Asia. They all rotted. One year, Lysenko even managed to persuade the government to send an army of peasants into the fields with tweezers to remove the anthers from the spikes of each wheat plant because he believed that his hybrids must be pollinated by hand. Under banners proclaiming 'Greater harvests with less dung', Soviet farmers also had to create artificial manure by mixing humus with organic mineral fertilizers in a rotating barrel. This method removed the phosphate and nitrogen, and when the muck was spread on the fields, it was useless. Ignoring Lysenko's repeated failures, the Soviet press continued to trumpet his endless successes: cows which produced only cream, cabbages turned into swedes, barley transformed into oats, and lemon trees which blossomed in Siberia.

Lysenko's greatest triumphs came after the Second World War when he dreamt up the 'Great Stalin Plan for the Transformation of Nature'. To create a new and warmer climate in the vast lands of Siberia, Lysenko proposed planting millions of trees. The peasants had to plant the seeds and saplings close together because, according to Lysenko's 'law of the life of species', individuals of the same species do not compete but help each other survive. Naturally all the seedlings died but not before the composer Shostakovich had written his choral symphony, *The Song of the Trees*, and Bertolt Brecht had penned this poem:

> So let us with ever newer arts
> Change this earth's form and operation.
> Gladly measure thousand-year-old wisdom
> By new wisdom one year old.
> Dreams! Golden if!
> Let the lovely flood of grain rise higher!

In China, Mao became greatly taken with the theories of Williams, Lysenko and Michurin. He read Williams' book on soil while still in Yanan and later frequently quoted both him and Lysenko. Mao, too, wanted the Chinese to plant seeds close together because, as he told colleagues, 'with company they grow easily, when they grow together they will be comfortable'.[14] Lysenko's theories meshed perfectly with Mao's obsession with class struggle. He readily believed that plants from the same 'class' would never compete against each other for light or food. While the Chinese Communists were still in Yanan, the chief Chinese Lysenkoist, Luo Tianyu, propagated the Soviet teachings: and in the 1942 rectification movement, a purge of Party members, Luo enthusiastically persecuted those who believed in genetics.[15]

After the Communist victory in 1949, Luo was put in charge of the new Beijing Agricultural University and Soviet-style science now reigned supreme. In the 1950s, all Soviet methods, textbooks and ideas had to be followed, while Western-trained scientists were either arrested or forced publicly to disown their 'fascist eugenics' theories. All research in genetics came to a stop. Lysenko's Soviet disciples toured China giving lectures, and Chinese peasants studied his theories at Michurin societies. China had her own Michurin, a peasant called Shi Yiqian who became a professor at the Henan Agricultural College after he grew grapes on a persimmon tree, and apples on a pear tree. In schools, children also set up a Michurin corner in their classrooms to study how to create such hybrids. Some reportedly managed not only to graft one vegetable on to another but also to cross-breed animals such as rabbits and pigs.

Soviet ideas also dominated other fields, notably that of medicine. Perhaps the most absurd notion introduced to the Chinese was the work of Olga Lepeshenskaya, who supposedly proved that living cells could be created from non-living organic material.[16] None of this could be challenged, as a former doctor in Beijing explained:

> We were told the Soviets had discovered and invented everything, even the aeroplane. We had to change textbooks and rename things in Lysenko's honour. So the Harving Cushing Syndrome – a disease of the adrenalin gland – became Lysenko's Syndrome to show it had been discovered by him. Since genetics did not exist, we were forbidden to talk about inherited diseases such as sickle cell anaemia, even to students. This meant that all through Mao's lifetime there was no policy to stop people in the same family marrying each other and passing down their genes. A lot of idiots were born as a result.[17]

Adherence to Lysenkoism meant that when a potato virus struck large areas of China in the 1950s, nothing could be done because, as in the Soviet Union, the changes had to be attributed to environmental factors. Chinese scientists who had invested years of research into the blight were ignored, and their work was not published until 1979. Some believe that potato output in the Mao era was half what it might have been had the cause of the problem been correctly identified.

Lysenkoism reached its apogee in the Great Leap Forward when in 1958 Mao personally drew up an eight-point Lysenkoist blueprint for all Chinese agriculture. Every farmer in every commune in the country had to follow it. The eight elements of this 'constitution', as it was called, were:

1. The popularization of new breeds and seeds
2. Close planting
3. Deep ploughing
4. Increased fertilization
5. The innovation of farm tools
6. Improved field management
7. Pest control
8. Increased irrigation

The Popularization of New Breeds and Seeds

All over the country in 1958 people began to announce remarkable achievements like those of China's Michurin, Shi Yiqian. In Guangzhou, children and teachers crossed a pumpkin with a papaya, and runner beans with soybeans. In Henan, they produced sunflowers crossed with artichokes. In Beijing, scientists crossed tomatoes with aubergines, corn with rice, and sorghum with rice. One of the most glorious claims was a cross between a cotton plant and a tomato – the result red cotton![18]

In addition to these vegetable freaks, the New China (Xinhua) News Agency also trumpeted claims that peasants were growing super-big plants – pumpkins weighing not 13 lbs, but 132 lbs, wheat with extra-large ears, and rice of exceptional weight. The country's top national agricultural worker, Yang Guangbo, set the pace by growing paddy rice with 150 grains per ear instead of 100. Others, too, were held up for emulation, amongst them Jiang Shaofang of the Yuli Botanical Normal School in Guangxi province whose achievements were described in *China Youth News*:

> The grains of sorghum are as big as those of corn, one full spike weighing as much as one pound, and one stalk may have several ears of corn giving a yield much greater than normal corn ... Jiang Shaofang now plans by crossbreeding and grafting sorghum and corn and sugar cane to produce a plant that will be all three – sorghum, corn and sugar cane. He is also preparing next year to plant a high-yield field of wet rice that will produce 600–1,000 lbs per 0.04 acre.* The methods he plans to use will be a) to breed a very high yield of wet rice and b) to apply highly advanced agricultural techniques.

Specimens of these miraculous plants appeared at exhibitions or on giant pictures paraded through every city. The Chinese also claimed to produce extraordinary animals. The Ministry of Agriculture boasted in 1960 how peasants at the Golden Dragon Commune near Chongqing had been the first in the world to cross a Yorkshire sow with a Holstein Friesian cow using artificial insemination. The Xinhua News Agency described how after a year the litter was still thriving: some of these curious creatures were white but others were patched like the Holstein and 'in general they had shorter snouts and sturdier legs than ordinary pigs'.[19]

These fantasies were not without consequences in the real world. One interviewee, condemned as a 'rightist', was sent to a farm near Shanghai where he ran the pig pen. Cadres ordered him to start the pigs breeding prematurely. Normally, pigs do not breed before they are a year old and weigh at least 160 lbs. Instructions came down from above first to start breeding when the pigs weighed 66 lbs and later to start when the piglets were just four months old and weighed only 33 lbs. There was also a scheme to cross Chinese pigs, which produce small litters of two or three piglets, with much bigger Russian sows which have up to fourteen piglets in a litter. The result was indeed larger litters but all the piglets died because the sow could not

* The Chinese measure of land is the *mu*, equivalent to 0.17 acres.

produce enough milk to feed them. The interviewee said he tried but failed to save the piglets by bottlefeeding them. Attempts in Inner Mongolia and Tibet to crossbreed local sheep and goats with Ukrainian breeds were no more successful because the offspring, ill-adapted to the harsher climate, died in the first winter.

Close Planting

Mao's faith in high-density planting led nearly every commune in China to start an experimental field growing grain in this way. These experimental fields were begun in 1958 and in many places were retained until 1980. In some provinces, like Guangdong, close planting was initially obligatory in all fields. A density of 1.5 million seedlings per 2.5 acres is usually the norm in the south, but in 1958 peasants were ordered to plant 6–7.5 million seedlings and the next year 12–15 million per 2.5 acres. The same close planting was done throughout China with wheat, cotton, sorghum, millet and every other important crop: the results were identical – the seedlings died. Yet the press published photographs apparently showing wheat growing so densely that children could sit on top of it. A retired Xinhua photographer later told the author that the pictures were faked by putting a bench underneath the children.

Fortunately, in most places the peasants knew that close planting was dangerous nonsense and avoided carrying it out on a large scale, otherwise there would have been no food at all in China. Party officials knew this too. One interviewee recalled that before Mao visited the Xinli experimental field in the suburbs of Tianjin in 1958, the cadres brought rice plants from other fields and pushed them close together by hand. 'They were so close together, you really could walk across them,' the interviewee remembered. When Mao left, the cadres immediately removed and replanted the shoots. Mao's doctor, Li Zhisui, recalls how the same thing happened in Hubei: 'Party Secretary Wang Renzhong ordered the peasants to remove rice plants from away fields and transplant them along Mao's route to give the impression of a wildly abundant crop . . . All of

China was a stage, all the people performers in an extravaganza for Mao.'

Deep Ploughing

Mao took the idea of deep ploughing to even greater extremes than had Stalin, in the belief that if it was good to plough deep, it was better to plough deeper still. In some places furrows dug by hand were ten feet deep although generally they were around three to four feet. The exhausting, backbreaking work was often done by crack teams of peasants who sweated around the clock. In 1958 Liaoning province's Governor, Huang Oudong, ordered 5 million people with tens of thousands of animals to toil non-stop for forty-five days to deep-plough 3 million hectares of land. Where the top soil was too shallow, he instructed the peasants to transport soil from fields elsewhere. All this was intended to treble yields in Liaoning.[20] In Heilongjiang in the far north, where for part of the year the soil is frozen solid, peasants blasted open furrows with dynamite. In labour camps on the high plateaux and mountains of Qinghai, the inmates tried to soften the iron-hard soil by digging little holes and filling them with straw and grass which were set on fire. In the rice fields of the south, peasant women waded through the deep paddies up to their waists and many caught infections as a result. In Anhui, where the soil is thin, the deep ploughing destroyed the fertility of the fields for many years to come. In some regions, fields were excavated to a depth of thirteen feet.[21] Indeed, in Guizhou province the trenches were so deep that peasants had to tie ropes around their waists to prevent themselves from drowning. Later, the same province claimed to have the biggest yield in the entire country, an absurd 130,000 *jin*, or 65 tonnes per 0.17 acres.[22]

Of course, there was never any real proof that any of this was effective, but agricultural halls displayed exhibits showing how much taller wheat plants grew the deeper they were planted. In February 1959, agronomists in Anguo county reportedly dug up wheat plants to prove that deep ploughing worked: 'Land ploughed 5 inches had roots only 13 inches long after two months' growth. Land ploughed 5 feet had roots 5 feet long and wheat plants growing in land ploughed 8 feet deep had roots 7 feet 8 inches long.'[23] The deep ploughing was not prac- tised everywhere all of the time, but in some places peasants kept it up for three years or more.

Increased Fertilization

Lysenkoist agrobiology ruled out the use of chemical fertilizers so the Chinese government halted investment in chemical plants and, instead, instructed peasants to use a new method to replace lost nutrients. The Russians claimed that earth when mixed with manure would acquire the qualities of manure and recommended a ratio of 10 per cent manure to 90 per cent earth. So all over China millions of peasants started mixing all sorts of earth and rubbish with real manure and laboriously hauled this to their fields and spread it. To ease the transport of massive amounts of this 'fertilizer', peasants built carts run- ning on wooden rails to carry it to the fields.

The most extraordinary rubbish was thrown on to the fields as fertilizer. People in Guangzhou took their household rub- bish to the outskirts of the city where it was buried for several weeks before being put on the fields. Near Shanghai peasants dumped so much broken glass that they could not walk in the fields in bare feet. Others broke up the mud floors of their huts and their brick stoves and even pulled down their mud walls to use as fertilizer. Elsewhere people tried to turn ordinary soil into manure by heating and smoking it for ten days. Some tried to collect manure by dragging riverbeds for the rich mud and weeds. An article in the *People's Daily* explained that, thanks to the Communists, China was now no longer short of fertilizer:

> Chinese scientists have said that in the past, many people only considered the mineral plant nutrients, that is the amount of nitrogen, phosphorus and potassium in the fertilizer and their relative proportions. They neglected the experience of the Chinese peasants over thousands of years in using organic fertilizer whose application in massive quantities produces high yields. Agronomists proved last year that they could supply the nutrients continuously and improve the physical properties of the soil.[24]

The Research Institute of Hydrobiology also claimed to have invented 'an everlasting fertilizer', described as a blue-green algae which assimilates nitrogen. *China Pictorial* boasted that when planted in a paddy field 'it is the equivalent of a permanent nitrogenous fertilizer'. Peasant scientists such as He Wenyi, 'who could neither recognize chemical symbols, nor understand laboratory reports, nor remember lists of ingredients', were also said to have invented a method for producing fertilizer from bacteria.

The Innovation of Farm Tools

Some of these incredible Heath Robinson inventions made of wood instead of steel have already been described. China also experienced major setbacks when she tried to mass-produce and use machinery based on impractical designs. One example was a rice planter designed to automate the delicate and back-breaking task of planting rice shoots which proved useless because it could handle only one variety at a fixed spacing. Another was a special Soviet plough designed for deep ploughing. The Chinese version, the double-share plough, cost ten times as much as a traditional plough but proved unsuitable for the terraces and paddy fields of southern China: 700,000 had to be withdrawn from use and melted down again. In addition, the Chinese began to manufacture big, heavy Soviet tractors and rejected the small walking tractors which were then helping Japanese farmers to reap record yields on their small plots. In the 1980s, these small tractors were produced in large numbers and were credited with transforming the work of Chinese peasants.

Improved Field Management

Improved field management referred to the field rotation system advanced by Williams. A communiqué issued at a high-level meeting at Wuhan in 1958 summarized its aims: 'We should try to reduce the area sown to various crops to about one-third the present acreage. Part of the land so saved can be left fallow or used for pasturage and the growing of grass fertilizers: the rest can be used for afforestation, reservoirs and the extensive cultivation of flowers, shrubs and trees to turn the whole land with its plains, hills and waters into a garden.'[25]

Though most provinces were not so foolish as to remove two-thirds of their fields from production, Mao's slogan of 'Plant less, produce more, harvest less' could not be completely ignored. Henan province reported cutting the area sown to grain by 14 per cent and Inner Mongolia and Qinghai by 21 per cent, while Shaanxi stated that it was allowing a third of its arable land to lie fallow.[26]

At the same time, the intensive effort put into those areas which were sown with grain sometimes had disastrous results. In provinces such as Hunan which normally grows two crops of rice, peasants were ordered to grow three. Farmers who had poor land were ordered to switch to growing crops which promised a higher yield but exhausted the soil. As a result, in northern Anhui the peasants planted maize in the summer, and in Shaanxi they had to grow corn instead of millet. Since the only crop that mattered to Mao was grain, the acreage devoted to cash crops was in some places reduced. And in Fujian, where China's best tea is grown, tea bushes were ripped out to make way for grain.

Pest Control

In the interests of pest control a new campaign to exterminate the 'four evils' – birds, rats, insects and flies – was launched in 1958. The whole country was turned out to make a noise, beating drums and pans to prevent sparrows from landing anywhere until they fell down dead with exhaustion. The war against the sparrows, as it was termed, was only called off in April 1960 and the birds were replaced on the list by bedbugs.[27] Without the birds to prey on them, insects multiplied, causing damage to crops. Peasants tried to kill the insects at night by setting up huge lamps in the middle of the fields so that the insects would fly around them until they dropped down dead. Everywhere people were ordered to fulfil a quota by catching and killing flies. The same had to be done with rats and field mice. Since Tibetans regarded the killing of a living animal as a grave sin, some imprisoned lamas killed themselves rather than meet their daily quotas. This campaign was also accompanied by an intensive hygiene campaign. Even at the height of the famine people's houses were still being inspected for cleanliness.

Increased Irrigation

At the same time, every county in China was ordered to construct a water reservoir by building a dam and water channels. A series of gigantic schemes were also conceived and the construction of those already under way, like the Sanmenxia Dam on the Yellow River, was speeded up. Almost without exception, the engineering schemes of this period neither worked nor lasted. A senior Ministry of Agriculture official speaking in the 1990s simply dismissed all the small reservoirs as 'completely worthless'.[28] Most of the county dams had collapsed within two or three years and the dam on the Yellow River quickly filled up with silt, rendering it next to useless.[29] Even today it barely functions. A few medium-scale dams did survive, only to collapse later with terrible results. In the worst dam disaster in history, the Banqiao and Shimantan dams at Zhumadian in Henan province burst after heavy rainfall in August 1975, releasing a wall of water which killed 240,000 people.[30]

The labour put into the construction of these dams was stupendous. Nearly all the construction work was performed by people using the simplest tools who worked day and night in shifts, living in makeshift tents and being fed only when they worked. The peasant labourers were organized in military units and marched to work following flags, with martial music blaring from loudspeakers. On the larger projects, tens of thousands were conscripted as labourers and paid nothing.

To make room for the reservoirs, uncounted numbers of people were evicted from their villages and forcibly relocated. In 1958, when the Xin'anjiang reservoir was built in northern Zhejiang province, 300,000 people were transferred *en masse*, and from one county alone, Chun An, 137,000 people were evacuated:

Along the road, many of the evacuated families had to eat and sleep in the open air or in rough tents. Freezing and starving, they ate uncooked grain to fend off hunger. People collapsed with illness on the roadside, some even died; pregnant women had to give birth during the journey. According to an old cadre who took part in the relocation work, the marching peasants resembled wartime columns of refugees.[31]

Inspired by the gigantic dams in the Soviet Union, such as that on the Dnieper, and schemes like the Volga–White Sea canal, the Chinese also planned 'the greatest construction undertaking in history'. This was a project to divert surplus water from the Yangtze to the Yellow River in the north. The water would be taken through a huge interlocking system of deep canals, dams, tunnels, ravines and lakes. Work began during the Great Leap Forward and it was envisaged that it would take millions of men seven years to complete it. As it was, the Xinhua News Agency reported that throughout China the peasants had shifted more rock and earth in a single day than had the builders of the Panama Canal in a whole decade: 'A total of 6,560 million cubic feet was excavated in the week ending December 12, 1959. This is more than 12 times the amount shifted for the building of the Panama Canal.'[32] The Party also planned to water the deserts of western China and plant millions of trees by melting the glaciers of the Tianshan mountains. Propaganda photographs even showed scientists dropping materials from aeroplanes to melt the ice.

In the countryside, the dams collapsed because they were made of earth not concrete, and were designed not by engineers but by untrained peasants. The Party took a peculiar pride in defying 'book learning'. One article in *China Pictorial* eulogized Le Heyun, a water conservancy engineer of peasant origin, as a 'bold innovator' and 'advanced worker': 'In 1959, when the construction of the county's Huangtan reservoir was in progress, he suggested that the culvert and conduit should be built of substitutes instead of reinforced concrete as originally planned, thereby saving 7,000 yuan.' Interviewees said concrete was rarely used and this explained why none of the dams lasted more than a year or two. Without a functioning reservoir, the canals and irrigation ditches were rendered equally useless. In later years a few were rebuilt using concrete and one in Sichuan now serves as a boating lake.

Even when the famine was over, Mao's faith in his agricultural methods does not appear to have been shaken in the slightest by their evident failure. On the contrary, in 1964, Mao established at Dazhai in Shanxi province a working model of his eight-point 'constitution'. Millions of visitors, both domestic and foreign, would be taken around Dazhai and told of the wonders of its amazing peasant scientists, their nitrogen-fixing bacteria, the splendid new varieties of plants, the home-made dams, and so on. Perhaps Mao's vanity prevented him from realizing what a fool he had made of himself.

Certainly, in 1958 and 1959, Mao seemed immune to any doubts, believing he had personally witnessed proof that his methods were succeeding beyond even *his* expectations. As a peasant song put it, the grain reached to the sky and paradise was at hand. For example, in 1958 he visited Xushui, one of the model communes, a convenient train ride away from the capital in Hebei province. As he was driven up to the commune centre, his car passed piles of vegetables, turnips, cabbages and carrots laid out for half a mile along the roadside.[33] Officials told him that the peasants had dumped the vegetables because they had grown so much food they did not know what to do with it. At the commune headquarters, the Party secretary told him that they were eating five meals a day free of charge and the autumn grain harvest had quadrupled to half a million tonnes. Mao was reportedly so staggered by this that he pushed up his cap and asked: 'How can you consume all this food? What are you going to do with the surplus?'

The *People's Daily* even started a debate on how China should cope with its food surplus.[34] Everywhere Mao went, Party officials told him of astounding successes: fields which did not produce 330 lbs of grain – the average before the Great Leap Forward – but 49,500 lbs or even 53,000 lbs per 0.17 acres. In fact, there was no way of knowing the real size of the harvest since the State Statistical Bureau had been dismantled and its local offices replaced by 'good news reporting stations'. Yet the propaganda machine churned out one triumphant claim after another. China had outstripped the United States in wheat and cotton production, she had beaten Japan in per unit yields of rice, and she had bettered the United States in cotton yields.

Mao was not alone in believing this nonsense. Liu Shaoqi, formerly an advocate of gradual progress, and his wife, Wang Guangmei, applied to join the Xushui model commune. Its 1958 harvest was double that of 1957, Liu asserted, and he urged the country to 'go right ahead and realize Communism. We must not think that Communism will only be realized very slowly. So long as we work properly, it will be very soon.'

Deng Xiaoping was equally optimistic. He expected per capita grain distribution in 1958 to be 1,375 lbs on the strength of a peasant's assurance that by using Mao's agricultural methods he had produced 77,000 lbs per 0.17 acres on an experimental field. Deng calculated that at this rate yields in 1959 would rise to 231,000 lbs per 0.17 acres and would by 1962 stand at 2.5 tonnes. 'We can all have as much as we want,' he concluded.[35] At Ya'an, in Deng's home province of Sichuan, people showed how much food they had to eat by leaving pots of cooked food on the roadside from which any passer-by could help himself.[36] Chen Boda, one of Mao's cronies, went so far as to declare that the time had come to abolish money; from now on not only should food be free but also clothing, haircuts and everything else.

Mao felt such achievements trumped those of the Soviet Union which had in 1957 launched the first satellite in space. The breaking of such records was therefore called 'launching a satellite' or 'launching a sputnik'. He also declared that China was achieving such success that she was overtaking the Soviet Union on the road to Communism. No one dared challenge these bogus claims directly and later every senior official would explain that, like Deng, they had been innocently duped by the peasants.

In the belief that China was awash with food, everyone in the autumn of 1958 was encouraged to eat as much as they wanted, and for free. In Jiangsu province the slogan was 'Eat as much as you can and exert your utmost in production'. In Guangdong, the Party Secretary Tao Zhu urged everyone to 'eat three meals a day'.[37] In Zengu village, peasants later told American anthropologists what it was like: 'Everyone irresponsibly ate whether they were hungry or not, and in 20 days they had finished almost all the rice they had, rice which should have lasted six months.'[38] In Shanxi, the American William Hinton heard the same thing: 'If there was one facet of the Great Leap Forward that everyone remembers, it was the food. "We lived well," said Wei-de. "We ate a lot of meat. It was considered revolutionary to eat meat. If you didn't eat meat, it wouldn't do . . . People even vied with each other to see who could eat the most . . ."'[39]

What was happening in China was almost identical to what had happened in the Soviet Union during Stalin's collectivization movement. In his semi-fictional novel *The Soil Upturned*, Sholokhov describes a similar scene: 'They ate until they could eat no more. Young and old suffered from stomach-ache. At dinner-time, tables groaned under boiled and roasted meat. At dinner-time everyone had a greasy mouth, everyone hiccupped as if at a wake. Everyone blinked like an owl as if drunk from eating.'

In China, where there had never been enough food for all, people ate so much that by the winter of 1958–9, the granaries were bare. Some far-sighted rural Party secretaries saved their communities by planting sweet potatoes but elsewhere people trusted that they, like the city folk, would under Communism be provided for out of the state granaries. Yet Mao refused to accept that there was a shortage and, since he was convinced that the peasants were hiding their grain, he refused to open the state granaries. Even worse, over the three years from 1958 China doubled her grain exports and cut her imports of food. Exports to the Soviet Union rose by 50 per cent and China delivered grain *gratis* to her friends in North Korea, North Vietnam and Albania.[40] This generosity spelt death to many in China.

The Chinese are still suffering from the greatest and most far-reaching consequence of Mao's illusions. Convinced that China had entered an era of unprecedented abundance, Mao rejected any thought of China limiting her population growth. The country's most prominent advocate of birth control was Ma Yinchu, the Chancellor of Beijing University. In 1958, he was dismissed and condemned as a Malthusian. Only a year earlier he had warned of the consequences if no limits were set on population growth. As with so many things, Mao took an orthodox Leninist view. From early on Communists had believed that modern science was the key to a limitless expansion of food supplies. In 1913 Lenin had declared that 'we are the implacable enemy of the neo-Malthusian theory' which he described as 'reactionary' and 'cowardly'. Mao repeatedly attacked the warnings not just of experts like Professor Ma but also of foreigners such as Professor Lossing Buck and the US Secretary of State, Dean Acheson, who feared that China's population growth would outpace any increase in her food supply. In the early 1960s, as China was starving, Mao wrote in yet another criticism of Acheson that: 'Among all things on earth man is the most precious. Under the leadership of the Communist Party miracles can be wrought as long as there are men. We are against Acheson's counter-revolutionary theory. We believe that revolution can change everything. China's big population is a very good thing.'[41]

Mao even feared that there would be a labour shortage. In December 1958, following a meeting of Chinese leaders at Wuchang, a communiqué was issued claiming that 'it will be found that the amount of arable land is not too little but quite a lot and it is not a question of overpopulation but rather a shortage of manpower'. So, from the start of the Great Leap Forward, the Chinese peasants were encouraged to have as many children as possible because, as Mao liked to remind listeners, 'with every stomach comes another pair of hands'. Within a generation, China's population would double to 1.2 billion.

In the winter of 1958–9, people in China began to starve in large numbers but another two years would pass before the Party would come to grips with the terrible disaster. Within the Party leadership, however, a struggle over Mao's policies was about to begin.

6

Mao Ignores the Famine

'The history of the Chinese Revolution in the
past decades has fully proved one truth. It is
that the execution of Chairman Mao's direct
orders is sure to lead to victories and that
contravention of the same is sure to lead to
failures.'

Wu Zhifu, First Secretary of
Henan province[1]

THE FAMINE COULD easily have been arrested after the first
year of the Great Leap Forward if enough senior leaders had
dared to stand up to Mao. Yet even before the first communes
were established, Mao warned in the *People's Daily* that dissent
would not be tolerated. An editorial in February 1958 bluntly
stated that 'Anyone who does not make a Great Leap is a
rightist conservative . . . Some people think that a Leap is too
adventurous. It is new, it may not be perfect, but it is not an
adventure. All must have "revolutionary optimism and revolutionary heroism".'

Naturally, no one dared utter a word of caution. Mao had
unveiled the Great Leap Forward at a meeting in January
1958 in Nanning, the capital of Guangxi province in southern
China, when he declared that the economic plans drawn up two
years earlier had been too cautious. In April, the first 'people's
commune' was established in Chayashan in Henan province,
one of China's poorer regions. There, for the first time, private
plots were entirely abolished and communal kitchens introduced for its 40,000 members. Soon the more left-leaning

provinces began to follow suit, amalgamating existing collectives into communes, although the term people's commune, or *renmin gongshe*, had yet to be adopted. This happened when Mao visited the Seven Li village collective in Xinxiang, northern Henan, in August and uttered the words: 'This name, the People's Commune, is good!' The room in which he said this was turned into a museum and the phrase 'The People's Commune is good!' became a rallying cry, and a slogan painted on walls all over the countryside.[2]

In Henan, Mao was impressed by the astonishing achievements of the new communes which Wu Zhifu, the province's First Secretary, showed him. Mao himself does not seem to have drawn up detailed plans on how they should function and even now it is far from clear who was responsible for their design. As Mao told his doctor, Li Zhisui, before embarking on his grand tour of Henan and other rural regions: 'There are lots of things we don't know. How is this people's commune organized? How does it work? How does it allocate income and verify how much people have worked? How do they implement the idea of uniting agricultural labour with military training?'

In Henan and everywhere else Mao went in the summer of 1958, he listened to reports designed to flatter him, which hailed the fantastic success in agriculture that he had wisely predicted. At the end of August when the Party leadership held its customary summer meeting by the sea in the colonial villas of Beidaihe, Mao was so confident that he issued a grand communiqué proclaiming that Communism was at hand. The great optimism continued as Mao went on to Anhui, where another favourite, Zeng Xisheng, turned out huge crowds to greet him. In the capital, Hefei, he was introduced to the wonders of the backyard furnace. By the beginning of November he was once more in Henan for another Party meeting to listen to further reports of dazzling success. Soon afterwards Party leaders gathered in Wuchang, Hubei province, where they discussed how much grain had been harvested. The weather in 1958 had been unusually good and the harvest was indeed the highest since 1949, but all pretence of dealing with genuine statistics had been abandoned. Mao was told that the national grain harvest had gone from 185 million tonnes to 430 million, even 500 million, tonnes. Disregarding such claims, he settled quite arbitrarily on a lower but still high figure of 375 million tonnes. By the end of the year, Mao felt sufficiently confident of his success to relinquish his post as President of the Republic to Liu Shaoqi. Perhaps he felt he no longer needed such honours.[3] No one dared challenge this atmosphere of heady optimism, not even the leader most sceptical of the Great Leap Forward, Chen Yun. He stayed silent, although he had wanted to adhere to the modest goals laid out in the second five-year plan that he had helped draw up. So did Premier Zhou Enlai, Mao's most urbane and brilliant follower, and another moderate, who had already made a grovelling self-criticism, retracting his censure of the 1956 little leap forward.

Yet in the autumn of 1958, the great harvest was not being gathered in by the peasants. Many were too busy making steel or working on reservoirs and irrigation projects. In some places they had even melted down their scythes to make steel, and the grain just rotted in the fields. More dangerously, officials began to procure grain on the basis of the inflated harvest claims. Now that the peasants had been collectivized, the grain was not kept in the peasants' homes but in communal granaries. No village cadre who had announced a record-breaking harvest could now back down and deliver less than a record allocation to the state. Provincial leaders, too, determined to demonstrate their achievements and their loyalty, increased deliveries to the central government. And China began to cut her imports of grain and to step up exports. Beijing wanted to show that it could repay Soviet loans ahead of schedule because Mao's policies were so successful.

During the autumn months, the peasants had been encouraged to eat as much as they wanted but, as winter progressed, the grain in the collective granaries began to run out and the food served in the communal kitchens became sparser and sparser. The peasants traditionally call this season 'between the green and the yellow', because around the Spring Festival, as Chinese New Year is called, the fields are bare of both ripe and newly sown crops. In many parts of the country, around the Chinese New Year of 1959, starvation set in and the weak and the elderly began to die. Many years later, the Party veteran Bo Yibo would write that 25 million were starving in the spring of 1959.[4]

When, after the glowing reports of a few months earlier, stories of food shortages reached Mao's ears he refused to believe them and jumped to the conclusion that the peasants were lying and that 'rightists' and grasping *kulaks* were conspiring to hide grain in order to demand further supplies from the state. He was therefore delighted when a senior official in Guangdong province delivered a report in February 1959 which exactly corroborated his suspicions. As one interviewee put it, 'It was as if he had found treasure.' The report was by Zhao Ziyang, who after Mao's death would order the first commune to be disbanded and as Deng Xiaoping's prime minister would oversee the rural reforms. In 1959 he was a senior official responsible for agriculture in the southern province and in January of that year he set out on an inspection tour of Xuwen county. If the peasants were hungry, he concluded that it was only because grain was being hoarded and so he launched 'anti-grain concealment' drives to ferret out the grain hoarders. This, according to a biography by David Shambaugh, resulted in 'numerous purges, suicides and criticisms of local cadres'.[5] In another county, Lei Nan, Zhao did the same, organizing a series of meetings which attacked brigade and production teams for 'hiding and dividing' 34,000 tonnes of missing grain.[6]

In response to such reports, Mao issued a decree ordering a nationwide campaign: 'We must recognize that there is a severe problem because production teams are hiding and dividing grain and this is a common problem all over the country.' During this 'anti-hiding production and privately dividing-the-grain movement', local officials had no choice but to turn a deaf ear to appeals for emergency grain relief. Mao himself continued to receive petitions from starving villages but discounted them. One letter from the Po Hu commune in Henan province requested an investigation into the behaviour of production team leaders who were savagely beating peasants for hoarding grain. It complained, too, that those who refused to beat the peasants were being condemned for exhibiting a low political consciousness.[7] Mao responded by instructing the provincial leader, Wu Zhifu, not to be too hard on 'those comrades who commit slight mistakes'. Interviewees have added that he consistently refused to condemn those cadres who behaved brutally and ruthlessly towards the peasants and that on one occasion he advised 'We only need to criticize them a bit – let them make a self-criticism – that's enough.'

In this climate of megalomania, make-believe, lies and brutality, only one major figure appears to have had the courage and honesty to say what was really happening. This was the Minister of Defence, Marshal Peng Dehuai, who toured parts of the country in the autumn of 1958 and began reporting that things were not as good as they appeared to be. In Gansu, he found orchards cut down to fuel furnaces and the harvest left to rot in the fields.[8] He went on to Jiangxi and Anhui and to his home village in Hunan province and sent telegrams to Beijing warning that the 'masses are in danger of starving'. On another tour in early 1959 he even went to Mao's home village in Hunan and found untilled fields, falsified production figures and peasants dying of starvation.

Peng Dehuai was the only senior leader who not only genuinely came from a poor peasant background but had himself experienced famine in his home village and lost several brothers to starvation. Other leaders, such as Mao or Liu Shaoqi, were the sons of rich farmers, wealthy enough to educate their children in private schools. As a boy, Peng had enlisted in a warlord army before leading a band of peasant rebels in the mountains of Hunan. When he joined the Communists, he rose to a senior position through sheer ability. After 1949 he went on to command the Chinese forces fighting in Korea and then in mid-1959, as Minister of Defence, attended the Lushan summit.

This key Party meeting in July and August at a summer mountain resort above the Yangtze River in Jiangxi province lasted for six weeks and was the best chance the opponents of the Great Leap Forward would have of stopping Mao. The crude, barely educated but forthright soldier was encouraged by some of the more sophisticated leaders to write a petition to Mao raising objections. Far from issuing a public challenge to Mao's authority, Peng privately gave Mao a handwritten letter running to 10,000 characters.

His mood at the time is evoked in a poem composed in the style of a verse from Beijing opera which is attributed to his pen:

The millet is scattered over the ground.
The leaves of the sweet potato are withered.
The young and old have gone to smelt iron.
To harvest the grain there are children and old women.
How shall we get through the next year?
I shall agitate and speak out on behalf of the people.[9]

At the Lushan meeting, Peng kept insisting on the most important point of all: the Party, which had won power on the back of peasants driven to revolt by hunger, must not now be responsible for a still greater famine. It was, as he later pointed out to his niece, a gross betrayal of trust: 'I have experienced famine. I know the taste of it and it frightens me! We have fought decades of war and the people, poorly clothed and poorly fed, have spilt their blood and sweat to help us so that the Communist Party could win over the country and seize power. How can we let them suffer again, this time from hunger?'[10]

He was backed by a small number of other leaders: the First Secretary of Hunan province, Zhou Xiaozhou; Huang Kecheng, Chief of the General Staff; and Zhang Wentian, an alternate member of the Politburo who had studied in Moscow. According to Mao's doctor, Li Zhisui, Zhang said they must 'pull the Emperor off his horse even if that means losing our heads'. Another member of this group was one of Mao's secretaries, Li Rui, who later published an account of the meeting which gives an unusually detailed picture of what happened.[11]

Peng's letter itself was mildly worded, not even referring to a famine. Instead, it praised the accomplishments of the Great Leap Forward, observing that there were more gains than losses, though it did warn against leftist tendencies and stressed the need to learn from mistakes. Mao, however, scented a conspiracy and decided to circulate the letter and demolish its criticisms. On 30 July, he summoned an enlarged meeting of the Politburo which he opened with a half-hearted apology:

The collective dining halls are not our invention. They have been created by the masses . . . Being basically not good at construction, I know nothing about industrial targets . . . It is I who am to blame . . . Everyone has shortcomings. Even Confucius made mistakes. In regard to speed, Marx also committed many errors. He thought the revolution in Europe would take place in his lifetime. I have seen Lenin's manuscripts, which are filled with changes. He too made mistakes . . . Have we failed? No, our failure has been only partial. We have paid too high a price but a gust of Communist wind has been whipped up and the country has learned a lesson.

Mao refused to recognize that there was anything intrinsically wrong with his goal of 'greater, better, faster and more economical results', or that the shortcomings of the Great Leap Forward were anything but minor. They were, he said, nothing but the 'tuition fees that must be paid to gain experience' and amounted to temporary defects. 'Come back in ten years and see whether we were correct.' All this talk of food shortages was no more than wild exaggeration:

China is not going to sink into the sea and the sky won't tumble down simply because there are shortages of vegetables and hairpins and soap. Imbalances and market problems have made everybody tense but this tension is not justified, even though I am tense myself. No, it wouldn't be honest to say I'm not tense. If I am tense before midnight, I take some sleeping pills and then I feel better. You ought to try sleeping pills if you feel uptight.

Using a singularly inappropriate metaphor, he castigated low-ranking officials for impetuously rushing things: 'There can be no room for rashness. When you eat pork, you can only consume it mouthful by mouthful, and you can't expect to get fat in a single day. Both the Commander-in-Chief [Zhu De] and I are fat, but we didn't get that way overnight.'

Mao expanded this line of argument by urging the others to recognize that they all shared the responsibility for any mistakes: 'Comrades, you must also analyse your errors and you will feel better after you have broken wind and emptied your bowels.' He even tried to persuade the Politburo that ignorance was actually an asset in this audacious endeavour: 'An illiterate person can be a prime minister, so why can't our commune cadres and peasants learn something about political economy? Everybody can learn. Those who cannot read may also discuss economics, and more easily than the intellectual. I myself have never read textbooks!'

The debate went from the almost comical absurdity of these remarks to a bitter and acrimonious row as Peng Dehuai's short temper exploded. Peng accused Mao of acting despotically, like Stalin in his later years, and of sacrificing human beings on the altar of unreachable production targets. He said that troops were getting letters from home that told them of terrible food shortages and that this could cause unrest. He warned that 'if the Chinese peasants were not as patient as they were, we would have another Hungary'. If there was an uprising, the loyalty of the troops could not be relied upon and the Soviet Army might, as in Hungary, have to be called in to restore order.

Mao retaliated by accusing Peng of being a 'rightist' and a 'hypocrite' and of trying to 'sabotage the dictatorship of the proletariat, split the Communist Party, organize factions within the Party and spread their influence, to demoralize the vanguards of the proletariat and to build another opposition party'. The attacks culminated in a furious exchange when Peng, referring to a much earlier argument, shouted: 'In Yanan, you cursed me [literally 'fucked my mother'] for forty days. Now I have been fucking your mother for eighteen days and you are trying to call a stop – but you won't.'[12]

Peng had only the timid backing of a small group of supporters, and most senior leaders avoided siding with him. Zhou Enlai, who a few months earlier had expressed concern that the reports of a great harvest were being falsified and that 'the lies are being squeezed out of the lower cadres by a higher level', did nothing. According to one biographer, he sat as silent as a stone and then returned to his room to drink 'until he was stuporous'.[13] Liu Shaoqi did not come to Peng's rescue and neither did Chen Yun. Deng Xiaoping was fortuitously away in Beijing nursing a broken leg.

By contrast, Mao enjoyed strong backing from his supporters, amongst them Zeng Xisheng, First Secretary of Anhui; Wu Zhifu, First Secretary of Henan; Ke Qingshi, the Shanghai Party boss in charge of the Eastern China Bureau; Xu Tong, First Secretary of Shandong; and cronies such as Kang Sheng and Chen Boda. These men denied that there was a famine and urged Mao to continue with the Great Leap Forward. Mao's trump card was the loyalty of the military chiefs who were summoned to a meeting and asked one by one to stand up and say whom they supported, Mao or Peng. Mao warned that if the Party were to split into two, he would organize a new one among the peasants, and that if the army were to split, he would go into the hills and recruit another army. The generals backed Mao.

In his memoirs Dr Li Zhisui recalled: 'Mao did want to be told the truth. Even in my disillusionment I still believe that had he fully understood the truth early in the Great Leap Forward, he would have brought a halt to the disaster long before he did. But the truth had to come to him on his own terms, from a modern Hai Rui. He could not accept it when it included criticism of him, or when it came from conspiring ministers . . .'[14]

Hai Rui was the subject of a Hunan opera performed when Mao had toured the province before the Lushan conference. The opera, called *Sheng si pai*, tells the story of the upright Ming dynasty official Hai Rui who risks his life to intervene with the Emperor to stop the execution of a woman wrongly accused of murder. Hai Rui himself is nearly executed for daring to challenge the vainglorious and misdirected Emperor. The subtle message of the opera was lost on Mao, who failed to grasp the connection between his own situation and that of the Emperor misled by the flattery of lying courtiers, but he was taken with the theme and encouraged other works about Hai Rui. Though he probably realized that some of his officials were exaggerating the success of his Great Leap Forward to curry favour, yet he never doubted that it was a success.[15]

Before the Lushan meeting, Mao had also gone back to his home village in Hunan, Shaoshan, where he felt his kith and kin would tell him the truth. Listening to their complaints, he disarmingly suggested that they could dismantle the collective kitchens, water conservancy projects and backyard furnaces if they did not work. His remarks were not published but the news spread to other Hunan villages. For a while parts of Hunan began to abandon the Great Leap Forward. But after the Lushan summit when the province's First Secretary, Zhou Xiaozhou, was dismissed as a rightist, his successor Zhang Pinhua reinforced all these measures. In Hunan the collective kitchens lasted in all three and a half years, longer than almost anywhere else.

Mao was willing to recognize that there were defects in what he was doing but his belief that there had been huge harvests remained unshaken. Before the Lushan meeting, he had ordered provinces to step up deliveries of grain to the centre and had approved new and higher targets for state grain procurement. As he remarked at Lushan, 'Achievements are great, problems are considerable but the future is bright.'

The Lushan meeting ended in a complete victory for Mao. The Party leadership resolved to return to the policies of the Great Leap Forward with redoubled energy and voted to condemn Peng as an 'anti-Party element' and a 'right opportunist'. A month later, Peng wrote a humbling self-criticism and was put under house arrest in a village outside Beijing where he grew vegetables. In the Cultural Revolution he would be imprisoned, tortured and killed.

Within a few weeks of Lushan, a new purge of 'right opportunists' began across the country. In the *People's Daily*, Deng Xiaoping made Mao's counter-attack clear to everyone:

Some of the rightist elements in our Party do not wish to recognize the remarkable achievements of the Great Leap Forward . . . They exaggerate the errors that have occurred during the course of the movement, which the masses have corrected. They use these errors as a pretext to attack the Party line. The movement of 1958 hastened our economic development. But the rightists ignored this and insisted that the movement manifested catastrophic consequences. The people's communes work well but the rightists ignored this, and attacked this movement as a step backward. They contended that only by abolishing the communes could the living standards of the population be raised. The masses, on the contrary, believe they have made great strides forward . . . The rightist opportunism quite obviously reflects the bourgeoisie's fear of a mass movement in our Party.

The provincial leaders returned from Lushan to institute a campaign of terror. All over the country large numbers of low- and high-ranking officials were dismissed or arrested as 'little Peng Dehuais' if they had betrayed even the slightest doubts about the Great Leap Forward. In Anhui, for example, Zhang Kaifan, a senior official who had written to Mao about the

terrible famine in Wuwei county, was named as a 'right opportunist' by Mao. In the Anhui purge anyone whose conscience
had pricked them was rounded up as a 'small Zhang Kaifan'.
Throughout the countryside, large numbers of peasants were
put in prison where they would starve to death in the next
phase of the famine. No national figures for the victims of this
campaign are available but it was one of the worst in the Party's
history and extinguished any hope that the next and most awful
stage of the famine could be prevented.

Instead, a new hysteria about the Great Leap Forward was
whipped up. Higher and yet more absurd grain targets were
put forward and still greater successes announced. Sichuan
declared that its sputnik fields were producing 7.5 tonnes of
grain per hectare, ten times the normal grain yield. More and
more effort went into farming the experimental plots, while in
provinces such as Henan and Sichuan officials were ordered
to reduce the area sown with grain. The Party did quietly abandon the backyard furnaces so that the peasants were freed from
the burden of mounting round-the-clock steel-making, but by
then there was in any case almost nothing left to melt down
because the peasants had already been stripped of everything
they owned. And the collective kitchens were resumed in those
parts of the country which had abandoned them in the wake
of Mao's remarks at Shaoshan.

In the autumn of 1959, the grain harvest dropped by at least
30 million tonnes over that of 1958 but officials reported that
it was higher, much higher. (This estimate takes into account
sweet potato plantings, so the fall in real grain output was in
fact still sharper.) To make their lies stick, local officials began
to requisition all the grain they could find. The state procurement targets were set at 40 per cent of total output, the highest
level ever, and in many places the entire harvest was seized.
Sometimes, officials reported a harvest so big that even after
taking away everything they could find, including all livestock,
vegetables and cash crops, they still continued to search from
house to house. Mao had ordered officials not only to deliver the
grain quotas, but also to set quotas for pigs, chickens, ducks and
eggs. Party leaders went from village to village leading the search
for hidden food reserves. It was a brutal and violent campaign in
which many peasants were tortured and beaten to death.

In China, most peasants practise subsistence farming, so most of the grain grown is consumed at home by the peasants themselves. Only a small part is normally delivered in taxes or, under the Communists, to meet procurement quotas. Thus, when their grain was seized, the peasants knew they had nothing left to eat. Most hoped that under socialism the state would provide for them but since no grain had been forthcoming the previous winter, many feared they might be left to die. In the countryside, mere survival became a desperate struggle. By the end of 1959 much of the peasantry was starving to death but the hardest time in the entire famine came in January and February 1960 when the greatest number perished.

Throughout this period Mao continued to claim that the peasants had buried the grain deep in the ground and that they stood sentry guarding it.[16] To throw the search parties off the scent, he said, they ate turnips by day and after dark secretly ate rice. In fact, the peasants ate only the gruel served up by the communal kitchens which was mixed with grasses and anything else they could forage that was edible. The peasants, as they queued for food, began to resemble the inmates of concentration camps, skeletal figures dressed in rags, fighting with each other to get equal portions.

The *People's Daily* suggested at the end of 1959 that 'the peasants must practise strict economy, live with the utmost frugality and eat only two meals a day – one of which should be soft and liquid'. In other words, one meal was to consist of buns of maize or wheat, and the other, a watery soup. The Party described this as 'living in an abundant year as if it were a frugal one'. Mao himself made a small gesture by giving up eating meat. Meanwhile, the country's main grain surplus provinces – Sichuan, Henan, Anhui and Shandong – delivered the most grain to the centre and it was in these regions that the peasants starved in the greatest numbers.

At the same time a bizarre political situation existed. Most of the Party leadership clearly knew what was going on but no one dared acknowledge the famine until Mao did so. Chen Yun, who had been to the Henan countryside and had realized what was happening, decided to retire to his villa in picturesque Hangzhou. He told Mao he was suffering from ill-health and, accompanied by a nurse, took up the study of local opera. He did not return to Beijing until 1961.[17] Liu Shaoqi, President of China and another member of the Politburo Standing Committee, also withdrew from the scene, in this case to the semi-tropical island of Hainan where he spent much of 1960, claiming that he was studying economics.[18] Deng Xiaoping appears to have spent most of his time involved in the growing ideological dispute with Moscow. The final rupture between the two fraternal Parties came in July 1960 when the 15,000 or so Soviet experts at work in China suddenly left. It is quite conceivable that Beijing wanted them to leave so that they could not report to Khrushchev that the entire country was starving.

After their departure, China lapsed into an eerie isolation. Few Chinese leaders travelled abroad and few foreign guests were made welcome in China. The foreign community was reduced to a smaller number than at any other time in a century. From the beginning of 1960, the Party banned any domestic publication from leaving the country apart from the *People's Daily* and the bi-monthly magazine *Red Flag*.[19] The world could only guess at what was happening to a fifth of humanity. Those inside the country knew as little as those outside. All mail was controlled by the local authorities and checked to prevent news of the famine spreading. Few Chinese had telephones and domestic travel came to a standstill. The number of flights and train departures was cut by half because there was no fuel. Travel by any other means was difficult without ration tickets that were valid nationwide.

In the China presented by *Red Flag* all was well. Mao wrote in September 1959 that the great leap in agriculture was even greater than in 1958. Henan's First Secretary, Wu Zhifu, whose province was one of the epicentres of the famine, declared that rich peasants had instructed the rightists to make the collectives smaller but 'now the masses feel much more comfortable'. In the first issue of 1960, he wrote again, saying that 'although there has been a serious drought, the communes are still very prosperous and people are very happy'. A month earlier, the leader of Anhui, Zeng Xisheng, had remarked that production increases were not to be reckoned in a few percentage points but in double digits and that thanks to the Great Leap Forward natural disasters had been overcome.

In the first half of 1960, Mao and his supporters were still calling for another great leap forward, including a giant jump in steel production. Mao ordered the mobilization of 70 million people to achieve a target of 22 million tonnes of steel, a ludicrous goal since only 8 million tonnes had been produced in 1957 and 11 million tonnes claimed in 1958. He even proposed raising total output to 100 million tonnes within ten years, but this time his orders were ignored.[20] Mao also insisted that the peasants continue eating in the collective kitchens, describing these as the 'key battlefield of socialism'. The fog of unreality with which he surrounded himself defied any efforts to penetrate it until the end of 1960. Much of what he did or said in this year still remains a mystery. Some accounts suggest that he retreated into his study for long periods because he could not bear to admit to himself what was happening.[21]

Even in Beijing there was nothing to eat, while in the countryside just outside the capital peasants who had survived were too weak to plant the new crops or harvest them. In villages a few miles outside Beijing, most peasants were grotesquely swollen by oedema and were dying in sizeable numbers. Grain output plummeted. The reality must have been impossible for anyone to escape. Yet Mao refused to halt the continuing export of grain and rejected suggestions that grain be imported. An extraordinary paralysis gripped the Party. The peasants sank deeper and deeper into a pit of numbing horror as winter approached once more. They and the Party knew they would now die in even greater numbers. No one in a position of authority dared tell Mao the truth. One source claims that he only began to respond on receiving desperate pleas from members of his own family.[22] He Xiaoqu, a cousin from his own village, reportedly sent his son together with other villagers to see Mao and tell him of the famine. They thrust a handful of grain vouchers at him, saying 'Unless you stop, we won't go back home. We ask you to take these ration tickets and see what you get to eat with them in our village.' The following chapters attempt to describe the extraordinary scale of the disaster for which Mao was responsible.

Part Two

The Great Hunger

7

An Overview of the Famine

'The evil deeds of evil rulers are the source
of disorder.'

Mencius

THE FAMINE OF 1958–61 was unique in Chinese history. For
the first time, every corner of this huge country experienced
hunger, from the cold wheat-growing lands of Heilongjiang in
the far north to the lush semi-tropical island of Hainan in the
south. It was a situation which, even during the famines of the
1920s, experts had said was impossible. They had believed that
even if one part of the country suffered shortages, China was
so big and varied that there would always be a surplus somewhere else. Yet this time people starved everywhere.

Dynastic records describe how other great calamities had
reduced the population of China by as much as half, but these
were the consequence of great convulsions such as the civil war
which followed the Qin dynasty's collapse some 2,000 years
earlier, or brutal invasions, like that of Genghis Khan's Mongols
in the fourteenth century. In 1959, China was at peace, unified
under one government, with a modern transport and communications system. Moreover, the Communist government
was the first since the seventeenth century to be entirely in
the hands of ethnic Chinese acting independently of outside
forces. The Manchu rulers of the Qing dynasty, who had
regarded themselves as a separate race of conquerors, had been
swept away. The Western powers' influence had come to an
end, and the Japanese invaders had been defeated. Even Russia,
with the departure of her experts in 1960, no longer exerted

any influence over the Chinese government. For the first time the Chinese Communist Party was free of the influence of the Comintern which supervised the affairs of other Communist Parties.

The famine left no one in China untouched but it did not affect the country uniformly. Many factors played a role – geography, the policies of local leaders, nationality, sex, age, political affiliation, class background, and whether one lived in the city or the countryside. Geography was important but this famine was peculiar in that its effects were not concentrated in the traditional famine belt. Indeed, some of the richest regions suffered more than others. The traditional famine belt lies between the two main river systems of China, the Yellow and Yangtze Rivers, which flow from west to east. The Yellow River rises deep inland and flows through Gansu and Shaanxi provinces and on through the provinces of Shanxi, Shandong, Hebei and northern Henan across the North China plain. This is the ancient heartland of Chinese civilization but the river has been called China's Sorrow. Its silt-laden waters bring fertility to the lands through which they flow but also disastrous floods.

Further south, the Huai River is still more notorious because for much of its length through the provinces of Henan and Anhui, it winds through flat land, prone to extensive flooding. In times of drought, the soil is baked rock hard but in good years this region, like the North China plain, produces important grain surpluses to feed the coastal cities. Yet while all the provinces along these rivers have experienced severe famines, their fate between 1958 and 1961 depended as much on the acts of their leaders as on natural conditions. Henan and Anhui fared the worst, being governed by two ultra-left-wing leaders whose fanaticism led to both terrible atrocities and an enormous death toll. Events in both provinces are described separately in the following two chapters.

China's greatest river is the Yangtze. It rises in the Tibetan plateau, gathers in the fertile basin of Sichuan province, perhaps the most arable region in China, pours through narrow gorges and then meanders across the richest parts of central China until it reaches the sea near Shanghai. Historically, mass famines were rare in Sichuan, but in 1958–61 this great granary recorded the highest number of deaths of any province: it too was controlled by another Maoist stalwart, Li Jingquan. His enthusiasm for the Great Leap Forward ensured that food shortages hit the Sichuanese earlier than the peasants in some other provinces. On the other hand, Sichuan recovered more quickly than the northern provinces because in the south peasants can grow two or more crops a year. Events in Sichuan and the rest of south-west China are described in Chapter 10.

Some of the last territory to be conquered by the Han Chinese lies south of the Yangtze and is still inhabited by large populations of minority peoples. During the Long March in the 1930s, even the Communists were astonished by the poverty of some minority peasants who could barely afford to clothe themselves. In these regions, Han Chinese tend to farm the flat valley lands. Though generally more prosperous than the indigenous peoples, in 1958–61 they had less to eat. Since they lived in the most accessible districts, the authorities were able to seize more of their food supplies and so they died in greater numbers than the minorities living in the remote hills.

In the west of China, Tibetans, Mongols, Uyghurs and other peoples are scattered over steppes, mountains and deserts. In some ways, these minorities were better off during the famine because the authorities, however ruthless, found it harder to enforce their demands; and when the grain was taken away, they could forage in the mountains, forests and grasslands. This was not the case among the deeply religious and independent Tibetans. Communist policies there provoked a major revolt, and repression combined with famine wrought a terrible disaster described in Chapter 11.[1]

The three provinces of Manchuria – Liaoning, Jilin and Heilongjiang – and Inner Mongolia had been settled by Han Chinese in large numbers only in recent times. The famine of 1958–61 brought another wave of settlers fleeing hunger to the south. Inner Mongolia alone absorbed an extra million refugees and Heilongjiang province saw its population increase from 14 million to 20 million between 1958 and 1964, largely because of immigration. Yet even in Manchuria people starved, despite the fact that the region normally has a surplus of food, though the famine there seems to have struck later than in Sichuan and many other provinces.

The coastal provinces and cities traditionally import grain, relying on the inland provinces for up to a third of their needs, but are prime exporters of cash crops such as tea, cotton, silk and fruit. When the customary grain imports from inland ceased, their inhabitants starved. However, in the later stages of the famine many of those living in Fujian, Zhejiang and Guangdong had the advantage of receiving food packages from overseas relatives, for their provinces are the ancestral homes of the majority of Chinese living abroad. One interviewee recalled how her mother travelled regularly by fishing boat from Malaysia to Guangdong carrying barrels of pork fat steeped in oil which saved her home village from starvation. Yet although these provinces are geographically similar, their experiences during the famine differed. Zhejiang had, before the launch of the Great Leap Forward, been a stronghold of private farming. In the campaign against opponents of collectivization, those who abandoned the collectives were subjected to brutal suppression. In 1958, in one county alone, Yongjia, near the city of Wenzhou, 200,000 peasants were 'struggled' as 'right opportunists' and many were killed or sent to labour camps.[2] Neighbouring Fujian province had to bear the burden of being the first line of defence against a possible invasion by the Kuomintang across the straits from Taiwan. Between 1959 and 1963, the province was placed under strict military control and had to feed the large numbers of troops quartered there. Many people were arrested as suspected spies after the authorities required a considerable part of the population to report on their neighbours.[3] In Fujian, Zhejiang and Guangdong, the government also took absurd measures to boost grain production. Peasants were ordered to cut down their orchards and uproot their tea bushes and instead plant grain. And to open up more land for grain, the hills in the lightly wooded interior were set on fire as part of a crude slash-and-burn programme and then sown with grain. The first year's crop was good because ash enriches the soil, but the following year the harvest was poor. By 1960 the Fujianese were eating nothing but sweet potatoes. These regions are also noted both for breeding freshwater fish and sea fish but interviewees said that in the midst of the famine peasants and fishermen were strictly forbidden to engage in any private fishing.

Generally, those who lived in the great cities on the coast

and along the main waterways, such as Wuhan on the Yangtze, suffered least for they received ration tickets. Moreover, plans to establish urban communes were never implemented and the urban population was never forbidden to cook at home. Many did die, though, especially the old and the very young, but the famine took longer to affect them, as Chapter 15 explains. Even in the very worst provinces, such as Anhui, the urban population was sheltered to such an extent that often they had no knowledge of what was happening in the villages.

The most vulnerable section of China's population, around five per cent, were those whom Mao called 'enemies of the people'. Anyone who had in previous campaigns of repression been labelled a 'black element' was given the lowest priority in the allocation of food. Landlords, rich peasants, former members of the Nationalist regime, religious leaders, rightists, counter-revolutionaries and the families of such individuals died in the greatest numbers. During the Great Leap Forward, many more people were placed in these categories and often imprisoned. As Chapter 12 explains, the penal system underwent a huge expansion as millions were arrested without trial. Most of the new penal colonies were established in the frozen northern wastes of Heilongjiang or in sparsely settled lands in the west, where it is hard to grow food at the best of times. Up to half the prisoners dispatched to provinces such as Qinghai or Gansu died. Indeed the inmates of the penal colonies suffered a double misfortune. The provinces where they were imprisoned were led by hard-line extremists whose policies devastated the local population and prisoners alike.

Not surprisingly, those who suffered least throughout China were Party members. They consistently had first call on the state's grain reserves, they lived in separate compounds closed off from the outside world, and they ate in separate canteens. Even in labour camps, prisoners who had been Party members received more food than their fellow inmates.[4] Members of the families of officials admitted in interviews that they often had little inkling of the misery outside their privileged world and what they did know came from their servants. In the country-side, the commune leaders did not eat in the collective kitchens with the peasants but in separate canteens. Many sources have testified that the food there was always adequate and often very good, with the cadres receiving not only sufficient grain but also meat of all kinds. Zhang Zhongliang, the First Secretary of Gansu, where at least a million people starved to death, travelled with his own personal cook. In Henan's Xinyang prefecture, one of the worst affected areas in the country, the Party Secretary Lu Xianwen would travel to local communes and order in advance elaborate banquets of twenty-four courses, according to Party documents. Only at the village level did the lowest officials such as production team leaders sometimes starve to death.

The death tolls during the famine will be discussed later, but broadly speaking the bulk of those who died were the ordinary Han Chinese peasants living in the new communes. By the end of 1958, virtually the entire rural population of some 500 million was under the control of this new and bizarre form of organization which formed the institutional framework of the Great Leap Forward. Mao and his cronies boasted that the communes were the gateway to heaven and Kang Sheng composed several ditties for the peasants to repeat:

> Communism is paradise.
> The People's Communes
> are the bridge to it.

> Communism is heaven.
> The Commune is the ladder.
> If we build that ladder
> We can climb the heights.

The peasants soon came to regard the communes as an instrument of terror. They were set up in a great rush in the summer of 1958, often within a month, sometimes within forty-eight hours. The source of their inspiration was the *Communist Manifesto* in which Marx envisaged organizing the peasants into industrial armies based in 'agro-cities' which would close the gap between town and country. Around 10,000 peasants were grouped into each commune, although sometimes they contained two or three times that number. To create a commune, the local authorities merely merged the 'higher collectives' which had been set up in 1955–6. The first commune established in April 1958 at Chayashan in Henan province brought together 27 collectives, 9,300 farms and 43,000 people. As the Party put it, 'In 1958, a new social organization appeared fresh as the morning sun above the broad horizon of East Asia.'[5] The communes formed one of the Party's 'Three Red Banners' – the other two being the Great Leap Forward and 'the general line for socialist construction' which would propel China into Communism. They set out to achieve the abolition of all private property, the industrialization of the countryside and the complete fusion of the state bureaucracy, the Party and the peasantry into a militarized and disciplined organization. Early each morning, the peasants would march to work behind a red flag, in some cases even carrying rifles. Within the commune they were formed into production teams, which sometimes comprised the entire workforce of a small village, and these production teams were grouped within a larger unit called a brigade. Special detachments of exemplary workers were drafted as 'shock troops' who would work twenty-four hours without a break, while the rest of the commune worked two shifts. There were even militarized teams of shock women workers.

For a few months in 1958, commune leaders actually separated men and women into different living quarters. (Indeed Mao even wondered whether it would suffice for men and women to meet twice a month for the purposes of procreation.) This separation first took place at the Xushui commune in Hebei but was later extended to many parts of the country, including Henan, Hunan and Anhui, as well as to battalions dispatched to work on dams and other construction projects.[6] In one commune in Anhui province, men and women lived in dormitories at opposite ends of the village. The commune leaders believed that this separation was good for production and stressed that men and women, including married couples, could 'collectively' attend meetings and work in the fields.[7] The Communist Party's explicit aim was to destroy the family as an institution:

The framework of the individual family, which has existed for thousands of years, has been shattered for all time . . . We must regard the People's Commune as our family and not pay too much attention to the formation of a separate family of our own. For years motherly love has been glorified . . . but it is wrong to degrade a person from a social to a biological creature . . . the dearest people in the world are our parents, yet they cannot be compared with Chairman Mao and the Communist Party . . . for it is not the family which has given us everything but the Communist Party and the great revolution . . . Personal love is not so important: therefore women should not claim too much of their husbands' energy.[8]

To this end, the elderly were sent off to live in 'happiness homes' portrayed as retirement homes, while children were separated from their parents and placed in nurseries or boarding schools. In most communes, such plans were only briefly realized, if at all, but the cadres were almost universally successful in destroying domestic life by banning cooking and eating at home. Collective kitchens were set up everywhere and operated for at least three years. Usually the largest house in the village was turned into the kitchen where the food was cooked in large pots. A few places had communal dining halls but, more often than not, people squatted on the ground to eat their food. Only later on in the famine were they allowed to return to their huts to eat as families.

The agro-cities never actually existed as such, but in many places ambitious plans were set in motion. In Anhui's Fengyang county, cadres decided that they would refashion the county town by straightening out its twisting lanes. 'The streets should run in straight lines with four lanes, and in the middle there should be gardens and flowers,' urged a planning conference.[9] The dissident journalist Liu Binyan, who was exiled as a rightist to a village in Shanxi province in the north-west, recalled even more ambitious plans:

There was no underground water in the mountain village but orders came for a fountain to be set up on the main street. The people rarely ever had a scrap of meat but were ordered to carve out cave dwellings in the mountainsides to house a zoo containing tigers and lions. Their carefully tended terraced fields were destroyed to erect a miniature Summer Palace.[10]

Many more such wonderful institutions were supposedly set up overnight. Fengyang county claimed that by the end of 1958 it had established 154 specialized red universities, 46 agricultural middle schools, 509 primary schools, 24 agricultural technical schools, 156 clubs, 44 cultural palaces and 105 theatrical troupes.[11] The latter helped to provide a relentless programme of revolutionary songs which continued while the peasants worked and ate. If they were working around the clock, there were performances or broadcasts all night. Even when they were supposedly at rest, the peasants were obliged to attend political meetings and rallies.

In theory, the fantastic harvests were supposed to create unprecedented leisure for the peasants. When Mao visited Hebei's Xushui commune and heard of the great autumn harvest expected, he recommended: 'Plant a little less and do half a day's work. Use the other half for culture: study science, promote culture and recreation, run a college and middle school.' Yet such was the reality that, at the end of 1958, the *People's Daily* ran an article headlined 'See that the Peasants take rest'. It pointed out that an experiment had been carried out which compared the achievements of peasants forced to work four or five days without sleep, with those of a team which stopped at midnight and had two rest periods during the day. More was achieved, it said, by those allowed to rest. So the paper recommended that the peasants should not be overworked but allowed to sleep.

At the same time, the peasants were forced to hand over virtually all their private possessions. In some places, a Utopian madness gripped the villagers. One senior leader, Bo Yibo, later described what happened in a town in Hubei province:

The Party Secretary of Paoma town announced in October 1958 that Socialism would end on November 7th and Communism would begin on November 8th. After the meeting, everyone immediately took to the streets and began grabbing goods out of the shops. When the shelves were bare, they went to other people's homes and took their chickens and vegetables home to eat. People even stopped making a distinction as to which children belonged to whom. Only wives were safe from this sharing because the Party secretary was unsure about this. So he asked the higher-level authorities for instructions on whether people should continue to be allowed to keep their own wives.[12]

Even the bodily wastes of the peasants became public property. In the communes, communal latrines replaced private ones because the excrement had to be used on the communal fields. Any individuality in clothing was discouraged and men and women dressed alike in unisex baggy cotton trousers and jackets. And, as has been described earlier, a great effort was made to eradicate every aspect of religion and folk culture. All these policies amounted to nothing less than an attempt to expunge every and any visible difference in wealth and status between individuals, as well as between villages and counties.

The administration of the peasant's life underwent a great change too. In the past the villagers themselves had controlled many aspects of their lives. Now the commune took charge not just of all matters to do with farming, but also marriages, funerals, travel and the distribution of food and other goods. The language itself was transformed: shops were renamed 'material supply offices'; instead of cash, there were 'certificates of purchase'; and money kept in banks on deposit became 'public accumulation funds'. Chen Boda had envisaged the complete abolition of money and this almost came true. The peasants had to use ration tickets for just about everything, including hot water.

Within each commune, a new unified administrative structure was set up which was responsible for every decision, no matter how trivial. The commune Party secretary ran a handful of committees which supervised agriculture, food and trade, political, legal and military affairs, science and technology. In addition, another office was responsible for drawing up a daily plan for work, education, culture, health and welfare. Under this highly centralized administration, the individual was powerless – nothing could be done without permission from the commune headquarters which often lay several days' journey away.

Through the communes, a direct line of command reached from Mao right down to the individual peasant. Such a militaristic structure of control had, perhaps, never been so absolute at any other time in China's history. Above the communes stood the county administration, the prefectural Party committee, the provincial Party and then Mao and his cronies at the centre. Each of the twenty-eight provinces, autonomous regions and municipalities was designed to be a self-sufficient and autonomous entity. This meant that the provincial Party boss acted as a kind of regent answerable only to Mao. The civilian administration, such as the national ministries responsible for education, health, agriculture and so on, no longer functioned, nor did the administration of local government. The Party was everything and no one could challenge or appeal against any decisions taken because no other authority existed.

With money virtually abolished, the communes substituted an extraordinarily elaborate system to compute the value of work done and to achieve an egalitarian distribution of wealth. In the first stage of the communes, the cadres were supposed to apply the principle of each according to his work, so each facet of work was calculated on a point system. First, each peasant was graded on a scale of 1–10, according to the individual's physical strength and health. Skill, knowledge or experience were not taken into account. Then each type of work was graded separately with different accounting systems for each crop, for the various jobs in the construction of dams and irrigation works, and for sideline work such as raising chickens or repairing tools.

At first, the contract system was employed, under which each peasant, production team or brigade agreed to carry out a fixed amount of labour in a given period to meet the production targets set by the state. Surplus output was then divided among the different levels according to another complicated formula. At the beginning, there was, therefore, an incentive to work hard since income was linked to productivity. But then, in the autumn of 1958, Mao was so bowled over by what he was shown in model communes in Anhui and Henan that he decided China was ready to move to the next stage of Communism in which each would receive according to his needs. Touring Anhui province, Mao declared: 'Since one commune can put into practice the principle of eating without pay, other communes can do likewise. Since rice can be eaten without pay, clothing can also be had without pay in the future.'

In Henan's communes not even work points were awarded.

Food was distributed in communal mess halls free of charge according to individual requirements. Everything was free, from clothes to haircuts. Under this supply system, the expenses of seven of the ten 'basic necessities of life' were borne by the commune: food, clothing, housing, childbirth, education, medical treatment and marriages and funerals. No one was even paid pocket money. The communes also began to redistribute wealth between the villages, so that the richer villages had to hand over some of their tools and animals to the poorer ones as well as anything else they possessed, including cash. When the harvest was gathered in, it was delivered to the commune headquarters which then divided it up as it saw fit. In some parts of the country this redistribution of wealth took place between counties.

Inevitably, all this caused a great deal of resentment among the peasants but by the winter of 1958–9 the whole experiment was, in any case, beginning to fall apart. In many places, therefore, it is possible that the final stage was never carried out. Nevertheless, the effect of these policies on peasant attitudes to farm work was always the same. They felt there was no longer an incentive to work hard, to care for the fields or tend the animals, because the fruits of their labour would in any event be taken away. Instead, the peasants assumed that since Communism had arrived the state would provide everything they needed. In fact, this was only true as far as the local cadres were concerned – they did indeed live well on what the state provided.

The psychological impact of the system must also be viewed in the light of traditional Chinese farming practices. Despite the backward technology employed, the Chinese peasant who farmed his small plot of land was a model of efficiency. With the advent of the communes, the Communists treated farming as if it were akin to manufacturing and could be organized like an assembly line. This approach took no account of the peasant's skill in minutely tailoring his work to suit local conditions. Even in the eighteenth century, Jesuit priests working in China had been deeply impressed by the way in which most peasants constantly fine-tuned their plots of land to get the maximum out of them: 'Most farmers have a refined knowledge of weather and time, or, in other words, of the sequence of seasonal change, as it applies to their own small area.' The peasant's knowledge of farming techniques was considerable: 'They are not content to determine what sort of manure is suitable for each soil. They go on to desire what account should be taken of what has been harvested, and what is to be sown, of the weather that has gone before, and that chosen [for a particular operation].'[13]

Now that the peasant no longer considered the land his own, there was no need to nurture it carefully in order to provide the maximum output over an extended period of time. Instead, orders came from a distant bureaucracy which tried to extract the maximum in the shortest possible time by sowing early, or by trying to reap two crops instead of one, or by trying to grow unsuitable crops. With the full power of the Party behind the orders to apply Mao's innovations such as close planting, deep ploughing and so on, the peasants had no choice but to obey. They knew that these methods were wrong but now each had only to concern himself with collecting work points.

After the first terrible winter of famine in 1958–9, apathy set in. The Party cadres had increasingly to rely on force and terror to get the peasants to obey their orders. At the height of the famine, they wielded the power of life and death because they controlled the grain stores and could kill anyone by depriving them of food. In many places, the cadres ordered that only those who worked could eat and left the sick, the old and the young to die. In Sichuan and some other provinces, it took a mere six months for the communes to make the journey from Utopia, where each could eat his fill, to a hell where it was 'work or starve to death'.

8

Henan:
A Catastrophe of Lies

'This is a holocaust and massacre committed
by our enemies.'
Party report on Xinyang prefecture

WHAT HAPPENED IN the quiet rural province of Henan in
central China between 1958 and 1961 is so extraordinary that
even beside the other horrors of the twentieth century, it stands
out. After Mao's death, the Communist Party allowed the publication of heavily disguised versions of the events in Henan,
such works being briefly encouraged to discredit the Maoists
resisting Deng Xiaoping's rural reforms. A local opera by Du
Xi called *Huang Huo* or *Catastrophe of Lies* appeared in 1979,
and the novelist Zhang Yigong published *The Case of Criminal
Li Tongzhong*, the story of a rural cadre who secretly raids a
state granary to distribute food during the famine and is then
caught and punished for his 'crime'. However, after 1982 such
works were quietly shelved and the full story of the 'Xinyang
incident', as the events in Henan are euphemistically termed,
has never been made known beyond the inner circles of the
Communist Party. This is the first attempt to describe the
horror which consumed this otherwise unremarkable rural
backwater.

The prefecture of Xinyang lies in a plain watered by the Huai
River. At the time it was made up of 17 counties and
was home to about a fifth of Henan's population of some

50 million. In April 1958, Xinyang shot to fame when the first commune in China was formed within the prefecture at Chayashan in Suiping county.[1] In response to this singular honour, the prefectural Party leadership became fanatically devoted to Mao and his dreams and, to sustain them, launched a reign of terror in which tens of thousands were beaten and tortured to death. A Communist Party report published in 1961 described the events not just as mass murder but as 'a holocaust'.[2]

The great terror began in the autumn of 1959 when, in the wake of the Lushan meeting, the prefectural Party committee declared war on the peasants. Those who failed to fulfil their production quotas were condemned as 'little Peng Dehuais' and no mercy was shown towards them. Although the provincial Party Secretary, Wu Zhifu, had lowered the year's grain target for the province in view of a local drought, the zealous Xinyang leadership was determined to show that nature would not be permitted to force a retreat. The leadership insisted that the harvest of 1959 would be as good as that of 1958, so county officials strove to outdo each other in reporting good results. After the summer, the First Secretary of Xinyang prefecture, Lu Xianwen, declared that despite the drought, the 1959 harvest in his region was 3.92 million tonnes, double the real figure. Grain levies, hitherto set at around 30 per cent of the harvest, now amounted in practice to nearly 90 per cent. For example, in one county within the prefecture, Guangshan, cadres reported a harvest of 239,280 tonnes when it was really only 88,392 tonnes, and fixed the grain levy at 75,500 tonnes. When they were unable to collect more than 62,500 tonnes, close to the entire harvest, the local cadres launched a brutal 'anti-hiding campaign'.[3]

Lu Xianwen declared that anyone who even suggested that the 1959 harvest was lower than that of 1958 was an enemy of the people, a criminal who opposed the Three Red Banners. He went on to claim that since the villagers were hiding plenty of grain, the Party was confronted with an ideological conflict, a struggle between two different lines. As he told one meeting in the early autumn: 'It is not that there is no food. There is plenty of grain, but 90 per cent of the people have ideological problems.'[4]

At a meeting of his deputies Lu Xianwen announced that a

class struggle was now beginning in which all the peasants were the enemy. This struggle against the peasantry must, he said, be waged even more ruthlessly than had been that against the Japanese. When county Party secretaries returned from their meeting in Xinyang city, they passed the same message down to their subordinates. The secretary of Gu Xian county told his cadres that during this period the peasants must be considered as anti-Party and against socialism. The peasants, he said, were the enemy, and this was war.

Some low-ranking cadres, local peasants themselves, were appalled by this, but dissent was impossible. No one, however humble, was allowed to remain neutral in this struggle. In Guangshan county, First Party Secretary Ma Longshan publicly 'struggled' one of his deputies, Zhang Fuhong, beating him so severely that his scalp was ripped off and he died from his wounds.[5] In similar struggle sessions which took place all over the prefecture, no Party member could refuse to take part and all had to join in the beating and torture of those suspected of hiding grain. Even prospective Party members were warned that if they did not participate, they would be barred from membership. To enforce the terror, the Public Security Bureau began to arrest both officials and peasants accused of being 'right opportunists'. Over 10,000 were detained, many of them subsequently dying from beatings or starvation.[6]

All over Xinyang, local officials also began to organize mass rallies which sometimes masqueraded as public entertainments to intimidate the peasants. On one such occasion, 10,000 people were invited to attend an opera performance, but when it was over the county Party Secretary, Lian Dezhu, went on stage and personally beat four peasants accused of hoarding grain. On other occasions, cadres demonstrated to the already starving peasants that some had indeed hidden grain by staging fake searches. In one commune, Ji Gong Shang, they secretly buried grain which they had first taken from a state granary. Then they summoned the peasants to watch an on-the-spot inspection in which the cadres duly discovered the 'secret' cache. All over the prefecture, cadres staged house-to-house searches, turning everything upside down to unearth the reserves which the peasantry was supposedly hiding from the state.[7]

At some rallies organized by the prefectural Party, every peasant attending had to hand over a quota of 5 lbs of grain. Later, when cadres were convinced that there really was no grain left, they would hold another rally at which the peasants were ordered to donate their chickens, ducks, pigs and other livestock. Finally, the peasants had to hand over their remaining possessions, everything from quilts to bronze door knockers – even, if they had nothing better, their cotton winter coats. In schools, teachers and pupils also had to take part in the campaign and deliver whatever grain or food coupons they possessed. Cadres in some places had to report three times a day on their achievements in the anti-hiding-grain production campaign. The prefectural Party committees even organized a competition to see which county could obtain the most grain. Huang Chuan county urged its inhabitants to eat less for three days so that it could rise higher than ninth place, its leaders declaring that it was better to let a few hundred people starve to death than sacrifice their honour.

To force the peasants to hand over their last remaining reserves, the officials did not simply beat the peasants but created a nightmare of organized torture and murder.[8] In its unpredictable terror, this rivalled the land reform campaign of 1948. Lu Xianwen issued orders to his cadres to crack down on what he termed 'the three obstacles': people who declared that there was no grain left; peasants who tried to flee; and those who called for the closure of the collective kitchens. In implementing the crackdown, each place invented its own methods of torture. In Guangshan county, local officials thought up thirty different tortures while Huang Chuan county had a list of seventy. Party documents drawn up after the arrest of the Xinyang prefecture's leadership in 1961 give details.

Many involved tying up and beating to death the victims, whose numbers in each locality ran into the hundreds. One Public Security chief, Chen Rubin, personally beat over 200 people in the Yidian production brigade of Dingyuan commune, Luoshan county. Han Defu, Second Secretary of the Segang commune, thrashed over 300 people. Guo Shouli, head of the militia of Nayuan brigade in Liji commune, Gushi county, beat 110 militiamen, 11 of whom were left permanently disabled and 6 of whom died. The same official arrested a commune member, Wei Shaoqiao, who had left one of the dam construction sites and returned home without permission. He was beaten to death, and when his wife came to look for him, she too was tied up and beaten until she died. She was three months pregnant. Guo Shouli then wanted to cut off the 'roots' of the family and killed the couple's 4-year-old child.

Others were buried alive or deliberately frozen to death: 'At the headquarters of the reservoir construction site of Ding Yuan of Luoshan commune, peasant Liu Nanjie had all his clothes removed and was then forced to stand outside in freezing snowy weather.'[9] In another case at Huashudian commune in Guangshan county, thirteen orphans were kept in water outdoors until they all froze to death. A common form of punishment was for cadres to drag people along by their hair. In one case in Huang Chuan county, a peasant woman was dragged for sixty feet over the ground until she died. Officials are also recorded as having tortured people by burning the hair on their heads, chins or genitals. The peasants tried to escape this form of cruelty by shaving off all their hair but then the cadres began to cut off the ears of their victims. In the Da Luying production brigade in Fan Hu commune, Xixian county, cadres hacked off the ears of seventeen people. A 20-year-old girl, Huang Xiu Lian, who was president of the commune's Women's Association, cut off the ears of four people, one of whom later died. Elsewhere women were humiliated by having sticks inserted into their genitals. Others were forced to sit or stand motionless for long periods, or made to run long distances.

Party records list still more grotesque methods of instilling fear and terror. The Party Secretary of Qisi commune in Gushi county, Jiang Xue Zhong, is said to have invented a method of boiling human flesh to turn it into fertilizer and was rumoured to have boiled more than a hundred children. Subsequent investigations revealed that he *had* boiled at least twenty corpses. Equally harsh punishments were meted out to those working in labour gangs on various huge reservoir and irrigation projects within the prefecture. According to figures for Gushi county, of the 60,000 workers sent to work on one dam project, 10,700 perished from exhaustion, hunger, cold or beatings.

There was almost nothing the peasants could do to save themselves in the face of this terror. When the collective canteens ran out of grain, some began slaughtering the remaining livestock. Retribution was savage after Lu Xianwen denounced this as 'sabotage of production' and demanded the punishment of offenders. Cadres in Xiangyang Dian commune in Pingyu county ordered the culprits to be dressed in mourning. Some had their noses pierced and wire pulled through the nostrils. They were then forced to pull a plough in the field like an ox. Others were stripped naked and beaten, and an oxhide still covered in fresh blood was tied around them. When the hide dried, it was torn off, ripping the victim's skin with it. An 18-year-old student, Wang Guoxi, was similarly treated when he was accused of stealing a sheep belonging to the Party Secretary of the Zhaoluo production brigade in Fan Hu commune, Xixian county. Strung up in the sheepskin, he was dragged from village to village for three days without food. When it was pulled off, the sheepskin, which by then had shrunk, took off much of his own skin as well and he subsequently died. An official account comments that

> Various kinds of counter-revolutionary atrocities of unparalleled savagery took place in almost all counties and communes and, according to the records, they took place not only in rural areas but in cities, factories, government units, schools, shops and hospitals. Eight headmasters of Guangshan county's 12 middle schools committed murder and it has been discovered that 28 teachers and students were beaten to death or forced to commit suicide in two middle schools.[10]

Even when, at the start of winter, it was clear that the peasants had nothing to eat but tree bark, wild grass seeds and wild vegetables, Lu Xianwen declared that this was merely 'a ruse of rich peasants' and ordered the search for grain to be redoubled. Party cadres were also incited to smash the cooking pots in every household to prevent them from being used at home to cook grass soup.

Some tried to flee but Lu ordered the arrest of such 'criminals' after seeing children begging by the roadside. Militiamen were instructed to guard every road and railway and to arrest any travellers, even those staying in hostels. All government organizations were given strict orders not to provide refuge to the fleeing peasants.[11] In Gushi county, the militia arrested at least 15,000 people who were then sent to labour camps. In Huang Chuan county, the head of the Public Security Bureau allowed 200 to starve to death in prison and then dispatched the 4 tonnes of grain he had thereby saved to the Party authorities.

The most extraordinary aspect of these events is that throughout the famine the state granaries in the prefecture were full of grain which the peasants said was sufficient to keep everyone alive. Several sources have stated that even at the height of the famine, the Party leadership ate well. By the beginning of 1960, with nothing left to eat and no longer able to flee, the peasants began to die in huge numbers. In the early stages of the famine, most of those who died were old people or men forced to do hard labour on inadequate rations. Now, it was women and children. Whole villages starved to death. In Xixian county alone, 639 villages were left deserted and 100,000 starved to death. A similar number died in Xincai county.[12] Corpses littered the fields and roads as the peasants collapsed from starvation. Few of the bodies were buried. Many simply lay down at home and died.

That winter, cannibalism became widespread. Generally, the villagers ate the flesh of corpses, especially those of children. In rare cases, parents ate their own children, elder brothers ate younger brothers, elder sisters ate their younger sisters. In most cases, cannibalism was not punished by the Public Security Bureaux because it was not considered as severe a crime as destroying state property and the means of production. This latter crime often merited the death sentence. Travelling around the region over thirty years later, every peasant that I met aged over 50 said he personally knew of a case of cannibalism in his production team. One man pointed to a nearby cluster of huts and said he recalled entering a neighbour's house to find him eating the leg of a 5-year-old child of a relative who had died of starvation. The authorities came to hear of what he had done but although he was criticized, he was never put on trial. Generally, though, cannibalism was a secret, furtive event. Women would usually go out at night and cut flesh off the bodies, which lay under a thin layer of soil, and this would then be eaten in secrecy. Sometimes, though, the authorities did intervene. In one commune, a 15-year-old girl who survived by boiling her younger brother's corpse and eating it was caught. The Public Security Bureau charged her with 'destroying a corpse' and put her in prison where she subsequently starved to death. In Gushi county, in 1960, the authorities listed 200 cases of corpses being eaten and charged those arrested with the crime of 'destroying corpses'.[13]

Among the peasants little blame or stigma was apparently attached to breaking such taboos. Bai Hua, one of China's most famous contemporary writers, recalls that while living in another part of China, he heard the following story from a workmate who returned from a visit to Xinyang.[14] There, the man had discovered that all his relatives bar one had starved to death. This was his aunt who had managed to survive through chance because a pig had run into her hut one night. She quickly closed the door, killed it and buried it under the ground. She did not dare share the pork with anyone, not even her 5-year-old son, for she was convinced that if she did so, her son would blurt out the news to the other villagers. Then she feared that the authorities would seize the meat, beat her to death and leave her son to die anyway. So she let him starve to death. Neither Bai Hua nor his workmate condemned the aunt for her actions.

Deaths were kept secret for as long as possible. What food there was was distributed by the collective kitchen and generally one family member would be sent to collect the rations on behalf of the whole household. As long as the death of a family member was kept secret, the rest of the household could benefit from an extra ration. So the corpse would be kept in the hut. In Guangshan county, one woman with three children was caught after she had hidden the corpse of one of them behind the door and then finally, in desperation, had begun to eat it.[15]

The Xinyang prefectural leadership did everything it could to hide what was going on from the world outside. The Party ensured that all mail and telephone calls were monitored and censored. No one could leave the region without written permission from the Party leaders who even posted cadres at the railway station in Zhengzhou, the provincial capital. They were

accompanied by guards who searched and usually arrested anyone getting off a train from Xinyang. While in other parts of
China the authorities issued starving peasants with 'begging
certificates' which allowed them to try their luck elsewhere,
this was strictly forbidden in Xinyang.[16]

The provincial authorities in Zhengzhou did send inspection
teams to Xinyang but they were prevented from gathering
information. In one instance, the inspection team was simply
not allowed to get off the train. Even when, in the autumn of
1959, the provincial authorities offered to send grain to relieve
the shortages caused by the drought, it was refused. Some grain
was delivered but it was returned by the Xinyang leadership
who continued to insist that they were enjoying a bumper harvest. In the atmosphere of terror, no cadre at any level dared
admit the truth: Liang Dezhen, the First Secretary of Huang
Chuan county, turned back relief grain because he suspected
that it was a ruse to trap him into making a political mistake,
and one production brigade in the county that did take the
grain sent it back as the fruits of its 'anti-hiding-grain production' work.[17]

Much of the blame for what happened in Xinyang must rest
with Wu Zhifu, the head of the Henan Party organization. A
short, tubby man, the son of local peasants, Wu had joined the
Party early on and became a student of Mao's at the Peasant
Movement Training Institute in the mid-1920s. After the Communists had driven the Nationalists south of the Yangtze in
1948, he rose to be a senior member of the Party in Henan. As
such, he was responsible for carrying out land reform in the
province, which was marked by exceptional violence. Not only
were landlords stripped of all their possessions, but so were
rich peasants and large numbers of so-called middle peasants.
According to one account, the peasants 'carried off and divided
everything that could be moved. Beatings and killings were
widespread and not all victims were landlords.'[18] Indeed, the
violence was so great that the Party was obliged to halt the
process. Partly as a result, the post of First Secretary went not
to Wu but to a more moderate figure called Pan Fusheng. Over
the next few years, the Henan leadership was split between

radical leftists loyal to Mao, who wanted to press ahead with collectivization as fast as possible, and moderates under Pan. The Maoists began to drive the peasants harder and harder, forcing them into ever larger co-operatives and pressurizing them to promise to deliver ever larger quotas of grain to the state. Such men were singled out for praise by Mao in July 1955 when he compiled his book *The High Tide of Socialism in the Chinese Countryside*. Henan suffered from famine in 1956 and Pan responded by splitting the co-operatives into smaller units and allowing peasants to leave if they wished. He criticized the collectivization, saying, 'The peasants are the same as beasts of burden, yellow oxen are tied up in the stall and human beings are harnessed in the fields. Girls and women pull ploughs and harrows with their wombs hanging down. Co-operation is transformed into the exploitation of human strength.'[19] In the 1957 Anti-Rightist purge, Pan was accused of following in the footsteps of Bukharin – the Soviet leader shot for opposing Stalin's rush into collectivization – and dismissed.[20] In his place Mao appointed Wu Zhifu, who turned Henan into the pace-setter for Maoist agriculture. As a result, many provinces adopted the slogan: 'Learn from Henan, catch up with Henan, press ahead consistently and win first position.'

Chen Boda, who spent much time in Henan, made Wu his protégé and asked him to write articles about his successes in *Red Flag*, the ideological journal which Chen edited. Henan was rewarded for its loyalty by being chosen as the site for both the country's first tractor factory and a giant hydro-electric scheme on the Yellow River.

Mao toured the new model communes in Henan several times in 1958, admiring their agricultural miracles and the speed with which some communes had apparently reached the final stage of Communism. In his wake, thousands of officials from around the country came to study the Henan model. Among the innovations launched in Chayashan was a technique called 'launching a sputnik'. Unlike the Soviet Union's satellite, this sputnik required no technology or science, just peasants pushed into working for twenty-four hours at a stretch to achieve extraordinary feats of industry. The American journalist Anna Louise Strong claimed that in one such twenty-four-hour sputnik, peasants produced a staggering 1.2 million tonnes of iron, more than the United States poured in a whole month. By launching sputniks, Wu promised to make Henan the first province to achieve full literacy, complete irrigation and full Communization. He also claimed that the Chayashan commune's sputniks were lifting grain yields to astronomical levels. Yields allegedly shot from an average of around 330 lbs per 0.17 acres to 3,300 lbs and sometimes even 11,000 lbs. After Mao visited these fields, he told a top-level meeting in Zhengzhou that such yields could now be reached by everyone. It was of course all lies, for everything Mao saw was a staged pantomime. Before each visit, local officials prepared fields for Mao to inspect by digging out shoots of wheat and replanting them all in one experimental field. When Mao arrived they put three children on top of the grain to show that the wheat was growing so closely together that it could support their weight. When he left, they put the grain back in the original fields. The same trick was used to demonstrate how successfully agriculture was being mechanized. At each commune Mao visited, he was delighted to see electric irrigation pumps watering the fields, but they were always the same pumps, which had been taken from the last commune and which were then installed in the next while he slept.[21]

Trapped by their own lies, local officials then had to order the peasants to try to reach exceptional grain yield targets using methods such as deep ploughing and close planting. Some peasants genuinely believed that close planting would work if it was done with great accuracy. They cut up endless copies of the *People's Daily* and on the pages spread out over the fields they marked out exactly where individual seeds should be placed. Experience dictated a limit of 12 lbs of seed per *mu* (0.17 acres), but now they tried to plant 88–132 lbs per *mu*. In some places, layer upon layer of seeds were forcibly pressed into the ground. Naturally, the seeds suffocated each other and the fields remained barren. No one dared openly admit that Mao's ideas did not work, so they literally covered up the emperor's nakedness with their coats. They went to their huts and took out their cotton coats and bedding, and added seeds and water. In this way the seeds quickly sprouted. When the new seedlings were high enough, the mattresses and coats were buried under soil.[22]

In Henan, everything was taken to extremes. When the nation was ordered to exterminate the four pests and clean up their villages and latrines, the peasants in Xinyang set a new standard in this orgy of cleanliness by brushing the teeth of their oxen and sheep. Henan's irrigation projects were the grandest and most ambitious in China and work on them went on around the clock. In the fields, too, peasants worked at night by electric light; when that was not available, they used oil lamps and candles.

Henan's enthusiasm for the Great Leap Forward made Zhengzhou a favourite venue for a number of key top-level meetings in 1958. That year Wu reported that the Henan grain harvest was 35 million tonnes of grain, triple the real total of 12.5 million tonnes.[23] To Mao this was a vindication of his policies and substantiated what he thought he had himself seen in Henan. In internal Party circulars, he described those who doubted him as 'tide-watchers', 'bean-counters' and 'right opportunists'. After the Lushan summit, Mao was equally pleased when at a meeting in November 1959, again in Zhengzhou, Wu Zhifu told him that Henan's agriculture was doing even better. Wu had returned from Lushan and had immediately organized a huge conference with cadres from the village level upwards. They were ordered to spare no effort to hunt down 'right opportunists'. Wu made a list of those who should be attacked. He said rightists included those who talked about the limitations of nature and predicted disaster, and divided them into five categories – among them the 'push-pull faction', the 'wait-and-see faction', the 'shaking-heads-in-front-of-the-furnace faction' and the 'stretching-out-hands faction'.[24] These categories were so vague and so open to interpretation that anyone could be persecuted depending on the whim of their superiors. Fear and panic swept the province.

Wu Zhifu set a new and equally unrealistic grain target of 22 million tonnes for 1959. Though lower than the 1958 target of 35 million tonnes, because parts of Henan were stricken by drought, it was more than double what was actually harvested in 1959, estimated at 10.3 million tonnes of grain.[25] At the same time, Wu reduced the acreage sown to grain by 14 per cent in line with Williams' theories. In early 1960, he raised production targets still higher and commissioned more irrigation projects, reporting to Beijing that Henan's grain output that year was again very high and joining in the chorus of Maoist loyalists who were urging another 'Great Leap Forward'.

The blame for these acts of criminal folly cannot entirely be laid on Wu's shoulders, or on those of Xinyang's Lu Xianwen. The fanaticism with which they pursued these goals derived in part from Henan's past which had created a fertile ground for Utopian fantasies. In a region notorious for its famines, the peasants were psychologically receptive to millenarian movements. Dynasties had come and gone, but their way of life had changed little. Most lived in the same kind of crude huts made of mud and straw as had their forefathers 2,000 years before, and across the same fields the patient ox pulled a wooden plough just as its ancestors had done. By the twentieth century, Henan was a backward and impoverished region known as the 'land of beggars'. The exhausted soil could not feed the growing population and many periodically fled elsewhere. Among those who stayed, many turned to secret societies and religious sects – it is no coincidence that in the first half of the twentieth century American missionaries built hospitals and churches in great numbers in the province. Throughout the late 1930s and early 1940s, disaster after disaster struck Henan. In April 1938, Generalissimo Chiang Kai-shek breached the dykes of the Yellow River to halt the Japanese army's southward advance. Some claim that as a result between 1 and 3.9 million peasants drowned or starved and another 11 million were left homeless. Nonetheless, war continued to rack the region. In the plains the Nationalists and Japanese armies fought. In the Dabie mountains in the south of Henan, the Communist Red Army established a base and each army fought viciously for control of the peasantry. In 1943 Henan was the epicentre of what was then considered the worst famine in Chinese history when between 3 and 5 million died. This was the famine which the American journalist Theodore White witnessed and which he appealed, successfully, to Chiang Kai-shek to stop. It convinced him that the peasants were right to go over to the Communists after the Japanese defeat: 'I know how cruel the Chinese Communists can be: but no cruelty was greater than the Henan famine, and if the Communist idea promised government of any kind, then the ideas of mercy and liberty with which I had grown up were irrelevant.' In the light of what subsequently occurred in Henan under Mao, his comment has a terrible irony. The famines did not end with Japan's defeat in 1945. The following year another famine, witnessed by the *Daily Telegraph* correspondent John Ridley, carried off a further 5 million people in Henan.

Ultimately, responsibility for what happened in Henan in 1958–61 rested with Mao himself. He had personally sanctioned the orgy of violence and had held up Xinyang as a model for the rest of the country. As early as the beginning of 1959, Mao had received letters from peasants in some counties in Henan protesting that people were starving to death.[26] He disregarded them and in response to complaints that production team leaders were brutally beating peasants who refused to hand over their hidden grain, he addressed a meeting of provincial leaders in February 1959 as follows: 'We should protect the enthusiasm of cadres and working-class people. As for those 5 per cent of cadres who break the law, we should look at them individually, and help them to overcome their mistakes. If we exaggerate this problem it is not good.'[27] Officials were effectively given *carte blanche* to take any measures they wished to seize the fictitious hoards of grain.

However, reports of what was really happening in Henan were reaching the centre, and some influential figures in the capital were becoming concerned. Mao was guarded by a special unit of bodyguards, some of whom were recruited from the Xinyang region which had been an important military base for the Red Army during the 1940s, and they received letters from their relatives. Another source of information came from inspection tours by Mao's secretary Tian Jiaying and by Chen Yun, one of the most senior figures in the Party. Despite the efforts made to deceive them, both expressed scepticism about Henan's claims. Yet Mao only believed what he wanted to hear. He dismissed reports from these sources and instead accepted as the truth a report from the Xinyang leadership that insisted there was no grain crisis. It admitted that there were problems with falling grain supplies but claimed that this was only due to widespread sabotage by former landlords, counter-revolutionaries, revisionists and feudal elements. The Xinyang Party leadership (who appear to have had a direct channel of communication with Mao) proposed to solve the grain problem with a harsh crackdown. Mao was delighted to hear that, as he had always maintained, class struggle lay behind China's problems. He issued a directive to the rest of the country urging all Party members to deepen the struggle against such class enemies. The Xinyang report was copied and distributed to the whole Party as a model of what was wrong and what should be done about it. To support the Xinyang leadership, he dispatched some members from his own circle to the prefecture in January 1960. According to his doctor, Li Zhisui, Mao sent his confidential secretary, Gao Zhi, and his chief bodyguard, Feng Yaosong. He told them to come back if the assignment became too hard, saying, 'Don't worry, no one will die.'

For the entire summer of 1960 Mao did nothing, although it was by then becoming clear even to him that China was starving. The rest of the Chinese leadership was paralysed, waiting for Mao to change his mind. At the beginning of the winter, inspection teams led by senior Party leaders set out from Beijing to gather evidence of what was going on in the countryside. What happened next in Xinyang is not entirely clear. According to one version, an inspection team led by Chen Yun and Deng Liqun arrived in Xinyang but were detained as they got off the train and confined to a small room. They returned to sound the alarm. Another version has it that an army colonel from Beijing came home on leave and discovered that his relatives in Guangshan county were starving.

Whatever the truth of the matter, the famine was broken in early 1961 when about 30,000 men from the People's Liberation Army (PLA) were ordered to occupy Xinyang, distribute the grain in the state granaries and arrest the prefecture's leadership. The army stayed for three or four months. One source said that in Huang Chuan county, people were so weak they could only crawl across the ground to get to the grain. Some died only feet away from it. The troops also distributed 1.17 million winter coats and 140,000 quilts, and provided emergency accommodation. A report on Xinyang revealed that in places nine out of ten dwellings had been abandoned: the troops set about repairing a total of more than half a million dwellings and opened 80,000 government buildings as shelters for the peasants. A massive effort to gather fuel for fires was undertaken and an edict was promulgated to ensure that the peasants were not asked to do more than half a day's work.

Mao had himself authorized the PLA's intervention and, in a brief letter distributed within the Party, he wrote that it was necessary to do this even if he risked being accused of rightism. The PLA, together with cadres from Zhengzhou, launched an investigation into what had happened in Xinyang. About fifty of the top officials were arrested and interrogated, and a report was drawn up and widely distributed. The official version which Mao authorized blamed the whole episode on counter-revolutionaries and class enemies:

> There are two reasons why our enemies could act so recklessly. On the one hand, they disguised themselves as the Communist Party and draped their counter-revolutionary souls with the banner of socialism and threw dust in the eyes of some people. On the other hand, there is a social basis for the counter-revolutionaries. As counter-revolutionaries were not thoroughly suppressed and land reform was not properly carried out, some landlords, rich peasants and bad men were left untouched and many of them sneaked into revolutionary organizations, collaborating with each other to carry out the restoration of the counter-revolutionary class and to conduct cannibalistic persecution of the masses.[28]

Mao's views notwithstanding, the 'Xinyang incident' became widely known amongst the senior levels of the Party throughout China and was used to push for a reversal of policies in 1961. Versions of the findings of the investigation were circulated and have since reappeared in different publications that form the basis of the above account. It seems likely that one version containing higher death tolls was restricted to the top levels of the Party and that another was distributed to lower-ranking cadres to minimize the damage to morale. Evidence that morale was indeed damaged within the army comes from a document drawn up by the PLA's General Political Department, a copy of which the US State Department obtained in 1963. It expressed strong fears that the loyalty of the army was in doubt because some of the troops were openly blaming Mao for the death of their relatives.[29]

Different versions of the official report on the 'Xinyang incident' would explain why different sources give conflicting figures for the death toll. Some claim that the total population of Xinyang* was about 8 million in 1958 and that the final death toll was 4 million out of a provincial death toll of 7.8 million. A former Chinese Party official, Chen Yizi, who lived in Xinyang during the Cultural Revolution and, after 1979, took part in an official investigation into famine deaths, has said that the Henan provincial death toll was 8 million. When I visited the worst-hit counties, such as Luoshan and Guangshan, people readily admitted that two-thirds of the population had perished during the famine. Even in the less severely hit counties and communes, death rates of 20 or 30 per cent were standard. At the Chayashan commune, the first in China, the death rate was 33 per cent.

Other sources, including such books as Ding Shu's *Ren Huo* and Su Luozheng's *July Storm*, put the death toll in Xinyang at 1 million and the provincial total at around 2 million. Such sources provide detailed death tolls for each of the counties in Xinyang. Even if, in the absence of conclusive documentary proof, the lower figure of 1 million is accepted, this still means that around one in eight died, a figure which remains horrifying.

Few were punished for this holocaust. One version of the official report on Henan states that 130,000 cadres were investigated and ordered to reform their work-style. Of these, 8,000 were considered to have made 'serious mistakes', 983 were discharged from their posts and disciplined, and a mere 275 were arrested and brought to justice. Among them were 50 senior cadres. A handful, including the Xinyang Party secretary Lu Xianwen, were given the death sentence but were reprieved on Mao's orders.[30] Instead, Lu and the others were assigned to posts elsewhere in the country. Some of those responsible are still living in Zhengzhou over thirty years later. Wu Zhifu was protected by Mao and, though demoted to Second Secretary in 1962, was later given a high position in the South-West China Bureau. He reportedly wrote a self-criticism in which he said 'my crimes are very great. Whatever punishment is announced,

* Since then Xinyang has been divided into two prefectures.

I will not protest even if it is death.' Even today, many in Henan still consider him to have been a good man forced to do bad things. He died in the early 1970s and was praised by the Party as an honoured patriot. His mother still lives in Zhengzhou and is dignified with gifts at Qingming, the Chinese festival honouring the dead. Wu's sons have been given good jobs in the government and allowed to study abroad. Few now want to remember Xinyang's bitter history or to try to understand what happened there.

9

Anhui:
Let's Talk about Fengyang

'Let's talk about Fengyang.
Once it was a good place to live,
But since Emperor Zhu was born there
There's been famine nine years out of every
   ten.
The wealthy sold their horses,
The poor sold their children.
I, who have no children to sell,
Am roaming the world with a flower drum.'[1]
                              Popular Chinese song

THE FIRST BEGGAR to become Emperor of China buried his
mother in style. She had starved to death in a little hamlet just
outside Fengyang, an obscure town in the poor countryside of
Anhui province. After her son Zhu Yuanzhang became
emperor, he returned to Anhui and built a burial complex for
his mother so gigantic that it covered a dozen square miles. Six
hundred years later, the tomb is still there but its imperial
grandeur has crumbled into ruins: peasants have used the
bricks to build their homes, the avenue of stone spirit guardians
stands deep in grass, and ducks paddle in the moat around
the wooded burial mound. Emperor Zhu is one of the most
memorable figures in Chinese history. After the death of his
parents he became first a beggar and then a Buddhist monk.
He later joined a secret visionary sect, led an army to victory

over the occupying Mongols and founded the Ming dynasty, almost the only ethnically pure Chinese dynasty in the last thousand years.

Mao considered Zhu his precursor and model. Like Zhu, Mao had been a peasant, a beggar and the leader of a secret sect. He too had led an army which threw out the foreigners and had unified the nation. Mao also admired Zhu for his achievements as Emperor. To prevent the recurrence of famine Zhu had ordered the reform of agriculture, the planting of trees, the construction of irrigation works and, above all, the establishment of granaries: '*Shen wa dong, guan ji liang,*' he declared – 'Dig deep tunnels and store grain.' Peasants were resettled in underpopulated or virgin lands, absentee landlords were dispossessed and even his troops were ordered to grow grain. Yet, as a popular song about Fengyang's most famous son suggests, Zhu was soon hated. He became a tyrant and in his paranoia turned China into a vast police state. Each morning his officials, terrified by his sudden and bloody purges, would bid farewell to their families before leaving for the court, in case they never saw them again.

In honour of Emperor Zhu, Fengyang was privileged after 1949 and became a model county. Like Xinyang in neighbouring Henan, it lies in a rich plain watered by the Huai River and is vulnerable to both floods and droughts. During the Sino-Japanese War, it was ravaged and in the civil war that followed it witnessed fierce fighting between Communists and Nationalists over a key strategic prize, the railway linking Beijing to Nanjing which runs near Fengyang. During the fighting soldiers buried villagers alive, massacred the families of enemy fighters and ate the corpses of their prisoners.

The Communist victory in 1949 brought peace to the county. Fengyang took the lead in collectivizing agriculture and even had a machine tractor station run by Soviet advisers. The county of 335,000 people was soon boasting impressive grain yields. After Mao's death, it continued to be a model, this time for the redivision of communal land. As such, it has been the subject of numerous studies. One, a compilation based on county Party records, was smuggled out of China in the wake of the pro-democracy demonstrations in 1989. The 600-page document, entitled *Thirty Years in the Countryside*, was never intended to be circulated outside the top echelons of the Party, for it paints a detailed and appalling picture of the famine. What happened in Fengyang is significant because it reflects the role that Anhui played in the events of 1958–62. At the height of the famine, Anhui abandoned collective farming. At first Mao welcomed Anhui's policies but later, suspecting a plot, he abruptly changed his mind and dismissed the province's leader. Had he not done so, the recent history of China might have been very different.

The man responsible for both Anhui's terrible famine and its reforms was a paunchy, aggressive former peasant called Zeng Xisheng. Zeng was a bully with a violent temper but during the Long March he had proved his courage as one of Mao's bodyguards. He was slavishly loyal to Mao who trusted him, perhaps because he too was a Hunanese. Zeng had joined the Party in its early days, attended the Whampoa Military Academy and first met Mao in 1923. He achieved prominence as a signals intelligence officer in the Red Army and by the 1940s he was in charge of the Fourth Route Army in northern Anhui. When the Communists triumphed, he became the First Secretary of Anhui, a large rural province with a population of 33.5 million in 1953. As Mao pushed China faster and faster along the road to collectivization, Zeng was right behind him. When the Great Leap Forward started, he spared no efforts to show his devotion, and when Mao visited Anhui's capital, Hefei, in 1958, Zeng brought the whole of the city's population out to cheer him. When Mao called on the Chinese to make steel, Zeng showed this could be done not just in big furnaces but in every backyard. Soon small 'backyard furnaces' were melting down pots and pans all over China. Zeng penned numerous articles for *Red Flag* praising the Great Leap Forward and when Mao felt threatened at the Lushan summit, Zeng was outspoken in defending his policies against the objections of Peng Dehuai and others. In 1960 Mao promoted him, entrusting him with the leadership of both Anhui and Shandong.

The Great Leap Forward began in Anhui, as everywhere else, with claims of extraordinary success. In Fengyang that year one sputnik field supposedly grew a national record of 62.5 tonnes of tobacco in just 0.17 acres of land.[2] Fantastic pressure was exerted at every level to meet the quotas that Zeng set. Local

Party secretaries were kept locked up in rooms for weeks until they agreed to meet their grain quotas and other targets. They in turn put their deputies through the same ordeal. So it went, from prefecture to county, from commune to brigade, from production team right down to the individual peasant. If a peasant didn't agree to double or treble or quadruple his harvest the production team leader would beat him until he gave in. Nobody believed these targets could be reached but cadres reported that they had been. The lies went back up the pyramid from peasant to production chief, to brigade leader, to commune Party secretary, to county secretary, to prefectural leader and finally to Zeng Xisheng who reported to Mao. With each repetition, the lies became more and more fantastic, a ghastly parody of Chinese Whispers. All over the province, grain yields which were at best 726 lbs per 0.17 acres were inflated to an astonishing 33,000 lbs (14.7 tonnes).

Poor, impoverished Anhui now claimed to be flush with a fantastic bonanza and Zeng began to deliver large amounts of grain to other parts of the country and even abroad – in 1959 alone Anhui exported 200,000 tonnes although its grain harvest had shrunk by 4 million tonnes from the record 10 million tonnes harvested in 1958. In 1959, the state demanded that the peasants of Anhui hand over 2.5 million tonnes, that is 40 per cent of the harvest.[3]

In Fengyang, the year before had been bad enough. In 1958, the county had harvested 89,000 tonnes but reported 178,500 tonnes to cover up a sharp decline in output. Some of this grain was not even gathered in, but rotted in the fields because too many peasants were out making steel or building dams. After the peasants deducted what they needed to eat and to keep for seed, a surplus of only 5,800 tonnes was left to deliver to the state, but the grain levy was fixed at 35,000 tonnes on the basis of the false harvest reported. The missing 29,200 tonnes had to be extracted by force. In 1959, the county authorities lost all touch with reality. The county reported that 199,000 tonnes were harvested, a little higher than the reported figure for 1958, but in fact the harvest had further declined from 89,000 to 54,000 tonnes. Of this, the state demanded 29,464 tonnes.

In 1958 and 1959, Fengyang officials lied not just about grain production but also about the amount of arable land sown, the area of virgin land ploughed, the number of irrigation works created and practically everything else. They said they had raised 166,000 pigs when the true figure was only 43,000. One production team claimed it had grown 19.6 acres of rapeseed when it had grown none at all. The brigade chief thought this lie was too modest and informed his superior that the team had grown 10 acres.[4] As the communes in the county trumpeted their new riches, the cadres were busy seizing whatever the peasants owned. All private property had to be handed over, including private land, draught animals, carts and even milling stones and houses. In Fengyang, the cadres commandeered over 11,000 houses, and to feed the backyard furnaces they took bicycles, scissors, knives, cooking utensils and even iron fences. When the Party needed more carts for its schemes, the cadres simply knocked down houses to take the necessary wood. Some peasants were left entirely homeless, others forced to live ten to a room. Even the huts that remained were stripped of their wooden doors and furniture to fuel the backyard furnaces. In the most fanatical villages, men were not even allowed to keep their wives who were forced to live separately.

In the run-up to the creation of the communes in 1958, the peasants went into a frenzy, eating as much of their food as they could and selling their livestock. People chopped down trees, dug up their vegetables and did everything to ensure that as little as possible was handed over. When the communes were established, the entire administration of daily life changed. Every minor decision or arrangement previously decided by the villagers now had to be passed to the commune headquarters which looked after around 5,000 households. By the end of September 1958, the communes were in full operation, and eating at the collective kitchens was compulsory.[5] By the Spring Festival of 1959, peasants in Fengyang and everywhere else in Anhui were starving. As food supplies dwindled fights broke out at the collective kitchens. The only food that was served was a watery soup. Those who were unfortunate received the thin gruel at the top of the pot, those who were lucky got the richer liquid at the bottom. Those too weak to collect their soup went without. Amidst this desperate struggle for food in early 1959, the Party launched the first anti-hiding-grain campaign in Anhui which, in its brutality, rivalled that in

Henan. After the harvest of 1959 was taken away in the autumn, people began to starve to death in large numbers.[6] A sense of what life was like in Anhui in the winter of 1959–60 is evoked by one survivor, now a grandmother, who then lived in another county near Fengyang on the Huai River plain:

In the first year [1958–9], we earned work points and the communes distributed grain to each family. This we kept at home. But in the second year [1959–60], there was nothing left at home, it had all been taken away. Nevertheless the village cadres came to every household to search for food. They searched every street and every building. They took away everything they could find, including our cotton eiderdowns, several bags of carrots and the cotton we had saved to make new clothes.

Our family still had one jar of food and we had to hide it behind the door. This jar was full of sweet potatoes which we had dried and ground up. When the cadres came, Second Aunt sat on the jar pretending to sew clothes and so they missed it. This jar helped us a lot. I think it saved our lives because in our household no one died. You could not cook the dried sweet potato but if you were very hungry, you just grabbed some of it with your hands. Almost every day the cadres came. They searched every home for nine consecutive days. Later, we buried the jar underground but the cadres came and poked the ground with iron rods to see if we had buried anything. Then we hid it somewhere else. This went on until February.

The communal canteen did not serve any proper food, just wild grasses, peanut shells and sweet potato skins. Because of this diet we had terrible problems. Some were constipated but others had constant diarrhoea and could not get beyond the front door. Yet the cadres still regularly inspected each house for cleanliness and if they found that a house or the area around it was dirty, they would place a black flag outside. If it was clean, they put up a white flag. I had to try and clean up the mess but at the time I had difficulty walking.

My legs and hands were swollen and I felt that at any moment I would die. Instead of walking to the fields to look for wild grass, I crawled and rolled to save energy. Several old women tried to get grass from ponds or rivers but because they had to stand in the water their legs became infected.

All the trees in the village had been cut down. Any nearby were all stripped of bark. I peeled off the bark of a locust tree and cooked it as if it were rice soup. It tasted like wood and was sticky.

At the time the villagers looked quite fat and even healthy because they were swollen but when they were queuing up at the canteen to eat, they would suddenly collapse and could not get up. Some could only walk using a stick.

One sister lived in a house that had been turned into the public canteen and her family were okay. Another sister became so weak she had no strength to draw water from the well. One day she suddenly fell down because her legs could not support her. In those days the ground was slippery because it was raining a lot. Her leg became inflamed and covered with running sores. She drained them with a knife. Our younger sister was only 10 then and was well enough to walk so she went to the older sister at the canteen to beg for food. She was given some buns which she hid by tying them around her waist and secretly brought her the food.

Another relative lived with her mother-in-law, who refused to give her any food. She stole grain to eat but had to go a long way to do this. Actually, there was food hidden under the *kang* but her mother-in-law kept this from her. She was only saved when her brother-in-law took pity on her and told her. So she could raid the pot and eat something.

No one in our family died. By February 1960, Grandpa's legs were completely swollen. His hair fell out, his body was covered in sores and he was too weak to open his mouth. A friend came and drained off some of the sores and this helped. We still had three small goats and an aunt killed two of them secretly to help him. Unfortunately, the cadres discovered this and took the carcases away.

More than half the villagers died, mostly between New Year [1960] and April or May. In one of our neighbours' houses, three boys and a girl starved. In one brother's family two children died. Another family of sixteen died. Many families disappeared completely with no survivors at all. The production team chief's daughter-in-law and his grandson starved to death. He then boiled and ate the corpse of the child but he also died. When the village teacher was on the verge of death, he said to his wife, 'Why should we keep our child? If we eat him then I can survive and later we can produce another child.' His wife refused to do this and her husband died.

When people died, no one collected the bodies. The corpses did not change colour or decay because there was no blood in them and not much flesh. After people died, their families would not report the death to the production team. This was because they could get another portion of food. One family had three children and they died. The father hid the bodies and claimed their rations. In the whole village only seven or eight families did not suffer any deaths but some fled.

Later, when the wheat was harvested the situation improved, but we had to carry on eating at the canteen all through 1960. It was a good harvest and there were far fewer mouths to feed. The autumn harvest was also good and later we were allowed to eat at home. We had nothing to cook with and went to our neighbours to borrow pots. Some of the houses I went to were empty because everyone had fled.[7]

This woman's account, extraordinary though it is, is by no means unusual. Records at Fengyang show that the entire population of some villages perished. In Xiaoxihe commune, where enthusiasm for collectivization was extreme, all the inhabitants of twenty-one villages died. In such villages, people frequently resorted to cannibalism but even this did not ensure survival because the corpses provided so little sustenance. Finally, when there was not even human flesh left to eat, all died. According to official records, there were 63 cases of cannibalism in Fengyang. *Thirty Years in the Countryside* recounts examples, among them the following: 'Chen Zhangying and her husband from Wuyi brigade of Damiao commune strangled their 8-year-old boy, boiled and ate him ... Wang Lanying of Banjing brigade of Wudian commune not only took back home dead human bodies and ate them but also sold 2 *jin* [just under 2 lbs] as pork.'[8]

Just how extensive cannibalism was may never be known. It was official policy to cover up such incidents, even when arrests were made. Zhao Yushu, Fengyang's Party Secretary, insisted on describing cannibalism as 'political sabotage'. The Public Security Bureau was ordered secretly to arrest anyone connected with such practices. Of the 63 who were arrested, 33 died in prison. An interviewee from another county in Anhui recalled that a traditional practice called *Yi zi er shi* – 'Swop child, make food' – was common.

The worst thing that happened during the famine was this: parents would decide to allow the old and the young to die first. They thought they could not afford to let their sons die but a mother would say to her daughter, 'You have to go and see your granny in heaven.' They stopped giving the girl children food. They just gave them water. Then they swopped the body of their daughter with that of a neighbour's. About five to seven women would agree to do this amongst themselves. Then they boiled the corpses into a kind of soup. People had learned to do this during the famine of the 1930s. People accepted this as it was a kind of hunger culture. They said: 'If your stomach is empty, then who can keep face?' One woman was reported and arrested by the Public Security Bureau. No one in the village criticized her when she returned from a labour camp a few years later.

At first, the villagers tried to bury their dead in coffins but later, when the wood ran out, the living just wrapped the dead in cotton. Finally there was no cloth left, so at night people mounted guard over buried relatives until the flesh had sufficiently decomposed to prevent others from eating the corpse. In parts of Fengyang, officials issued regulations on the disposal of corpses to try and keep the scale of the deaths secret. An example of such regulations is cited in the report on Fengyang:

1. Shallow burials are prohibited. All corpses must be buried at least three feet deep and crops must be grown on top.
2. No burials are allowed near roads.
3. All crying and wailing is forbidden.
4. The wearing of mourning clothes is forbidden.

In the Zhangwan production team of Huan Guan commune, the regulations were even stricter. Peasants were told that they must not wear white clothes, the colour of mourning, but red ones. In China, red is the colour for celebrations. Another cadre in Wanshan brigade also insisted that peasants must pay a tax of 2 *jin* of alcohol before burying their dead. He would then strip the corpses of their clothes and take them home.

In many places where there was no one left to bury the dead, the bodies lay where they had fallen. One man I met recalled how as a child living in a small town, he and others had even played with the corpses. He remembered, too, how a villager went insane and wandered around for days ranting and raving with four or five heads tied around his neck. Elsewhere the bodies were buried beneath a thin covering of soil but the stiffened corpses were so bent that often the feet and head stuck out of the ground. For years to come, he said, the carelessly buried skeletons would re-emerge from the ground during a drought.

The first to die were often the strongest and most active members of a village who were worked the hardest. Left behind were the elderly and the children. By the end of 1961, Fengyang county was left with 2,398 orphans of whom 247 were given shelter by the authorities. Some were abandoned by parents who despaired of being able to feed them. Some were brought by their parents to Hefei, the provincial capital, to exchange for grain coupons. Sometimes they simply died on the streets. One interviewee remembered that as a child she had walked past small corpses covered with maggots lying at one of the main intersections in Hefei.

Zhao Yushu, the Fengyang Party Secretary, tried to stop people abandoning their children by forbidding Party officials from giving them succour. The Fengyang report quotes an official:

A lot of children were being abandoned and Zhao Yushu forbade people to pick them up. He said, the more you pick them up, the more children will be abandoned. Once he said that he had seen a landlord abandon his child so he got the idea that anyone who did this was a bad class element; if a cadre rescued an abandoned child, it meant that he was bad too.

The authorities denied most orphans any shelter. In the winter of 1962 when they implemented a new policy and began rounding up orphans, they found 3,304. Most of the children were under 10 years old and usually boys. The shortage of females from that generation is striking in Anhui. One village that I visited had around forty men who had been unable to marry because there were only two or three women survivors of their generation. Now in their mid-forties, they had been in their late teens during the famine. According to Ding Shu's book *Ren Huo,* the People's Liberation Army also later issued a regulation forbidding the recruitment of orphans. They were considered politically unreliable because it was feared that they might one day take revenge for the disaster which had befallen their families. The author also describes how he met a man who had been at a state boarding school in Anhui during the famine. The school had enough food but the parents of many pupils were starving and some decided to make their way to the school. He recalled how they arrived at the gates to beg for food from their children but the school refused to let them in.

A handful of brave souls risked their lives to speak out against what was happening. The Party Secretary of Yinjian commune in Fengyang, Zhang Shaobao, wrote a letter to Mao in 1959. Since he dared not use his own name, he signed himself 'Shi Qiu Ming' meaning 'To pursue clarity':

To the Central Party and Chairman,

I write this letter without seeking any personal gain. All I care about is the interests of the Party and the people. I am therefore resolved to report the massive deaths which have taken place in Fengyang county this winter and spring. To my knowledge four villages in three communes have had shocking mortality rates. In one village it is 5 per cent, in the second 11 per cent, in the third 15 per cent and in the fourth more than 20 per cent. In some villages 5–6 people are dying each day. Other villages are completely deserted because the people have either died or fled. I have seen with my own eyes 300 or 400 orphans whom the authorities have gathered together. Of these about 100 have died.[9]

Those who addressed such letters to the county Party Secretary were arrested and accused of 'spreading rumours and slandering the Party'. One local doctor, Wang Shanshen, the head of the Kaocheng hospital in Wudian commune, was arrested for telling the Party Secretary Zhao Yushu the truth. Zhao had asked the doctor if nothing could be done about the many people who had fallen sick. Dr Wang told him that people were dying not from any illness but from hunger. At one point a third of the population of Fengyang – 100,000 – was listed as sick, many of them with oedema.[10]

Protests did not just come from the county level. In 1959, Zhang Kaifan, Deputy Governor of Anhui, reported what he had discovered when he returned to his home town in Wuwei county. This town lies near the Yangtze River in the far south of Anhui, in one of the richest regions in China. Zhang approved a local decision to abolish the communal kitchens and then, at the Lushan summit, gave Mao letters and petitions that he had received. Mao condemned him as a 'right opportunist' and he was dismissed from his post. Others, too, were purged as rightists for advocating more moderate policies, including Li Shinong, another Deputy Governor, and Wei Xingye, the deputy propaganda chief for Anhui.

The case of Zhang Kaifan was significant because at Wuwei the local officials had independently decided to abandon the collective kitchens and the communes early in 1959. As a result, Anhui's leader Zeng Xisheng had a number of officials arrested as 'right opportunists'. A year later the complaints from Wuwei reached the ears of Premier Zhou Enlai in Beijing. A Party history book includes a letter which Zhou wrote to Zeng in March 1960 urging him to investigate allegations that people had starved to death in Wuwei.[11] In 1961, a report on Wuwei was used by Liu Shaoqi and Deng Xiaoping to urge the dismissal of Zeng. After 1979, when Deng Xiaoping overturned Mao's policies, Zhang Kaifan was one of the first Party officials to be rehabilitated.

For many lower-ranking officials such a reversal of verdicts came too late. After the Lushan summit in July 1959 and the launch of the campaign to root out 'right opportunists', Zeng set quotas for victims. Anyone who had made any kind of negative comment would be targeted. In the autumn of 1959 tens of thousands in Anhui were labelled as anti-rightists. In Fengyang, even the magistrate, Zhao Conghua, was arrested on a charge of opposing the people's communes. According to Party documents, he had said that the communes were premature and should have been tried out and tested before they were introduced throughout China. He also opposed collectivization and recommended dividing up the land again as well as abandoning the canteens and the steel-making campaign.[12]

To be labelled as a 'right opportunist' was in some places tantamount to receiving a death sentence. Anyone so labelled, and his entire family, was ostracized along with other outsiders such as landlords, counter-revolutionaries, Kuomintang followers and rich peasants, collectively known as the 'five types of bad elements'. These received the lowest priority in the distribution of food. When ordinary peasants were dying of hunger, such a label spelt certain death. Tens of thousands of people in these categories fled their villages, many of them trying to get to the railway that would take them to Beijing and from there to the north or south-east to Shanghai. Few succeeded in boarding the heavily guarded trains. One source recalled how those trying to escape were locked in a cell at a 'reception centre' in Bangpu station, Anhui's largest railway junction. There they were kept without food and each day the dead were taken and thrown into a pit. Those who did manage to board a train heading south-east were pulled off before they got to Shanghai. The authorities set up a camp on the outskirts of the city which provided food for work. No one was allowed to enter the city to beg. The most extraordinary attempt at flight took place in Wuwei county, on the north bank of the Yangtze River. Several sources claim that tens of thousands of starving peasants from the county decided to march to Nanjing, across the river to the east, in search of food and that to stop them crossing, the Party massed troops who opened fire, killing many.[13]

Anhui peasants also dreamt of reaching the rich and thinly populated lands of Manchuria and Inner Mongolia. A few managed to get as far as Harbin, in Heilongjiang province, over a thousand miles to the north. A doctor in Harbin recalled that each day the stationmaster had to remove a dozen or more bodies of starved wretches who had expired in the railway station. In Fengyang, the authorities made every effort to stop the peasants from escaping. As early as December 1958, the Party set up road blocks to arrest fleeing peasants. The Fengyang report claims that the militia were successful, since only around 4 or 5 per cent of the population managed to escape during the famine. Of these, a few returned and were punished, but most did not. In contrast to Henan, many Anhui peasants had a tradition of vagabondage. In the slack season, peasants would set off as beggars, pedlars or labourers. So, in some parts of Anhui, the local Party Secretary would organize begging expeditions, issuing all those who wanted to leave with certificates and a little food. Such a certificate entitled one to buy train tickets. If this was not possible, then at least the peasants could take to the road. These journeys were fraught with danger, however, because peasants in other villages would sometimes seize outsiders, forcing them to work for nothing, or abduct the women.

On the other hand, flight could mean the difference between life and death. Ding Shu in *Ren Huo* recounts the story of one daring Anhui peasant who sneaked into the local Party Secretary's office to steal a blank sheet of paper stamped with an official chop. With this he forged himself a travel permit and managed to reach remote mountains in Jiangxi province where he farmed some uncultivated land and survived the famine. When he returned to his village some years later, he discovered that his two brothers, who had stayed behind, had died of starvation.

Perhaps the most horrible aspect of the famine in Anhui was that throughout it the state granaries were full. The existence of these granaries was confirmed by Zhou Yueli, the former secretary of Anhui's leader, Zeng Xisheng, and by a number of county-level officials.[14] Just as in Henan, the famine was entirely man-made and its chief cause was the state's excessive levy of grain. The Party cadres obeyed their orders and extracted double or triple the usual grain levy in accordance with imaginary grain harvests. Once this was done, the grain lay safely guarded in state granaries. A part was exported, but most of it did not travel far, indeed could not, because China lacked the means to move large quantities of grain. Some was held in emergency granaries controlled by the military, in accordance with Emperor Zhu's motto 'Dig deep tunnels and store grain', and there it rotted. Mao adapted this dictum by adding his own words: 'Dig deep tunnels, store grain and oppose hegemony.' The latter referred to the perceived threat from either a US-backed Kuomintang invasion, or an attack by the Soviet Union.

But how, in Anhui and elsewhere in China, did the Party ensure discipline during the famine? Why did lower-ranking officials continue to obey orders? And why did the peasants not revolt?

Fear and terror explain their behaviour. A cadre who questioned orders faced death. The anti-right opportunist campaign had clearly demonstrated this fact but it also showed that opposition not only endangered the official but also his family, his relatives and even his friends. On the other hand, as long as an official held on to his position, he and his family could eat because they had access to the state supply system. In many villages, the only people to survive the famine were the Party Secretary and his immediate family. Peasants interviewed said that only if the village Party Secretary was either an honest man or too frightened to steal grain, would he and his relatives die of hunger.

The terror was also possible because the Party had already reduced a section of society to the status of slaves. During the land reform campaign, landlords and their families had been treated as outcasts. Now, those condemned by their class ancestry or by a political mistake had no rights at all, not even to food. They could be subjected to any cruel or inhuman form of punishment. If one section of society could be treated in this way it was but a short step to relegating peasants who were unable to comply with the demands for grain to the status of political criminals. They too became the enemy who could be treated without mercy. Zhao Chuanju, a deputy brigade chief quoted in the Fengyang documents, spelt this out: 'The masses are slaves, they won't listen or obey if you don't beat or curse them or deduct their food rations.' Zhao Chuanju personally beat thirty peasants to death.

As the famine worsened and the peasants lost hope, the cadres also found that they could only keep order by creating more and more terror. According to Fengyang statistics, 12.5 per cent of its rural population – 28,026 people – were punished by one means or another. The report lists the punishments: some were buried alive; others were strangled with ropes; many had their noses cut off; about half had their rations cut; 441 died of torture; 383 were permanently disabled; and 2,000 were imprisoned, of whom 382 died in their cells. Sometimes torture was used to force the peasants to give up their food supplies, sometimes to punish them for stealing food. The Fengyang report gives examples:

The famine in the Ukraine in 1932–3 was to presage an even greater disaster in China
during the Great Leap Forward: (*above*) collecting the emaciated corpses of Ukrainian
famine victims for cremation; (*below*) on the streets of Kharkov, the capital of the
Ukraine, pedestrians pay scant attention to the starving

At the height of the Great Leap Forward peasants all over China were marshalled into massive labour-intensive projects: (*above*) members of the Gangkou commune in Jiujiang, Jiangxi province, march off to work behind red flags. This photograph was taken in the autumn of 1959 when the slogan was 'Go all out and continue the Great Leap Forward and defeat rightism'; (*below*) peasants in Guangdong province at work on the Xinxihe reservoir. Armies of such peasants built reservoirs in every county in China but most collapsed within a few years

China's propaganda boasted of miraculous agricultural yields: (*above*) close planting of wheat reputedly produced a crop so dense that children could stand on top of it. This picture from *China Pictorial* was, like so many others, a fake – the children are standing on a bench hidden beneath the grain. Nevertheless, as the photograph below shows, China claimed she had outstripped even America in wheat production

China Surpasses U.S.A. in Wheat Production

The men responsible for the worst excesses during the Great Leap Forward included (*above*) Chen Boda, the editor of *Red Flag*. The son of a wealthy landlord, he became the most influential ultra-leftist thinker around Mao and his ideas inspired both the Great Leap Forward and the Cultural Revolution; (*below*) Li Jingquan, the Party Secretary of Sichuan province. Under his leadership between 7 and 9 million people starved to death in a province famous for its agricultural surpluses. He was never criticized for his actions but lost power during the Cultural Revolution

(*Above*) A rare photograph of Zeng Xisheng, Party Secretary of Anhui province. Up to a quarter of the population of Anhui perished during the famine but Zeng lost power in 1962 for pioneering reforms which saved many more lives; (*below*) Henan province was the pace-setter during the Great Leap Forward and its Party Secretary Wu Zhifu was Mao's devoted follower. Under Wu's leadership millions starved, especially in the Xinyang prefecture, but Wu's crimes were never publicly condemned

(*Above*) Mao inspects an experimental field in the famous Seven Li commune in Xinxiang county, Henan province, in 1958. It was here that he declared: 'this name, the People's Commune, is great'; (*below*) among the alleged scientific successes of the Great Leap Forward was the creation of giant vegetables. Here peasants parade a giant pumpkin

(*Above*) In Anhui Mao Zedong shows his approval for an innovation intended to help triple steel output – the backyard furnace. City-dwellers had to melt down whatever metal objects they could find to make steel; (*below*) peasants in even the remotest regions had to do the same in much larger furnaces. This propaganda photograph shows crude smelters built near Xinyang in Henan province. Party documents later described what happened in Xinyang as a 'holocaust'

(*Above*) The most hated part of the communes were the communal kitchens. This propaganda photograph of a village communal canteen shows peasants eating together – the reality was much harsher; (*below*) the communes were run as militarized units and were intended to be effective both in war and in peace. In some places this was taken literally to mean arming the peasants. Here members of the Dongjiao commune near Zhengzhou, Henan province, work with their weapons close at hand

(*Above*) As part of the Great Leap Forward's attempt to wipe out all pests in a massive public hygiene movement, sparrows were exterminated. Here peasants parade the bodies of those killed during a single day; (*below*) all over the country peasants were inspired to create homemade tools and machines as part of the promised mechanization of agriculture. Since the steel produced in the backyard furnaces was useless, all these devices were made out of wood, like this truck built in Gaotang county in Shandong province. It was powered by a kerosene engine

(*Above*) The Great Leap Forward was, above all, an attempt to master nature. Nothing was impossible if the masses were mobilized to perform extraordinary feats of manual labour. To symbolize this peasants painted murals on their houses. This one, entitled 'Making the mountains bow their heads and the rivers give way', was painted in the Spring Flower commune near Xi'an in Shaanxi province; (*left*) one of the greatest of these senseless endeavours was the construction of the Red Flag Canal in Henan province. To divert water to a poor region, peasants spent years constructing a channel through mountains and along steep hillsides using the most primitive tools

(*Above*) The slightest opposition to Mao's policies led to condemnation as a rightist. In this scene Zhang Bojun, Chairman of the Democratic Party of Peasants and Workers, is condemned as a rightist at a public meeting. His party was a remnant of political parties which had existed before 1949 but which were allowed to continue to give an impression of tolerance; (*below*) in the communes, peasants were made to work day and night and often slept in the fields. These peasants from Xianyang county in Henan province are engaged in deep ploughing which Mao believed would create bigger and better crops. In some places, furrows twelve feet deep were dug

Those who benefited from the Great Leap Forward included (*above left*) Hua Guofeng, who later became Mao's successor after denying that peasants were starving in Mao's home county; (*above right*) Zhao Ziyang, who first reported that the peasants were hiding grain – under Deng Xiaoping he later became General Party Secretary and launched the rural reforms; (*below right*) Hu Yaobang, who was promoted after inspecting Mao's home county and lying about what he saw there – he later regretted his actions and in 1979, after Deng Xiaoping made him General Party Secretary, he began to dismantle the communes; (*below left*) Kang Sheng, one of the few to die while still in favour – he implemented Mao's purges before 1949 and after, and gave his enthusiastic backing to the Great Leap Forward

The chief victim of the Great Leap Forward was Marshal Peng Dehuai (*top*) who presented a private letter to Mao during the Lushan summit in mid-1959 that criticized the Great Leap Forward (*middle*). The blurred photograph below was taken during the Lushan summit when Mao attacked Peng as a rightist

Two of the men who helped end the famine and earned Mao's hatred: (*above*) President Liu Shaoqi and his wife Wang Guangmei, photographed setting an example during the famine by picking wild fruit and grasses in the wooded hills of Wenquan near Guangzhou; (*left*) Zhang Wentian, one of those who spoke out at the Lushan summit in support of Peng Dehuai and who had evidence of the famine in Anhui

(*Above*) The tenth Panchen Lama of Tibet was one of the very few who dared to speak out during the famine. His report came close to accusing the Party of attempted genocide against the Tibetans. Soon after his report was delivered, he was imprisoned and did not regain the trust of the Communist Party until shortly before his death in 1989; (*right*) the writer Deng Tuo was among the first victims of the Cultural Revolution. Deng had written a history of famine relief in China which was republished in 1961 when he and a small group of intellectuals openly ridiculed Mao and his catastrophic policies

Mao Zedong, architect of the famine

In the spring of 1960, Li Zhonggui and Zhang Yongjia, Secretary and chief of Qiaoshan brigade, began to bury four children alive and they were only pulled out when their families begged for mercy. The children were buried up to their waists before being taken out and were traumatized by the experience.

Su Heren, chief of the Liwu brigade, buried alive a commune member, Xu Kailan, because she was crying and begging him to give her some rice soup to eat.

Cadre Hua Guangcui refused to give peasant Chang the noodles she had begged for her sick mother. He said the mother was so ill that she would soon die anyway. He told Chang to bury the old woman before the others returned from working in the fields. Hua said that if she did not do this immediately he would force her to bury her mother in the house when she died. Chang had no choice but to bury her mother alive.

Ding Xueyuan was arrested for slaughtering his pig. He was forced to work at a reservoir construction site in the daytime and then handcuffed in a cell at night. He died in his prison cell of torture.

Wang Yuncong, chief of Fengxing production team in Zongpu commune, detained Li Yijun and accused him of being a thief. He thrust a burning iron bar into Li's mouth.

Han Futian, chief of Zhaoyao production team of Yingjiang commune, captured a thief and chopped off four of his fingers.

Zhang Dianhong, chief of Huangwan production team of Huaifeng brigade in Huangwan commune, caught Wang Xiaojiao, a peasant who had stolen grain. He pushed iron wire through his ears, strung him up and beat him.

Huang Kaijin pushed iron wire through the ears of children and then connected the wires and joked that he was 'making a telephone call'.

Zhong Kecheng, secretary of Xinghuo brigade, raped a woman, Xiao Qing, by blackmailing her after catching her stealing.

Sun Yucheng, chief of Zhetang brigade of Banqiao commune, caught a woman stealing and shoved his gun up her vagina.

Zhang Yulan, deputy chief of Xinhua brigade, ordered an elderly woman and her two grandchildren to hand in 70 *jin* [67 lbs] of wild vegetables and grasses every day. He said that otherwise they would not be given any food. Eventually, the old woman and the two children died of illness and starvation.

In each county in Anhui, tens of thousands were beaten and imprisoned by kangaroo courts. Even after the cadres had forced the peasants to hand over their grain during the winter of 1959–60, the violence did not abate. The cadres had to use whips and sticks to force the emaciated and enfeebled peasants to plant food for the next harvest and to stop them from eating the grain that they were supposed to sow. It is quite likely that if the Party had not halted the Great Leap Forward, the rural cadres would have carried on irrespective of the cost in human lives. Zhao Yushu, the head of Fengyang county, is alleged to have said: 'Even if 99 per cent die, we still have to hold high the red flag.'[15]

What happened next is equally incredible. The whole machinery of terror came to a stop and its perpetrators were put on trial. In January 1961, Anhui mounted a full-scale 'rectification' campaign and the peasants were summoned to testify against those who had terrorized them. A Fengyang Party document records the trial:

> In the extended meeting of five levels of cadres of Fengyang county, the atmosphere was intense and solemn. More than 90 per cent of the speakers at the meeting came from the families of people who had died. All of them voiced their complaints of wrong-doing and cried miserably and bitterly. The overwhelming majority of comrades in the meeting were moved to tears. Some told their stories from the morning until 7 p.m. and until their tears became dry . . .[16]

The trial established the exact number of cadres who had 'made mistakes'. In the two worst communes of Xiaoxihe and Wudian, 39.1 per cent and 22.2 per cent respectively of the officials were declared guilty. In the entire county, the figure was 34 per cent, or 1,920 cadres. The rectification followed the classic pattern of such internal purges: the Communist Party decided that 70 per cent of its cadres were 'good' and that a further 25 per cent were 'good in nature' but had made mistakes. That left a mere 5 per cent as scapegoats, the 'bad elements' who had sabotaged Party policies. Only a handful of these, all low-ranking officials, were tried and sentenced as criminals. The county Secretary, Zhao Yushu, had only to make a self-criticism. Two senior county-level Party members were found guilty of making mistakes but neither was punished or expelled from the Party. Out of Fengyang's 91 commune leaders, only one was expelled and another tried in a civil court. Among the 787 cadres at the brigade level, 50 were arrested but only 9 were given prison sentences. At the team level, only 17 out of 3,318 cadres went to prison. The documents mention only one case where the 5 per cent quota was exceeded, that of Wudian commune where the county's first collective had been set up in 1955 and which became a provincial model. There, 26 per cent of the population had perished in the famine and cadres had murdered peasants just for stealing sweet potatoes: 13 per cent of its cadres were punished and 95 were executed.[17]

Another object of the rectification campaign was to return what had been forcibly taken from the peasants. This too was a failure. The communes had no cash or other resources with which to compensate individuals for their losses and the state would not help. Wudian commune gave its peasants little more than a quarter of what they were owed. The commune should have paid each household about 1,000 yuan, a tidy sum when monthly urban wages averaged 50 yuan. Fierce arguments broke out when it came to dividing up whatever tools or pots the communes possessed. Sometimes people insisted on getting their original possessions back and no others. Or they became angry when the communes handed back broken or damaged tools. The peasants refused to accept such tools, saying that they would now have to spend their own money repairing them. Some peasants were accused of lying and cheating in order to grab more than they were entitled to. Then there was the problem of households which had fled or died out. Who was entitled to their compensation? In some cases, cadres sold off the possessions of those who had fled and spent the money on funerals or other necessities, only to be confronted later by the original owners who came back demanding the return of their goods or compensation.

As well as instituting the rectification campaign, in 1961 Anhui also discarded the central tenet of the Great Leap Forward – complete public ownership of land. As Mao later remarked bitterly, the province reverted to capitalism. Just why the provincial Party Secretary Zeng Xisheng swung from an extreme 'leftist' position to one on the 'far right' is not clear. Perhaps, sensing that the tide was turning, he was motivated by self-interest. Perhaps he felt genuine revulsion at what he had done. For much of 1960 he had been in Shandong province to the north, where he had enforced Mao's policies as brutally as in Anhui. In August 1960, he came back to accompany the senior leaders Deng Xiaoping, Liu Shaoqi and Peng Zhen on a tour of Anhui. It was at this moment that Zeng first proposed giving the land back to the peasants and abandoning Mao's great endeavour. According to his doctor, Li Zhisui, Mao was still unwilling to confront his failures and was so depressed that he retreated to his bed. Zeng cautiously began to try out what came to be known as *ze ren tian* or 'contract field farming' under which peasants were given back partial control of their land and grain levies were reduced.

What Zeng attempted to do created a split in the Party that would tear it apart. One camp supported Zeng's *ze ren tian* and a return to private farming. The other camp, grouped around Mao, would admit no compromise and insisted on continuing with collective farming and the communes. Tensions rose in the winter of 1960–1 as central Party inspection teams produced incontrovertible evidence of the famine's terrible cost. The events which followed are described later but, ironically, Zeng Xisheng lost his position, and later his life, not for causing the death of so many people but for introducing the reforms which saved many more lives. He was dismissed in 1962 and appointed to a lowly position in Shanghai before being brought to work in the South-West China Bureau in Chengdu alongside Peng Dehuai. In 1967, Red Guards were sent from Hefei to seek him out. They accused him of causing the deaths of millions. He was dragged from his home and beaten to death. Officially, the cause of death was high blood pressure. When he was cremated at the Babaoshan crematorium for revolutionary heroes in Beijing, Mao praised his achievements.

In Anhui, Zeng Xisheng and his victims have been forgotten, wiped from the official memory. No photograph of him has been published for many years but older peasants still curse his memory. They say he held dancing parties at the height of the famine and forced women into his bed. Only a few will credit this crude, fat tyrant with daring to introduce reforms which in 1961 probably saved the lives of many of them.

How many did die in the famine in Anhui? Officials now claim that 2 million died and that a similar number fled. The 1989 *Anhui Statistical Yearbook* indicates a death toll due to the famine of 2.37 million out of a population of 33 million. Chen Yizi, the senior Party official who defected in 1989, claims the real figure is 8 million, a quarter of the population. Chen based his figure on the research he carried out after 1979 when he was given access to internal Party records. This enormous figure seems entirely plausible. In Fengyang, 51,000 are recorded as having starved to death just in the winter of 1959–60, and altogether a quarter (83,000) of its 335,000 people are estimated to have perished. If anything, the death toll might be higher still. Ding Shu estimates that in Fengyang 90,000 died while Chen Yizi has said that one in three perished. Interviews in other parts of Anhui suggest that Fengyang's death toll was not exceptional.

10

The Other Provinces

'With a basket of fragrant flowers, let me sing for you.
I came to the fair country of Nanniwan.
This is a good land where nature is beautiful,
With crops, cattle and sheep everywhere.
Once, the mountains of Nanniwan were barren without
   a trace of human habitation
But now it is different, the new Nanniwan has changed,
It is like the rich farmland south of the Changjiang River.'
                                    Popular Communist song from the 1940s

THE IMAGINATION BALKS at picturing a famine which brought hunger and fear to 500 million people across the vast territory of one of the world's largest countries. For the first time, even in Sichuan which possesses some of the richest arable land in the world, peasants perished in their millions. Those in the rich and empty lands of the north, where life is usually easier, were reduced to a ration of 9 ounces of grain a day.[1] In Liaoning province, a centre for heavy industry, peasants who fled to its cities starved to death. In *A Mother's Ordeal,* which recounts the life of a woman who grew up there, the author Steven Mosher paints this picture:

Conditions must have been desperate in the countryside, for the streets of Shenyang [the capital of Liaoning] were full of hungry beggars. There were patched and tattered scarecrows with hollow cheeks and lifeless eyes who resembled living skeletons. There were children with pipestem limbs and swollen stomachs crying piteously for food. There were young men so crazed with hunger that they would snatch a leaf pancake out of your hand if you ventured too close.

In Hebei province, which surrounds two of China's richest cities, Beijing and Tianjin, conditions were equally bad. The Chinese journalist Ge Yang, who was exiled as a rightist to one rural area of Hebei, recalled how on the streets people said peasants were selling the flesh of dead children.[2] The authors of *Chinese Village, Socialist State*, the history of another rural district in Hebei, described what happened there:

By late 1959 Wugong villagers were reduced to eating cornstalks. There was little fuel and no cooking oil. It would be two decades before cooking oil became readily available. That winter, vegetables grown in fields fertilised by excrement often had to be eaten uncooked . . . In the worst-off regions, weak, dispirited villagers left some of the meagre crop to rot in the fields . . . by winter and into next spring, there was no nutrition and no medicine. Sick people died: so did infants and the elderly. In Raoyang, a few husbands sold wives for food and cash.

Perhaps the most terrible aspect of the famine was that there was nowhere to escape from it. Even in the most remote corners of the high mountains of Tibet or in the distant oases of Xinjiang in the far west, there was no sanctuary. An exodus was impossible because the country's borders were closed and tightly guarded. People in Guangdong died trying to swim to Hong Kong just as Kazakh nomads in Xinjiang were shot trying to ride across the mountains to their fellow tribesmen in the Soviet Union. Since peasants had no way of knowing how widespread the famine was, many who fled their homes perished on the road, exhausted. Interviewees recalled seeing such beggars dying by roads in Gansu, Hubei and Guangzhou. Those who could tried to turn off the highways and venture on tracks up into the hills where the Party's control was weaker and the chances of survival greater.

Flight had always been the traditional response to famine and so it was in 1958–61. Although some provincial leaders in Anhui, Henan and elsewhere set up roadbocks, they could not always prevent the peasants from escaping. At least a million fled Anhui;[3] a million and a half escaped from Hunan, equal to 4 per cent of the population; and in one year alone at least 1.6 million emigrated from Shandong.[4] Henan peasants followed tradition and headed for the north-western provinces. Sichuan peasants set out for minority regions in the surrounding mountains or trekked across the border to Guizhou province. In Hebei, some local governments even organized a migration to Manchuria which was reputed to have land to spare and jobs in its giant iron and steel works. Minority areas lured many, both because they were less densely populated and because the Party dealt more leniently with the ethnic Hans within them, as its first priority was to control the indigenous peoples. At least a million refugees made their way to Inner Mongolia in just twelve months.[5] Several hundred thousand are thought to have moved to the Tibet Autonomous Region, prompting Western newspapers to suggest that the rebellious Tibetans were being deliberately swamped with immigrants.[6] It is difficult to put a figure on this mass internal migration but it may have been in the order of at least 10 million.[7]

These migrations were often accompanied by the break-up of families. In Gansu the divorce rate rose by 30–40 per cent and in a few counties by as much as 60 per cent during the famine.[8] The peasants frequently sold their wives in exchange for food or money. Sometimes the wives had no choice but to leave when the last food was reserved for blood relatives or when, though there was nothing to eat, their husbands felt bound to stay and tend the graves of their ancestors. In some areas of China, a woman could easily find a new husband. In Heilongjiang, with its large labour force of immigrant workers, marriageable women were in short supply and it was common for two or even three men to share a woman between them. Often two brothers would agree to cohabit with one woman.[9] Another source states that in general, 'the poorer the region, the greater the amount of wife selling. To hide the shame, the wives were called cousins . . . If the chief family earner died, a teenage daughter might be sold to the highest bidder in a distant place to obtain grain to keep the rest of the household alive.'[10]

When the famine was over, local governments in parts of Sichuan and Gansu negotiated agreements with authorities elsewhere, requiring them to force the wives to return to their original homes. Often they refused to go back to husbands who had sold them.[11] In Hebei, one such husband went to court to recover his 'property rights' but the court decided for the wife.[12] Prostitution was also frequently reported. In Gansu, one former prison inmate recalled how local peasant women came to the gates to prostitute themselves in the hope of obtaining a *wotou*, or bun, to eat. In Anhui, too, there were so-called 'brothel work teams' where cadres kept women who would sleep with them in exchange for food.[13] At the end of the famine, some women migrated to areas of Henan or Gansu where large tracts of arable land had been depopulated. After the dismissal of Gansu's hard-left leader in 1961, women made up two-fifths of the immigrants in the province and in Hebei peasants moved to resettle farmland in the Xinyang district.

In their bid to find a place of safety, women had to abandon children whom they could no longer feed. Some children were sold in the cities or dumped at railway stations or in hospitals. A nurse in Lanzhou, capital of Gansu province, recalled one such incident:

> During that winter of 1959, there was an event which occurred in my hospital. The nurse of the night shift went upstairs to go to bed. She stumbled over something and screamed in panic. People came running, thinking she had been attacked. After a while, when she could speak, she said she had found a strange object on the stairs leading to the third floor. Others followed her there and found a small cardboard box in which a baby lay wrapped in cotton rags. On a scrap of old newspaper were written the words: 'To kind-hearted people, please look after her. From a mother who regrets her faults.' At the beginning, only female babies were abandoned but later on boys were left behind by those who hoped the hospital would feed them.

Other infants were left by the roadside. In the yellow-earth country of north-west China, people abandoned their children by the roadside in holes dug out of the soft soil. One interviewee described what happened:

> Those who still had the strength left the village begging and many died on the road. The road from the village to the neighbouring

province was strewn with bodies, and piercing wails came from holes on both sides of the road. Following the cries, you could see the tops of the heads of children who were abandoned in those holes. A lot of parents thought their children had a better chance of surviving if they were adopted by somebody else. The holes were just deep enough so that the children could not get out to follow them but could be seen by passers-by who might adopt them.[14]

Still others were abandoned in caves and mine-shafts in the mountains. Stories also circulated about how, in some places, villagers would kill and eat such infants. In western Xinjiang parents gave their children to the nomadic Mongol or Kazakh herdsmen to look after as they were thought to have enough milk and other food. Many children who were adopted or purchased met unhappy fates. One interviewee from Nanjing told the story of how his neighbour, a childless worker, bought a 6-year-old girl from a starving Anhui peasant. She was cruelly teased by other children in the housing block as a 'stray dog' until her life was made so unbearable that she finally killed herself. Another source recalled that a writer and Party member in Hefei, Anhui province, was dismissed after purchasing a young girl from a starving peasant and later using her as his concubine.

When the peasants could not flee, the only alternative was to rebel. All over China, desperate peasants organized attacks on local granaries. Sometimes the peasants fought each other: one source recalled a battle between Hebei and Henan peasants armed with sticks and rocks in which 3,000 were killed. It is hard to be certain about the scale and frequency of such attacks and fights but they were certainly not rare, especially in 1960. According to Chen Yizi, there were numerous attacks on lower Party officials: 'There were some small-scale rebellions and even cases when whole counties rose up against the government, sometimes, as in Guizhou province, led by a village Party Secretary.'[15] In Hebei province, Muslim Hui robber bands mounted an attack on a granary at Hejian which led the authorities to equip the militia with machine guns and to encircle the granaries with barbed wire.[16] In Fujian, when a hundred peasants stormed a grain store under the leadership of a village

Party Secretary, the authorities called out the army.[17] In Shandong, former Kuomintang officers were accused of organizing the rebellions there and were executed.[18] There are also reliable reports of riots and small-scale attacks on state granaries in Anhui. In Sichuan, a similar attack which has been widely recorded occurred in 1961 in Ruijin county. There, in the mountains east of Chengdu, peasants successfully stormed a granary and carried off the grain. Later, the head of the local militia was arrested and imprisoned for failing to order his men to open fire on the peasants. A similarly successful attack took place at Zhengya in the same province because the local militia, whose own families were starving, did nothing to prevent it.[19]

In addition to the granaries, starving bands of peasants frequently attacked trains. After one such band blocked a train on the line from Hebei province to Shandong and pilfered it for food, the authorities installed twelve guards on each train. Heavily armed guards also manned the trains carrying export grain to the Soviet Union. In Gansu, desperate peasants even attacked army trains. An eyewitness related how a garrison was cut off when the local populace stormed one train:

> The starving people behaved as if they had discovered a 'new continent' and crowded around the train begging for food. The soldiers raised their rifles with sharp bayonets and confronted the crowd. These people knew they had little to lose. Their only hope of surviving was to seize the grain on the train. The crowds erupted like boiling water and the soldiers trembled although they had rifles in their hands. One of them nervously pulled the trigger and the explosion shocked and agitated the crowd. They rushed on to the train and grabbed sacks of grain. The desperate guards fired their guns into the air, but this did not work. The train was quickly looted. A few days later, another train approached the station and many, many starving people flooded the place. They were agitated and carried guns, buckets and so on. But this time the soldiers fired their guns directly at the people. The station became a battlefield. People had to run away. How could the 'people's army' now shoot its own people? Later, it was said that the military garrison had itself been without food for three days.[20]

In a similar case, the local populace stormed a military train carrying grain for starving soldiers and scientists working to create China's first nuclear bomb. In the middle of Qinghai, a gigantic complex of laboratories and workshops called the Ninth Academy had been established on a desolate plateau. Surrounding China's 'Los Alamos' was a complex of labour camps and state farms. Despite the priority given to building the bomb, especially after 1959, both scientists and prisoners ran out of food. In 1960, Marshal Nie Rongzhen, who was in charge of the project, reportedly held a telephone conference begging all military commanders to donate food. A train carrying these supplies was blocked by starving villagers before it arrived. When the armed guards did not open fire, the villagers ransacked it. According to an article published in China in 1989, when the peasants discovered the food was going to the People's Liberation Army, they returned and put the sacks of grain back on the train.[21]

Such attacks and rebellions were numerous enough for President Liu Shaoqi to issue a dire warning in 1962. If nothing was done, he said, China would face a civil war as severe as that of the Soviet Union in 1918–21. He issued instructions to prepare for the imposition of martial law, although he stopped short of authorizing troops to open fire on civilians. Yet no matter how rebellious the peasants felt, the majority were usually incapable of organizing concerted resistance. They could not gather in sufficient numbers and almost always lacked arms. Indeed, at the height of the famine, they possessed virtually nothing and hunger had gravely weakened them. The militia guarding the grain stores were invariably stronger and better fed, and could usually rout them. If the militia failed to suppress an uprising or joined it, then the army was always available. Most army troops were well provided for and so did not starve during the famine. The only real threat to the government might have come from urban dwellers but they never became as desperate as the peasants.

The famine may have tested the loyalty of Communist cadres but few of them dared break ranks either to join a rebellion or to distribute state grain on their own authority. One well-known exception was the author Zhao Shouli in Shanxi. He used his authority in Yangcheng county to persuade the authorities to distribute grain and is credited with having thus saved many lives. Ding Shu in *Ren Huo* recounts that for this 'crime', Zhao was seized by Red Guards during the Cultural Revolution. They then asked local people to come forward and testify against him. Although the locals refused, he was still struggled and later killed.[22]

Not everyone lacked the courage to speak out on behalf of the peasants. In *Ren Huo*, Ding Shu recounts the example of a woman worker called Liu Guiyang who went to Beijing and pasted up the slogan 'Get rid of the people's communes' outside Zhongnanhai, where Mao lived. Such stories are credible. One interviewee said he saw a wall poster put up in the campus of the Agricultural University in Changsha, Hunan province, where he was studying in 1959. It ran to nine pages and described how the peasants were starving and how they hated the communal eating. It went on to accuse village leaders of stealing grain and oil to feed themselves. The poster attracted the attention of hundreds of people who stood around reading and discussing it. The next day it was torn down, but the interviewee said similar posters appeared at other universities in the city. People also spoke out against the Great Leap Forward in open meetings in Changsha. The same thing happened in Nanjing University and at Wuhan in Hubei province where students and teachers put up posters. People also used the meetings which the Party organized to criticize Peng Dehuai and 'right opportunism' after the Lushan summit as occasions to speak out. Students, because they were often sent out to work in the countryside, had seen what the real harvests were and had witnessed for themselves the children with swollen bellies and the cruelties inflicted by village leaders. They knew that the entire Great Leap Forward was both a sham and a catastrophe. Even so, the great majority of the population were terrorized into silence. Obedience was ruthlessly enforced by an all-pervasive surveillance apparatus. In Anhui, one interviewee recalled the reaction when a small handwritten notice was pasted up in a toilet in an office in Hefei. It said 'Down with Tyrant Zeng, capture his demon wife alive!' The police were called in with dogs to try and track down the author.

Gansu

In all China the worst-hit province was probably Anhui, but poor and backward Gansu ranked a close second. The province straggles along what is called the Gansu Corridor to the far west and in 1958 it had a mixed population of around 12 million Han Chinese, Hui Muslims, Tibetans, Mongols and other minorities.[23]

Before the Great Leap Forward, some local leaders, including the Deputy Governor Sun Diancai, had been expelled from the Party or demoted for resisting collectivization.[24] Gansu's First Secretary was another Red Army veteran, Zhang Zhongliang, who was devoted to Mao. After the Lushan summit, he wrote articles heaping praise on the Great Leap Forward and insisting that its policies were so successful that even his poor province had grain to spare. In the winter of 1959, Zhang went to Beijing to meet Zhou Enlai and offered to send his surplus to more needy provinces. Zhou took him at his word. When Zhang returned, he organized his urban officials into work teams and sent them out to collect grain from every village. According to one eyewitness the requisition teams adopted a strategy called 'politeness first, forcefulness second'; he described what happened in one commune:

The commune Secretary shouted at the peasants, telling them to hand in the grain in response to the Party's and Chairman Mao's call. The peasants kept silent but were clear in their minds that if they did so, it was as good as giving up their lives. This kind of mobilizing speech by the commune leader did not work. He saw in the eyes of the peasants anguish, sadness and disappointment. Actually, the commune leader himself was not at all happy with his superior's order but he dared not disobey him. He knew how he would end up if he refused.

Nevertheless, the work teams began their action. When they looted a village, it was termed 'imposing grain levies'. The sound of crying, begging and cursing echoed everywhere. Afterwards, the peasants were consumed by anger and hatred and a sad feeling of impotence. They had only a very small amount of beans and potatoes left in their houses. Young people now left their home village while the elderly and children scavenged for grass seeds, tree bark and so on to eat. Within a month, the famine began to worsen. The villages became silent, bereft of human activity.

In 1988 the Chinese magazine *October* published an article describing how the work teams in Gansu used 128 forms of torture to extract the grain: 'People were either tortured or starved to death. Some were tied up and beaten, or left hanging until they died. People were not allowed to eat grains and [were] stopped from digging wild vegetables. All they could do was starve.'[25]

An article by a demographer, Peng Xizhe, alleges that not only did Gansu have no surplus grain, it did not even have enough to feed its own population.[26] In 1958, per capita grain output fell by 19 per cent. In 1959 it fell by a further 32 per cent. In the following two years it was half the size of the 1957 harvest, which had barely been sufficient. Even in 1965 the grain harvest was still 25 per cent below that of 1957. In some areas, a third of the population starved to death between 1958 and 1961. In the Zhangye region of western Gansu this amounted to 300,000 people, including some 40,000 in the city of Zhangye itself.[27] There the local authorities set up a special department charged with collecting and counting the corpses. Ruan Dingmin, head of the Zhangye propaganda office, sent a daily report to Lanzhou which was read by Gansu's Party Secretary Zhang Zhongliang. When, in 1961, Beijing sent Wang Feng, a senior official in the Central Committee's Organization Department, to investigate the famine, he could not believe the contents of these reports and summoned Ruan Dingmin to testify in person. Wang Feng also dispatched a medical relief team to the area around Zhangye and one of its members recalled what they witnessed there:

Early one morning, we stopped at a big village but found few signs of life around the low mud huts. A few people could be seen who were so weak, they could hardly beg for food. The team leader raised his voice, shouting: 'Old folks, come out now! Chairman Mao and the Communist Party have sent us doctors to rescue you!' He shouted over and over again. Eventually, those still alive crawled out of their houses. These were people struggling on the edge of death. If they fell over, they were unable to get up again.

The team found one group of dead bodies after another. I pushed open the floor of one hut and had to draw back because of the stink. A low groan came from inside and I saw two or three people lying still in the darkness on a *kang*. At the front lay an old man and one of his hands pointed at something. Together with him lay a woman who had long been dead and whose decomposing body was the source of the stench. The old man's hand was pointing at a small human body, four limbs spread out, mouth open wide. It looked as if the child was crying out but in fact the body had been lying dead for days.

The medical team had brought syringes with them to inject a mixture containing glucose. The famine victims were then given sorghum or bean soup but this caused more deaths. The starving swallowed the food but their stomachs were unable to absorb it and burst. Most of them died.[28]

Other severely hit counties in Gansu included Dingxi and neighbouring Tongwei. Zhang Shangzhi, a reporter from the *Gansu Daily*, recounted in an article how on a journey to his home village in Tongwei county, he saw dead bodies along the roadside, in the fields, indeed everywhere he looked. No one had buried the corpses. He reached his own village only to find that three members of his family had already starved to death. Around 100,000 people died of hunger in Tongwei.[29]

In 1994 *Kaifang*, a Chinese magazine published in Hong Kong, reported that in the Longxi area of Gansu during the famine, people ate children including their own.[30] The article relates a case where parents ordered their 7-year-old daughter to boil some water to cook their little son. When the baby was eaten, the daughter was told to boil some more water. Realizing that she would be next she knelt down, 'begging her father not to eat her and saying "I will do anything if you do not eat me."' Such stories of cannibalism in Gansu have appeared in other Chinese publications, sometimes thinly disguised as fiction. One such novel, *Hungry Mountain Village* by Zhi Liang, describes how during the famine a Beijing journalist was exiled as a rightist to an unnamed province in the north-west. There peasants not only ate children but adults too.

The report which Wang Feng drew up on the famine in Gansu led to the dismissal of Zhang Zhongliang but he was not otherwise punished. Later, the report fell into the hands of Red Guards who travelled across China to find him in Jiangsu province where they struggled him. He survived and, according to some sources, died peacefully on Hainan Island (and according to others in Nanjing) in the early 1980s.

It is hard to find a reliable figure for Gansu's death toll. The lowest figure of 696,000 out of a population of 12 million appears in Gansu's official population statistics. Chen Yizi, whose team investigated Gansu after 1979, states that 1.2 million died. In a biography of Qian Ying, a senior Party official who accompanied Wang Feng on his visit to Gansu, a figure of 1.3 million is mentioned. I was told by other Chinese sources that the true figure is 3 million.

Under Wang Feng, Gansu, like Anhui, became in 1961 a laboratory for experiments in private farming. Mao stopped these at the end of 1962 and four years later Wang Feng was toppled and severely beaten by Red Guards. Gansu once again became a bastion of ultra-leftism. It did not recover from the famine during the Mao era and there was another severe famine in 1974 and 1975 when peasants tried to flee elsewhere in search of food.[31]

Other provinces in the north-west of China suffered equally during the Great Leap Forward but fewer details have emerged. The small neighbouring province of Ningxia to the north of Gansu seems to have been hard hit. Life in a labour camp there during the famine is powerfully described by the author Zhang Xianliang in his autobiographical book *Grass Soup* (see Chapter 12). He recounts that those outside the labour camps had less to eat than those inside. Travelling in Ningxia during the 1980s, I was told that during the famine cannibalism had become common among the peasants living in the barren mountains to the south of the capital, Yinchuan.

In the adjacent province of Qinghai, the ultra-leftist Party Secretary Gao Feng was also dismissed in 1961. After an investigation by Wang Zhao, a senior official sent from Beijing, he was accused of causing 900,000 deaths. Qinghai is part of the Tibetan plateau and was at the centre of the Tibetan revolt described in the next chapter. Huge numbers of Chinese prisoners were sent to its bleak uplands to work in a chain of large labour camps. There they built roads, railways and the nuclear research centre, the Ninth Academy. At least 200,000 of the prisoners in these camps starved to death.

The famine was no less harsh in the south-west of China. In Guizhou province, next door to Sichuan, out of a population of around 16 million, 1 million died. In the region of Zunyi, in northern Guizhou, the site of a famous Party meeting during the Long March, only one in eight survived. In other places, such as Jinsha county, a quarter of the population died. Most of the deaths occurred not among the province's minorities but in the valleys populated by Han Chinese, such as the counties of Sinan, Yuqing and Yinjiang. The main cause was the violent appropriation of grain. An investigation by a team sent from Beijing later led to the execution of the Party Secretary of Sinan county and the suicide of two other leaders in charge of counties with large death tolls.[32]

Sichuan

The province of Sichuan was crucial to the success of the Great Leap Forward. If Mao's agricultural policies worked there, then China would have huge surpluses, for the Sichuanese tradition-ally boast that in a good year they can produce enough to feed five other provinces. Equally, a famine in 'Heaven's Granary', as Sichuan is called, would be hard to explain or justify. Within the province, Mao put his trust in a tough ultra-leftist called Li Jingquan. A Shanxi peasant who became Mao's devoted fol-lower during the Yanan period, Li had ruled Sichuan with an iron fist since entering the province after the Kuomintang's defeat. Land reform was successful and popular but when in the early 1950s the state began to monopolize the important grain market, things soon began to go wrong. Party cadres banned private trading and imposed ever higher grain quotas. Li was determined to show that the first stages of collectivization would result in more grain. A violent and aggressive figure, he tolerated no dissent or opposition. Grain purchasing targets became excessive as the incentive to grow grain diminished. When the state exerted pressure on local leaders and peasants to deliver more grain to the state, some killed themselves or died in struggle sessions.[33]

Li implemented the 1957 anti-rightist campaign in Sichuan vigorously and even wanted to raise the quota of arrests beyond that recommended by the centre. In some cultural units, two-thirds of the staff were labelled as rightists. Inevitably, Li also threw the province into the Great Leap Forward and dismissed any officials who questioned what was going on. One victim was the provincial deputy propaganda minister, Ye Shi, who is reputed to have said that the exaggerated reports of the success of the advanced co-operatives were like people who slapped their own cheeks to make themselves look healthier.

In Sichuan, people seem to have begun to die in large numbers during the first winter of 1958–9. Cadres were sent to seize large amounts of grain but most of the autumn harvest was never collected. In rural Sichuan most of the men had to work round the clock making steel and building dams. Accounts of what happened in Sichuan mirror those from Anhui or Henan. For instance, in different parts of Sichuan I was told the identical story of how peasants artificially created an 'experimental field' by moving the rice or wheat plants closer together. A goose egg was then placed on top of the crop to demonstrate its density. This was what happened in 1958 when Mao visited the model Red Splendour commune. Li Jingquan went to great efforts to ensure that the truth behind this charade was not revealed. When, a year later, Liu Shaoqi went to the same commune, local officials locked up anyone who might have been ready to give the game away and hid them in an old temple. After an informant revealed this to Liu, he walked past the temple and asked to look inside. There he questioned the peasants but they were too terrified to do more than smile and mumble.[34] Many of the peasants in this commune subsequently starved to death.

As in Anhui and Henan, fantastic reports of bumper harvests, called the 'exaggeration wind', led in turn to the brutal seizure of grain. Those who refused to hand over all their grain were beaten and tortured. After the Lushan summit, Li Jingquan also set about trapping officials who might be guilty of disloyalty. On his return, he circulated a document containing Marshal Peng Dehuai's criticisms and then asked all cadres at grade 17 and above whether or not they agreed (all officials are graded from 1 to 24, with 1 being the highest). Most realized what was afoot but some endorsed what Peng had said and were arrested as 'right opportunists'. Sichuan officials who spoke out or tried to ameliorate the consequences of the famine later met with the most violent persecution. One such was the father of Jung Chang, the author of *Wild Swans*. A dedicated revolutionary and a senior official in Chengdu, Wang Yu was horrified at what he saw in the countryside although local officials prevented him from seeing the worst. He later suffered from oedema and fell into depression. In 1961, he withdrew from his work and spent months in hospital. This was enough to provoke persecution during the Cultural Revolution when he was attacked for 'the waning of his revolutionary will'. He died in 1974 half insane after a long period in a work camp.

Many eyewitnesses have said that, as elsewhere, at the height of the famine in Sichuan the granaries were full even though some of the province's grain and livestock was exported to other regions of the country. Just how much grain left the province remains a secret, perhaps because, unlike Gansu's First Secretary, Li was not dismissed in 1961. Despite Sichuan's huge death toll, he was protected by Mao and may have won the gratitude of other leaders for supplying them with food in their hour of greatest need. Li was also careful to keep a low profile when, in 1962, he freed his peasants from some of the restrictions of collective farming under a national policy that Liu Shaoqi introduced as the 'three freedoms, one guarantee', or *san zi, yi bao*.

Sichuan's death toll was enormous. Estimates range from 7 to 9 million out of a population of at least 70 million.[35] The lowest figure revealed by official population statistics is 7.35 million but other sources, including Chen Yizi and the Chinese demographer Peng Xizhe, suggest a figure of around 9 million. This last estimate suggests a death rate among the rural population of close to one in seven. This seems plausible, for in just one prefecture, Yibin, there were 1 million famine deaths. Some villagers, living in a fertile part of the province, thought that 20 per cent or even a third of the population had died.[36] Cannibalism was widespread, especially in the worst-hit districts such as Yanan, south-west of Chengdu. Even in Deng

Xiaoping's home village of Guang'an, peasants went to beg for food in the cities.

Li Jingquan's decision to implement Liu Shaoqi's policies may explain why Mao encouraged his downfall in the Cultural Revolution. Red Guards waged particularly violent battles in Sichuan's cities. Li survived, but one of his sons was beaten to death and his wife committed suicide. Li was rehabilitated and given an honorary position by Deng Xiaoping when he returned to power in 1978. Yet he was never allowed to go back to Sichuan, where public discussion of the famine is still taboo.

11

The Panchen Lama's Letter

'When we heard there was large-scale famine,
it was a new thing. In Tibet food supplies had
been sufficient for centuries. Agriculture
was old-fashioned but sufficient. In the past,
one or two individuals may have died from
starvation, that is possible. Otherwise it was
unheard of.'

The Dalai Lama, 1995

IN 1962, TIBET'S second highest religious leader, the Panchen Lama, wrote a report in which he came close to accusing
the Chinese Communist Party of attempted genocide. No other
group in China suffered more bitterly from the famine than
the Tibetans, of whom perhaps one in five died during these
years. In the birthplace of the current Dalai Lama, Ping An
county in Qinghai province, at least 50 per cent of the population starved to death.[1]

The Tibetans have traditionally lived scattered across an
enormous region that spills over the borders of present-day
China, farming the valleys between the highest mountains of
the world and roaming with their herds across a vast and desolate plateau. After the eleventh century, their conversion to
Tantric Buddhism, imported from India, turned a warlike
people into the most intensely religious society on earth. The
focus of religious and economic life became the large monasteries subject to the rule of reincarnated lamas. This theocracy
was little changed by the Mongols or Manchus who occupied
China. When the British invaded Tibet in 1905, they found a

medieval society cut off from the outside world. The Nationalists failed in their turn to impose their rule over Lhasa and
the Tibetans lapsed into a self-imposed isolation that was only
shattered by the invasion of the People's Liberation Army in
1950–1.

The Chinese Communists created an autonomous region
in central Tibet and divided the rest of the Tibetans among
different provinces. The majority now lived within the newly
drawn borders of Sichuan, Qinghai, Gansu and Yunnan provinces. There they were subject to the same policies, the 'democratic reforms', which were applied all over China. The
monasteries were dismantled, the land and livestock they controlled were given to the poor peasants, individuals were
labelled according to their class and, after the initial stages of
mutual-aid teams and co-operatives, communes were set up.
Under the terms of a seventeen-point agreement that the Dalai
Lama signed with Beijing in 1951, inner Tibet (which in 1965
would formally become the Tibet Autonomous Region or TAR)
was, temporarily, excused from introducing these democratic
reforms. No such concessions were made to the rest of the
Tibetans who rose in revolt, some as early as 1952. When collectives and higher collectives were established in the mid-1950s,
resistance turned into large-scale bloodshed, especially among
the Tibetans in Sichuan who are known as Khampas. Many
retreated to Lhasa from where, in 1959, the Dalai Lama was
forced to flee amid fierce fighting. The rebellion was put down
with great brutality and up to 100,000 Tibetans fled to India
where the Dalai Lama had sought sanctuary. For those who
remained behind, the effects of the Great Leap Forward
brought fresh hardships.

Although the collectivization which sparked off the rebellion
was a nationwide policy, many Tibetans are still convinced that
the ensuing famine was a deliberate attempt to punish them
further for their revolt. The majority of Tibetans had the misfortune to live in those provinces – Sichuan, Qinghai and Gansu –
which were devastated by some of the most brutal and fanatical
leaders in the whole country. Here, Han Chinese and Tibetans
suffered alike from the famine. In the Dalai Lama's birthplace
in Ping An county, as many Chinese as Tibetans died of hunger.
Even Chinese who were resettled in Qinghai died. Out of 5,000

Henanese dispatched in 1959 to Tongren county in Qinghai, only 2,000 were left when the group was sent home two years later, the majority having starved to death.[2] Yet many Tibetans still feel they were subject to a far harsher fate than the Chinese. First, they were the victims of policies imposed on them by alien conquerors. Second, the wholesale destruction of their monasteries and the arrest of their lamas which took place in the 1950s and not, as is generally believed, during the Cultural Revolution, were viewed as a deliberate attempt to erase the basis of Tibet's civilization. And finally, the Tibetans were peculiarly vulnerable to the destructive consequences of Maoist agricultural policies.

Tibetans were either nomadic herdsmen or farmers dependent on barley. In the Great Leap Forward, the Party forcibly settled the nomads and this, as in Kazakhstan under Stalin, led to the death of most of their animals. In some places, Tibetan peasant farmers, who knew only how to eat barley, which they roast over a fire and grind into a paste called *tsampa*, were now forced to grow unfamiliar and unsuitable grains. Much like the peasants in Ireland, who could not make bread from the wheat imported after the potato crop failed, the Tibetans, especially the nomads, had no idea how to eat wheat or maize. And, while many Chinese peasants knew from experience how to endure famine, this was a hardship virtually unknown among the Tibetans. Many said they would have died had Han Chinese immigrants not taught them to eat leaves or wild grasses.

The Khampas of eastern Tibet, now part of Sichuan province, grew barley and reared livestock, taking their animals in the summer to graze on high mountain pastures.[3] Like the Sichuanese peasants, in the 1950s the Khampas were coerced into joining mutual-aid teams, then higher co-operatives and finally communes. Their large monasteries became centres of resistance and when they were bombed, armed Khampas took to the hills to wage a guerrilla war. Those who stayed behind were forced into communes which were relatively small, with little more than a thousand members. Life was as harsh as elsewhere. Members had to hand over their entire possessions, including their spare clothes and quilts. Metal articles, including the large amounts of jewellery which Khampa women traditionally wear, were all melted down to make 'steel'. Even in these distant mountains, steel furnaces were erected and, for the first time, Khampa women were made to plough the land. The new agricultural policies made no allowances for the high altitude and local conditions. So wheat was grown instead of barley and sometimes two or three crops were planted in a year, quickly exhausting the soil. The entire population was mobilized in winter, which is very severe in this region, to labour outdoors building unnecessary irrigation canals and digging redundant wells. The Khampas were also forced to eat in collective kitchens and these were retained until 1964, far longer than in other parts of China. One interviewee gave this description of her life in the Huo Shi Tang commune at the foot of the 22,000-foot-high Gongga mountains during this period.

> The worst years were from 1961 to 1963. Every day five or six people would be found dead in the morning. The bodies of the children and old people were always swollen with hunger. Since most men had been arrested, about 60 per cent of the adult population were women. We would collect grasses from the fields, boil them and force this mixture down our throats. If you didn't, then you would die. Although we were dizzy and faint, we still had to keep working and then we would try and pick up grain or grass to eat. But you had to keep an eye out for the guards. If they caught you, then they would grab you by the throat and choke you to make you spit out the grass seeds. They would body-search all of us when we returned from working in the fields. There were also special teams which searched people's homes for grain, digging up the floors, breaking open walls and looking through the fodder for the horses. The searches went on all through the famine. If they discovered any food, even a few grains, then they would organize a big meeting of 500 or 600 people. The guilty person would have a big wooden sign hung on him and then he would be paraded round, beaten and spat on. Some people were beaten to death in these struggle sessions. Anyone accused of damaging the fields or tools was also beaten. The former landlords were beaten the worst and sent to work more often. Even if they were dying, they still had to work.

An eyewitness from another commune in the same region described much the same situation: 'The famine lasted from

1962 until 1965. My brothers went around picking up whatever food they could find. Sometimes they found bones, which might have been human, and ground them into a kind of paste, adding barley husks. We did not have *tsampa* but we ate this instead. We had to work very hard and were very hungry. Many people died at this time.'

As elsewhere in China, the authorities began seizing grain from the Khampas in early 1959. Those caught hoarding grain were sentenced to long prison terms as 'rightists'. In prison, the majority starved to death. The inmates of one prison were fed a ration of just 11 lbs of grain a month.[4] Out of 300 inmates, 160 died. In another prison at Barkham, half of the 1,000 inmates perished.[5]

Another part of Sichuan, the Aba prefecture, had been detached from Qinghai after 1949. Here, the 'democratic reforms' started later and the monasteries were closed only in 1958. The worst year of famine was 1961. One monk recalled in an interview what it was like there:

Everyone opposed what the Han cadres did, so there was a rebellion. Two-thirds of the men were arrested and were sent to labour camps, mostly at Guanxian near Chengdu. About 70 per cent died of hunger because they were fed only three ounces of food a day. A few returned in 1964 and others in 1977. Those who remained at home had to work from early in the morning until night. People were frightened to talk to each other, in case they were called counter-revolutionaries and beaten. Many people were beaten. No one could leave the commune. There was enough food but it was taken away by the Chinese. A few of us fled to the mountains and lived there for years.

Ironically, this remote region of grasslands is where Mao and the Red Army would have perished on the Long March but for the food provided by the local Tibetans. 'Some day we must pay the Mantsu [another tribe] and the Tibetans for the provisions we were obliged to take from them,' Mao later told the American journalist Edgar Snow. According to Rewi Alley and Wilfred Burchett, two Maoists who worked in China after 1949, the formation of the communes in minority areas 'was one way of repaying the debt'.[6]

For all the Tibetans in Sichuan, the famine lasted longer than among the Chinese because the reforms that followed the famine were delayed until 1965 when one yak and a small plot of land were distributed to households of three to five people. The overall death toll among the Khampas is thought to have been very high. One source said that in the Kanding district, out of one million inhabitants which included Han Chinese, 400,000 died. Another source estimated that a fifth of the Tibetans in Sichuan perished, largely from hunger.

The first Tibetans to rebel were the nomads in the region known by the Tibetans as Amdo. Most of Amdo lies in Qinghai province but a part, Gannan, is in Gansu and another, Aba, is in Sichuan. Among the nomads of Qinghai, the fiercest and most independent are known as the Goloks, or 'heads turned backwards', because they ignore even the authority of Lhasa. They began fighting as early as 1952 but their rebellion was eventually put down by the People's Liberation Army who used planes to hunt them down. In many cases neither the pilots nor the troops on the ground could distinguish between a group of nomads on the move and a band of guerrilla fighters. They were also ignorant of Tibetan customs and mistook anyone carrying a knife or a sword, as Tibetans customarily do, for a dangerous rebel. And the women who carried infants inside their voluminous sheepskin coats were sometimes killed because soldiers suspected them of concealing weapons. In 1956, there were 140,000 Goloks, but by the 1964 census, their numbers had dropped to 70,000.[7] The Golok warriors escaped on horseback to the mountains or to India but the women and children remained and were forcibly settled into communes. In 1958, the tribe was brought together to live in a city of tents in Qinghai laid out in straight rows and traversed by streets named 'Liberation Road' or 'Beijing Road'. Instead of roaming in small groups over the thin pasture, which grows on a bleak plateau 12,000 feet above sea level, the herds of each family, usually numbering around a hundred yaks, were concentrated in one spot. There was no forage prepared and what pasture there was was soon eaten bare. Before long the animals were starving. Normally, nomads slaughter animals in the autumn when they are fat to provide food for the winter. Now no animals could be killed without the express permission of the provincial authorities, hundreds of miles away, who made no allowance for the customs of the herdsmen. By early 1959, the animals had either died of starvation or were so thin that their emaciated bodies could provide little sustenance.

For the first time, the nomads also had to learn how to till the region's stony soil. All over Amdo, efforts to plough the thin soil of the plateau failed, leaving a legacy of long-term environmental degradation. Overgrazing and deep ploughing destroyed the thin layer of top soil and exposed the barren black rock beneath. The ground was often so hard that the Tibetans had to use picks to break up the soil. Even so, they had to 'deep plough' to a depth of three feet and to 'close plant'. The harvest of the autumn of 1959 failed, even in the arable regions where wheat and other crops unsuited to the short growing season were sown. On good farming land, yields fell by half. Without draught animals, women often had to pull the ploughs themselves. In the winter, when temperatures fall to minus 30° Centigrade or lower, they were turned out to dig irrigation canals. The poor harvests were reported as enormous successes. One interviewee, from a place called Xiahe, recalled how it happened:

> Grain production per *mu* was 250 *gyama* [330 lbs] but the Chinese officials reported that it was 1,000 *gyama* [1,320 lbs]. According to the Chinese, if in the past you could travel a few miles a day, now you could travel 300 miles a day. So likewise with the harvest: if you worked hard, it could be increased. If the leader of a particular hamlet gave a true figure, then, in another, they would give one 60 times or 600 times higher and the Chinese would say 'Why can't you produce this much?' And then he would be struggled. So everybody told lies. At first an individual got eighteen ounces of food a day, but later, there was so little grain in the store that they reduced it to nine ounces. With this you cannot make steam buns, so they made a soup, a kind of gruel. Later, when they closed the collective kitchens, it was better. When people cooked their own food, they could supplement their diet with mushrooms, sweet potatoes and things gathered from the mountains and forests.

Interviewees from Amdo also reported the endless house searches for grain, the seizure of all personal property and the smelting of all metal objects to make 'steel'. Some also recalled eating food substitutes, known as *daishipin*. In winter people ate stalks, husks and cobs, and even boiled their boots and other articles made of leather. Several interviewees recalled incidents of cannibalism but these were generally among the Han Chinese. The death rate was extremely high in Amdo. One interviewee said that out of 906 inhabitants of his village in Tongren county, 20 fled and 267 died of hunger. A further 67 men were sent to the Delingha labour camp in Qinghai province, and only 24 ever returned. In all, one in three villagers died. The interviewee said that out of eight members in his house, four starved to death and two fled to India. Three uncles were also beaten to death in struggle sessions. Another interviewee from the same county said that in 1958 his village consisted of 35 households with 210 people. By 1964, only 127 people were left. Most of the men had been arrested and never returned.

Adult males died in the greatest numbers. Many were arrested simply because they were lamas. Generally a quarter of the male population were reckoned to be monks, although this includes those who were labourers attached to the monasteries which controlled much of the land and livestock. Amdo is famous as a religious centre of the dominant Gelugpa, or Yellow Hat, sect because its founder, Tsongkapa, as well as the current Dalai Lama and the tenth Panchen Lama, were all born there. The demolition of nearly all the region's monasteries provoked widespread unrest. In several incidents, the People's Liberation Army machine-gunned crowds of Tibetans attempting to free lamas under arrest. In 1958, 2,000 rioting Tibetans were gunned down in such circumstances in Wendu county.[8] Almost every family contained one member who, as either a lama or a rebel, was classified as a 'black element'. This had terrible consequences for the rest of the population. Virtually everyone could be labelled as a 'rightist' because they had someone in their immediate family who had been killed as a rebel, arrested as a lama, or classified as a landlord for belonging to the local aristocracy. Some sources claim that during this period, one in seven Tibetans were penalized as 'rightists', compared to a national average of one in twenty.[9] Worse still, those arrested were sent to labour camps in Tibet,

Qinghai, Gansu and Sichuan which had the lowest survival rates in the country. Few ever returned. For example, out of 400 monks arrested from a monastery in Gannan county, Gansu, only 100 survived.[10] Many eyewitnesses testified that the death rate for Tibetan prisoners ranged from 40 to 90 per cent.[11]

It was against this background that the tenth Panchen Lama drafted a 90,000-word report for Mao. Apart from Peng Dehuai, he is the only prominent leader known to have dared to do so during the famine.

In 1961, the Panchen Lama toured many counties in Amdo and was shocked by what he discovered. He went to his birthplace, Xunhua, as well as to Gonghe (also known as Hainan, where in 1958 the rebellion in Amdo began), Tongren, Guide, Haibei, Haixi and the labour camps at Gangca, to the north of Lake Koko Nor. At each place he asked how many had been shot, starved or beaten to death. According to another source, who refers to the report, the Panchen Lama concluded that up to 15 per cent of the population had been imprisoned, 800 to 1,000 from each town or village, and that in prison nearly half of these had died.[12]

At the Spring Festival in 1962, he returned to Qinghai, to a place near the Gangca labour camps. There he flew into a rage, angrily rounding on officials who had prepared a field for feasting, dancing and other New Year festivities. Had they no feelings, he asked, to dance on a spot beneath which the bodies of thousands of men, who had been starved or beaten to death, had recently been buried?

Chinese propaganda insists that after 1949 the Panchen Lama co-operated and supported the Chinese Communists, while the Dalai Lama turned traitor by fleeing the country in 1959. It is true that the Panchen Lama gave credence to Chinese propaganda reports that in Tibet a 'new socialist paradise on the roof of the world' had been created. In a report to the Standing Committee of the National People's Congress in December 1960, he declared that 'a wonderful situation prevails in Tibet today. Prosperous scenes of labour and production are to be found in every corner of the vast countryside and the towns. This is the main trend of our work today.' Yet what he saw on his journeys shook him deeply and he determined to write a hard-hitting report to Mao. Many of the various Tibetan advisers who surrounded him tried to dissuade him, but without success. They included Rinpoche Enju, his teacher and Abbot of the Tashilhunpo monastery, the seat of the Panchen Lamas. The latter had consulted oracles which predicted disaster but he also tried to put forward rational arguments to sway his pupil: 'If they [the Party leadership] had wanted to solve the problem, they would have done so earlier. If they do not want to solve the problem, then it will do no good just to send letters of opinion, because they will pay no attention. I worry that handing in this letter will not only not help the Tibetans, but will bring trouble to you. Now that the Dalai Lama has gone, everyone depends on you.'[13] Another of his advisers, the Abbot of Sera monastery and a Deputy Governor of Qinghai, Geshe Sherab Gyatso, urged the Panchen Lama to tone down the report and to 'make his words smoother'.

The Panchen ignored their counsel and in mid-1962 finished the report, adding four policy recommendations for Tibet. The report was written in Tibetan, translated into Chinese and then translated back again into Tibetan to make sure it contained no mistakes. Teams of interpreters worked on it, each only seeing a portion. In the report, the Panchen Lama alleged that Buddhism was being virtually annihilated and he warned that, if current policies continued, the Tibetan nationality would either cease to exist or be completely assimilated. The text of his report has never been published, but an official biography, *The Great Master Panchen*, contains this extract: 'In the last few years, the Tibetan population has fallen drastically. Apart from the women, children and the elderly who could not fight, the majority of the rest have all been arrested. All healthy, normal young men have been seized. The Tibetans living in Qinghai, Gansu, Sichuan and Yunnan lead an unspeakably difficult life.'[14] The report went on to charge the Communist Party with 'making serious mistakes in the suppression of the rebellion'.

After it was delivered, he met with Mao in person. Senior Chinese officials, including Premier Zhou Enlai, had from the beginning encouraged the Panchen Lama to write the report and the text had been approved in meetings with Li Weihan and other senior officials from the United Front Department, the Party body responsible for Tibet. Their encouragement was part of the general rollback of Great Leap Forward policies which began in early 1961. That year the ultra-leftist Party secretaries of Qinghai and Gansu were toppled, and in other parts of the country such as Anhui, various forms of private farming were being tried out. Mao, however, was unrepentant. The Panchen Lama was being used in the continuing political struggle to overturn Mao's disastrous policies and when this failed, he became one of the first victims of the losing side. At a meeting at Beidaihe in late August 1962, Mao decisively turned against the 'reformers' and insisted on a return to Communism. The Panchen Lama was immediately arrested and charged with organizing a rebellion. Although he was struggled, he refused to make a self-criticism and remained under house arrest or in prison until 1977. During the Cultural Revolution, Red Guards accused him of being a 'reactionary slave-owner' and the 'biggest parasite and blood-sucker' in Tibet. For some years he was held in solitary confinement. He is later reported to have said that without Zhou Enlai's intervention, he would have been killed. Only in 1988 did the Party repeal the verdict that he was an 'anti-Party, anti-people, anti-socialism element'. In the early 1990s, his officially sanctioned biography was able to describe his report to Mao 'as the most glorious page in Master Panchen's political life'. When he returned to Qinghai for the first time in 1982, he was greeted by huge crowds.[15]

Meanwhile, in 1962, other Tibetans associated with the report also fell, including Li Weihan, who was dismissed and accused of being a 'capitulator' for 'kowtowing' to the Panchen Lama. Many were arrested as 'little Panchens'. In 1968, during the Cultural Revolution, Geshe Sherab Gyatso was beaten to death by Red Guards at the age of 86. Rinpoche Enju, Abbot of the Tashilhunpo monastery, died in similar circumstances in 1969 aged 60. The Party Secretary of Qinghai, Gao Feng, also fell victim to the Cultural Revolution and died in 1968, after he had been dismissed and moved to a post in Jiangsu province.

The tragedy of the Tibetans does not end there. The Party drew no lessons from the tens of millions of famine deaths, and the Tibetans in the TAR, who had been exempted from establishing communes, later had to follow the same disastrous path. In the TAR, famine was endemic for twenty years.

After 1959, most of the peasants were forced to form mutual-aid teams and then co-operatives. Starvation soon set in. Dawa Norbu in *Red Star in Tibet* describes what happened:

> Immediately the harvest was over, the Chinese exaggerated the results as usual. They claimed that the yield was about ten times the seed . . . it followed that if we could produce a bumper crop in the first year of our liberation, there was no reason why we could not double this year's yield in the following season. We were made to sign a pledge to the effect that we would obtain a yield of twenty times the seed in the next season.[16]

As in the rest of China, the same ill-conceived irrigation schemes and the same insistence on using organic fertilizers and planting second and third crops were instituted. The fields were not rotated and were exhausted after the first year. Canals were built which proved useless because they relied on unpredictable glacial meltwater. Sometimes even existing water supplies were damaged by draining small pools and lakes. The Chinese introduced some successful innovations, among them steel instead of wooden ploughs, but most of the trumpeted achievements, such as the development of special 'high-altitude wheat' and other new varieties, were bogus. Grain output in the TAR temporarily rose in 1959 but then fell. A tough rationing regime began and Tibetans said they ate only a third of their normal diet. Dawa Norbu gives details: 'A working person was allotted a monthly ration of 22 lbs of *tsampa*, half a pound of oil or butter, a third of a brick of tea and a little salt. Only the tea was sufficient, the rest was a starvation diet to us. Old people and children received even less.'[17]

In the cities, people were given monthly ration tickets for 18 lbs of grain, as low as prison camp rations. In consequence, as one account describes, 'People ate cats, dogs, insects. Parents fed dying children their own blood mixed with hot water and *tsampa*. Other children were forced to leave home to beg on the roads. Old people went off to die in the hills alone. Thousands of Tibetans took to eating the refuse thrown by the

Chinese to the pigs that each Han compound kept, while those around PLA outposts daily prised apart manure from the soldiers' horses, looking for undigested grain.'[18]

Anyone who admitted the existence of food shortages was violently punished and declared an 'enemy of socialism'. The Tibetans in the TAR had the additional burden of feeding a garrison of some 200,000 Chinese troops and another 100,000 civilians.[19] These were entitled to national grain tickets and access to state grain reserves. However, several Tibetan interviewees said that many Han Chinese also resorted to eating grass and leaves and had heads and legs swollen by oedema. As in other regions, the Tibetans saw their grain being taken away as 'national patriotic wealth' after every harvest. 'Some was taken away to China in trucks as "preparation for war". We were told that a war with Russia, or the USA, was imminent. Another part was left in Tibet to sell to the Chinese officials and their families,' said one interviewee. It is not certain, though, if this grain really was transported to China, or if it was held in granaries and tunnels for a war which never happened. Most of it probably just rotted away uneaten. Some Tibetans are convinced it was shipped to the Soviet Union to pay for help with the building of China's first nuclear bomb. It is certainly plausible to link the food shortages with an accelerated effort to build a nuclear bomb, as it was developed in Qinghai. Some Tibetan prisoners worked on the construction of China's nuclear research centre near Lake Koko Nor in Qinghai and others worked on the railways, roads and mines connected with this and Mao's other preparations for a nuclear war with the Soviet Union.

Labour camps in the TAR had extraordinarily high death tolls. In Drapchi prison outside Lhasa, one survivor claimed that between November 1960 and June 1961 out of 17,000 prisoners, 14,000 died.[20] According to a joint statement by two nuns who fled to India in 1961, two-thirds of those in this prison died: 'Cartloads of dead bodies were taken away daily for burial or for use as manure on the fields. People were not allowed to say that those deaths were caused by starvation. If they were caught saying so they would be punished severely.'[21]

Among the rest of the population, most interviewees from the TAR reckoned that the death rate from famine in the years of the Great Leap Forward was around 10 per cent, although a few estimated a higher figure of 15 per cent. Yet more were to die of hunger later on. From the mid-1960s, the TAR authorities began to set up communes. The first was established in 1965 in Damzhung county. The Cultural Revolution delayed the spread of the communes but by around 1970 most nomads and peasants belonged to one. This was also the highpoint of the 'study Dazhai' campaign. The leader of the Dazhai model commune in Shanxi province, Chen Yonggui, toured Tibet as well as the rest of China. His commune became the model for the Tibetans, as one of the slogans of the time declared: 'For nomads, study Red Flag, for agriculture study Nyemo. The whole country should learn from Dazhai.'

Red Flag was the name of the model commune for Tibetan nomads in the Nagchu district, north-east of Lhasa. The Nyemo commune in Lhuntse county, about 280 miles north-west of Lhasa, was the model for Tibetan peasants, and its Party secretary, Rigzin Wangyal, was the Tibetan counterpart to Chen Yonggui. Tibetans had to imitate the large-scale terracing and irrigation techniques practised in Shanxi. There, the loess soil is soft and easy to terrace but the Tibetans had to slave for twelve hours a day trying to create terraces on the rocky slopes of towering mountains and then carry water up to irrigate the fields. The ill-fed peasants simply collapsed and died from exhaustion, or were beaten to death in struggle sessions for failing to meet their quotas. One source claimed that at the Nyemo commune, 30 per cent of the population died in these circumstances. It was sheer madness from the start. The terracing of mountains over 12,000 feet had already been tried during the Great Leap Forward in the Qilian mountains bordering Gansu. These and others built in Qinghai and elsewhere proved equally useless and have now been abandoned.

For the nomads in the TAR, the communes brought disaster just as they had for the Goloks ten years earlier. A former official from western Tibet described the folly of what took place:

They were forced to start farming the high pastures. Old and young were yoked to the plough because their yaks were not domesticated and so could not be trained to plough a field. The nomads were also forced to build drystone walls, four or five feet high, to protect the grass and the fields from wild animals and the wind. Of course, they only lasted two or three days and then fell down. Because it was so high, 14,000 feet or more above sea level, they did not sow wheat but highland barley. However, even this could not grow at such altitudes. They planted 100 lbs per *mu* but gathered almost nothing at harvest time, perhaps a pound per *mu*. The officials had to do this otherwise they would be disregarding Mao's orders. The attempt at farming was only stopped in 1978 or 1979 and a lot of the pasture was ruined.

In *New Tibet*, Dorje Gashi claims that 'out of three or four years, there was only one year in which the Tibetans could say there was a barley harvest. In most cases, 80 per cent of the barley crop was destroyed by frost.'[22]

The collectivized yak herds died because the nomads were forbidden to move them to their summer or winter pastures. Soon there was no butter, milk or cheese. The authorities forbade, too, the hunting of wild animals, another standby of the nomads. As one source put it: 'We hardly saw meat because of the dialectical argument that ran thus: if you killed your animals that worked and reproduced, you were killing the national economy and you were committing anti-motherland sabotage.'[23] Every animal had to be registered and, before it was slaughtered, permission had first to be obtained from the prefecture's headquarters. 'The herds constantly declined, but officials had to report that they were increasing,' one former official recalled. Many nomads died not from hunger but from the tremendous cold. They no longer had yak hair to make tents with which to keep out the fierce winds. The Chinese also copied Soviet cross-breeding ideas, interbreeding the tough Tibetan mountain sheep with Ukrainian sheep. The crossbreeds were supposed to produce a heavier, coarser wool but the new sheep were not hardy enough to survive the winters.

The growing hunger and desperation of the peasantry led to a number of revolts in the countryside within the TAR. At a place called Nyima, about 50 miles north-west of Lhasa, a former nun called Ani Trinley Choedron led a revolt in 1969 which lasted for three or four months. Troops were sent in and reimposed control after heavy fighting. In Lhasa, the Party had the leaders of this revolt and others publicly executed. In one case, nine members of a group called the 'Gelo Zogha', or 'Association against the Rulers', were shot. In another case, a senior Party member, Ada Chongkok, was shot for, amongst other crimes, writing a poem ridiculing the food shortages.[24]

No one can understand the continuing enmity between Tibetans and Chinese without grasping the bitterness created by these artificial famines. It is conceivable that in many places one in four Tibetans died of hunger although it may never be possible to arrive at a definitive statistic. No one is sure how many Tibetans there were before the famine, particularly since the national census did not extend to the TAR either in 1953 or in 1964. Official Chinese population statistics show a 10 per cent decline in the number of Tibetans between the 1953 and 1964 censuses. According to *Forty Years of Work on Nationalities,* published by the Nationalities Commission, the number of Tibetans fell from 2.78 to 2.5 million.[25] This is partly because up to 100,000 Tibetans fled to India after the abortive 1959 revolt but one must also remember that, as in the rest of China, the population may have grown after 1953. It is revealing that the same book shows that from 1953 to 1964, the number of ethnic Mongolians rose by 400,000 to 1.97 million, despite the famine. If the Tibetan population grew at a similar rate from 1953, it might have peaked at 3.4 million in 1959. Since by 1964 the population had decreased to 2.5 million, this suggests that some 900,000 are missing. If one subtracts the 100,000 refugees, then the rebellion and famine may have cost 800,000 lives. In his 1962 report the Panchen Lama talks of the population of Tibet numbering 3 million. This indicates that the population may have declined by 500,000 and that one in six may have perished.

Whatever the true figure, the evidence for the enormous scale of the famine and its long-term effects is considerable. Food supplies in Tibet only began to improve after 1980, when General Secretary Hu Yaobang and Wan Li, who introduced reforms in Anhui, visited Lhasa and replaced the Tibetan leadership. The communes began to be dismantled and a measure of religious freedom was restored, but fifteen years later Beijing admits that in a quarter of the TAR's counties people cannot feed or clothe themselves. A third of all children do not attend school and the literacy rate is the lowest in China at around 30 per cent. Despite the subsidies pumped into the TAR, put at 35 billion yuan between 1952 and 1994, the Tibetans are still among the poorest people in China. Long after the famine, life expectancy is still the lowest in China and scientists continue to debate how to restore the large areas of pasture ruined in this period. In 1995, the Chinese government estimated that it would take twenty-five years for Tibet to catch up with the rest of the country.[26]

12

In the Prison Camps

'The Buddhist classics speak of six ways one
can be reincarnated. There is hell, hungry
ghosts, animals, Asura, humans and heaven,
and the worst of these is to become a hungry
ghost.'

Zhang Xianliang, *Grass Soup*

MILLIONS WERE SUCKED into China's vast network of
prisons and labour colonies during the Great Leap Forward,
indeed more than in any other period after 1949. And, with
the onset of the famine, these institutions became in effect
death camps.[1] In his book *Laogai: The Chinese Gulag*, Harry Wu,
who himself spent nineteen years in the camps, estimates that
during this period the number of political prisoners peaked at
close to 10 million. (By comparison, in the forty years up to
1989, he estimates that a total of 30–40 million were arrested
and convicted for political reasons.[2])

During the Three Red Banners movement that began in 1958, anyone who expressed dissatisfaction with the hardships caused by Mao
Zedong and the Communist Party leader's impractical policies, or
anyone who showed resentment over the following three years of
hunger and food shortages, was seen as directly threatening the
stability of the Communist Party's dictatorship. The Communist
Party responded with draconian measures of suppression.

The majority, around 70 per cent, of those imprisoned were
sentenced to 'reform through labour' and held in the labour

reform camps of the Ministry of Public Security. Such prisons contain both common and political criminals. As in the Soviet Gulag, intellectuals and political prisoners were treated more harshly in these labour camps than real criminals, who were considered easier to reform and indoctrinate. Harry Wu claims that political prisoners were given longer sentences, reprimanded and beaten more often and given lower food rations. They also found it harder to adapt to the treacherous dog-eat-dog environment in the camps and were not able to cope with the physical demands made on them which, in turn, led to punishments for failing to meet their work quotas and still lower rations.

In exceptional cases, life could be better for intellectuals. One interviewee from Guangzhou said both her parents were sent to labour camps during the famine. Her father never returned, dying in a camp in 1975, but her mother was sent to the Yingde labour farm in Guangdong province which grows tea. As a professional player of the *erhu*, a Chinese musical instrument, she was invited to join a prison orchestra which toured other camps. She was given four meals a day and ate better than did her children left behind in Guangzhou. Gao Ertai, a painter, only survived the camps because he was summoned by the Gansu Party Secretary, Zhang Zhongliang, to paint a tableau celebrating the tenth anniversary of the Daqing oilfield. At that stage, his legs were so swollen by oedema that he had to be lifted up on to the scaffolding to complete the huge tableau.[3]

However, most of those arrested were not intellectuals but rather, as Harry Wu points out, 'peasants driven to drastic acts or rebellion by hunger and dissatisfaction with living conditions'. The severity of these peasants' punishments was linked to their class status:

Suppose someone steals twenty pecks of corn from a commune. If this person is from a landlord family, it is possible his sentence could be as high as ten years, the rationale being 'his act should be considered a counter-attack by the landlord class, a hostile and destructive counter-revolutionary act against socialist public property'. If this person is from a poor or middle-class peasant background, or from the family of a Party cadre, it is possible that no disciplinary action would be taken.

Most of the peasants, however, were not transported to distant labour reform camps. During the Great Leap Forward, the Party created another form of imprisonment called 're-education through labour'. This was not organized by the Ministry of Public Security but by provincial, municipal and county-level authorities. Wu writes that from 1958, such makeshift re-education-through-labour camps were set up at every level down to that of the local village commune. The inmates were not subject to any judicial procedure and were not imprisoned for a fixed term but conditions were otherwise usually identical to those in the labour camps. Arrests under the 're-education through labour' system began in 1957, when perhaps 550,000 counter-revolutionary rightists and another 400,000 rightist sympathizers were dispatched to the camps. The system became fully effective the following year and, according to Wu, was 'undoubtedly one of the most important methods the Communist regime employed to weather the storm'. Inevitably, there are no comprehensive records of the fate of these re-education-through-labour prisoners but a Party document from Fengyang, Anhui, gives some idea of their circumstances:

> Peasants were forced to work extra hours at the construction site of the hydro-electric power station. The cadres, including the county Party Secretary and deputy magistrate, treated the peasants harshly. If the peasants did not work, they were not given food. Some sick peasants were sent back home and died on the way . . . In the construction site of the reservoir, a prison was set up where 70 peasants were imprisoned of whom 28 died. There were many methods of torture, including being forced to stand, being tied up by ropes, or suspended by ropes. One of the worst methods was to thread iron wire through people's ears.[4]

Since there are so few other accounts of 're-education through labour' from the rest of China, one cannot be certain how representative this example is. Much more, though, is known about life in the labour reform camps. Many of these camps were established in remote and uninhabited regions in Heilongjiang, Gansu and Qinghai, and a handful of surviving inmates who later emigrated have written about their horrifying experiences there. The death rate in these camps was staggeringly high, ranging from an average rate of 20 per cent to places in which only one in ten survived. The painter Gao Ertai was arrested as a rightist in 1957 and found himself in such a camp with 3,000 others at the Jiabiangou state farm near Jiuquan in Gansu: 'More than 90 per cent of us perished. For 15 hours a day, we dug a gully in a futile bid to render the wasteland fertile. We were given two bowls of thin gruel every day in addition to an insubstantial bun . . . Years later, when local peasants wanted to convert the site into a seed farm, they discovered hundreds upon hundreds of bodies.'[5]

The highest death rate was probably experienced by the Tibetans imprisoned after the abortive revolt of 1959. One survivor, Ama Adhe, describes in *A Strange Liberation: Tibetan Lives in Chinese Hands* what happened at the Dartsedo camp bordering Sichuan. By the roadside the authorities opened a mass grave which was filled with corpses and gave off a terrible stench. 'Every day,' she recalls, 'they would deliver nine or ten truck loads of bodies to put there. Some days less, some days more. Usually, eight, nine, ten trucks.' Of the 300 women arrested with her, only 100 survived. The survivors were then made to walk to another prison, a gigantic lead mine, which was still worse. This camp, called Gothang Gyalpo, was filled with Tibetans and Kuomintang prisoners: 'So many prisoners were working all over this huge lead mine, they looked like bugs, like ants going in every direction. There were thousands and thousands of them swarming over the mine. And, when I looked round, they were all Tibetan. And their physical condition was the same as at Dartsedo, starvation. Many were leaning on walking sticks, otherwise they would not be able to hold up their heads.' Only 4 out of the 100 she arrived with survived this second camp. In 1962, a fellow prisoner overheard a new prison warder being told that in the last three years, 12,019 Tibetans had starved to death at the mine.

John Avedon, in his book on the Tibetans, *In Exile from the Land of Snows*, quotes former prisoners who reported similar death rates in Gansu. One claimed that of the 70,000 Tibetans taken to camps north of the provincial capital, Lanzhou, only half survived. At Jiuzhen prison in the same province, more than half the 76 Tibetan prisoners died of starvation and at least half of the 1,000 Chinese inmates perished. At the Vebou camp complex, ten hours' drive west of Xining, the capital of Qinghai, 14,000 of the 30,000 inmates died. In another camp at Shen Mu, half the 12,000 inmates died.[6]

One interviewee from Shanghai told me that at the Mazong Shan coal-mine in Gansu province where he was sent, only 2,000 of the 5,000 Shanghainese he arrived with survived. Altogether there were 100,000 prisoners, half of them Tibetans, and at least 20 per cent died of hunger. Another interviewee estimated that one in five died at the Qi Ling state farm in Qinghai province where he worked with 4,000 others. Han Weitian, who was arrested in Shanghai as a former Kuomintang member and whose experiences are recorded by the Taiwanese-based writer Pu Ning in *Red in Tooth and Claw*, was sent to the Delingha labour camp complex in the same province. Han believes one-fifth of the 100,000 inmates died and that in all the camps in Qinghai 200,000 died.

Such specific figures are not available for those sent either to camps in the far north or, nearer home, to places such as Qinghe in Hebei province. The accounts of former inmates are no less terrible, though. Jean Pasqualini, part French, part Chinese and the author of *Prisoner of Mao*, relates how since so many prisoners were dying, the guards took the weakest to a special camp known as Section 585 or the Patient Recovery Centre to improve the morale of the rest. Harry Wu was one of the few ever to return from Section 585. In his autobiography *Bitter Winds*, he remembers that 'dead bodies went out and live bodies came in almost daily'. Chi Chunghuang, now a professor of English in America, was also there: 'When people were dying in their hundreds, the bodies were carried from all over the state farm to one camp. They stacked all the corpses in three rooms and piled them up to the ceiling. Then, in the evening, convicts were ordered to take out the corpses and bury them.'[7]

Peasants living outside the camps somehow became convinced that those inside had greater access to food. A former journalist from Shaanxi, sent to a state farm in the Qilian mountains on the border of Gansu and Qinghai, remembers how peasants even came to beg to be allowed to work in the camp, settling in caves outside and trying to steal the prisoners' food.[8] Dr Tensing Choedak, the Dalai Lama's physician, has said that at his camp in Gansu he gave food to a starving village girl. Next day there was 'a mass assault on the prison walls by scores of men and women from Jiuzhen camp demanding food. A full-scale mêlée ensued, until they were beaten back with rifle butts by the guards and then the townspeople retreated across the fields.'[9] By contrast, the Chinese writer Zhang Xianliang, in his autobiographical work *Grass Soup*, writes that he escaped from his camp in Ningxia province only to discover that the villagers outside had less to wear and eat than the prisoners themselves.

Before the famine, rations in the labour reform camps were not designed to starve the prisoners. In the autumn of 1958, prisoners in some camps even shared with the peasants the joy of being able to eat as much as they wanted. This happy state lasted for several months. Most Chinese prisoners are fed *wotou*, buns made of baked and steamed corn. When Jean Pasqualini first arrived in the camps, the minimum monthly grain ration was 31 lbs, but top workers could get 43 lbs. He was required to spend his days folding sheets of paper in his prison cell and the more he worked, the more he ate. The prisoners were classified into categories according to their work rate, and every few weeks their status and rations would be reassessed. The amount of food was determined not just by productivity but by a prisoner's political attitude. Political prisoners almost never received the top rations.

Dr Benjamin Lee, who now works in the United States but was then a prisoner in the Lake Xingkai camps in the far north, says that inmates there had a monthly ration of 83.7 lbs of cereals and over an ounce of soybean oil.[10] This diet of 2.7 lbs a day provided over 4,000 calories but, after deducting food stolen or wasted, the ration in fact amounted to only 2.2 lbs, or 3,520 calories a day. This is the barest minimum needed to sustain life in the region's harsh environment where in winter temperatures fall to minus 20° Centigrade and sometimes even lower. In this cold, prisoners dug canals for twelve to sixteen hours a day. A pair of prisoners would together have to carry loads of 330–440 lbs of muddy earth on shoulder poles, up and down steep and slippery banks, hundreds of times each day. This was devastating for intellectuals unused to the mildest form of physical labour.

Generally, prisoners in the labour reform camps began to die in large numbers at the end of 1960, when grain rations were cut by half and adulterated with 'food substitutes'. These *daishipin* consisted of wild grasses, the otherwise inedible by-products of crops, such as corncobs, chaff and potato leaves, and the residue of pressed oil seeds, as well as innovations such as algae and seaweed. To make the food go further, the buns were also steamed twice, making them heavy with water. In some places, prison rations were cut a year earlier. Zhang Xianliang, imprisoned in Ningxia, writes that in the winter of 1959–60, the grain ration dropped from 22 lbs a month to 16.5 lbs, amounting to a couple of buns a day. Eventually, prisoners were getting a mere 9.9 lbs a month. Even this was not pure food, but unhusked grain. In Jiuzhen camp in Gansu, the ration dropped still lower, first to 16.5 lbs a month and then to 8.5 lbs, or just 1.5 oz per meal.

As food supplies dwindled in the winter of 1959–60, camp commandants, like commune leaders in the countryside, decreed that only those who worked would be fed. On the Qinghe state farm in Hebei, prisoners considered beyond work – the elderly, the weak and the sick – were brought to the special unit described above by Jean Pasqualini and left to die. The working hours of the rest were shortened so that they could preserve their energy for the vital sowing season in the spring. When spring came, prisoners who were sent out into the fields often died from the extreme demands made of them. Han Weitian recalls how in Qinghai he saw 'healthy' prisoners carrying bags of seed weighing 60 lbs and dropping down dead with exhaustion from the effort of running behind the sowing machine. In Hebei province, prisoners died in a similar fashion in the spring of 1962 when hundreds of the healthiest had to answer Mao's call for an all-out effort on sowing.

From early 1961, the labour reform camp authorities changed the rules and began to allow inmates' relatives to send or deliver food parcels. Prisoners were even encouraged to write home and ask for food, and to go out scavenging. Much of what they gathered consisted of wild grasses, bark and tree leaves which ended up as soup. And in their struggle to survive, prisoners began to eat far worse things. They hunted living creatures: field-mice, rats, frogs, toads, snakes, lizards, cockroaches, the eggs of praying mantises and worms of all kinds. These things were caught, taken back to the camp and boiled. Some creatures, such as snakes, they ate raw. Others searched through horse and ox dung for worms and pieces of undigested grain which could be cleaned and eaten. Prisoners also ate the worms from their own stools and, at Delingha, searched through the excrement of other prisoners for undigested grains. This was because those prisoners who were former Party members were given the best jobs which allowed them to pilfer grain from the camp granary; the uncooked grain passed through them undigested. In some camps, prisoners were seen eating their own excrement. Inmates also searched the refuse of the guards for pieces of old cabbage, the rind of fruit, rotten meat and bones. Ama Adhe recalls how the guards would watch, laughing, as prisoners fought over used tea leaves that they had thrown on the ground.

More appalling than any of this was cannibalism. Eyewitness reports of cannibalism appear in all accounts of prison life during this period. In one camp in Gansu, it was called 'eating the crops of Jiuzhen'. A Tibetan who was in Jiuzhen, Tenpa Soepa, describes how he tried, but failed, to eat one of his companions: 'I couldn't even get a piece off the body. First of all, I was very weak, and the corpse was stiff and frozen. We didn't have any knives. I tried to pull off an ear but couldn't. You just had to put your mouth down and try to bite a piece off. But when I was about to bite, in my mind I felt this strong feeling. I felt I could not possibly eat this. I tried twice but in the end I was not able to eat anything.'[11]

The most terrible story appears in *Red in Tooth and Claw*. In the Delingha camp, prisoners sent out to fetch water would dig up fresh corpses buried beneath a thin layer of sandy soil. They would then cut the flesh off the thighs, arms or breast to sell as meat from a horse or camel: the buyer, though suspecting the meat's true origin, would not inquire too closely.

There was also a lively trade in tobacco, clothes and food pilfered from the kitchens or caught in the fields. While some prisoners arrived in camps without winter clothing, or even bowls and eating implements, others, especially the city-dwellers, came with watches that were exchanged for food. A few traders had wads of money tied around their waists when they died. For the majority, the obsession with food was so all-encompassing that some hesitated to eat all their food at once. Psychologically, it was better to keep some food in reserve rather than endure the torture of watching others eat or live with the knowledge that there was nothing more left to eat. Professor Chi Chunghuang saw the most poignant example in Qinghe. He was lying in the infirmary next to a young college student from Sichuan who had oedema and was plainly close to death. His mother had sent him a box with cake inside but he would not eat it. Instead, he just opened the box and looked at it while his neighbours watched with envy. He died a few days later with the cake still uneaten. Professor Chi states: 'One has to understand the psychology of hunger. Every evening we would sit on the *kang* for supper. No one would eat first because then they would finish first and have to watch the others eat. This was a great suffering. When hungry you hate to eat so fast because afterwards there is nothing left.'

In some camps, prisoners sewed themselves little bags in which to keep food. They would then hang these around their necks just to keep this fear at bay. Perpetual hunger led to another obsession over the division of rations. This was difficult to do fairly. Prisoners did not have receptacles of equal size. Some got the watery food from the top of the pail, others the thicker gruel from the bottom. Certain types of food, such as a pile of cucumbers of different sizes, simply could not be divided into identical portions. In Dr Choedak's camp, some prisoners had no bowls but only pieces of wood in which crude indentations had been carved. Others had tin cans or metal ashtrays which the guards had handed out.[12] Zhang Xianliang in *Grass Soup* records:

Among the 18 men there were eighteen different standards of measurement. Splitting up a pile of food was infinitely more difficult than writing a poem . . . Whether or not a man kept on living, or whether he was able to live one more day or two, appeared to depend on whether he was given two extra or two fewer grains of rice. One's survival did not depend on the vitamins or protein in one or two grains of rice – but it did depend on the spiritual sustenance, the encouragement those grains gave a man. After every convict had received his portion, he would stir it around his basin for a long time, glancing at everybody else's basins and comparing their amounts to his own.

Suspicion and envy led to fights and thieving on all sides. Prisoners stole from each other to find things to trade for food. The strong bullied the weak to get the best food. As the rations were cut, the prison camps became less and less controllable. Groups of prisoners began to attack the food being carted to other cells, or to grab the food of another before it was eaten. Harry Wu describes how he organized his squad to protect their supplies:

> I told my squad we would walk back from the kitchen together to protect each other's food. Even then, our rations were at risk. Three men came after one of my squad members the next afternoon and two of them grabbed him while the other stole his *wotou.* They had organised to work together. Then other squads including mine began organising against the band of three. I went out with four of my squad members the following day. We found the three and gave them a beating.[13]

In Delingha, Qinghai, conditions were still worse, as Han Weitian records in *Red in Tooth and Claw*:

> On our farm, many stronger fellows gathered there to rob the food senders. It is hard to believe that men on the brink of death could still be so energetic, but they struggled out of their beds, staggered up to the kitchen door, and lay in ambush waiting for the moment when the bamboo hampers of loaves were carried out of the kitchen. They were all prepared to steal. One day these starving plunderers snatched the loaves away, and afterwards many suspects were imprisoned in special cells, and kept constantly in close custody until they died. Strife was inevitable among these men. Three to five people died every day fighting one another for food at the kitchen door, or in the yard. They did not fight with clubs or fists, but merely pushed each other with their remaining strength. That push was often enough to knock down one's opponent and deprive him of his life.

As the conviction grew among the prisoners that they were all doomed to die in the camps, they grew fearless with desperation. Order began to collapse throughout the prison system and guards feared a mutiny. In August 1961, the Minister of Public Security, Luo Ruiqing, authorized all labour reform camps to 'use strong management to prevent vicious and malignant incidents involving prisoner uprisings'.[14]

Punishments became more brutal. In Ningxia, prisoners were tied to a carrying pole and suspended upside down, or bound to a tree to allow clouds of mosquitoes to feast on them. Another punishment was to tie a man's hands together and let other convicts drag him along the ground.[15] In Jiuzhen, Gansu, there were frequent executions. Dr Choedak remembers that 'with hundreds dead, executions continued to be carried out. The charges were never specified. The names of those to be shot would simply appear on small posters periodically glued to the prison walls with such observations as "stubborn" or "suffers from old brains".'[16]

Yet at the height of the famine in Ningxia, the guards made no effort to stop the prisoners from escaping. The prison walls were only four feet high, but there was little point in escaping when there was even less to eat outside. In *Bitter Winds* Harry Wu writes that in Hebei's Qinghe camp one prisoner who did escape found that even in Beijing there was nothing to eat so he walked up to a police kiosk, turned himself in and was sent back to the same prison.

The brutal nature of the prison system may have encouraged prisoners to beat each other in struggle sessions, but this did not always prevent them from showing humanity towards one another. The Tibetans, in particular, reported how older prisoners would give younger ones their food if they thought that they themselves had no chance of surviving. Ama Adhe stole food and tossed it into the cells of starving lamas, and when a relative brought her food, she divided it up amongst her fellow prisoners. Yet, in general, such gestures were rare. The struggle to survive overrode all normal feelings. Prisoners noticed how the dehumanizing effect of hunger extended even towards their wives and children for whom they lost all concern. Spouses who travelled long distances to bring gifts of food, even though they had deprived themselves of their meagre rations to do so, inspired little gratitude. Some prisoners committed suicide when they became aware of the dehumanized state into which they had fallen.

The behaviour of the guards in the labour reform camps is rarely described as intentionally cruel. It was merely that they did not care whether the prisoners lived or died. One exception is mentioned by Ama Adhe who remembers the well-fed guards of the Gothang Gyalpo lead mine taking a deliberate delight in mocking their prisoners:

> When prison staff saw the cook carrying the soup to the prisoners, they gathered together and followed along behind the cook to watch the scene for their amusement. When all the soup was served out, the empty pot would be placed in the centre of the prisoners. The prisoners would watch the pot and wait, and the guards and officials would stand around and watch with glee. Then, on a signal, the prisoners would go all out for the pot, desperately trying to get something out of it, sticking their hands in and licking their fingers. As the prisoners were so weak they would fall over and stumble and roll around, and the pot would be pushed and pulled in every direction and the prisoners would be fighting together for a chance to lick this empty pot. The Chinese officers would roar with laughter, it was a very funny show for them, and they would shout and laugh and encourage the prisoners to fight over the empty pot.[17]

As long as Mao denied the existence of the famine, the guards had no choice but to continue working the prisoners to death. After all, since there was no famine, prisoners could not be dying of hunger. Once a prisoner failed to fulfil his work quota, he was given less food, or none at all. With less food it was harder to continue working and death almost inevitably followed. Dr Choedak saw guards kicking prisoners who were dying, cursing them for being 'too lazy to work'. Tenpa Soepa recalls that 'When a prisoner became ill or exhausted he would just lie under his blanket in the morning. Then the guards would drag him out to the fields, right out to his work place. But these prisoners couldn't do any work, they couldn't even stand up. They would just lie there in the field, and there they would die. Many died just like that, lying helpless in the fields.'

Han Weitian reports that the same thing happened in Delingha: 'Sometimes when a poor wretch fell dead on the ground, the "leaders" would go over and examine him to determine whether he had really ceased to breathe, but they wouldn't allow death to provide an excuse for malingering.'

The absolute insistence that there was no famine when all around were dying was not merely macabre, it was surreal. Zhang Xianliang recalls that it was a political crime to note how many were dying:

> People in our group began to die one after another. If you got up in the morning and discovered that the person beside you had died, the thing to do was make a report to the Group Leader in the following manner: 'Group Leader, so-and-so has died.' Whatever happened, you never wanted to say 'Oh! Group Leader, another person has died!' This subtle linguistic difference is something that people who were not in the camps in the 1960s cannot understand . . . You had to forget all about the man who had died beside you right away. Next time, when 'another' died, you had to think of him as the first. It was necessary to get accustomed to this method of accounting, for no matter how many died in the camps, they were all the only one who died.

The prison authorities made every effort to carry on as if nothing was amiss. In Qinghe the camp loudspeakers continued to blare out waltzes and tunes such as 'The asters are in bloom' while the emaciated prisoners staggered across the bleak fields in search of food. Political indoctrination, with lectures, study sessions in the cells, the compilation of lengthy self-criticisms and even the occasional performance of an agit-prop play, went on without respite. One interviewee remembers how in his camp throughout the famine the gaunt skeletons had to assemble each day and stand with heads bowed to listen to a speech about ideology: 'This was the thought reform, the re-education of the camps, which was supposed to turn us into New Men to fit into the New Society.'

In May 1961 the Chinese government imposed a new policy, establishing fixed sentences for counter-revolutionary rightists undergoing re-education through labour. In study sessions Harry Wu and other rightists were told to make a confession, think again about their crimes, and state the punishment they thought they deserved. At study sessions Dr Choedak had to repeat that 'the Chinese Communists are the vanguard of all Communists. This is because Mao is the leader of the whole world. Right now he is the only one worthy of even being called a leader!' In Qinghe in 1960, Jean Pasqualini heard the camp director tell them that 'The situation at home and abroad is very good. At home the production has never been so high and all efforts are being bent to overcome any economic hardships that linger on. Improvement is assured for 1961. What I have come to tell you is that you have more reason than ever to be grateful to the government. The government realises we have been living through a temporary period of difficulty caused by abnormal factors beyond our control.'

Prisoners were warned not to tell visitors that there was famine or that inmates were dying from starvation. When the brother of Ama Adhe arrived to meet her in one camp, she was warned that she must 'show a happy face'. If she said anything about starvation or suffering there would be 'serious consequences'. Like officials elsewhere in China, the prison authorities dared not speak out or betray what they thought. For a while, the guards were able to insulate themselves from the famine by consuming the prisoners' rations or what they grew. However, their wives and children, who often remained in the big cities, starved on the same diminishing rations as the rest of the population. Eventually, the food shortage did affect the prison guards. In the Qinghe camp prisoners were invited to tour the kitchens of the guards to see what they were eating – sweet potato flour mixed with ersatz corncob. A Shanghainese sent to work at the Mazong Shan coal-mine in the deserts of Gansu recalls how his starving guards repeatedly sent out desperate messages to the provincial government headquarters begging for food. When there was no reply, a party set off to walk to the railway line. From there, they used a hand-operated railway cart to travel hundreds of miles to the provincial capital of Lanzhou. In response to their appeal, the Lanzhou authorities sent a truck which arrived one day containing 5 tonnes of grain. The guards kept half and gave the rest to the prisoners, who each received half a cup of grain.[18]

If the Great Leap Forward had not been abandoned, it is

likely that in this camp and others many more inmates would have died. Thanks to Liu Shaoqi's emergency measures, which will be discussed in Chapter 16, conditions began to improve at the end of 1961 and were still better in 1962. And in 1961, when the Party secretaries of Qinghai and Gansu were replaced, some prisoners began to be sent home. Even Tibetan prisoners held in Sichuan, Gansu and Qinghai were re-housed in prisons in Tibet. Elsewhere, the change was less marked. In Qinghe near Beijing food rations increased slightly in late 1961 and the amount of food substitutes fell. In 1962, Liu Shaoqi made preparations to rehabilitate the rightists and allow them to return to their old jobs. Although Mao blocked this move, the commandants of many camps were replaced and a more humane regime was introduced. Some prisoners even began to be paid for their labour.

13

The Anatomy of Hunger

'In those years, starvation became a sort of
mental manacle, depriving us of our freedom
to think.'

Han Weitian

STARVATION CAN BE one of the most prolonged and humiliating forms of death. Its immediate effect is rapid weight loss
as the body consumes reserves of fat and then muscle tissue.
On a diet of 1,600 calories a day, equivalent to a pound of
cereals, the body will lose a quarter of its weight in two to three
months.[1] This, the first stage of starvation, is familiar from
news pictures. Adults often have emaciated bodies and concave
stomachs while the bellies of children are distended by the
gases created by bacteria growing in the stomach and intestine.
In tropical countries and especially among refugees living in
camps, famine victims in this state are often carried away by
disease before they reach the stage of terminal starvation.

However, in China the famine was different. The vast majority of people remained in their own homes. Standards of public
health continued to be vigorously enforced. Even in the depths
of the famine, people in villages or labour camps were
inspected to see if they were obeying the sanitation regulations
zealously laid down during the Great Leap Forward.

As the famine intensified, a large part of the population
reached the second stage of starvation. The *Encyclopaedia Britannica* describes it thus: 'Activity will be reduced and general
lethargy will occur. If there is a further reduction in food intake,
further weight loss will occur and the death rate will rise.

Psychologically the mind is dominated by a desire for food. Other emotions are dulled. Moral standards are lowered and in extreme conditions murder and cannibalism may occur.'

In this second stage, the body stops shrinking and begins to swell. In medieval Europe, this was called the 'dropsy'. It is now known as oedema (or edema), defined in the *Encyclopaedia* as 'a swelling due to the effusion of watery fluid into the intercellular spaces of connective tissues'. A lack of protein means that fluid escapes from the blood into the tissues which, when punctured, 'secrete a thin incoagulable fluid'.

During the height of the famine, various sources suggest that around 10 per cent of the urban population and 10 to 30 per cent of the rural population suffered from oedema. In Fengyang, a report claimed that 37.8 per cent of the population was sick, largely from oedema.[2] It is a condition easily detected. It is present if, when a finger is pressed against the skin, the skin preserves the indentation rather than reverting to its unmarked state. In Changsha, Hunan province, one writer recalls that 'Many of the old people and almost all the children I knew had the "water swelling disease", dropsy. Our bodies puffed up and wouldn't recede ... When acquaintances met, they squeezed each other's legs to see how swollen they were, and examined each other's skin to see if they were yellow. It was a game for me to poke Nai Nai's cheek and leave a hole that would fill up only very slowly like dough.'[3] Even in Beijing, which as the capital received the highest priority in the supply of food, oedema was present. One doctor who worked there reckoned that it affected 10 per cent of the population. A health survey conducted in 1961 estimated that the same proportion of Heilongjiang's population likewise had oedema.[4]

Since officially there was no famine in China, only bumper harvests, doctors were forbidden to tell patients that they were starving. The usual Chinese terms for malnutrition and lack of food are *yinyang bu liang* and *quefa yinyang.* Instead, the government resorted to euphemisms. Doctors were told to talk about fictitious diseases such as *fuzhong bing* or *shuizhong bing,* that is swollen sickness or water illness. Oedema is, however, a symptom not a disease. At the same time, it was forbidden to record a death as due to starvation. Even in the prison camps this could not be done, and in some places all medical terms were dispensed with and oedema was simply referred to as 'Number Two Disease'.

Emmanuel John Hevi, an African student studying medicine in Beijing during the famine, records how his teachers claimed that the Chinese are physiologically different from the rest of humanity. His American-trained biology professor gave a lecture on the metabolism and explained that 'because proteins, fats and carbohydrates are inter-convertible during human metabolic processes, the people of China do not suffer any nutritional loss in consequence of their diet's deficiency in fats and proteins'. As Hevi comments, 'She was not telling us what she knew to be a fact but rather what she had been ordered to tell us as a political necessity . . . Faced with a shortage of protein and fats, the Party declares that these things are no longer necessary but are luxuries which the Chinese people can well do without.'[5]

Fortunately, one authoritative medical description of the reality behind such nonsense has been written by Dr Benjamin Lee who now works in the Department of Pediatrics at the Louisiana State University Medical Center.[6] In 1958 he was sentenced as a rightist and spent the next four years on the Sino-Russian border in Heilongjiang province at the Lake Xingkai state farm. There he took notes of the effects of the famine on over 5,000 prisoners. Although Dr Lee only recorded what happened to camp inmates, his description applies equally well to millions of others outside the camps:

> An inmate would become malnourished within a few weeks of arrival. Usually, the first sign of severe malnutrition in a prisoner was incontinence. However little water he had drunk, the victim would find himself having to urinate one or even two pints of colourless fluid a night. Prisoners had to get up at one- to three-hour intervals and, even more humiliating in crowded cells, they would often pee in their pants before they made it to a pot or the latrines. Some gripped their penis to try and stop themselves.

> Equally degrading was the way in which the starving lost control over their bowels, developing acute diarrhoea. Their stools would become milky and jelly-like, and often bloody. Terminal cases excreted reddish brown watery faeces in large

quantities. Food would pass through the intestine within an hour, often without undergoing any change. Victims would also suffer from severe flatulence and at night they would sweat so severely that their bedclothes would become drenched.

The outside of the body would also change. In a third of the inmates, big patches of brown skin appeared, especially at the elbows, the spine, the feet and thighs. Some long-term prisoners found the skin inside their cheeks drying up and turning green. The skin would also fissure, creating crevasses in the hands and feet which became infected. The skin became particularly painful at the fingertips and the sides of the nails. Often the first sign of malnutrition was the appearance of fine parallel yellowish lines which appeared on the fingernails. The upper nail would flatten out and become thin and brittle, while the lower part turned thick and soft like dirty rubber. Sometimes the nails bled, causing intolerable pain. As they weakened, prisoners found that they could no longer make fine movements with their fingers and the tendons around the wrists became inflamed.

Starvation also changed the body in other ways. Large joints, like the shoulder, moved with a dull clanging noise. Joints thickened and became enlarged. Even the cartilage at the end of the nose thickened so that the bridge of the nose widened into a crest. Much the same thing happened to the sternum. Other parts also swelled in strange ways. In some prisoners, the parotid glands under the neck and in front of the ears grew to the size of a hamburger. Others complained of swellings behind the knees, or at lymph nodes in the groin or under the arms. Veins in the eyeballs hardened and became inflamed. Fissures in the teeth appeared. In some cases, the chest collapsed and became compressed like a child's rib-cage to half or even a third of its normal extent.

Most inmates suffered from a terrible hacking cough. One former inmate said that this condition became worse at night when he would cough continuously, unable to catch his breath: 'My chest cavity seemed to have been packed with dynamite – explosion after explosion would erupt from within me.' Many famine victims also fell into a high fever with severe headaches and cramps. High blood pressure, hypertension and bradycardia, when the heart beats very slowly, became common, while broken bones did not heal but swelled up dangerously.

Dr Lee could always tell when a prisoner was going to die. He would lose his appetite, the skin around his swollen body would turn translucent and his face would become corpse-like. However, the actual manner of death varied. Some would suddenly drop dead of heart failure while out walking or after dinner. Others died in a general convulsion. A few would begin to spit massive amounts of blood from their lungs as if they had severe pneumonia; or they would show signs of suffering from severe jaundice because their liver had failed. Often, death was heralded by violent diarrhoea after which the patient would collapse in a coma. When the authorities began to replace real food with food substitutes, many prisoners also died from perforation of the intestine.

Dr Lee's observations are borne out by others who survived the camps. Harry Wu noted that 'The heart does not stop beating from lack of nourishment. Depending on your overall health, you can survive for a week, even two, with no food or water at all. In such a depleted state, it is other things that kill you. Sometimes you catch cold, your lungs fill with fluid, finally you stop breathing. Sometimes bacteria in the food cause continuous diarrhoea that leads to death. Sometimes infection from a wound becomes fatal. The cause of death is always in your file as pleurisy or food poisoning or injury, never as starvation.'

Dr Tensing Choedak, while in the Jiuzhen prison camp in the Tenger Desert, Gansu, observed that in the first stage of starvation 'one and all resembled living skeletons. Ribs, hips and shin bones protruded, chests were concave, eyes bulged, teeth were loose, black hair turned russet, then beige and then fell out.'[7] Prisoners' eyes also weakened and they lost the ability to see properly at night. This stage was followed by oedema, and inmates like Harry Wu quickly learned what would happen next: 'For the first time I saw a person with one leg swollen and the other thin as a stick. I began to recognise the symptoms of oedema. First someone's foot would swell so that he could not wear his shoe. Slowly the swelling moved up through the ankle, the calf, the knee, the thigh. When it reached the stomach and made breathing difficult, a person died quickly.'[8]

A professor of English, Wu Ningkun, describes in *A Single Tear* his feelings of horror as he realizes his own body is changing: 'I was the first to come down with a serious case of oedema. I became emaciated, my ankles swelled and my legs got so weak that I often fell while walking to the fields for forced labour. I did not know what I looked like as there were no mirrors around but I could tell from the ghastly looks of the other inmates that I must have been quite a sight.'[9]

Children came down with the same symptoms even in the cities. In *A Mother's Ordeal*, Chi An, who was then a small girl in Shenyang, the provincial capital of Liaoning province, describes what happened to her family:

With the exception of the baby, all of us swelled up and turned a whiteish yellow, like pale turnips. We had so much fluid under our skin that if we cut ourselves, we no longer bled. Instead of blood, little beads of faintly pink liquid would ooze out. A scab never formed, and even the smallest scrape took a long time to heal.

In Ningxia province far to the west, prisoners believed that once the swelling reached the head, a person was doomed: 'The person soon resembled a balloon that had been filled full of air – the eyes would swell so that they became small slits: light couldn't penetrate them and one could not see out. But simple, straightforward oedema could still not be described as a death mask. If the skin on the part that was swelling began to split and a yellow glandular fluid oozed out, then death was not far away.'[10]

All remarked that in the final stage a person would develop this 'mask' which signalled that death must follow in a day or two. In *Grass Soup*, Zhang Xianliang describes this phenomenon vividly:

Needless to say, men with such death masks were emaciated. In addition, the skin of their faces and entire bodies turned a dull, dark colour; their hair looked dried-out and scorched: the mucus of their eyes increased but the eyes themselves became exceedingly, strangely bright. They emitted a 'thief's glare', a kind of shifty, scared yet crafty, debilitated but also poisonous light. No one felt afraid when they saw it though, for they knew that their own eyes were not much different.

A similar description comes in *Red in Tooth and Claw*, in which Han Weitian recalls, 'If you saw us, you would find each face starved into a pale mask, without flesh or life. Such faces were little different from those of the departed. No matter its shape, the face of the starvation victim is covered by only a fragile layer of skin. The eyes are hardly eyes but rather the pits of nuts fitted into sockets of bone. Such eyes shed no light.'

Strangely enough, people appeared to get better just before the end. Harry Wu was surprised by this when he watched the death of his friend Ma, a peasant arrested for stealing grain to feed his family. 'I had watched the swelling travel up Ma's body. His skin stretched so tight it became bright and smooth like glass. During his last days he seemed to experience increased energy and cheerfulness. His thin pale face regained some rosy colour. I later recognised those changes as typical of the last days of oedema. "The last redness of the setting sun" we said.'

Although all these descriptions of oedema come from writings about prison camps, peasants in villages in Anhui and Henan and just outside Beijing gave me identical descriptions. One man who grew up in Fengtai, a suburb of Beijing, recalled that as a child he knew that those people around him with heads swollen from oedema were certain to die within weeks.

Incredibly, some people did come back from the dead. When I was in a village in Anhui, a woman pointed to a man working outside, saying that he had literally returned from death. As a boy of about 9 during the famine, his family had given him up for dead but then someone forced some nourishing soup down his throat and he recovered. In some instances, even prisoners taken away for burial recovered. This happened to the Tibetan Ama Adhe, as she relates in *A Strange Liberation*:

My condition deteriorated, until finally I couldn't even walk. I would just sit there, maybe saying mantras. And one night I felt that my nose was getting very cold . . . I thought maybe it is my turn to die of starvation . . . the next morning I heard rushing water like a waterfall or a stream. And when I looked up, I saw that I had been thrown into the wooden cage that they built to hold the dead bodies. I realised where I was and I felt so sad, and I made a final prayer to His Holiness and the triple gem. Then the workers came round to carry away these corpses, and when they saw me they yelled out, 'Hey, this one has her eyes open!' And I was carried back to my cell.

Han Weitian was actually taken to the morgue in his labour camp: 'There were times when I sensed I was at last parting from the world. It was not a sense of pain, but only a feeling of yielding. The ache of hunger induced a feeling of suffocation so keen that one day I suddenly lost consciousness. I was later told that after I had passed out they found I had stopped breathing and was stiff and cold.' A friend of his who was the camp doctor came to hear of what had happened and went to examine him in the morgue. Han had already been lying there for half an hour when the doctor arrived. At first, the doctor failed to detect any sign of life but then, using a stethoscope, he heard faint breathing and brought Han to a fireside where he administered an injection and fed him some thin lukewarm gruel. Miraculously, Han recovered. Dr Lee, too, managed to save several patients on the point of death by injecting them with thiamine, a form of vitamin B1.

Living on the verge of death produced a strange state of mind, as Han Weitian recalls:

In those years, starvation became a sort of mental manacle, depriving us of our freedom to think. We could not for a moment forget its threat. It seemed to be continuously putrefying the air and making it difficult to breathe ... it is strange that hunger can cause so much pain in your body. It seems like a vice pinching all your bones which feel dislocated for lack of flesh and sinews. Your head, hands, feet, even your belly and bowels are no longer where they normally are. You are tempted to cry out loud but haven't the strength. When experiencing extreme hunger, one can barely utter an audible sound.

In *Grass Soup*, Zhang Xianliang remembers the feeling of suffocation:

This problem was not a result of some illness of the central respiratory system nor was it caused by injury to the head or lung disease. The fatigue of my body simply led to an exhaustion of my lungs as if they were too worn out to work. I often did forget to breathe and found that I would suddenly be dizzy, with pricks of light behind my eyes. Darkness would rise up before me as I fell over. Later I became accustomed to remembering to take in oxygen.

The final moment of death was often peaceful. The Tibetan Tenpa Soepa remarked: 'Dying from hunger can actually be an easy way to die. Not very painful. People would be sitting, and then fall over and die. No moans of agony.'[11] Dr Choedak also noticed how calm the final moments were. People lay immobile on the *kang* and then 'their breath became softer and more shallow until, at the last moment, bubbles of saliva slipped over their lips and they died'.[12]

Many were not so fortunate and died painfully from the food substitutes which were introduced in 1960 and 1961. At times 80 per cent of the food served to prisoners was made up of substitutes. Such substances split the digestive tract or the sphincter. Outside the prisons people died in the same way. Like the prisoners, the peasants ate tree bark, corncobs, the chaff from soybeans, sorghum, wheat and other grains, ground-up roots and corn stalks. They also ate large amounts of grasses and weeds and anything else they could find which looked edible. This was all collected and thrown into the pot – the grass soup of Zhang's book. Tenpa Soepa, who like many others survived by eating wild grass, noticed that 'if you looked in the toilet it didn't look like a human being's toilet. All the stools were green from the grass and undigested leaves.'

Some prisoners were even fed sawdust and wood pulp. Jean Pasqualini describes in *Prisoner of Mao* what happened in the Lake Xingkai camp in Heilongjiang in 1960. Dark brown sheets of the stuff arrived at the kitchens:

We prisoners had the honour of being the guinea pigs for the various ersatzes the scientific community came up with. The warder describing the new nutritional policy told us that paper pulp was guaranteed harmless and though it contained no nutritive value, it would make our *wo'tous* fatter and give us the satisfying impression of bulk. The new flour mix would be no more than thirty per cent powdered paper pulp. It will go through your digestive tracts easily, he said with assurance. We know exactly how you will feel.

The experiment led to mass constipation and a number of deaths among older and weaker prisoners. The wood pulp was abandoned although the government also tried out another variety of food substitute on the prisoners – marsh-water plankton.

They skimmed the slimy, green stuff off the swampy ponds around the camp and mixed it in with the mush either straight or dried and powdered, since it tasted too horrible to eat unaccompanied. Again we all fell sick and some of the weaker ones died. That particular plankton, they discovered after a few autopsies, was practically unassimilative for the human body. End of plankton experiment. At length our daily ersatz became ground corncobs, mixed in with the *wo'tou* flour. Afterwards it was adopted as the standard food supplement for the country at large.

In the countryside people also ate the straw of their huts, the cotton in their coats or mattresses, tree leaves and blossoms, and the feathers of ducks and chickens. Prisoners recounted how they chewed their shoes and boots, belts, coats and anything else made of leather. In Lanzhou, people actually raided the local tanneries for leather to eat.

The worst substitute of all derived from an ancient and mistaken belief that eating compounds of earth and weeds would fill up one's stomach and provide enormous endurance. This soil was known as 'Buddha's soil' or 'Guanyin soil', Guanyin being the goddess of mercy. In Gansu, peasants boiled the soil before eating it. One doctor recalls how he went to a Gansu village where the entire population, 800 in all, had died after eating Guanyin soil.[13] When the medical team dissected some of the corpses, they found the soil had blocked up the intestine and it could not be digested or excreted. Another doctor, working elsewhere in China, believes such a practice was common:

People mixed it [the Guanyin soil] with corn flour and the bread made of this mixture was edible and, more important, very filling. As the news spread, tens of thousands of people copied this invention. But once in the stomach, the soil dried out all the moisture in the colon and the patients could not defecate for days. I had to open up their stomachs. I did this operation on about fourteen people every day. Many people never made it to the hospital and others died on the operating table. I had a note typed out and took it to the street committees in the district around the hospital. I saw people dropping dead with my own eyes. Nobody was interested in what I had to tell them. All they thought about was food.[14]

Those in the cities were driven to forage for food like the survivors of some apocalyptic disaster. In *Son of the Revolution*, Liang Heng describes his childhood in Changsha, Hunan: 'I grew accustomed to going with my sisters to the Martyr's Park to pull up a kind of edible wild grass that could be made into a paste with broken grains of rice and steamed and eaten as "bittercakes". Gradually, even this became scarce and we had to walk miles to distant suburbs to find any.'[15] Far to the north in Shenyang, Chi An made pancakes out of leaves picked from the poplars which lined the streets. The leaves were soaked overnight to remove tannic acid, then dipped in flour and browned in a wok without oil.

The smell of these leaf pancakes frying made my mouth water, but they didn't taste nearly as good as they looked. Despite the soaking, the poplar leaves retained an acid bite that made my salivary glands scream in protest. The worst part was the constipation they brought on. A day after Mother added them to our diet, we stopped having bowel movements. For a week after that, we felt increasingly bloated and crampy. Finally mother told us we would have to dig the hard little balls of faeces out with our fingers. My brother and I were too hungry to mind very much, though; we continued to devour the pancakes without protest.[16]

In the desperate search for food many died from eating poisonous mushrooms, berries or leaves. A doctor who worked in one city hospital said that the emergency department was filled with people who had eaten poisonous wild vegetables.

Alcoholics, unable to satisfy their addiction, also died from drinking methanol, industrial alcohol and any number of other substitutes. To stop people from eating seeds after they were sown, the leaders of some communes and labour camps had the seeds dipped in poison. Sometimes scavenging children died from eating them.[17]

Overeating could also kill. When better food became available at harvest time or after 1962, people ate more than their enfeebled digestive systems could cope with. Han Weitian has estimated that 2,000 fellow prisoners died from 'gourmandizing' in his camp in Qinghai. Prisoners there tried to build up their health by eating in a single sitting up to eighteen loaves of a black bread made out of pea powder. Then they returned to their heavy work: 'They more often than not ended up with stomach-aches. Some of these greedy eaters simply died in the field from violent stomach-aches. Such victims howled with pain while holding their swollen bellies.' One interviewee in Sichuan, who had been sent as a rightist to Ya'an, a poor region in the mountains west of Chengdu, recalls how many peasants died of overeating at the Spring Festival in 1962. On this rare occasion the peasants could fill their bellies with dumplings made of wheat and beans but their digestive systems broke down, often with fatal results. Even a medical team sent to treat famine victims in Gansu killed many patients by giving them too much food.

Since no one was permitted to acknowledge the reality of the famine, medical efforts to deal with the crisis were doomed to failure. Even in the hospitals in major cities, doctors were provided with few resources. Since they themselves were often starving, they could not stand up to the strain. At times as many as a third of the staff of one Beijing hospital were off sick. The one remedy available to doctors was to recommend a special diet for their patients. Those who contracted tuberculosis, which was very common, were given extra coupons to buy two ounces of sugar a month as well as milk and pig's liver.

Prolonged starvation left lasting effects on its victims. Many children developed rickets. A few became mentally retarded. Most found themselves to be shorter and smaller than normal when they matured. Several interviewees who had been young children during the famine claimed that they were six inches shorter than they would otherwise have been. Very few women were able to have children during the famine. A large proportion stopped menstruating because of the lack of protein in their diet. Some students sent down to the countryside said that they stopped menstruating for as long as five years. Women who did give birth often died because they did not stop bleeding. Mothers who survived found that they could not produce enough milk to feed their babies. Statistics from Fengyang in Anhui also reveal that many women suffered from prolapse of the uterus, the collapse of the womb. Those female peasants who were forced to work in the paddy fields also contracted infections from spending long periods up to their waists in water.

Even when in early 1961 medical teams were sent to some of the worst-affected areas in the countryside, the fiction about the famine was maintained. One doctor who spent three months on a relief mission in Gansu recalls that the Party organized a meeting on their return at which they were warned not to talk of the deaths they had witnessed. A Party official insisted that not a single death had occurred and that to deny this would constitute treason.[18]

14

Cannibalism

'I take a look at history: it is not a record of
time but on each page are confusedly written
the characters "benevolence, righteousness,
and morals". Desperately unsleeping, I carefully look over it again and again for half the
night, and at last find between the lines that
it is full of the same words – "cannibalism!"'
Lu Xun, *Diary of a Madman*, 1918

WHEN, 2,000 YEARS ago, the Han dynasty was established
amidst enormous upheaval, it was recorded that nearly half the
people in the empire died of starvation. This prompted the
founding emperor Gao Zu to issue an official edict in 205 BC
authorizing people to sell or eat their children if necessary.
Over two millennia later his words were still being obeyed in
Anhui. There, peasants practised a tradition of swopping their
children with those of their neighbours to alleviate their
hunger and to avoid consuming their own offspring. Villagers
in Anhui described this practice in a phrase of classical Chinese
– *i tzu erh shih*, or *yi zi er shi* in the modern pinyin spelling –
that dates back still further.[1] Nothing better demonstrates the
remarkable continuity of Chinese culture than the fact that
this phrase was first employed 2,500 years ago. In May 594 BC,
the Chu army besieged the Song capital. Eventually its starving
inhabitants sorrowfully recorded that 'in the city, we are
exchanging our children and eating them, and splitting up
their bones for fuel'.

During the famine of the Great Leap Forward, peasants killed

and ate their children in many parts of China. In *Wild Swans,*
Jung Chang recounts the story told by a senior Party official
about an incident in Sichuan:

> One day a peasant burst into his room and threw himself on
> the floor, screaming that he had committed a terrible crime and
> begging to be punished. Eventually it came out that he had killed
> his own baby and eaten it. Hunger had been like an uncontrollable
> force driving him to take up the knife. With tears rolling down his
> cheeks, the official ordered the peasant to be arrested. Later he
> was shot as a warning to baby killers.

At the other end of the country, in Liaoning province, the
Shenyang provincial Party newspapers also reported cases of
cannibalism. In *A Mother's Ordeal,* a classmate of Chi An, whose
story it tells, records what happened in her own hamlet:

> A peasant woman, unable to stand the incessant crying for food
> of her two-year-old daughter, and perhaps thinking to end her
> suffering, had strangled her. She had given the girl's body to her
> husband, asking him to bury it. Instead, out of his mind with
> hunger, he had put the body into the cooking pot with what little
> food they had foraged. He had forced his wife to eat a bowl of the
> resulting stew. His wife, in a fit of remorse, had reported her
> husband's crime to the authorities. The fact that she voluntarily
> came forward to confess made no difference. Although there was
> no law against cannibalism in the criminal code of the People's
> Republic, the Ministry of Public Security treated such cases, which
> were all too common, with the utmost severity. Both husband and
> wife were arrested and summarily executed.[2]

In interviews, peasants readily acknowledged that they had
witnessed cannibalism at first hand. 'It was nothing exceptional,' a local official told me in Anhui, while in Sichuan the
former head of a village production team said he thought it
had happened 'in every county and most villages'. Official Party
documents bear this out. In one county in southern Henan,
Gushi, the authorities recorded 200 cases of cannibalism in a
population of 900,000 at the start of the famine. In Anhui's
Fengyang county, with 335,000 people in 1958, the Party noted

63 cases of cannibalism in one commune alone. Interviewees also spoke of cannibalism occurring in Shaanxi, Ningxia and Hebei provinces. Former inmates of labour camps personally witnessed cases of cannibalism in camps in Tibet, Qinghai, Gansu and Heilongjiang. In the Qinghai prison camps, prisoners regularly cut the flesh off corpses and sold or ate it. Outside the camps, it was the same. A Tibetan peasant from Tongren county in Qinghai remembers that among the youths from Henan who were settled there, one girl killed an 8-year-old child and ate the corpse with three others. All four were arrested. In another case, a Tibetan family was caught eating the flesh from a child's corpse.

There are enough reports from different parts of the country to make it clear that the practice of cannibalism was not restricted to any one region, class or nationality. Peasants not only ate the flesh of the dead, they also sold it, and they killed and ate children, both their own and those of others. Given the dimensions of the famine, it is quite conceivable that cannibalism was practised on a scale unprecedented in the history of the twentieth century. Moreover, it took place with the knowledge of a government which is still in power and which wields considerable influence over world affairs. This startling fact is all the more plausible when one looks at the documented history of cannibalism in China and other parts of the world.

In the West, cannibalism is considered the ultimate taboo, the worst act of savagery, but it is far from unknown. Greek literature and the records of ancient Egypt frequently mention famine-related cannibalism. In Western Europe it often occurred during famines and the wartime sieges of the sixteenth and seventeenth centuries. In this century, two major incidents of recorded cannibalism in the West stand out: those in the Nazi concentration camps and in the Ukraine.

At the trial of the Treblinka concentration camp commandant after the Second World War, a former British internee testified that while clearing away dead bodies, he and his staff noted that a piece of flesh was missing from as many as one in ten cadavers:

> I noticed on many occasions a very strange wound at the back of the thigh of many of the dead. First of all I dismissed it as a gunshot

wound at close quarters but after seeing a few more I asked a
friend and he told me that many of the prisoners were cutting
chunks out of the bodies to eat. On my next visit to the mortuary
I actually saw a prisoner whip out a knife, cut a portion of the leg
of a dead body, and put it quickly into his mouth.[3]

The cannibalism which occurred during the Ukrainian
famine of 1932–3 has closer parallels with China during the
Great Leap Forward. Faced with an almost identical set of circumstances, Ukrainian peasants behaved much as the Chinese
were to do nearly thirty years later. The Italian Consul in the
then capital of Kharkov wrote in June 1933 to his embassy in
Moscow that 'at present some 300 cases of cannibalism have
been brought before a tribunal in Kharkov. Doctors of my
acquaintance have noticed human flesh on sale at the market
place.'[4]

An eyewitness who testified in an inquiry into the famine
held by the US Congress in 1988 said that 'if a person was
selling meat, the police would immediately seize the meat to
check if it was human or dog meat. There were people who
had no qualms about cutting off a piece of flesh from a dead
body which they would sell in order to get money for bread.'
Cannibalism was so common that the secret police, the OGPU,
issued instructions on how to deal with it. In May 1933 the
Vice-Commissar of the OGPU and the chief procurator of the
Ukraine told their subordinates:

> The present criminal code does not cover punishment of persons
> guilty of cannibalism, therefore all cases of those accused of canni-
> balism must immediately be transferred to the local branches of
> the OGPU. If cannibalism was preceded by murder, covered by
> article 142 of the Penal Code, these cases should be withdrawn
> from the courts and from the prosecution divisions of the People's
> Commissariat of Justice system and transferred for judgement to
> the Collegium of the OGPU in Moscow.[5]

The Italian Consul reported a number of cases in which
parents were arrested for infanticide and subsequently went
mad:

Very frequent is the phenomenon of hallucination in which people see their children only as animals, kill them and eat them. Later, some, having recuperated with proper food, do not remember wanting to eat their children and deny even being able to think of such a thing. The phenomenon in question is the result of a lack of vitamins and would prove to be a very interesting study, alas one which is banned even from consideration from a scientific point of view.[6]

Such terrible thoughts were prompted by a famine in which over 5 million died. Yet the Ukraine has some of the richest agricultural land in the world and famine there, although not unknown, was rare. By contrast, famine was such a regular occurrence throughout Chinese history that there existed a sort of 'famine culture' passed down through the generations. As many observers quoted in Chapter 1 pointed out, people knew what sort of wild vegetation could be eaten, what should be sold first to raise money and which members of a family should be sacrificed before others. Anhui peasants even believed that they knew how to detect cannibalism – those who ate human flesh smelt strange and their eyes and skin turned red.

The consumption of human flesh in China was not, however, limited to times of famine. Indeed one authority on the subject has concluded that cannibalism holds a unique place in Chinese culture and that the Chinese 'have admired the practice of cannibalism for centuries'. The American academic Kay Ray Chong has found numerous references to the practice in Chinese historical records and literature as well as in medical texts. In *Cannibalism in China*, published in 1990, Chong looked at cannibalism under two main headings: 'survival' cannibalism which took place as a last resort; and 'learned' cannibalism undertaken for other reasons. It is the latter which sets the Chinese apart. They are, he writes, 'quite unique in the sense [that] there are so many examples of learned cannibalism throughout their history'. In many periods of Chinese history, human flesh was considered a delicacy. In ancient times, cooks prepared exotic dishes of human flesh for jaded upper-class palates. Enough accounts of the various methods used to cook human flesh have been preserved for Chong to devote a whole chapter to them. For example, a Yuan dynasty writer, Dao Qingyi, recommends in *Chuo geng lu* (*Records of Stopping Cultivation*) that children's meat is the best-tasting food and proposes eating children whole, including their bones. He refers to men and women as 'two-legged sheep' and considers women's meat even more delicious than mutton.

Chinese literature is filled with accounts of Epicurean cannibalism. One of China's most famous works of literature, *Shui hu zhuan*, or *The Water Margin* (also translated as *Outlaws of the Marsh* and *All Men are Brothers*), contains frequent references to the sale of human meat and descriptions of cannibalism. Cooking methods are described in graphic detail. For example, when one of the main characters, Wu Sung, visits a wine shop, he is led into a room 'where men were cut to pieces, and on the walls there were men's skins stretched tight and nailed there, and upon the beams of the roof there hung several legs of men'.

Human flesh was regarded as part food, part medicine. In 1578, Li Shizhen published a medical reference book (*Ben cao gang mu*, or *Materia Medica*) which listed thirty-five different parts or organs, and the various diseases and ailments that they could be used to treat. Some parts of the body were especially valued because they were thought to boost sexual stamina. In the Ming dynasty, powerful eunuchs tried to regain their sexual potency by eating young men's brains. During the last Chinese dynasty, the Qing, numerous Western accounts testified to the Chinese belief that drinking human blood would increase a man's sexual appetite. Whenever a public execution took place, women whose husbands were impotent would buy bread dipped in the fresh blood of the executed. As late as the nineteenth century, it was not unusual for Chinese executioners to eat the heart and brains of criminals.

Cannibalism was also a gesture of filial piety. Records from the Song dynasty (AD 420–79) talk of how people would cut off part of their own body to feed a revered elder. Often a daughter-in-law would cut flesh from her leg or thigh to make soup to feed a sick mother-in-law and this practice became so common that the state issued an edict forbidding it.

Throughout Chinese history, cannibalism was also extremely common in times of war. Not only was it the last resort of inhabitants trapped in besieged cities or fortresses, but in addition, prisoners of war or slain enemies often became a staple source of food. Under the Emperor Wu Di (AD 502–49) prisoners were purchased in cages. When there was a demand for meat, they would be taken out, killed, broiled and consumed. During the Yellow Turban rebellion in the Tang dynasty (AD 618–907), thousands were butchered and eaten every day. A century later Wang Yancheng of the Min kingdom was said to have salted and dried the corpses of enemy soldiers which his men would take with them as supplies.

Such practices continued into modern times. During the Taiping rebellion of 1850–64, the hearts of prisoners were consumed by both sides to make them more bold in combat. Human flesh and organs were openly sold in the marketplace during this period and people were kidnapped and killed for food. Chinese soldiers stationed on Taiwan before the Sino-Japanese War of 1894–5 also bought and ate the flesh of aborigines in the marketplace.

Cannibalism is also an expression of revenge and was recommended by Confucius. It was not enough, he said, to observe the mourning period for a parent murdered or killed in suspicious circumstances. Heaven would praise those who took revenge. Killing alone, however, was not sufficient. Enemies should be entirely consumed, including their bones, meat, heart and liver. Chinese historical records are littered with examples of kings and emperors who killed and ate their enemies, among them some of the greatest figures, such as the Emperor Qinshihuangdi, who first unified China. Liu Bang, the founder of the succeeding Han dynasty, distributed small pieces of his enemies for his vassals to consume as a way of testing their loyalty. Traitors were chopped up and pickled. In some cases, the victor of a struggle would force his enemy to eat a soup made from his son or father. Even buried enemies were not safe.

Little had changed by the nineteenth century. James Dyer Ball in *Things Chinese* recorded what happened when Cantonese villagers fell out over water rights in 1895. After armed clashes, the prisoners who had been taken were killed. Then their hearts and livers were distributed and eaten, even young children being allowed to participate in the feast. During the civil war between the Communists and the Nationalists in the 1940s, there are also recorded instances when prisoners were killed and eaten in revenge.

Under Communist rule, cannibalism to obtain revenge continued, notably during the Cultural Revolution in Guangxi province in the far south of China. According to official documents obtained by the Chinese writer Zheng Yi, in some schools students killed their principals in the school courtyard and then cooked and ate their bodies to celebrate a triumph over 'counter-revolutionaries'. Government-run cafeterias in the province are said to have displayed bodies dangling on meat hooks and to have served human flesh to employees. One document relates that 'There are many varieties of cannibalism and among them are these: killing someone and making a big dinner of it, slicing off the meat and having a big party, dividing up the flesh so each person takes a large chunk home to boil, roasting the liver and eating it for its medicinal properties, and so on.'[7]

The documents obtained by Zheng Yi suggest that at least 137 people, and probably hundreds more, were eaten in Guangxi. The cannibalism was organized by local Communist Party officials and people took part to prove their revolutionary ardour. In one case, the first person to strip the body of a school principal was the former girlfriend of the principal's son. She wanted to show that she had no sympathy with him and was just as 'red' as anyone else. Harry Wu, in *Laogai: The Chinese Gulag*, records a similar incident while he was at the Wang Zhuang coal-mine in Shanxi. A prisoner called Yang Baoyin was summarily executed by firing squad for writing the words 'Overthrow Chairman Mao' and his brains were eaten by a Public Security cadre.

In *Cannibalism in China*, Chong concludes that cannibalism probably occurred on a massive scale in times of great convulsions. There is every reason to believe that this also holds true for the Great Leap Forward, a dark and secret legacy of China's ancient culture which few inside or outside China wish to confront. This chapter began with an extract from a short story by one of the most famous twentieth-century Chinese writers, Lu Xun. Since it is written in the style of Nietzsche,

Western readers assume it is allegorical, but Chinese readers would surely read it as a tirade against the unchanging realities of life in China.

15

Life in the Cities

'There were tens of thousands of people
roaming the streets and looking for food.
When you sat down to eat . . . all these people
would be watching you.'

Interviewee, Chengdu

THE GULF BETWEEN town and country in China is so wide
that most city-dwellers were only dimly aware that people were
dying in the countryside during the famine. One member of a
group of Shanghai students who went on holiday to Gansu to
visit the sites of the Silk Road at the height of the famine
recalled that when they saw emaciated wretches dying in the
streets they simply assumed that this was normal. Even the
journalist Zhu Hong, wife of the dissident Liu Binyan, failed
to grasp that millions were starving to death in Sichuan when
in 1960 she was sent to Chongqing to research an article about
the spirit of self-reliance. And a former student in Beijing is
still stricken with guilt because he encouraged his girlfriend to
go back to her home in the countryside since he was worried
that she was losing weight. Months later a letter arrived
informing him that she had starved to death.[1]

The barriers separating the 90 million people privileged to
live in the cities and the rest of the population – around 500
million – went up within a few years of the Communist victory
in 1949. The state undertook to provide those living in the
cities with food, housing and clothing. With the introduction
of food rationing, the corollary measure, the internal passport,

became essential. This ensured that anyone registered as living in a village could not enter a city without permission and could not obtain state grain rations. Urban or rural status was determined at birth and was usually hereditary. In effect, the state had reduced the majority of China's population to the level of passport-holders from a separate and foreign country.

In the Soviet Union, Stalin had introduced the internal passport in 1932, as a way of dealing with the consequences of the famine. Without urban residency, starving peasants seeking food were turned back or arrested by militia posted at railway stations and checkpoints on all roads leading into the cities. The system served the same purpose in China and the results won praise from foreign visitors in the 1950s. They were no longer troubled by the sight of beggars and starving wretches on the streets of wealthy Shanghai as they had been before 1949, a sight which had come to symbolize the immorality of capitalism. Chinese city-dwellers, too, appreciated the change. Fixed rations brought security because the state would feed them no matter how bad the harvests were.

Within the cities, not everyone received the same rations. Urban society was carefully stratified and high status was rewarded with higher rations. As in imperial times, a member of the state apparatus was graded on a scale from 1 to 24, according to his or her political loyalty; and depending on his or her grade, each individual was allocated one of three kinds of ration books. In all cases, women were given lower rations than men. Those in the top grades, from 1 to 13, were entitled to the largest grain rations and in addition received 4 lbs (or *catties*) of pork, sugar, eggs and yellow beans, and four boxes of cigarettes a month. Second-class people received less grain, no sugar and half as much pork, eggs and beans. Those in the bottom class were given no pork or eggs, but one box of cigarettes and 2 lbs of yellow beans. Other food and goods could be bought in the marketplace with the pocket money given as wages, but during the Great Leap Forward the city markets were closed down.[2]

In the push towards Communism, the number of goods distributed by the rationing system grew and grew. Cloth, cotton, matches, soap, candles, needles, thread, cooking oil, wood, paper, coal and other fuels, fish, meat, beancurd and so on could only be acquired with coupons. The soap ration was one bar per month and in some places a ticket was necessary to obtain hot water or a bath.

This rationing system was complicated still further by the fact that some coupons were only valid in a certain province, city, county or commune. Local ration tickets often became worthless if they were not used within a month, a measure designed to prevent hoarding or trading. Other goods such as biscuits could be purchased with cash but only if accompanied by a voucher. The most precious tender was a national grain ticket because it could be used to obtain food anywhere and it amounted in effect to an alternative currency. A national voucher for a pound of grain was worth 2.5 to 3 yuan but in famine-stricken regions such vouchers became more treasured than gold. City-dwellers sometimes answered appeals from rural relatives by posting them grain vouchers but joy would turn to despair when, as sometimes happened, the recipients discovered that no grain could be obtained at any price.

As China moved to realize full Communism, the urban rationing system began to break down. As happened during the Soviet Union's first five-year plan, China's Great Leap Forward was accompanied by a massive internal migration of labourers to man the hastily erected factories or help finish crash building projects. In Beijing, ten huge building projects, including the Great Hall of the People in Tiananmen Square, were completed in time to celebrate the tenth anniversary of the Communist victory in 1959. The sudden extra burden of these tens of millions of additional mouths imposed an immense and intolerable strain on the rationing system. According to statistics released in 1985, the urban population of China doubled from 99.4 million in 1957 to 187.2 million in 1958. If these figures are reliable, a staggering 87 million peasants took part in the greatest organized migration in Chinese history. Other sources suggest a much lower but still impressive total of 30 million.[3] (It is possible that the larger statistic indicates that 87 million people received state grain for working in the cities *and* on various dams and other public works in the countryside.)

At the end of 1959, as the famine deepened, most of these peasants were sent home. A further 10 million went back to the countryside in 1960 when the Party began to empty the cities to lessen the burden on state grain stores. This mass movement in and out of the cities makes it difficult to interpret official statistics on urban birth and death rates. Chinese statistics purport to show that there were no 'excess deaths' in the cities during the famine although the birth rate halved and the death rate rose steeply. These figures are contradicted by interviewees who made it clear that many *did* die of hunger but over a shorter time span than in the countryside.

In the cities, the gravest food shortages began in the winter of 1959. Shenyang, capital of Liaoning province, abandoned monthly food rations in late 1959 and stopped issuing cooking oil in early 1960 when all vegetables, including the ubiquitous winter cabbage, vanished from the shops.[4] The same was true in most other cities where, by the spring of 1960, there was nothing but grain to eat. At that time the grain ration began to be cut. In Shenyang, the authorities reduced the adult grain ration from at least 28 lbs to just over 13 lbs a month. Children received half as much. In Beijing's universities, male students who normally received top-grade rations saw their monthly allotment dwindle from 33 lbs a month to 26 lbs and then still less. (Rations for female students fell from 28 lbs to 22 lbs.) A former student of the Beijing Institute for National Minorities, Tsering Dorje Gashi, recalled the effect this had: 'Students' monthly ration fell to 22 lbs of food grain. No matter how carefully the students eked out their food, their ration would stretch to at most 25 days. For the remaining 6 to 7 days, the students had to survive on spinach, leaves or anything remotely resembling vegetables. Such a miserable diet drained both health and strength.'[5]

A diet consisting of nothing but a pound of cereals a day contains only 1,600 calories. As has been noted, this is a starvation diet which causes weight loss and eventually oedema from a lack of protein. Those with a lower status and those living in smaller cities had still less to eat. In Anhui, people living in the town of Fengyang had a monthly grain ration of 22 lbs in 1960 supplemented with 6 lbs of food substitutes.[6] As in other provincial cities, rice and other good-quality grains soon disappeared. In Fengyang, the town's granary switched to bean powder and finally to flour made from dried sweet potatoes. Not all parts of the city benefited even from this. One place with four communal canteens serving a thousand people provided nothing but food substitutes. In Xining, the capital of Qinghai, a province filled with state farms worked by convicts, the adult monthly grain ration fell to as low as 13.6 lbs per month.[7]

Shanghai seems to have had a better supply of food even than the capital, Beijing. Throughout the famine, Nien Cheng, who worked for the Shell Oil company and would later write *Life and Death in Shanghai*, received a grain ration of 40 lbs a month. In addition, her employer sent her hampers from Harrods filled with tinned sausages, Knorr soup and canned Australian butter. She recalls that in Shanghai restaurants remained open and there was a flourishing black market where you could buy an egg for 1 yuan and 4 lbs of mutton for 60 yuan – the average monthly wage. At the Shanghai Zoo, the animals continued to be fed while in nearby Anhui province millions died of hunger.[8] On a commune outside Shanghai, the painter Fu Hua remembers that he ate the slops intended for the pigs and fed them boiled-up human excrement instead.[9]

The most protected social group in the cities were Party members. As in the Soviet Union, they could buy scarce goods, above all food, in secret and unmarked shops. Although Party members claimed to share the same rations as others, this privilege shielded them from the worst hunger. One doctor, who continued to work long hours on shorter and shorter rations, recalls operating on an important Party official:

> He must have noticed my haggard face and unsteady feet. He asked me if I had had anything to eat that day and I told him I had not had a proper meal for two days. He said he would see to it, if his operation was successful. It must have been the most careful operation I ever did. Sure enough, a sack of rice and three pounds of pork were delivered to my house. I don't remember my children ever being so happy with me, as if I were the almighty Goddess of Mercy, sent from heaven to save them.[10]

Nien Cheng's sister, who was a Party member in the municipal health department, continued to eat full meals in work canteens that included luxuries such as pieces of pork. In many places, top officials and their families lived in special compounds with their own canteens, shops and supplies of provisions. The army and navy used their special status to supplement their rations in other ways. Army officers in Beijing took jeeps, machine guns and spotlights to the Mongolian grasslands to hunt wild animals. Navy vessels spent their time fishing.[11] In hospitals, the staff would cook and eat human placentas, and pharmacists sold dried and powdered placenta which was highly sought after as a source of protein.

As the shortages worsened, access to these special shops was vital because the mere possession of a ration ticket no longer guaranteed a supply of grain. Queues became longer and longer and started earlier and earlier because those who came last might leave empty-handed. Fights frequently broke out and people resorted to various stratagems to reserve a place in the queue. Meat became absolutely unobtainable without special connections.

As in the countryside, the food shortages in the cities caused terrible mistrust between family members. Initially, the old would give the young a portion of their food but by 1960 people had begun to steal from each other. In many families, members watched with eagle eyes as the food was divided. This became a matter of such bitter contention that many, even in Beijing, used scales at each meal to ensure that everyone knew they were getting exactly their fair share. Matters were made worse if families had to send their portions of rice to be cooked at a communal canteen. In Guangzhou, schoolchildren had to bring their lunchtime rice to school where it would be cooked. One interviewee recalled how the school cooks would steal from the children by scooping back some of the cooked rice. Often men stole their wives' coupons and parents took food from their children. Divorces and separations became common as tensions rose and tempers were lost. There were cases of sons beating or even killing their own mothers. Several former prisoners remember sharing a cell with inmates who had murdered one of their parents for a bag of grain. The reverse happened, too. In Tianjin an interviewee recalled how when his younger brother stole a *wotou*, their father discovered this and beat the boy with such violence that his retina was permanently damaged. In Xining, Qinghai, a father cut his own throat after beating a son who had stolen his food.[12]

Despite the efforts of the militia, peasants did sneak into the cities in search of food. One interviewee told of the terrible feeling of oppression that this created in Chengdu: 'There were tens of thousands of people roaming the streets and looking for food. When you sat down to eat something in a restaurant – they had nothing except boiled noodles without fat – all these people would be watching you. When you left, the plate would be snatched away by these beggars who would then lick the plate thoroughly.'

When, in 1961, the Shanghai authorities tried to win over former capitalists as part of an attempt to restart the economy, they took Nien Cheng and other once wealthy Shanghainese on a luxury cruise up the Yangtze. There she noticed how difficult it was to keep the beggars at bay. When the party ate in restaurants, the doors were locked to prevent starving peasants rushing in, but they watched the guests eat elaborate meals of meat and fish with their faces pressed against the windows.[13]

In Changsha, another interviewee recalled, if anyone in the street raised a hand to their mouth, dozens of people would start staring, and if they saw that someone was eating, then they would crowd around, asking where the food had come from. In canteens, beggars would deliberately spit into the food of people eating there in the hope that they would then leave it. One interviewee who grew up in Fuzhou, capital of Fujian, remembered that people would snatch food from anyone whose attention wandered even for a second: 'I was playing at the entrance to a police station when four men dragged another in. They were carrying a bun from which this man had taken a bite. While they were struggling, the beggar grabbed it like a tiger. He didn't care how much the others cursed and kicked him as long as he could eat.'

Little mercy was shown to those caught stealing grain. In Beijing, some university students caught stealing were sent to labour camps. In Chengdu, Tsering Dorje Gashi stopped to change trains on his way home:

> Stuck up on street walls everywhere we saw posters of men crossed out in red, and on enquiring what these meant, we discovered

that these were thieves and robbers, shoplifters, people who robbed and stole from communal grain stores . . . Out of all this misery the sight which saddened me most was the spectacle of two children of tender years lying down on the pavement, their emaciated bodies shivering. They looked as if they were going to die at any moment. I was moved and wanted to give them some food but I clearly saw that they lacked the power even to open their mouths. Those living nearby related that the father of the children had stolen from the grain store and was killed and that the mother had starved to death not many days before. 'It is better that these two die. They have neither the energy nor the strength to live,' they said.[14]

Between 1958 and 1961, it was an offence to buy or sell anything privately and pedlars were often sent to jail. One man recalled what happened to his grandfather in Beijing:

We decided to raise chickens to sell. At that time this was strictly forbidden and the police patrolled the black market. My grandfather looked after the chickens – seven hens and three cocks. Once he wanted to buy some chocolate for his grandchildren. It was terribly expensive – 25 fen for a tiny bar in Wangfujing Street. So he decided to sell a chicken on the black market. He was soon caught by the police who were ready to send him to jail. My mother went down on her knees to apologize and said he was so old that he didn't know that it was illegal. So they let him go. If he had gone to prison, he would have died.

To raise money to buy food, however, people did sell their family treasures and heirlooms. Paintings, books, jewellery, furniture, porcelain and anything else of value all went to special state shops. These closely resembled the Soviet *torgsin* shops in the Ukraine in the 1930s, where people traded precious goods and hard currency for food vouchers. The state bought these goods at rock-bottom prices and they later reappeared in Hong Kong antique shops.

By 1960, people in nearly all the major cities in China were beginning to peel the bark from the trees and pluck the leaves. In Jinan, capital of Shandong, the police started special patrols to protect the acacia and birch trees that lined the streets. In

Beijing, the trees were stripped bare. In Shenyang, the idea spread rapidly: 'Soon dozens of people were climbing the trees every day, stripping entire branches clean. Even green twigs were broken off. In the end not a touch of green life remained on any of the trees. It looked as if winter had set in again.'[15]

Some local newspapers even printed recipes for 'leaf pancakes' and advice on edible wild grasses and mushrooms. Sugar became the greatest and most sought-after delicacy. In Lanzhou, one interviewee wrote, 'the most serious problem was the shortage of sugar. Each person could only get four *liang* [eight ounces] a month. Sugar was vital for people's daily life. When people felt desperately hungry, they would drink a bowl of water with sugar and it would work. Therefore sugar was like gold and people had to acquire it somehow.' Another recalled that in Changsha he once walked eight miles just to buy a cube of sugar.

In 1960 the government introduced food substitutes. People in semi-tropical Fuzhou were given ground-up banana tree roots and stems which were mixed with rice flour and then steamed. They also tried to cook with coconut oil and cod-liver oil. One interviewee recalled how in his school, the headmaster forbade his pupils to mention the substitutes when they wrote to their overseas relatives because he said they were a brilliant Chinese invention which must be kept secret. This led the interviewee, then a child, to reflect that 'We Chinese are the most intelligent people in the world. That's why we know how to make this and the stupid foreigners don't.' Elsewhere, people were given cakes made of rice husks, sugar cane fibre, beetroot and turnip tops, and other substitutes. Newspapers advised people to double-steam their food in order to enlarge its bulk and make it go further. In the cities, cats and dogs disappeared from the streets. In Guangzhou, people hunted rats, sparrows and cockroaches.

Just as in the prison camps, the authorities in the cities experimented with ersatz foods. One of the most bizarre was a green fungus called *xiaoqiu zao*, or chlorella, officially described as a unicellular hydrophyte with a 'phenomenal yield of albumin, fats, carbohydrates and vitamins' which multiplied so fast that 'thirty crops a year can be expected'. This was used for everything from making biscuits and sauces to replacing milk powder for babies. People were ordered to grow the stuff in pots filled with urine and placed on window sills. Then it was collected, dried and sprinkled on rice. In *Wild Swans*, Jung Chang recalls how 'people stopped going to the toilet and peed into spittoons instead, then dropped the chlorella seeds in: they grew into something looking like fish roe in a couple of days, and were scooped out of the urine, washed, and cooked with rice. They were truly disgusting to eat, but did reduce the swelling [from oedema].'

In Tianjin, all schools and colleges were closed down. Students spent the whole of each day trying to collect grass, tree bark and anything else they could find. Schoolchildren in Shenyang were told to put their heads on their desks, close their eyes and sleep. In Beijing, the government instructed employees not to work too hard to prevent more people from coming down with oedema. One man living in Beijing recalled that in his office 'they often checked the staff and told people to rest to prevent the entire workforce collapsing'. Factories in Guangzhou sent home workers who were weak with hunger; and in schools there daily physical exercise was stopped and children just performed ear and eye exercises. To further conserve energy, children were told to lie down at home and to go to bed early. The authorities in Guangzhou even tried out acupuncture on schoolchildren in a bid to stem their hunger pangs. So serious was the malnutrition among the city's schoolchildren that in 1961 the authorities issued pupils with a single sugar lump twice a day. Children in rural areas of the province ate papaya leaves and roots and were sent into the hills to find other wild vegetation and to catch snakes, birds, snails and grasshoppers.

Yet, amidst all this, no one was ever allowed to mention publicly or privately that there was a famine or even hint at the fact. Propaganda encouraged people to make a virtue out of eating less while newspapers reported great strides in agricultural production. In Chengdu, the authorities declared that 'a capable woman can make a meal without food', reversing an ancient saying that 'no matter how capable, a woman cannot make a meal without food'. In the north, the *Beijing Daily* reported what could be achieved by 'alternating liquid meals with solid meals'. It recounted the example of a man with a family of seven who had managed to save a third of his household's monthly ration of 217 lbs by allocating each person no more than half a pound of grain a day.

In most cities, a large proportion of the inhabitants had oedema in 1960. Several interviewees recalled that their teachers' legs were so swollen that they could no longer stand up in front of their pupils and had to sit down to teach. In Beijing universities many students had swollen limbs, and in the canteens the porridge had so little rice in it that, as one former student put it, 'you could almost see your own reflection in it'. One interviewee who grew up in Fengtai, a suburb of Beijing, remembered that many neighbours died after their limbs swelled up. His parents told him not to go outside because he might be caught and turned into dumplings. Rumours of cannibalism were rife – people told stories of buying dumplings and finding a fingernail inside.

The utter failure of the cotton harvest in Shandong and other provinces where peasants were forced to try out vernalization led to further emergency measures. In 1958 China had boasted that its cotton crop was the biggest in the world, even bigger than that of the United States, but in 1959 cotton yields fell drastically. The growers, left with nothing to eat, refused to produce any more cotton, creating an acute shortage of cloth. The authorities began to dream up ways of making what was available go further. Tailors were urged to adopt a new method of cutting cloth using a cardboard pattern. The *Worker's Daily* reported that the 'broad masses of the people deeply love the advanced method of cutting' which was hailed as a 'technical revolution'. The newspaper calculated that if each of China's 650 million people saved one foot of cloth a year, an extra 65 million suits could be made.[16] The annual cloth ration was cut by 60 per cent to 4½ square feet per person and people were told how to make old clothes into new. For those outside the ration system, cotton cloth was often impossible to find and peasants sometimes resorted instead to using dried straw and grasses.

To make room for the huge influx of peasants into the cities, local authorities had earlier appropriated and reallocated all housing. Expecting that, like the peasants, they would soon be forced to join communes and lose all their possessions, many city-dwellers had hurried to sell off their furniture. When fuel supplies in the cities dwindled, those with no furniture left to chop up for firewood froze.

Transportation also ground to a halt: there was no petrol for cars or trucks and no coal for trains. Flights from Beijing to Guangzhou were cut from six to two a week. By early evening city streets were empty. Building lights were dimmed and light bulbs flickered with the erratic power supply. Hotels and guest houses were empty and visitors few. Without traffic, markets, birds or dogs, the cities were shrouded in an oppressive stillness.

As the famine deepened, the Party began to empty the cities. From Beijing alone, about 100,000 inhabitants were sent into the countryside in February 1960. One young girl, arriving at the famous Seven Li commune in Henan where in 1958 Mao had approvingly said 'This name, the People's Commune, is good', found peasants and guests subsisting off as little as 17 lbs of grain a month:

> At first I found the food inedible and threw away one of the *wotou*. People ran to eat it. I was struggled and accused of having 'bourgeois thinking'. Most of the men had oedema and the women had stopped menstruating. Most trees had been felled. People caught stealing the bark of the remaining trees were punished. People could no longer grow their own vegetables and tried to steal food from others. The leader of our group, Yuan Mu, told us that 'the spirit makes food'.[17]

Part Three
The Great Lie

16

Liu Shaoqi Saves the Peasants

'Even if there's a collapse that'll be all right.
The worst that will happen is that the whole
world will get a big laugh out of it.'
Mao Zedong in the winter of 1959[1]

BY THE END OF 1960 Mao still refused to believe that death
was stalking the countryside but his colleagues realized that
the regime was in danger of collapse and that they must act.
In early 1961, senior leaders began to dispatch inspection teams
to the countryside to gather evidence that they could present
to Mao. When Mao continued to insist that the famine was not
the result of his policies but of the actions of counter-
revolutionaries and landlords, some of the leadership led by
Liu Shaoqi took matters into their own hands. Mao believed
that their policies amounted to a challenge to his leadership
and, by the end of 1961, a power struggle was under way between
Mao and his followers on the one hand and Liu, Chen Yun and
Deng Xiaoping on the other. In provinces such as Qinghai and
Gansu, Liu and his colleagues managed to install new leaders
who were able to modify the communes, but elsewhere the provincial leadership remained firmly on Mao's side. The evidence
for what exactly took place during this period is patchy, but in
August 1962 Mao staged a comeback which culminated in 1966
with the start of the Cultural Revolution in which he eliminated
his enemies and almost destroyed the Party itself.

In February 1961, Zhou Enlai returned from three weeks in Hebei province and told Mao that the peasants were simply too weak to work and that villagers were determined to abandon the communes. At about the same time, Deng Xiaoping went to Shunyi county outside Beijing and returned to deliver an identical message – not only were the peasants starving but the village cadres had to steal from the communal granaries to ensure that they and their families could eat. Peng Zhen, the Mayor of Beijing, also went to the countryside together with the writer Deng Tuo and composed a report which bluntly accused Mao of ignoring reality.

Mao, however, still wielded considerable power over rural Party cadres who did their best to thwart these inspection teams, nowhere more so than in his home province of Hunan. This was sometimes called the cradle of the Party because so many of its leaders, including Liu Shaoqi and Peng Dehuai, had been born there. Parts of the province had been hit by drought in 1959, and a policy of trying to reap two rice harvests a year instead of one had caused a serious food shortage. By 1960 many were struggling to survive on half a pound of grain a day. In the Hengyang district 'nearly an entire production team had died of hunger, and there was no one left with the strength to bury the bodies. These were still lying scattered about in the fields from which they had been trying to pull enough to stay alive.'[2] Yet when Liu Shaoqi and his wife, Wang Guangmei, visited Hunan to see for themselves, local leaders went to extraordinary lengths to try and deceive them. Along the road leading to Liu's home town of Ningxiang, starving peasants had torn the bark off the trees to eat, so officials plastered the tree trunks with yellow mud and straw to conceal the scars.[3] As the *People's Daily* reported in an article published in December 1989, 'the grassroots Party organ interfered in everything to cover up the death toll'. Liu only managed to discover the truth in the village where he had been born, Ku Mu Chong, when some villagers dared to tell him that twenty of their number had starved to death, including a nephew of Liu's, and that a dozen more had fled. Liu was not the only senior leader to receive this treatment. That year the President of the Supreme Court, Xie Juezai, also returned to his birthplace in the same county where local officials solemnly told him that things were going so well that they were breeding two million pigs. In fact, as he later wrote, there was mass starvation.[4]

Just as many local officials lied to visiting senior leaders, so too did some prominent figures when reporting to Mao. The Party Secretary in Mao's birthplace in Xiangtan, Hunan, was Hua Guofeng, a 38-year-old from Shanxi who was determined to prove his loyalty to Mao at all costs. Hua had already earned Mao's gratitude at the Lushan summit by refuting the claims of the provincial Party leader, Zhou Xiaozhou, that there was widespread hunger in Hunan. Afterwards he wrote an article in the provincial Party newspaper headlined 'Victory belongs to those people who raise high the Red Flag of the Great Leap Forward'. And in the anti-Peng hysteria that followed the Lushan conference, he personally supervised the brutal persecution of Peng's family who lived in the Xiangtan prefecture.[5]

Mao himself did not go to Hunan but instead sent another senior Party official, Hu Yaobang, who had been born in the same district and who now headed the Party's Youth League. Hu soon realized that most of the province's population was starving to death and returned to Beijing to deliver his report to Mao. In 1980 Hu, by then General Secretary of the Chinese Communist Party and responsible for the break up of the communes after Mao's death, told an audience of Party officials how, on the eve of his audience, he paced up and down smoking, unable to sleep. Should he tell Mao the truth? Hu's courage failed him. As he later explained, 'I did not dare tell the Chairman the truth. If I had done so this would have spelt the end of me. I would have ended up like Peng Dehuai.'[6]

Liu Shaoqi sent inspection teams to Gansu and Qinghai which were more successful and quickly managed to bring down their Party leaders and introduce reforms which helped to end the famine. As in Xinyang in Henan, the support of the local army commanders was crucial, or it would not have been possible to arrest such fanatics.

In Anhui, Zeng Xisheng tried to hold on to power by switching sides early on. As one of the most aggressive promoters of the communes, he was a pivotal figure and his reforms, the *ze ren tian* or contract field farming system, became central to the struggles within the Party during 1961 and 1962. Zeng had begun cautiously, by ordering cadres to try small-scale experiments on land outside the provincial capital, Hefei. By the spring of 1961, cadres all over the province were ready to issue every peasant household with two or three *mu* of communal land for the spring sowing. At the same time Zeng allowed the communes to abandon the collective kitchens, rehabilitated officials dismissed as rightists, and punished those who had committed the worst crimes. Yet to do all this Zeng had to have Mao's approval. In March 1961, Zeng attended a top Party meeting in Guangzhou and reported what he was doing to a working group of the East China Bureau. China was then divided into a number of such regional bureaux and East China was controlled by the radical leftist and Shanghai Party boss, Ke Qingshi. Ke wanted to block Zeng's *ze ren tian* system, so Zeng appealed directly to Mao. Mao himself was toying with various measures that might raise agricultural production but without openly retreating from socialism. Trusting that Zeng would not betray him, Mao gave him his blessing, saying 'if we do it right, we can increase national grain output by 491,000 tonnes [1 billion *jin*] and that will be a great thing'.[7] Mao's verdict was immediately relayed to Anhui together with instructions to promote the *ze ren tian*. A few days later, Mao changed his mind and said that only small-scale experiments were permitted. Zeng then wrote Mao a letter, again expounding the benefits of the system.

Much of what happened at this crucial juncture is obscure but Mao, although unrepentant, was under pressure from Liu Shaoqi and others who were horrified by what they had discovered in the countryside. Even hitherto loyal supporters such as Deng Xiaoping, then General Secretary of the Communist Party, believed that whatever Mao thought, there had to be a retreat. At the March meeting in Guangzhou, Deng had uttered his famous maxim: 'It does not matter whether a cat is black or white as long as it catches mice.' In other words, ignore the principles of socialism: what matters is whether people have enough to eat or not. This sentiment would come back to haunt him five years later during the Cultural Revolution. At the time, Mao seems to have been torn between heeding the advice of his followers and sticking to his convictions. He took an immense pride in his obduracy and his doctor, Li Zhisui, in his memoirs quotes him as boasting that 'Some people don't give up their convictions until they see the Yellow River and have nowhere to retreat to. I will not give up my convictions even when I see the Yellow River.'[8] Confronted with such obduracy, senior leaders attempted to find a way to disguise a retreat to private farming so as to preserve the face of the Great Leader.

When senior officials met again in May, however, the attacks against Mao were blunt. Chen Yun baldly asserted that the Party should disband the communes altogether and immediately return all the land to the peasants, adding: 'The peasants do nothing now but complain. They say that under Chiang Kaishek, they "suffered" but had plenty to eat. Under Mao everything is "great" but they eat only porridge. All we have to do is give the peasants their own land, then everyone will have plenty to eat.'[9] Chen Yun insisted that China import emergency grain and chemical fertilizers, and drew up plans for the construction of fourteen large and modern plants to ensure long-term supplies of the latter. At the same time millions of tonnes of grain were ordered from Australia, Canada and other countries.

It was also at around this time that Premier Zhou Enlai, Liu Shaoqi and Chen Yun, who had dominated much economic policy-making until 1958, introduced a series of policies on the communes aimed at reviving the peasant economy. These were accompanied by other new regulations relating to industry, science, handicrafts and trade, finance, literature and art, education, higher education and commercial work.

Liu Shaoqi's reforms came to be known as the *san zi yi bao* or 'three freedoms, one guarantee'. They did not extend to the abandonment of collective farming and the division of the communal fields but the peasants were now free to raise their own livestock and grow food on small plots of wasteland, and to open markets and trade in everything except grain which they had to continue to guarantee to deliver to the state. These reforms amounted to the sort of collective farming which existed in the Soviet Union under Khrushchev. A variation of Liu's policy, known as *bao chan dao hu* or the 'household contract responsibility system', permitted the peasants to grow a certain amount of grain for the state on communal land but also to sell the remainder. In Hunan the peasants had a simpler term for these measures, calling them 'save yourself production'.[10]

In the universities, the Lysenkoists were replaced with real scientists and serious work began again on agricultural sciences.[11] By the summer of 1961, teachers, professors, statisticians, musicians, playwrights and other intellectuals were reinstalled in their original jobs and were being encouraged to help the return to sanity. The Party Central Committee called for scientists to be given sufficient time for their research and numerous academic forums were convened where experts were encouraged to engage in free debate. Yet even in Beijing all talk of famine continued to be forbidden as experts and other citizens obeyed instructions to grow vegetables in the wasteland allotted to each work unit and to raise chickens on their balconies. Professor Wu Ningkun recalls how in Anhui's capital, Hefei, government workers instructed to grow food were told to show the 'Yanan spirit' of self-reliance and arduous struggle. At the university there, professors cultivated small plots of land on the campus, Wu himself planting soybeans.[12] Even in Zhongnanhai, the leadership compound next to the Forbidden City in Beijing, everyone except Mao tried to set an example by growing their own food. Liu Shaoqi planted kidney beans with his guards. Zhu De was noted for his pumpkins. Zhou Enlai's wife, Deng Yingchao, served guests hot water and fallen tree leaves instead of tea.

In 1961, too, the reformers were for the first time in three years able to seize control of parts of the press and turn them against Mao. Thinly disguised attacks on the Great Leader began to appear. A year earlier, the *People's Daily* had claimed that Mao had 'solved problems which Marx, Engels, Lenin and Stalin could not, or did not have the time to solve in their lifetimes'. Now it began to publish sarcastic articles, one of which suggested that some people had 'substituted illusion for reality'. Another implied that Mao suffered from a form of mental disorder which led to irrational behaviour and decisions, and warned that this affliction 'will not only bring forgetfulness, but gradually lead to insanity'. It even went so far as to suggest that such a person should take 'a complete rest'. Another essay ridiculed the story of an ordinary athlete who was so overtaken by delusions of grandeur that he boasted of breaking the Olympic record for 'the long jump'. And one attack bitingly referred to the split with Moscow: 'If a man with a swollen head thinks he can learn a subject easily and then kicks out his teacher, he will never learn anything'.[13]

Other articles in the national press talked directly of agriculture. One pointed out that in ancient times wise governments had guarded against shortages by storing grain; another urged officials to listen to the wisdom of 'sage old peasants', saying that 'traditions which have come down to us from our ancestors all contain some truth ... what crops to plant, when to sow, how to cultivate, when to harvest – these cannot be changed by man's will'.

In June the *People's Daily* published a translation into modern Chinese of a memorial to the Ming Emperor Jiajing by that upright official, Hai Rui. This was soon followed by the publication of a new play about Hai Rui, which pointedly focused on the plight of peasants whose land has been confiscated and who have been oppressed by local officials. The play was written by the Deputy Mayor of Beijing, Wu Han, an expert on Ming history. In it, Hai Rui orders that the land be given back to the peasants and executes an official for abusing his power by murdering an elderly peasant. Hai Rui praises the Emperor for past deeds, but dares to criticize him for wasting resources on pointless public works while the peasants starve: 'Your mind is deluded and you are dogmatic and biased. You think you are always right and reject criticism,' Hai Rui tells the Emperor.

Apart from Wu Han, the most vocal critic of Mao's catastrophic policies was Deng Tuo who in the 1930s had written a history of famine in China. He had risen to become chief editor of the *People's Daily* but Mao had dismissed him for opposing his policies. Now, Deng reissued his book on famine and, together with Wu Han and another writer, Liao Mosha, published a series of thinly veiled satirical essays. Deng also wrote commentaries on his own, entitled *Evening Talks in Yanshan*, in which he urged leaders to go to the countryside and see for themselves what was happening. At the end of 1961, the Mayor of Beijing, Peng Zhen, gave Deng and others access to all the directives issued by Mao during the Great Leap Forward so that they could study them and trace the responsibility for the disaster.

By the middle of 1961, Mao, in the face of hostility to his dreams, had decided that he would make a self-criticism and accept a small retreat, much as Lenin had done with his New Economic Policy after the first collectivization famine in 1921. In July, he met Zeng Xisheng again, this time on a train, and held another discussion about the Anhui reforms. Their conversation, reproduced in a Chinese book published in the 1990s, is a surreal exchange in which the deaths of tens of millions of people are discussed using bizarre euphemisms.[14] Zeng blames the failures on two 'directional' mistakes. One is described as 'considering the decrease in production as the increase in production', in other words lying. The second is termed 'regarding the left opportunist tendency in rural areas as right opportunist', meaning that the wrong people were persecuted. In this disguised and convoluted language, the Party did not make the peasants starve to death in huge numbers. Rather 'severe excess deaths' were not 'taken seriously' because of 'subjective bureaucracy'.

Throughout the exchange Mao sounds self-satisfied and places the entire blame on others. He accuses Peng Dehuai of 'messing up' his original plan for tackling leftists at the Lushan summit and he advises Zeng to draw the correct lessons from his mistakes of 'subjective bureaucracy' and be the first to make a self-criticism. At the end Zeng succeeds in flattering a suspicious Mao into agreeing to private farming. Mao agrees to both contracting out the fields and allowing private plots in order to raise production to 1957 levels:

Zeng: We discussed this . . . we think it will be a big problem to restore production to the 1957 level. We have decided to lend land to the masses . . .
Mao: This method is great! Allocating 5 per cent of the land as private plots is not enough, we should give even more land so that there won't be more deaths by starvation!
Zeng: We are prepared to fix the percentage of private land at 5 per cent and then each year give a little more to the masses and reach around 7–8 per cent . . .
Mao: What about 10 per cent?

This 180-degree turn by Mao was later hushed up during the Cultural Revolution when he ordered the punishment of his colleagues, including Zeng Xisheng, for taking the capitalist road. Indeed, even at this stage in mid-1961, he had secretly decided to write them off: as he lamented to his doctor, 'All the good Party members are dead. The only ones left are a bunch of zombies.'

In the meantime Zeng went ahead and spread the *ze ren tian* system throughout Anhui. By the end of 1961 grain production had risen dramatically from 6 million to 10 million tonnes. Other places followed suit and in around 20 per cent or more of the country, a diluted form of private farming began. However, many senior leaders were reluctant to confront Mao and back sweeping concessions to the peasants that would end the food shortages. At another Party meeting at Beidaihe in August, Tao Zhu, the provincial Party leader from Guangzhou, proposed giving 30 per cent of the land to the peasants but both Premier Zhou Enlai and Marshal Zhu De remained silent. Peng Dehuai reportedly sent a letter in which he begged to be rehabilitated and criticized Zeng's experiment. And according to Zhou Yueli, Zeng's former secretary, Hu Yaobang returned from an inspection trip to Anhui and likewise criticized the abandonment of collective farming.

Officially, Mao continued neither to recognize the crisis nor formally to approve Zeng's *ze ren tian*. Officials from other provinces visited Anhui to see what was happening for themselves but by the end of the year Mao was again talking of dropping the Anhui experiment. Matters came to a head at a huge meeting held in Beijing in January 1962 and called the 7,000 Cadres Conference. At the meeting, Liu Shaoqi declared that the famine was 70 per cent the result of human error and 30 per cent the result of natural causes.

Liu had summoned the meeting to push through further rural reforms, and Anhui's *ze ren tian* was a major topic of discussion. Yet Mao dug his heels in, determined to stop it. He said he had received letters from cadres in Anhui protesting against the change and he called upon the meeting to discover what was really going on in Anhui. With most delegates clearly on Liu Shaoqi's side, Mao was facing a critical challenge to his authority. At this moment, his most loyal follower, Marshal Lin Biao, who had been promoted to succeed Peng Dehuai as Minister of Defence, spoke out in favour of Mao. According to Dr Li's memoirs:

Lin Biao was one of the few supporters Mao had left, and the most vocal. 'The thoughts of the Chairman are always correct,' he said. 'If we encounter any problems, any difficulty, it is because we have not followed the instructions of the Chairman closely enough, because we have ignored or circumscribed the Chairman's advice.' I was sitting behind the stage, hidden by a curtain, during Lin's speech. 'What a good speech Vice-Chairman Lin has made,' Mao said to me afterwards. 'Lin Biao's words are always so clear and direct. They are simply superb! Why can't the other Party leaders be so perceptive?'

Hua Guofeng also demonstrated his loyalty, saying: 'If we want to overcome the difficulties in our rural areas, we must insist on going the socialist road and not by adopting the house-hold contract system or individualised farming, otherwise we will come to a dead end.'[15]

Most of the time, though, Mao did not attend the conference discussions. Instead, he remained in a special room in the Great Hall of the People, 'ensconced on his extra-large bed, "resting" with the young women assembled there for his pleasure, read-ing daily transcripts of the proceedings taking place'.[16] How-ever, he did manage to insist on the dismissal of Zeng Xisheng. Despite his reforms, Zeng had little support within the rest of the Party and Liu Shaoqi wanted to punish him for the crimes committed in Anhui and have him executed. In the Cultural Revolution, Zeng allegedly asked Mao to rehabilitate him because it was Liu who had dismissed him. Another of Mao's victims was Wang Feng, who in 1961 had been put in charge of Gansu province and had tried out similar experiments in free farming in one prefecture, Linxia. Wang was sacked as was Linxia's prefectural Party Secretary, Ge Man. Four years later both men were among the first victims of the Cultural Revolution.

Among the beneficiaries of the 7,000 Cadres Conference was Lin Biao, whom Mao later designated as his successor. Another was Hua Guofeng, promoted to head the Hunan Party sec-retariat. From his position there, Hua opposed Liu's reforms with a vengeance. According to the *People's Daily*, 'In 1962 in order to oppose the influence of Liu Shaoqi's *san zi yi bao*, Hua led a working team to every brigade and village where the *bao chan dao hu* was implemented in order to return them to the path of socialism.' In the end it was not Lin Biao but Hua Guofeng who succeeded Mao after his death for Lin Biao died in 1971 while fleeing China after an attempted *coup d'état.*

Though Liu Shaoqi and Deng Xiaoping lost a few pawns at this conference, they nonetheless went ahead with a nationwide emergency programme. This was a modified version of Zeng's *ze ren tian* which allowed production teams, although not individual peasants, to contract out fields. Individuals could have private plots if they were on waste ground. At the same time the state's purchasing price for grain was raised, and the peasants were permitted to trade animals as long as they were not, like oxen, considered a means of production. All over China, peasants were allocated materials to replace their traditional work tools, fishing equipment, boats and carts. Under the influence of Chen Yun, the production of cash crops was also encouraged. Each region no longer had to practise self-sufficiency in grain but was allowed to grow whatever best suited its natural conditions. The size of the communes was reduced and in many of them production teams were given more autonomy.

In April 1962, Liu and Deng also introduced guidelines to rehabilitate most of the cadres and intellectuals condemned as 'right opportunists'. Some political prisoners were released and in the camps new prison commandants took over.

To ease the food shortages, the Party also began encouraging people to write to their overseas relatives and beg for food parcels. Until then the regime had treated anyone who had relatives abroad with deep suspicion. Contact could lead to imprisonment on charges of spying and an anti-Party label. During the xenophobia of the Cultural Revolution, these charges were revived and some people who had received parcels during the famine were persecuted.

Overseas relatives in Hong Kong sent 6.2 million 2 lb parcels in the first six months of 1962 (equivalent to 5,357 tonnes). The massive outflow overwhelmed the colony's post offices where people stood in line for hours. Hong Kong Chinese were also allowed to visit their relatives again and bring food parcels, and there were long queues for the train to Guangzhou. The Chinese government extracted as much money as possible from these visitors, levying a 400 per cent duty on the 2lb packages. Relatives in other parts of the world sent money orders to be used for importing chemical fertilizer. In return their families in China obtained grain coupons. The grain imported in bulk from Canada and Australia had begun to arrive in the cities but its origin was often disguised. As Chi An recounts in *A Mother's Ordeal*: 'Our family received a special issue of ten pounds of wheat flour from the state grain store. The government had put the flour in locally made sacks to disguise its origin but the employees at the store whispered that it was from Canada. It shocked me that the Party, still touting enormous increases in grain production, would import grain from a foreign country – and a hated capitalist one at that.' In Henan, Xinyang peasants could, over thirty years later, still remember how good the Canadian grain tasted.

In Shanghai, the government decided that it was now necessary to regain the confidence even of despised members of the former capitalist classes and sent them on excursions where they were treated to the best food. The city markets began to re-open and peasants were allowed to come into the cities and sell food legally. Albert Belhomme, an American soldier who defected during the Korean War and settled in Jinan, Shandong, described what happened there:

> At first the peasants with grain, vegetables or meat to sell were very timid. They came to the outskirts of the city at two or three in the morning. Transactions were carried on by the light of a match. People bought all kinds of things they didn't usually eat like carrot and turnip tops. Prices were high. As conditions worsened, the peasants became bolder, coming right into the city at daylight. The police gave up trying to stop them. Soon parts of the city were so crowded with pedlars and customers you couldn't ride a bicycle through certain streets.[17]

Some peasants became rich from this trade but could buy nothing with their paper money. Industrial production had ceased and the shops were often empty. Others were more successful, as Belhomme relates: 'They bought bicycles and even radios in spite of the fact that their villages had no electricity. They also spent huge amounts eating in the "free" restaurants where you could order good meals without ration coupons at high prices. Once in one of those restaurants, I saw a peasant in patched homespun clothes reach into his pocket and pull out a wad of cash that would have choked a horse.'

China also began to open her borders. During the past three years, tens of thousands had repeatedly tried to escape south to Macao and Hong Kong. Those caught were imprisoned, the penalty usually two or three months in a labour camp, but many died in the attempt, their bodies later found drifting in the Pearl River. People said they died because they were too weak to swim the distance, or had been shot by border guards. Then, in the summer of 1962, 250,000 people were suddenly allowed to reach Hong Kong. According to some estimates, altogether 700,000 people in Guangzhou were preparing to leave, some of whom had come from other parts of the country to escape.[18]

In the cities, the worst of the food shortages were over by the autumn of 1962, although people still lived on subsistence rations. In some places many women did not begin to menstruate again until 1965. The state continued to send as many people as possible to the countryside to minimize the problem of collecting and distributing grain. The peasants were understandably reluctant to hand over their grain to the state and for the next few years it was sometimes they who lived better than the city-dwellers, especially if they were able to sell food to the cities. In 1965, just before the Cultural Revolution began, food parcels from abroad were banned.

New policies for China's minority peoples were also launched in 1962. The Panchen Lama was encouraged to draw up his report on the treatment of the Tibetans while Beijing attempted to address their grievances. In the far western province of Xinjiang, tens of thousands of Kazakh nomads were allowed to cross the border and join their relatives in Kazakhstan and other parts of the Soviet Union.

Nevertheless, none of this changed the fact that Mao was still head of the Communist Party, at the apex of the power structure, although he no longer attended government meetings. Indeed, he seems to have spent much of the first half of 1962 sulking in a villa in Hangzhou. However, at the annual August meeting at the seaside resort of Beidaihe, Mao returned to the political stage with a vengeance. He attacked Liu and Deng by name, shouting furiously: 'You have put the screws on me for a very long time, since 1960, for over two years. Now, for once I am going to put a scare into you.' With a gesture of disgust he reportedly swept the documents on the reform of the communes off the table.[19] Later, he would complain that the rest of the leadership had treated him like 'a dead ancestor' and would accuse Deng Xiaoping of not wanting even to sit near him at meetings.

It is not hard to understand the revulsion Deng and others must have felt towards Mao. The entire Party must have known of the terrible economic damage inflicted on China, even if a full reckoning of the death toll was not made available to all. According to a study by the US Department of Agriculture published in 1988, Mao's Great Leap Forward had caused overall grain yields to fall by 25 per cent, wheat yields by 41 per cent. The production of coarse grains such as sorghum, millet and corn was lower than it had been before 1949. Oil-seed production, the chief source of fats in the Chinese diet, had collapsed by 64 per cent, cotton by 41 per cent and textiles by more than 50 per cent. The number of pigs, the main source of meat in China, had fallen in the four years to 1961 from 146 million to 75 million. The number of draught animals, used to plough fields almost everywhere in China, had fallen drastically too, so that there were half as many donkeys in 1961 as there had been in 1956. At the same time, in the five years from 1957, China had at Mao's urging exported nearly 12 million tonnes of grain as well as record amounts of cotton yarn, cloth, pork, poultry and fruit.[20]

The new policies might have been popular but Mao's supporters were still in place throughout the Party hierarchy. In most of rural China, the power struggle had not been resolved. Instead, there were now 'two lines', and officials followed whichever line suited them. Often, they shifted from one to the other, depending on the local political situation and the prevailing wind from Beijing.

As Liu Shaoqi and Deng Xiaoping implemented their reforms, Mao continued to insist that the order of the day was

'Never forget class struggle'. Seemingly incapable of compre-
hending the scale of the disaster that he had instigated, he
continued to act as if he believed the peasants were wholly
behind him. The poor and lower-middle-class peasant associ-
ations, instrumental in the land reform campaign, were revived
and villagers were ordered to attend meetings at which peasants
would describe their hard life before 1949. At the same time,
just as Stalin had done when he abandoned the New Economic
Policy, Mao claimed that rich peasants and landlords had
regained power and were rebuilding capitalism.

In the continuing struggle for power and the attempt to root
out opponents, Deng Xiaoping launched the 'Four clean ups'
movement to purge cadres who had kept grain for themselves
while the peasants starved. This had mixed success because
Mao launched a counter-political movement – the 'Socialist
education campaign' – aimed at targeting cadres who could be
accused of practising capitalism. As before, the Party continued
to send city-dwellers to the countryside to force peasants to
comply with its sometimes contradictory demands. The students and officials who went were often ignorant of the real
nature of the famine and baffled by the experience. One
student dispatched to a village in Hebei recalled:

In 1962 I and my fellow students were sent down to the countryside
in a movement called 'Consolidating the People's Commune'. I
still don't understand what it was about. I think they wanted us to
go and be used as cheap labour for the peasants. A gong would
wake us up at 4 a.m. and then we would go straight to the fields.
It took several hours of walking to get to them. We arrived in the
winter and our job was to take compost – fertilizer – to the fields.
The stuff was made of human and animal wastes, ash and any
other rubbish, and this was to prepare the land for spring sowing.
Then, around 9 a.m., we walked back to the village for our soup.
We would try and drink as much water as possible because the
next meal would not be until around 4 p.m. Even now I can't eat
porridge. The memories of that time make me throw up. Then,
in the evening, we had to take part in meetings and everyone was
supposed to talk about how to improve the communes. We all felt
very tired and no one spoke. For hours twenty or thirty of us would
squat on a *kang* feeling angry and tired. There was no electricity,

just a flickering oil lamp. The cadre would ask people to speak but nothing happened for hours, we were all so tired. Some people just slept. Then, at 11.30 p.m., the cadre allowed us to leave. The peasants hated our presence there and we had little contact with them.

Mao was determined to revive the communes and abolish the contract responsibility system. The rehabilitation of Peng Dehuai that had been prepared was thrown out. The new agricultural ministry was dismantled and its leader, Deputy Premier Deng Zihui, dismissed, Mao declaring that 'Marxism will vanish if we implement his household responsibility system'. He went on to announce that China was now ready for a new Great Leap Forward and justified himself by saying that 'Good men who make mistakes are quite different from men who follow the capitalist road.'

From August 1962 until the beginning of the Cultural Revolution in 1966, the split within the Party was hard to disguise and it spread through every level of the bureaucracy. When Mao finally recovered complete authority in 1966 his agricultural policies once again became law, but in the meantime each side stood by their respective policies. This meant that village leaders had a choice of whether to follow Mao's 'Ten points on agriculture' or Liu Shaoqi and Deng Xiaoping's 'Ten points on agriculture'. Recovery from the famine was hindered by battles between the two factions as each tried to oust the other's followers from positions of power in the countryside. One interviewee recalled what it was like when he became part of a rural work team:

> When I was a student I was sent to this village in Zhouxian county, Hebei. It was 1964 and Mao was trying to prove to Deng Xiaoping and Liu Shaoqi that their methods were wrong, that the peasants were corrupt, although production was rising. So we had to go to production team leaders and interrogate them. We had to make one confess to falsifying figures, to hiding grain and cheating the government. Then we could say we – our team – did our work the best because we had caught a big fish.

Even high-ranking Communist officials took part in local power struggles. One known example involved Zhao Ziyang, then the leader of Guangdong province, who tried to oust Chen Hua, the Maoist leader of Shengshi brigade, forty miles south of the provincial capital.[21] Chen was a national labour model whom Mao had received in person, but in the late summer of 1964 he stood accused of rape, corruption, extortion and 'suppression of the masses'. A work team led by Zhao Ziyang finally persuaded two frightened old peasants to come forward and testify against Chen. However, once the team had gone, Chen had the two peasant informers beaten up. They then wrote a letter of protest to Zhao who sent a second work team. When they in turn left, the two peasants were beaten up again. A third work team was dispatched but this time headed by no less a person than Liu Shaoqi's wife, Wang Guangmei who, somewhat bizarrely, turned up in disguise. At this point Chen Hua decided the game was up and boarded a boat to flee to Hong Kong. However, he was caught and soon afterwards died horribly, electrocuted by a high-voltage transformer at the brigade headquarters. The authorities said that he had committed suicide.

That year Wang Guangmei also turned up incognito at another commune called Taoyuan, in Hebei province. There she gathered evidence of the success of her husband's agricultural policies. Mao ridiculed this research and countered it by promoting his own model village, Dazhai, in Shanxi province. Chen Yonggui, its peasant leader, claimed that by applying Mao's ideas he had performed miracles and had turned a hillside wasteland into a paradise. As with all such model communes and villages, the claims were entirely fraudulent. Dazhai's 'miracle' had been the result of a massive injection of state funds: as a model it was meaningless. Nevertheless, Mao presented Dazhai's achievements as 'proof' that his ideas worked. Liu Shaoqi repeatedly tried to discredit Mao by sending in work teams, each consisting of up to 70 cadres, to gather evidence that its claims of high grain yields were bogus. Only in 1980 was it finally admitted in the *People's Daily* that Dazhai had accepted millions of dollars in aid and the help of thousands of soldiers, and that in fact its grain production had declined year by year and Chen Yonggui had executed 141 people during the mid-1960s.

Unbelievably, even in Xinyang the Maoists were able to make

a comeback.[22] After 1962, new cadres were assigned to take over from those responsible for the huge death toll. A middle-aged PLA veteran, Wang Zhengang, was appointed to run Gushi county. He began by organizing the delivery of Canadian relief grain because the peasants were too weak to labour in the fields and grow food. The *san zi yi bao* policies were implemented and the peasants were given a plot to grow food as they wished. The markets were reopened, as were schools, and Wang set up orphanages. Nonetheless, the political campaigns and purges instigated by Mao continued. Inspectors arrived and charged local cadres with under-reporting grain harvests to keep back food supplies. Peasants were summoned to accuse the very cadres who had saved them when they were on the brink of death. Wang, however, survived and was promoted to prefectural Party Secretary and moved to the city of Xinyang.

In 1966, Mao launched the Cultural Revolution to destroy those 'Party persons in power taking the capitalist road' and the entire province of Henan was torn apart. In this civil war, each side recruited Red Guards in the towns. One group, the Henan Rebel Headquarters, supported Mao, while their opponents supported Liu Shaoqi, naming themselves the February Second Faction after a strike Liu had led before 1949. In the summer of 1967, the Maoists went to Xinyang, seized Wang and brought him back to Gushi. There, in the main courtroom, Red Guards screamed abuse at him and interrogated him until he 'confessed'. He was accused of betraying socialism and of practising capitalism. When he was broken, the Red Guards announced that he had committed suicide by hanging himself and published a photograph showing his corpse with its tongue hanging out. As loudspeakers broadcast his crimes, the peasants in the villages who had been so passive during the famine became enraged and thousands came to Gushi. There, they surrounded the Red Guards and began beating them to death. Dozens were killed and the rest forced to don white mourning clothes and to crawl across the dirt to pay their respects in front of Wang's grave. Until 1993, this spot just outside Gushi remained a place of pilgrimage on Qing Ming, the festival at which the Chinese honour the dead. On such days, the peasants brought offerings of food and let off fireworks in his honour.

(In 1994 his grave was moved to make way for a new Christian church and apartment blocks.)

The same scenes were repeated all over China. In effect, the Cultural Revolution was nothing more than a purge of those who had been responsible for ending the famine, a device used by Mao to restore his authority, much as Stalin had done after the Ukrainian famine. It began with an attack on the play 'Hai Rui Dismissed from Office' and went on to target all those who had criticized the Great Leap Forward, defended Peng Dehuai and blamed Mao. Its chief target was Liu Shaoqi, who was so popular with the peasants that in some places they had begun to call *him* 'chairman'. Mao tried to whip up a campaign of hatred against Liu even in his home province of Hunan. Liang Heng, a former Hunanese Red Guard, describes in *Son of the Revolution* how, on arriving in a town in Hunan, 'I saw to my horror that in every doorway there hung a corpse! It looked like some kind of eerie mass suicide. Moments later I realised that the twilight had turned straw effigies of Liu Shaoqi into dead flesh.'

A bitterly worded propaganda document accused Liu of being a 'fanatical advocate of the rich peasant economy'. His 'sinister' policies were, it said, 'drawn from the rubbish heap of his forerunners Bernstein, Kautsky, Bukharin and the like'. His household responsibility system was an 'evil' device for the 'restoration of capitalism' and amounted to an incitement to cannibalism: 'These are the cries of a bloodsucker and in them we can discern the greed and ruthlessness of the exploiting classes, the rural capitalist forces, in their vain attempt to strangle socialism. From first to last this is the bourgeois philosophy of man-eat-man.'[23]

Liu was arrested, interrogated, tortured and then left to die half-naked and forgotten in a cellar in Kaifeng, Henan. Peng Dehuai was treated no better. Lin Biao had him taken to a stadium in Beijing where he was made to kneel before an audience of 40,000 soldiers. Then he was put in a cell where he was not permitted to sit down or go to the toilet and was subjected to incessant interrogations. He finally died in prison in 1973.

Many other leading figures who can be credited with saving the country by ending the famine met with an equally merciless death. One of the first victims was the writer Deng Tuo who died on 18 May 1966, supposedly by his own hand. Two days later, Kang Sheng decided that he would profit further from his victim's death and ordered his agents to raid Deng's home and remove his collection of antiques and paintings which he wanted for himself.[24] Wu Han, the author of the play about Hai Rui, died of medical neglect in 1969: his wife, daughter and brother were also persecuted to death.

A few opponents of Mao survived. Deng Xiaoping, condemned as 'the number two capitalist roader' and sent to the countryside in Jiangxi, managed to escape death, though it is not clear why. Chen Yun wisely dropped out of sight from the end of 1962. Mao's doctor Li Zhisui recounts how Mao's personal secretary, Tian Jiaying, secretly stopped a document in which Mao explicitly condemned Chen Yun as 'a bourgeois leaning to the right'. In Guangdong, Zhao Ziyang was seized and beaten by Red Guards who charged him with introducing the *san zi yi bao* policies and with being 'an apologist for rich peasants'. He survived, perhaps because Mao recalled his help in early 1959 when he started the anti-hiding and dividing grain campaign. Hu Yaobang also managed to escape retribution but spent six months labouring as a peasant in what was called a May 7th Cadre School. This was of all places in Xinyang, near Luoshan, and has since become Prison Farm No. 51.

17

Mao's Failure and His Legacy

'There are comrades who day in day out talk
about the Mao Zedong Thoughts, forgetting,
as they do so, the fundamental Marxist con-
cept of the Chairman and his basic method
which is to seek the truth from facts.'
                        Deng Xiaoping, 1978

FOR TWENTY YEARS after the famine China stagnated. The
population grew rapidly but little new was built. The airport in
every county, like the electricity, the telephones, the cars and
the roads that Mao had promised the peasants in 1958, never
materialized. In fact, over the next two decades, China managed to complete the construction of only one new railway line.
In the countryside, people did not starve but living standards
never regained the levels seen in the 1950s. After the famine,
Mao ruled for another fourteen years but remained obsessed
with justifying his Great Leap Forward and rooting out those
whom he felt had betrayed him. Huge numbers were killed or
imprisoned in the Cultural Revolution: how many is still not
known, but the victims ran into the tens of millions.

In launching the Cultural Revolution, Mao organized his
own army just as he had threatened to do at the Lushan summit.
These were the urban youth who enlisted as Red Guards and
worshipped him as a god. Under his auspices, the Red Guards
raided the army's munitions factories and armouries to equip

themselves with machine guns, and in places even with tanks, and then turned them against the Party leadership. Why Liu Shaoqi and his fellow leaders were unable to stop Mao is one of the most extraordinary and puzzling aspects of the famine, for Party members knew that Mao had allowed tens of millions to starve to death and that his Great Leap Forward had been a monumental failure. Perhaps part of the explanation lies in the Party's decision to keep the famine secret. Mao was only able to call upon the Red Guards to do his bidding because they, out of the whole population, knew the least about his crimes. In the climate of fear that pervaded the country, parents could not bring themselves to tell their children what had happened. Mao wanted the young to distrust and betray the older generation and praised those who exposed their parents. These so-called 'educated youths' would not find out what had happened in the countryside until Mao dispensed with them after 1969 and they were sent to live among the peasants.

As a group, the peasants did not participate in the Cultural Revolution and rural youths rarely left their homes to join the bands of Red Guards creating havoc around the country. Had the peasants answered Mao's call to anarchy, the economy would have collapsed but no peasant wanted to abandon his fields and go through another great famine. The Cultural Revolution did, however, leave its mark on the countryside. In some places, the Party further impoverished the peasants by levying an additional 5 per cent tax to pay for the cost of organizing these political campaigns and the accommodation of the Red Guards. And some peasants used the political chaos that followed to turn on the cadres responsible for the worst atrocities during the famine, sometimes simply publicly humiliating them but sometimes beating them to death. As in Xinyang, peasants tried to protect those local cadres who had ended the famine and were now attacked for restoring capitalism by introducing Liu Shaoqi's policies.

Though the countryside was largely unaffected by the political chaos of the Cultural Revolution, Mao's triumphant return to power was nevertheless a disaster for the peasants. The renewed effort to build a new society and make new men out of the starving and ragged peasantry meant a return to collective farming and the discouragement of any kind of private initiative. Mao's vision of a rural Utopia, embodied by the Dazhai model, was revived as if the famine had never taken place and teams of 'Dazhai inspectors' patrolled the communes to ensure that Mao's failed agricultural policies were closely followed. As one peasant from a mountainous region put it: 'Really, for us the famine lasted twenty years.' Though mass famine deaths ended after 1961, hunger remained endemic. Most peasants went without basic commodities such as cooking oil, meat, fruit and tea. One intellectual sent to work in the countryside of northern Henan from 1969 to 1973 recalled what life was like: 'Even at that time the peasants were not eating wheat. Their main food was still dried sweet potato and, twice a day, this was all they ate. They lived in complete destitution. No house had any doors left, all the wood had been taken away.'

Not until after Mao's death in 1976 did per capita grain production reach the level of 1957, and in the early 1970s food production actually fell once more to levels seen during the famine. As a Chinese expert wrote in 1980: 'For nearly twenty years from the Second Five-year Plan period (1958–62) to the downfall of the Gang of Four in 1976 there was little or no rise in living standards. Each peasant's annual grain ration remained at around 400 lbs of unprocessed grain . . . and consumption of vegetable oils, eggs, and aquatic products, according to our estimates, did not return to the 1957 level.'[1] Not until 1978 did the peasants eat as much as they had in the mid-1950s.

Up until Mao's death, China claimed that grain production had kept pace with the growth in population but the figures were falsified. Peasants grew sweet potatoes, the easiest and most reliable crop to plant, and local officials, under pressure to show that Mao's policies worked, calculated grain harvests by weighing the sweet potatoes. Since a sweet potato crop from one field weighs five times as much as wheat grown in the same field they appeared to meet their quotas. Yet once the sweet potatoes were dried, they shrank to a tenth of their original weight and even then were no substitute for good and nourishing wheat or rice. This type of fraud was widespread and villagers often drew up a false set of figures to show officials who came from outside to inspect their work. The system functioned but it barely enabled the cities to be fed and the peasants' diet was worse than it had been before the revolution. A study by the World Bank in 1985 concluded that peasants in equally poor countries had until recently a considerably richer and more varied diet than had the Chinese. Even in 1980–2, by which time the Chinese diet had become considerably more varied, 'the direct per capita consumption of grain [in China] is about 209 kg per year and is among the world's highest and exceeds that in India by 60 per cent and Indonesia by more than 30 per cent'.[2]

In the years after the famine, the peasants not only ate a poor and monotonous diet, they also lived in the same broken-down mud huts. Few were able to replace the wooden windows and doors and the household goods taken away during the Great Leap Forward. The Party outlawed all carpentry and handicrafts which were not undertaken by state-run units. Peasants in poor agricultural areas, who in the past had supplemented their income by carpentry, basket weaving and dozens of other trades, now had only farming on which to rely. Supplies of factory-made goods, even clothing, were often not available and many peasants were dressed in rags or in garments made of straw and grass. For years after the famine, the peasants lived little better than their draught animals, indeed they often had to pull their ploughs themselves.

Mao's policies stifled recovery from the famine. In the name of egalitarianism, no one was allowed to be seen to prosper from activities such as raising poultry or selling vegetables, even if they were permitted, without attracting censure and punishment as 'rich peasants'. Peasants could not, for instance, raise more than one or two pigs per household. Nor could they sell these animals privately. Anyone caught slaughtering a pig without permission would be sentenced to one or even three years in prison. The penalty for buying or selling oxen (regarded as a means of production) was even higher – five or six years' imprisonment. Peasant militia also patrolled the villages to stop the villagers from indulging in the most harmless pursuits if they smacked of bourgeois individualism. The small pleasures of life, even playing cards, became crimes against the state.

The peasants were also left to struggle with another legacy

of the Great Leap Forward, farming land that had often been ruined by deep ploughing, by ill-conceived irrigation projects or by growing unsuitable crops. In north China, the fertility of some 7.41 million acres of soil had been destroyed by wells and irrigation schemes which had caused the water table to rise. When the water evaporated from the sodden fields, a damaging deposit of salts and alkalis was left.[3] And the crudely built dams and irrigation works that they had created at great cost proved worse than useless, and in some cases even fatal – the collapse in August 1975 of two dams in Henan built during the Great Leap Forward has already been discussed in Chapter 5.

Despite the evident failure of the Great Leap Forward irrigation schemes, peasants continued to be sent to labour on still greater and more pointless projects, the most famous of which was the Red Flag Canal in northern Henan's Linxian county. There, tens of thousands toiled without machinery in the late 1960s to re-route a river by tunnelling a channel through a mountain and then along a bed built on the side of steep cliffs. Unaided by engineers the peasants built 134 tunnels and 150 aqueducts, and moved enough earth to build a road 42,480 miles long. Aside from these showcase marvels, peasants had to terrace mountainsides all over the countryside, as had been done at Dazhai, and since grain was the only agricultural product that mattered, peasants had to grow it irrespective of natural conditions. Finally, to open more land for grain, forests were cut down and lakes drained.

The reluctant peasants had also once again to follow the eight-point charter drawn up by Mao in 1958 (see Chapter 5). In *China: Science Walks on Two Legs*, the two American authors record how they were taken to Dazhai in 1974 and told of the benefits of using animal and human wastes instead of chemical fertilizer. Their hosts talked, too, of the advantages of close planting, the new hybrid species they had created and the innovative agricultural tools they had built.[4] Many others were taken around Dazhai and books poured forth about its success and the heroism of its peasant leader, Chen Yonggui. As late as 1976, Penguin Books published *China: The Quality of Life* by Rewi Alley and Wilfred Burchett which lavished praise on Dazhai's wonders.

In the real world, the peasants resorted to passive opposition and evasion in order to feed themselves, as the journalist and dissident Liu Binyan records:

> The starving peasants resorted to the only legal form of protest in China – a work slowdown – and they would continue to do this for the next thirty years. Every morning and every afternoon, after we set out to work collectively, we would sit down and chat for half an hour upon reaching the fields. After starting work, we often stood still leaning on our hoes and chatting for another half-hour. Then, when the regular break arrived, the peasants would take out their pipes and smoke for an hour.[5]

The peasants still talked about their hope that one day they would get their own land back, or that at least the Party would relent so that they could return to the policies of 1961 and 1962. 'They knew that if they could only divide the land once more, they would all eat well again,' said one writer who spent time in a village in Sichuan. In Anhui, a rural cadre told me that when he was obliged to go round the villages urging the peasants to grow more grain, they would tell him that the only way forward was to go back to the *ze ren tian*. In some places, the peasants secretly continued to farm the land they had divided up in that period or grew food on land in the hills, far away from official view. Some peasants even formed secret societies to fight for the return of their land. In one township in north-western Sichuan, a group of peasants banded together in what they called 'The Chinese People's Freedom Party'. In 1972, its twelve leaders were arrested and executed as counter-revolutionaries. It has been claimed that such movements were not uncommon and that they often had the backing of village-level cadres.

Meanwhile, the majority waited for Mao to die and hoped that, when he did, the communes would be abandoned. After his death in the autumn of 1976, his successor Hua Guofeng was determined to continue with Mao's policies but the peasants secretly started to share out the land. Anhui peasants say this began in 1977, and by the following year the Party had little choice but to go along with it. In 1978, 200 million peasants, or one in four, were not getting enough to eat and productivity had fallen to levels lower than during the Han dynasty. In 1978, an Anhui peasant grew 1,597 lbs of grain in a year, less than the average yield 2,000 years earlier when peasants had managed 2,200 lbs.

Official Communist Party history records that the first peasants to challenge Mao's policies were the Xiao Gang production team of Li Yuan commune in Fengyang county. The daring of this village derived from its experiences in the Great Leap Forward when 60 starved to death, 76 fled and only 39 people and one ox survived. The villagers were resolved not to suffer again, and on 24 November 1978, they attended a meeting organized by the production chief, Yen Chungang. The heads of eighteen households, most of whom shared the same surname as Yen, signed an agreement, solemnized by affixing their thumb print, under which they vowed to keep their acts secret. If discovery led to the arrest of the leaders, the rest promised to raise their children. The peasants then secretly split the production team's land amongst themselves under the household responsibility system or *bao chan dao hu*, a variant of Zeng Xisheng's *ze ren tian*. Soon, they were being held up as a national model for the whole country and later the original contract was enshrined behind a glass case in the Museum of Revolutionary History in Beijing.[6]

An alternative version of events suggests that the abandonment of the communes was instigated by Deng Xiaoping. One of his followers, Wan Li, soon after being promoted to Party Secretary of Anhui following Mao's death, issued six guidelines relaxing restrictions on private farming and trading. Peasants could now grow vegetables on 3/10ths of a *mu* instead of 2/10ths and did not have to pay pay taxes on wheat and oil-bearing plants grown on private plots. Deng Xiaoping, then Vice-Chairman of the Communist Party, gave his blessing to what were known as the *Anhui liu tiao*, or Anhui's Six Measures, and suggested that Zhao Ziyang, who had been appointed to take charge of Sichuan, should follow suit. The latter soon issued further measures of reform and even led a group of commune bosses on a tour of Western Europe to introduce them to the marvels of commercial farming.

The Third Plenum of the Eleventh Party Congress at the close of 1978 is now hailed as the beginning of a new era. At that meeting Deng was able to oust Hua Guofeng and begin to destroy Mao's communes. Wan Li, in a speech entitled 'Several key questions to be solved in agriculture', mounted a fierce attack on the failure of the communes in Anhui and ridiculed Dazhai. Cautiously, a few provincial leaders began to dismantle the system of collective agriculture that the peasants had lived under for a quarter of a century.[7]

The dismantlement of the first commune took place in August 1979 amid the greatest secrecy at Guanghan, a town forty miles from Chengdu, Sichuan. Nothing was announced in the press for at least another year and news of the daring act only became known when a Japanese journalist reported it. Nevertheless it took years for others to follow suit. In Sichuan, many communes waited until 1984 before daring to dissolve the system, and even in Anhui some places, such as Feixi county, did not allocate the land to households until 1985.

Mao's communes cost China dear. At a time when the agricultural productivity of other Asian countries was increasing in leaps and bounds, the Chinese peasant was hamstrung. Between 1960 and 1980, according to a World Bank study, the productivity of Japanese peasants rose twenty-fold and that of South Koreans sixty-fold. Even in 1980, Chinese peasants were half as productive as those in Indonesia, Pakistan and Thailand.

Chinese leaders constantly reiterate the fact that China feeds over 20 per cent of the world's population on 7 per cent of its arable land, and the shortage of arable land is used as the excuse for rural poverty. But on a per capita basis, China has more farming land than either South Korea or Japan, as the following table makes clear.[8]

	Population density per hectare	*Population density per hectare of arable land*
China	1.05	10
South Korea	3.89	17.3
Japan	3.15	23.9

Had Mao not reversed the initial redistribution of land after 1949 by establishing the collectives, China would not now be lagging so far behind. Peasant smallholders provided a good base for economic take-off in those countries which the United States dominated after Japan's defeat in 1945. In Taiwan, the

Sino-American Joint Commission for Rural Reconstruction set about boosting food output and winning the political loyalty of the peasants by giving them land. This resulted in the 1953 Land to the Tillers Act by which the amount of land cultivated by tenant farmers dropped from 40 per cent to 15 per cent. The Act forced many disenfranchised landowners to start up their own businesses which now form the mainstay of the island's economy. In Japan the Americans were similarly responsible for the 1952 Agricultural Land Law which consolidated and continued the break-up of large estates begun in 1946.

Under Mao, China also failed to capitalize on the new farming methods developed in the rest of the world. Cheap chemical fertilizers, new varieties of wheat and rice, and the use of plastic sheeting to extend the growing season all helped spur farmers in Japan, South Korea and Taiwan to reap once unimaginably high yields. Small so-called walking tractors, cheap enough for a household to buy and use for tilling and transport, vastly increased the household farmer's productivity. In Mao's China the peasants were stuck with large and unwieldy Soviet-style tractors.

After Deng Xiaoping's reforms, the peasants exploited these innovations with enthusiasm. The amount of chemical fertilizer applied in China doubled between 1977 and 1981 and had tripled by 1986. Grain production jumped from 286 million tonnes at Mao's death in 1976 to 407 million tonnes in 1984. By the mid-1980s China was once again a net food exporter. Peasants no longer subsisted on sweet potatoes but could now afford to use cooking oil and eat meat, vegetables, fruit and fish.

Though there is no doubt that Deng's reforms were of great significance, in fact they consisted of nothing more than the abandonment of a system which had failed catastrophically twenty years earlier, and indeed which had failed in the Soviet Union two decades before that. Deng must share the responsibility for ignoring the lessons of both these earlier failures. His reforms have consisted largely of returning the peasants to the situation they were in before the Communist revolution, and indeed for centuries before. The peasants are once again small farmers – although this time all land is nominally owned by the state – obliged to pay an annual grain tax.

To call Deng's policies reforms is in a sense a misnomer and it is also becoming clear that they have not solved China's Malthusian crisis. The Chinese are still confronted with a burgeoning population and hence the threat of famine, which may prove to be Mao's most bitter legacy. When the Communists fought the Nationalists during the 1940s, they were able to promise the 500 million peasants that they would be rewarded with a plot of land (its size varied from place to place) large enough to support a family. Thirty years later, Deng had the same amount of land to redistribute (or perhaps less given the environmental destruction that had occurred in the interim), but the rural population had nearly doubled. The post-1979 redistribution of land gave a temporary boost to the Party's popularity but it is still faced with the almost insurmountable problem of finding employment for a growing surplus of labour in the countryside. Throughout China's history, dynasties have been overthrown by landless and frustrated peasants who have risen up in revolt. Without more land to placate the peasantry, the Party now faces the possibility of its own overthrow. The growth in grain production has slowed since 1987 and output actually fell for the first time in 1994. In 1995, the Party panicked over a report by Lester Brown of the Worldwatch Institute in America which said that China is losing her ability to feed herself. By the year 2000 there could be a shortfall of 40 million tonnes. In just over fifty years, China's population will reach 1.6 billion and China may well need to import more grain than the rest of the world can supply. The last famine may, officially at least, be forgotten but the threat of another great famine will haunt future generations.

And what of Mao's Utopian vision of the future for Chinese peasants? In some ways, his fantasies are coming true although for reasons entirely contrary to his beliefs. In increasing numbers the peasants do have access to the marvels of twentieth-century technology. They have new houses made of brick and tiles and equipped with electricity and television. Their fields now produce three times as much grain per *mu* as in 1960. Mechanization has arrived with walking tractors and threshing machines. Chinese pigs now grow to four times the weight they did in 1960 and modern science is creating giant vegetables and genetically engineered hybrids. Mao's opposition to chemical fertilizers is now fashionable and foreign agronomists recommend natural fertilizers. It is not hard to imagine that if the famine is left out of the history books, Mao could continue to be worshipped as a great peasant emperor whose vision transformed China into a modern state.

18

How Many Died?

'Any society that is alive is a society with a *history.*'

Vaclav Havel

CHINA HAS NEVER officially acknowledged that the famine took place nor published an estimate of the death toll. The results of any internal investigations are a state secret and no public discussion of the famine is permitted.

Western experts made the first estimates of the death toll in the early 1980s, nearly a quarter of a century after the famine had taken place, and these calculations are only educated guesses, carried out on the basis of limited information. Yet given that the number of victims of the Holocaust and the Ukrainian famine are still being debated even though far more is known about them, such uncertainty over the death toll in China is hardly surprising. Moreover, in China the Party responsible for the famine is still in power and venerates the memory of Mao. Even in Russia, where the Communists have lost power, it is still proving difficult to determine how many died in Stalin's purges, the famines or the Second World War. Nor have the internal records of Mao's regime been scrutinized by an occupying power in the way the Allies were able to examine those of Nazi Germany.

However, reaching a reliable figure about a famine which lasted for years and extended over such a large country would be difficult even if China were to open all her archives. Many records were lost during the Cultural Revolution and a great deal of other evidence has been deliberately destroyed. In addition, only three censuses were taken in China between 1949 and 1982, one in 1953, another in 1964 and the third in 1982. And, as will be seen, data from that of 1964 must be treated with considerable caution.

During the Great Leap Forward, the State Statistical Bureau, set up in 1952 and modelled on its Soviet equivalent, simply did not function. Professional statisticians were relegated to other work and were only reappointed in July 1961. And only in the following year, on the instructions of Liu Shaoqi and Zhou Enlai, were plans drawn up for the establishment of a powerful, centralized and unified statistics system. At the same time, Party and government departments were forbidden to change statistical figures.[1]

Provisional regulations governing statistical work were issued in 1963 but the newly reconstituted bureau functioned only for another four years or so. On the eve of the Cultural Revolution, Wang Sihua, head of the State Statistical Bureau, was arrested and accused of implementing a revisionist line, 'seizing power from the Party' and 'asserting his independence'. At the same time, large quantities of material from the bureau were burnt. Wang had been in charge of organizing China's second national population census completed in 1964. The census had been conducted amid such secrecy that the outside world was unaware of it, and Mao refused to publish the results. Details of the 1964 census were only published in 1980. Thus for nearly a quarter of a century there was an effective blackout on all Chinese population statistics.[2]

These circumstances parallel those during collectivization and the ensuing famine in the Soviet Union. Stalin had ordered a new census in 1937 but its results were never released and lay buried in the central national archives for half a century. The director of the Census Bureau, O. A. Kvitkin, was dismissed and later shot. Stalin had estimated that the Soviet Union had a population of around 170 million people. However, the census itself counted only 162 million people, clearly showing that 7 million or more people had starved to death in the Ukraine and the northern Caucasus.

The parallels with China do not end there. Researchers have discovered that the Soviet Central Office of Statistics produced two sets of demographic statistics, one for internal use and one for publication. During the Mao era, China appears to have done much the same, at least as far as meteorological data is concerned. During the Great Leap Forward, the Central Meteorological Office continued to function accurately but the information it produced was restricted to senior levels of the Party. The meteorologists reported that there was no unusually bad weather or natural disasters in 1959, 1960 or 1961; indeed the weather was rather good. However, the official media reported claims by Mao and others that China had in this period experienced the worst natural disasters for a century. Official news reports even quoted experts as saying that China's climate had changed. In fact, the worst years since 1949 have been 1954 and 1980–1 when there was neither a severe grain shortage nor a nationwide famine.[3]

However, even if one is prepared to accept that the statistics released by China after 1980 were undoctored, there are doubts as to whether in the midst of a ruthless political struggle, an accurate census was taken in 1964. The count must have been made at the provincial level with the co-operation of the local Party organization and the results passed on to the centre only with the approval of the provincial Party Secretaries. In many provinces, the same officials who were responsible for the famine were still in power and would have had every reason to censor damaging information. In Sichuan, for example, Li Jingquan was still in power in 1964: the census would have revealed his responsibility for 7–9 million deaths. Nonetheless, the data from the 1964 census is crucial to making a proper estimate of the death toll for, without it, one is faced with a gap of twenty-nine years between the first census in 1953 and the third in 1982.

China began to publish a flood of statistical and demographic data after 1980, when the State Statistical Bureau was re-established and the country's few remaining statisticians returned from long years of physical labour in the countryside. It is now possible, using the data from 1953, 1964 and 1982, to track the progress of each age cohort from census to census and therefore establish how many of those born in 1950 survived until 1964 and then 1982. However, two factors in particular hinder a demographer from making a definitive study of the death toll during the famine – internal migration and the number of children who were born and died between 1958 and 1962.

In a famine people flee their homes and often do not return, but a census count does not show whether they have starved to death or whether they have moved away and failed to register elsewhere. Census figures for Shanghai, for example, show that 950,000 people left Shanghai between 1953 and 1964, but they do not reveal what happened to these people or where they went. During the famine, uncounted numbers fled the worst-hit regions, over 10 million settling in Manchuria and Inner Mongolia alone.

The other great challenge is to try and guess how many children were born during the famine years and, of these, how many died. This is not revealed by the 1953 and 1964 censuses although experts can make educated guesses based on birth rates and infant mortality rates before and after the famine. On the other hand, pre-famine trends are not a strong guide because it is clear that fewer babies are born in a famine. Many women stop ovulating altogether, and if they do give birth, they produce less milk and infant mortality rises sharply. One expert has calculated that Anhui suffered a fertility crisis for as long as two years during the famine but obviously the scale of the crisis varied from province to province.[4] With a population the size of China's, the margin for error is fairly high. Under normal conditions, China might in the late 1950s and early 1960s have seen around 25 million births a year. Even in famine conditions, the number of births might still have been 14 million a year. Thus in the four years from 1958 to 1962, the number of births could have ranged from a low of 56 million to a maximum of 100 million.

The censuses are not the sole guide to calculating the death toll in China because the local authorities also maintain registers of births and deaths. Given the rationing system which existed during this period, a careful record would have been made at times of the number of mouths to feed. On the other hand, at the height of the famine in the countryside, no one was burying the dead, let alone recording the number of deaths. The births and deaths of small children, in particular, would often have passed almost unnoticed. Nor would officials have kept track of those who fled and managed to survive or of those who died on the roads. And there is another, final question-mark about Chinese figures: how were the inmates of the labour camps and prisons recorded? And the millions in the armed forces? Generally, both groups are excluded from provincial population figures but during the famine there were perhaps as many as 10 million prisoners and the death rate in the camps was exceptionally high, on average 20 per cent and often far higher.

In the early 1980s, Dr Judith Banister undertook a major investigation of China's population statistics which was published in *China's Changing Population*. Taking all the above factors into account, she reached the following conclusion:

> Assuming that without the Great Leap Forward policies and experiences China would have maintained its claimed 1957 death rate of 10.8 during the years 1958–1961, the official data imply that those four years saw over 15 million excess deaths attributable to the Great Leap Forward in combination with poor weather conditions. The computerized reconstruction of China's population trends utilized in this book, which assumes under-reporting of deaths in 1957, as well as in all the famine years, results in an estimated 30 million excess deaths during 1958–1961.[5]

This figure, arrived at in 1984, is the most reliable estimate we have but it is not the only one.

While China has never formally rejected this total or put forward an alternative, a wealth of statistical information has been published which amounts to quasi-official recognition that millions did die of famine. One such work, *Contemporary Chinese Population* published in 1988, goes further by explicitly stating that the official data disguises the extent of the death toll. Official figures show that between 1959 and 1961, the population fell by 13.48 million but the authors say: 'The problem is that there are false figures and 6.03 million people during the three years of difficulty were not taken into account when the calculations were made ... If we take this into account, the death rate in 1960 should be 1 per cent higher at 3.85 per cent. So out of a population of 500 million, there were 19.5 million deaths in the countryside.'[6]

The authors also substantiate anecdotal evidence that large

numbers of girls were allowed to die or were killed during the famine. According to the 1964 census, 0.5 per cent more boys than girls aged 5–9 and 0.4 per cent more males than females aged 9–14 years survived the famine. Generally, even in normal times a higher proportion of male infants than female infants survive in China but the 1982 census indicates that the normal difference is only about 0.1 per cent. This means that during the famine 4.7 million fewer girls survived than would have done so in normal years. In other words, nearly a quarter of the 19.5 million famine victims were peasant girls, who appear to have been deliberately allowed to starve to death or were killed by their parents.

Articles published by some experts in China and by exiled dissidents claim that the death toll is far higher even than Banister's estimate. In 1993, a Chinese scholar writing under the pen-name Jin Hui published an article in a Shanghai academic journal, *Society*, which was later withdrawn. The author looked at inconsistencies in official statistics on birth and death rates, sex ratios, rural and urban populations and provincial and national figures, and concluded that the figures had been falsified to hide a death toll of at least 40 million. Unfortunately, it also true that Chinese statistics about any subject are rarely internally consistent so it is hard to know how significant these discrepancies are. Whether or not this figure of 40 million is to be trusted, it is now used, almost casually, by various authors inside China who lump deaths and the reduction in births together. Cong Jin of the National Defence University writes in *China 1949–1989: The Zig-zag Development Era* that 'From 1959 to 1961 the abnormal deaths plus the reduction of births reached about 40 million.'[7] Another book, *Disasters of Leftism in China* by Wen Yu, published in 1993, claims that 'from 1959 to 1961, the abnormal deaths plus the reduction of births reached altogether more than 40 million with direct economic losses of 120 billion yuan'.[8]

The estimates of American demographers are also challenged by Chen Yizi, a senior Chinese Party official who fled to America after the crackdown that followed the 1989 Tiananmen pro-democracy demonstrations. After 1979, Chen played an important role in the rural reforms as a member of a think-tank called the *Tigaisuo* or System Reform Institute patronized by Zhao Ziyang, then Premier and later Party General Secretary. The new Chinese leadership wanted to find out what had really happened under Mao, and one of the institute's first tasks was to draw up a picture of rural China. Chen was part of a large team of 200 officials who visited every province and examined internal Party documents and records. The institute's report concluded that between 43 and 46 million people had died during the famine and several sources said that an even larger figures of 50 and 60 million deaths were cited at internal meetings of senior Party officials.

The institute's report has never been released but in an interview Chen recalled the death toll for a number of provinces:

Henan	7.8 million
Anhui	8 million
Shandong	7.5 million
Sichuan	9 million
Qinghai	900,000

Thus, in these five provinces alone, 33.2 million people died. Chen argues that these figures are reliable because each province compiled detailed statistics on its population. In normal times, Chinese local officials keep records of household registration and these were particularly important when the commune system operated because with all food rationed, great care was taken in counting the number of mouths.

That such detailed records were kept is clear from the report on Fengyang county in Anhui. Such figures were also used when the Party compiled reports on the famine in each province at the end of 1960; and in places like Gansu officials kept a record of famine deaths as well as the number of mouths to feed. However, while it is clear that Beijing was aware of the scale of the disaster, the reliability of such figures is hard to ascertain. In addition, there is an added complication, because evidence suggests that the Party often produced different versions of the same report. Lower figures were released to lower-ranking officials. Until these internal reports are made public, we cannot be sure that they exist or, if they do, whether they take into account such factors as internal migration or include normal deaths in the totals.

From a moral perspective, the debate is meaningless. Whether 30 or over 40 million perished, China managed to hide the largest famine in history for twenty years. In terms of sheer numbers, no other event comes close to this. Until the Great Leap Forward, the largest famine on record took place in China between 1876 and 1879 when 9–13 million died.

In other great historical famines, a higher proportion of the population died than in China in 1958–61. At the start of the great Irish potato famine in 1845, Ireland had a population of about 8.5 million of whom around 1 million died of hunger and 1.5 million emigrated. Most historians recognize that the Irish famine was caused by a blight which destroyed the potato harvest on which the population depended for most of its food. Relief efforts were undermined by the slowness of communications and transport, and when grain was shipped from North America it did not relieve the hunger. The Irish economy was so dependent on the potato that it was not equipped to process the grain for human consumption. Indeed, before the famine bread was seldom seen and ovens virtually unknown. Even so, the British government still stands accused of acting with indifference to a subject people.

In more recent times, except during war, famines have become rarer. China is often compared to India but in this century India has not suffered a famine of comparable dimensions. India's largest famine in modern times took place between 1896 and 1897 when drought led to 5 million deaths. The Bengal famine of 1942, when around 1.5 million died, was caused by the Japanese invasion of Burma which cut off rice imports.

What sets Mao's famine apart from those in Ireland and India is that it was entirely man-made. China was at peace. No blight destroyed the harvest. There were no unusual floods or droughts. The granaries were full and other countries were ready to ship in grain. And the evidence shows that Mao and the Chinese bureaucracy were in full control of the machinery of government.

The event which most resembles Mao's famine is that in the Ukraine in 1932–3 where circumstances were almost identical, as has been shown in Chapter 3. A slightly larger proportion of China's population died in the Great Leap Forward than in the Soviet Union – 4.6 per cent (if one accepts a figure of 30 million out of a total population of 650 million) compared to 4.11 per cent (7 million out of 170 million). In China, deaths were concentrated among the rural population, so out of a maximum 550 million peasants 5.45 per cent died, one in twenty. Around a quarter of the population of the Ukraine perished in the famine there, largely in one year, 1933. However, in parts of China such as Anhui, it is likely that a quarter of the rural population died just as in the Ukraine.[9]

One can also compare China with Cambodia under Pol Pot. Inspired by Mao, the Khmer Rouge collectivized the entire population in the 1970s and it is reckoned that out of 8 million people, 1 million died. However, this number also includes the victims of a civil war and a war with Vietnam, so the extent of deaths due to famine alone is unclear.

If we look at Mao's famine as a deliberate act of inhumanity, then his record can also be measured against that of Hitler and Stalin. Some 12 million died in the Nazi concentration camps and a further 30 million were killed during the Second World War. Stalin is thought to have allowed 20 million to die in the gulags and overall he is believed to have been responsible for between 30 and 40 million deaths. However, an investigation into Mao's record by Daniel Southerland in the *Washington Post* suggests that Mao exceeded even these ghastly totals:

> While most scholars are reluctant to estimate a total number of 'unnatural deaths' in China under Mao, evidence shows that he was in some way responsible for at least 40 million deaths and perhaps 80 million or more. This includes deaths he was directly responsible for and deaths resulting from disastrous policies he refused to change. One government document that has been internally circulated and seen by a former Communist Party official now at Princeton University [Chen Yizi] says that 80 million died unnatural deaths – most of them in the famine following the Great Leap Forward.[10]

19

How to Record the Annals of a Place?

'Must we force ourselves to forget the
anguish and the wounds of the past so that
we can look to the future and move forward?
And by forgetting these wounds let them fes-
ter in our souls?'

Ba Jin, 1979

IN CHINA'S COLLECTIVE memory, the famine is the dog that
didn't bark. Though it was the greatest trauma experienced
by the Chinese people since 1949 and no one remained
untouched by it, even now it is barely discussed or referred to.
No books, no films, no plays are allowed to do more than make
a passing reference to the 'three years of natural disasters' or
the 'three years of hardship'. And the communes in which the
Chinese lived for a quarter of a century have been forgotten.

By contrast, all talk of the Cultural Revolution which followed
the famine is positively encouraged and the events of these 'ten
years of chaos' are often portrayed as a sudden deviation from
normality. The Cultural Revolution appears in films as an urban
phenomenon, a political upheaval in which high-ranking Party
officials were attacked and which brought anarchy to the streets
of the cities. It is remarkable therefore that the event which
dominated the lives of the vast majority of Chinese, the peasants, does not receive the same attention.

This neglect often appears to be a matter of mere chance.

Take, for example, the minor classic *A Cadre School Life: Six Chapters* by Yang Jiang, which appeared in the early 1980s. She and her husband, the prominent writer Qian Zhongshu, were sent from the Academy of Social Sciences in Beijing to the countryside in 1970. The book, modelled on the classical Chinese work *Six Chapters in a Floating Life*, tells of the hardships that these middle-aged scholars endured working among the peasants in Henan province.[1]

The poverty of the peasants is described well enough. They steal everything from the hopelessly incompetent literati, from old cabbage leaves to their faeces. Yet at no point does Yang Jiang hint at what she must surely have known – that they were living in Xinyang, an epicentre of the famine, alongside the peasants of Luoshan and Xixian who, ten years earlier, had eaten the corpses of their neighbours and, perhaps, even those of their own children. Though it is possible that the couple heard nothing of this during their stay, the former Party General Secretary Hu Yaobang and the dissident Chen Yi, both of whom were sent to May 7th cadre schools in Henan during the Cultural Revolution, became well aware of what had happened and why the peasants were still so hungry and impoverished. After all, it was surely no accident that so many were punished by being sent to this part of Henan to 'learn from the peasants' – in other words to copy their obedience and docility.

Another leading intellectual, the astrophysicist Fang Lizhi, who was also sent to the countryside during the Cultural Revolution, did find out what had happened in Anhui and was horrified. Dubbed 'China's Sakharov' for his outspoken criticism of the Communist Party and his advocacy of democracy, Fang Lizhi was a senior figure in Anhui's Science and Technology University in Hefei who started nationwide student demonstrations in 1987. These led to the dismissal of the General Secretary, Hu Yaobang, and were the precursor of the 1989 pro-democracy demonstrations in Tiananmen Square. While Fang and his wife sought refuge in the American Embassy after the Tiananmen massacre, he wrote in the *New York Review of Books*:

Much of the history of Chinese Communism is unknown to the world or has been forgotten. If, inside China, the whole of society has been coerced into forgetfulness by the authorities, in the West the act of forgetting can be observed in the work of a number of influential writers who have consciously ignored history and have willingly complied with the 'standardised public opinion' of the Communists' censorial system. The work of the late Edgar Snow provides one of the most telling examples of this tendency. Snow lived many years in China: we must assume that he understood its society. And yet in his reports on China after the Communists took power, he strictly observed the regime's propaganda requirements – including the forgetting of history. In *Red China Today*, he had this to say about China in the early 1960s: 'I diligently searched without success, for starving people or beggars to photograph. Nor did anyone else succeed . . . I must assert that I saw no starving people in China, nothing that looked like old-time famine and I do not believe that there is famine in China at this writing.' The facts, which even the Chinese Communists do not dare deny publicly, are that the early 1960s saw one of the greatest famines in more than 2,000 years of recorded Chinese history. In the three years between 1960 and 1963 approximately 25 million people in China died of hunger. As for beggars, not only did they exist, they even had a kind of 'culture' with Communist characteristics. In 1973 in Anhui I listened to a report by the 'advanced' Party secretary of a Chinese village. One of his main 'advanced' experiences was to organise his villagers into a beggar's brigade to go begging through the neighbouring countryside.[2]

Fang's attack on Western observers such as Snow is discussed later, but from what he has written it is clear that Fang is only one of many Chinese intellectuals whose disgust with their rulers was strengthened by what they discovered about the famine. Another is the dissident Ni Yuxian. In *A Chinese Odyssey*, Ni recounts how, as a young soldier from Shanghai, he discovered what was happening from fellow soldiers, who had received letters from home:

One evening, Ni Yixian noticed Xiao Liu, one of his new army friends, crying over a letter he had just received . . .
　'My whole family has starved to death,' his friend replied simply. Xiao Liu was from Anhui . . . Soon Yixian began to notice other of his fellow soldiers weeping when they received letters from

home. He began questioning his comrades. Their stories were always the same. The families of the soldiers were starving. Many were from Anhui . . .

In 1962, Ni Yuxian, then aged 16, took two weeks to write a letter of thirty pages to Mao in which he described the terrible famine, the underlying reasons and his remedy – private farming. He showed the letter to three friends and one night in the barracks they lay under a blanket and discussed it. Only one, Yang Guoli, was in favour of sending the letter to Mao: 'I know it's dangerous,' his friend argued, 'but we have to be responsible to the peasants. If you don't take responsibility, who will? If Chairman Mao really does read the letter, if he knows the true situation, then the results just have to be good. The policies will change . . .'[3]

The letter marked the start of Ni Yuxian's life as a dissident. The same is true of other major figures in the dissident movement such as Wei Jingsheng, the outspoken figure imprisoned during the 1979 Democracy Wall movement, who became one of China's most famous political prisoners. In his writings, he describes his horror at the poverty he witnessed as a Red Guard travelling through the countryside:

Eventually I went to my rural ancestral village in Anhui province. During my stay in the village, the aftermath of the Great Leap Forward was deeply impressed on my mind. Whenever the peasants talked of the Great Leap days, it was as though they were reliving 'doomsday' and could hardly hide their feelings of having been lucky enough to survive. Gradually, I came to understand that the so-called 'three years of natural disasters' were not really natural in origin, but caused by erroneous policies. Peasants recalled, for example, that during the Communising Wind in 1959–60, rice was left to rot in the fields because the peasants were too weakened [by hunger] to harvest.

During a gathering at a friend's house in the neighbouring village, I heard horror stories of villagers who had exchanged babies to eat. I pitied them all. Who had made these parents live to taste, inconceivably, of human flesh mixed with parental tears? By this time, I was able to discern clearly the face of the executioner, whose like would only come along 'once in several centuries in the whole world and once in several millennia in China' – and his name was Mao Zedong. It was Mao Zedong's criminal systems and policies that had made these parents, driven out of their reason by starvation, commit such acts to survive.[4]

Like others, Wei Jingsheng learned about the famine because, under Mao's instructions, peasants were urged to 'speak bitterness' in village meetings, in other words to remind their listeners of how hard life had been before 1949. Local Party committees were also ordered to compile written histories based on these memories. Many Red Guards were amused by this, as one recalled: 'When in the Cultural Revolution we attended meetings in villages, the peasants were asked to speak of their hardships under the old regime but they always talked of 1960. The cadres always became furious because they did not speak of the years before 1949.'[5]

For some Red Guards this was the first they had heard of the famine and such tales helped puncture their illusions about Mao. Even the better informed students were shocked to hear just how bad the famine had been. The peasants had fewer illusions. Fatalistic, ignorant of what had happened outside their own village and resigned to bad government, they were careful to keep their thoughts to themselves. Yet their faith in Mao was not necessarily shaken by the famine. One former Red Guard who lived in a poor village in Anhui said that 'The villagers didn't blame Mao. They said: "Buddha's doctrine is right but the monks read the scriptures with a wicked mouth." '[6]

For much of the Mao era, village loudspeakers blared out propaganda about endless successes in the rest of the countryside, and the official propaganda line swung erratically from one extreme to another, indifferent to logic or consistency. At the start of the Great Leap Forward, the *People's Daily* declared that 'Today, in the era of Mao Zedong, Heaven is here on earth.' Two years later the same paper instructed readers to behave 'as if the times of abundance were the times of shortage'.

Having told the Chinese that the Communist system had 'conquered nature' and that 'natural calamities' were now a thing of the past, the Party then blamed the famine on natural calamities. People were told that the country had suffered the worst natural disaster 'for a hundred years'; that unlike any other natural disaster in history, this disaster of droughts, floods, hurricanes, plagues and pests had affected every corner of China; and that this had happened for three consecutive years.

It is doubtful whether anyone in the villages or in the cities really believed this nonsense but fear ensured that no one dared point out such contradictions and fallacies. One interviewee, who was a student in Beijing at the time, recalled that 'If you said anything, you might be called a counterrevolutionary and put in prison. There were lots of rumours about the failure of the communes but it was impossible to call the people's communes into question. I made myself not question anything. I thought it was better not to think at all.'

In 1960, the official line changed again. The thousands of Soviet experts scattered around the country suddenly packed their bags. Within two weeks they had all gone and now the shortages were blamed on the Russians. In Beijing University, students were informed that 'The official reason for the shortages was that China had borrowed a lot from the Soviet Union. Now because of the ideological difference we had to pay back these debts.'[7] In Shenyang, Liaoning province, schoolchildren were told the same thing:

One day in the bleakest midwinter, a school assembly was held. Principal Gao, thinner and less effervescent than he had been, stood up and denounced the Soviet Union. 'Our one time "elder brother" has betrayed us,' he told us. 'Khrushchev the Revisionist has summoned home all the Soviet engineers and technicians who were in our country helping with socialist construction. He has torn up all the agreements calling for scientific and technical co-operation. He has called in all the loans that the Soviet Union had made to China.'[8]

Others were told that China had only borrowed these funds to fight the Korean War. The loans allegedly had to be repaid with food. Stories were circulated about how fussy the Soviets were, accepting only apples of a certain diameter. What really happened was quite the reverse. From 1958, China exported millions of tonnes of grain to the Soviet Union to demonstrate to the sceptical Khrushchev the success of Mao's Great Leap into Communism; and, convinced by her own propaganda, she also stepped up her exports of food and textiles to Hong Kong and many other countries and increased her aid to various allies such as Albania.

The Party also appealed to national pride. Children were told that 'Chairman Mao has said we must pay back our debts. China must not be a debtor nation. This is a matter of national pride. We must scrimp and save, until the loans are repaid. That is why we have no fruit, vegetables, or grain. They are being sold to raise money. The recklessness of the Soviet Union is responsible for our food shortage.'[9]

More or less the same stories were circulated in labour camps and in the villages. Party officials who debriefed doctors returning from Gansu's famine regions made false patriotism the cornerstone of their appeal. A Party leader told the medical team that

> The purpose of our meeting today is to improve and unify our thoughts. At present the imperialist and revisionist Soviet Union is taking advantage of our difficulties and forcing us to repay our debts. They are pressing us, the people, to oppose the Party and our Great Leader. They are saying that there are people starving to death. Haven't you got dignity? Do we help those imperialists and admit people died of hunger? Do we have our national pride? Do we want to disgrace our Party and Great Leader?[10]

In 1962, the Party also launched a great wave of propaganda to make an ordinary soldier, Lei Feng, who died when a telegraph pole fell on him, the model for the entire nation. His dearest wish was to be 'a rustless cog in the great machinery of socialism' and his most heroic attribute was a mindless, unquestioning obedience.

Five years later, the propaganda machine performed its most astonishing somersault. With the Cultural Revolution in full swing, Liu Shaoqi was blamed for the famine:

> A statement published in 1971 exonerated Mao from all responsibility for the Great Leap Forward. Liu Shaoqi was attacked for promoting excessive radicalism to sabotage Mao's policies in 1958

by urging the hasty nationalization of the communes and the abolition of wages based on the individual's work performance ... in other words the excesses of the Great Leap Forward and the initial defects of the communes were laid at Liu's door while Mao was depicted as the moderate.[11]

The official attitude to the truth changed greatly after 1979, when Deng Xiaoping set about overturning collective agriculture. For a brief period, sometimes called the Democracy Wall movement after a place in Beijing where free speech and wall posters were tolerated, people dared to break many taboos. They attacked the Gang of Four and the Cultural Revolution and, though direct criticism of Mao was still forbidden, writers were encouraged to expose the madness of the Great Leap Forward. In Henan, Yi Xu, the author of the opera *Catastrophe of Lies* mentioned earlier, was given access to internal Party documents. The work was performed and received praise from Deng's lieutenant, Hu Yaobang. Such openness, when the boundaries of what was permissible were undefined, ended in 1981 when the Party drew up its verdict on Mao's rule. The Democracy Wall was closed, *Catastrophe of Lies* was no longer performed, dissenting voices were silenced by harsh jail sentences and all discussion of the Great Leap Forward ceased. In the Party's official resolution on history, Mao was judged to have been 70 per cent correct. The Great Leap Forward was not considered part of the 30 per cent which constituted his mistakes. Instead, the Party declared that 'It was mainly due to the errors of the "Great Leap Forward" and of the struggle against "right opportunism" together with a succession of natural calamities and the perfidious scrapping of contracts by the Soviet government that our economy encountered serious difficulties between 1959 and 1961, which caused serious losses to our country and people.'[12]

Despite the slogan 'Seek truth from facts', the Party issued clear instructions to all concerned on how to handle the past in such internal publications as *How to Record the Annals of a Place*.[13] This particular Orwellian manual, edited by Zheng Zhengxi and published in December 1989, forms part of a series of handbooks for cadres to use when writing the history of their county or work unit. Its instructions apply equally to those supervising histories, plays, novels and films since they must all reflect Party policy. The book is particularly interesting because it recommends a shift in the rewriting of history: 'Some histories still use the old term "three years of natural disasters" as an explanation of the cause of the disaster but we should now make it clear that it was caused by human error. We should not leave people with the impression that judgement has been suspended.'

Indeed, most officials have now stopped pretending that the food shortages were caused by a continual series of disasters. In interviews with the author, senior officials dismissed the notion with a chuckle as if to say, who could be so gullible as to believe such a tall story? In keeping with this change, data on droughts and floods compiled and published by the national meteorological office now show that there was no abnormal weather between 1958 and 1962. Compared to most other years during Mao's rule, there were fewer natural disasters during the famine. In 1960, less than a third of the country's 120 meteorological stations recorded a drought. Of these only eight places posted a severe drought. These official figures were also corroborated by all those interviewed.

In *How to Record the Annals of a Place*, historians are told to treat the Great Leap Forward as an economic, not a political error. This means that the very phrase 'Great Leap Forward' must be written between inverted commas in order to make it clear that there was no increase in production. Those who have done otherwise (the author cites the compilers of histories in Nanjing and Wuxi) are urged to change their texts to delete the earlier view that the Leap brought economic benefits: 'We must start with the fundamental assumption that the "Great Leap Forward" was a bad thing ... We should record what happened in the perspective of the whole situation, to show that people blindly launched new projects. Although some were successful, it must be clear that in its entirety it was a failure.'

Such successes as there were must be shown to be the consequence of people rejecting, not following, the methods of the Leap. The author urges other historians to demolish the myth that production rose steeply and, above all, he says historians must differentiate between 'blind fervour' and 'revolutionary spirit'. They should reveal the connection between the anti-right opportunist movement, leftist mistakes and the disasters of the Leap.

The book is particularly interesting when it speaks of the differences between the Great Leap Forward and the Cultural Revolution. While the Great Leap Forward is a forgivable mistake 'in the Chinese people's pursuit of the road of socialist construction led by the Communist Party', the Cultural Revolution must be treated as 'a severe and disastrous event wrongly launched by leaders and manipulated by a counter-revolutionary group'. It points out, too, that the Cultural Revolution lasted for ten years but the Great Leap Forward only lasted for three, so in terms of damage inflicted the Cultural Revolution was by far the greater catastrophe: 'The "Great Leap Forward" damaged economic life but the Cultural Revolution began in the ideological field so everything was affected.'

Given this emphasis the book talks of the famine chiefly in terms of damage to the Party, so that it is 'only an error in the process of socialist construction of our economy which was solved by readjustment'. In the Cultural Revolution, but not the famine, Party member was set against Party member in an internal war. So the book goes on to spell out how the Great Leap Forward must be recorded so as to put the Party in a good light. The author puts forward an example from his own compilation of the history of Guizhou: 'Even before the Spring Festival there was a food shortage and only enough stored food to last two months. So I recorded what the county Party committee did in a very positive light. I said, for example, that they started an "anti-grain-hiding campaign".' In reality, it was precisely this forcible seizure of grain that caused so many deaths. The moral dimension of what the Party did in creating an artificial famine is entirely avoided by omitting any mention of the price paid in human lives. This absence of any reference to the toll of human misery is in keeping with the general practice in Chinese reporting. While economic losses are always carefully calculated when reporting disasters, similar care is never taken in counting lives lost.

Finally, the book makes it clear that it is still taboo to talk of a famine. This means that official accounts of recent Chinese history still cannot be relied upon. Indeed the degree to which the Party remains in firm control of the past inside China is astonishing, particularly since this also requires the complicity of overseas Chinese, few of whom have been willing to speak out, either from a distorted sense of patriotism, or to protect relatives. Nevertheless, accounts of the period are emerging both within and outside China. One thinly disguised record of the famine was published in China in 1994.[14] *Hungry Mountain Village* tells the story of a Beijing journalist who is labelled as a rightist and then sent to live in a village in the north-west. In this bitter and angry account, no horrors are spared. The local Party officials are portrayed in a particularly harsh light. The village Secretary is an ex-army man who feeds himself and the rest of his family as others starve to death, and exploits his power to force women to sleep with him. Before the spring sowing, he dips the seeds in poison to prevent children eating them and many die as a result. The peasants, too, behave like savages, chopping the bodies of children into meat which they eat. Although this is hardly flattering to the Party, the book avoids all mention of Mao himself. Even for this author, the Great Leader remains beyond explicit criticism.

These official and semi-official restrictions have not blunted the readiness of peasants to talk privately, without inhibitions, about the past. They are well aware of Mao's role, yet they share a genuine reluctance to condemn him. Conversations with peasants follow a circuitous pattern: Mao cannot be entirely blamed because he was deceived by false reports sent by ambitious officials. As always in China, the Emperor is never wrong, only misled by his ministers who flatter him and who in turn are deceived by dishonest lower-ranking officials. On the other hand, they cannot be blamed either, because they have no choice but to follow orders from above. So in the end no one is responsible.

Indeed, hardly anyone was ever punished for the famine. Lower-ranking officials who were initially arrested were often released on Mao's orders. Those condemned as right opportunists were rarely fully rehabilitated after 1979, apart from key figures such as Peng Dehuai who were already dead. The peasants, who lost all their possessions, were generally not compensated. No monuments commemorate the victims and some

Chinese are still not willing to believe that a famine costing so many lives ever took place.

Yet the famine does have a ghostly existence in the collective consciousness of the Chinese. Events in the period are projected back into the pre-1949 past. Films such as the award-winning *Yellow Earth* about the life of drought-stricken peasants in the loess plateau of Shaanxi contain subtle references. Most tellingly of all, when the pro-democracy demonstrators took over Tiananmen Square in 1989, they chose to show their contempt for the Party and to rally support by going on hunger strike. This form of protest is not common in Chinese politics and many Beijing citizens expressed their sympathy by bringing food to the hunger-strikers. Amongst rural Chinese, this symbolic gesture must have tapped a deep well of feeling. How could anyone willingly allow themselves to starve? The effect on the conscience of leaders such as Zhao Ziyang or Deng Xiaoping, men who were so intimately involved with the famine, can only be imagined.

20

The Western Failure

'I think the time will come when historians
will properly analyse the issue of collectivization.'

Nikita Khrushchev

A FAMINE ON such an enormous scale would never have
occurred had it not been kept secret. As the economist Amartya
Sen was the first to point out, famines are caused by censorship
and are the result of political decisions.[1] If Mao had not gone
to great lengths to deny that there was a crisis, then however
great the shortage of food, the famine would have been averted.
However, since 1949 China had become a closed and tightly
controlled state in which the Party wielded an absolute monopoly over information. With the press in China silenced, the
role of Western observers became of vital importance. Had they
alerted the world to what was happening, then the famine
might have been averted or at least shortened.

At the beginning of the famine, there were only a few foreign
journalists and diplomats stationed in Beijing. Still fewer journalists had permission to tour the country. The largest group
watched China from Hong Kong where they interviewed refugees, read the mainland press and listened to broadcasts. Only
these small groups of people had the time and patience to
analyse the fragments of information which became available
and they thus exerted an unusually strong influence on both
public opinion and the reactions of Western governments.
Above all they influenced the United States, whose citizens
were kept out of China but which was reluctant to trust what

its ally, Taiwan, said was happening. The China-watchers' views also influenced the newly independent countries of the Third World as they sought new allies and fresh ideas on development. Neighbours such as North Vietnam and Cambodia were particularly swayed by the reported successes of Mao's policies but so too were revolutionaries in Africa, Latin America and the Middle East.

During the famine, the role of these China-watchers became still more important as the world tried to evaluate the truth behind rumours filtering out. Was there really a famine? Should the West offer help? Would the Communists fall?

In Taiwan, Chiang Kai-shek became convinced that there was a famine, and intelligence reports of uprisings among the peasants on the mainland encouraged him to believe that the population would welcome his army as liberators. Around 1960, he ordered the Nationalist army to prepare for an invasion to recapture the mainland and his government broadcast promises of support to the insurgents and rewards for any Communist officers who changed sides, offering them high positions in a new government. *The New York Times* reported that in 1962 all Taipei was gripped by feverish expectations of an imminent return.[2]

Chiang repeatedly pressed the American government to back his invasion but was always turned down. The invasion never took place and Chiang missed perhaps his only chance of regaining the mainland. In reaching their decision the Americans were confused by the conflicting reports of relations between Beijing and Moscow. If an invasion went ahead would Khrushchev defend China against an American-backed invasion? Fantastic theories were spun which turned on whether there was a real split between the two Communist giants or whether it was merely a ruse to deceive the West.

The risk of sparking off a global conflict was one factor in Washington's decision not to aid Taiwan but American domestic politics also played a part. In the early 1950s Senator Joseph McCarthy had led a vicious campaign to root out supposed left-wing sympathizers within America. Old China hands came under suspicion and were accused of having 'lost' China to the Communists, a loss that became particularly grievous when soon afterwards American troops died fighting the forces of the new Chinese regime in the Korean War. Many China experts in the State Department were purged in an atmosphere of suspicion and anger. Thus, for years to come, those academics and journalists who wrote about China risked embroilment in a war between two bitterly divided camps, and reports of the famine in China appeared in a highly politicized, if not partisan, context. Any invasion of mainland China needed first to have the support of the American public: the more horrible the famine, the more support there would be for tough action. American reporters therefore came under pressure from different sides to show China in a particular light.

As it now appears, the mainstream American press reported the famine accurately. In December 1958 the Scripps-Howard newspapers printed a series of articles entitled 'Chain Gang Empire', one of which stated that

> the abolition of the family is an avowed, primary sociological objective of Red China's new commune system – the first serious effort in history to put a whole nation on what amounts to a prison chain gang . . . We may suspect that no people has ever been forced to work so hard and for so little as the Chinese people . . . They have suffered much in these years and have been regimented as has no other people in modern times by the most totalitarian regime of the twentieth century.

A report in 1959 by the *New York World Telegram and Sun* described how in 'famished Red China slaves steal pig's slop'.[3] In the following year *Time* magazine reported that in 1960 'hunger stalks mainland China for the third straight year'.[4] In 1961, the *Weekly Post* recorded that 'China must endure an ordeal of famine and pestilence on a scale which even this unfortunate country has not had to face in this century'. In 1962, *The New York Times* claimed that 'Communist China is a land of massive malnutrition and hunger. Three successive years of poor harvests have reduced the food available to most Chinese to little above the barest subsistence level.'[5]

At the time, however, such reports were ridiculed by many, not least by the respected BBC journalist Felix Greene, brother of the writer Graham Greene. Though based in New York he visited China in 1960 and in his subsequent book, *A Curtain of Ignorance*, he denigrated these reports in the American press, accusing their authors of exaggeration and misinformation, and of having been duped by warmongers in American Intelligence.

The most outspoken and influential figure to argue that something truly terrible was happening in China was Joseph Alsop, a Washington columnist. Throughout the famine he published articles which have turned out to be accurate. At one point, he gave serious consideration to a report that the famine was so bad that the amount of food available per capita had dropped to 600 calories a day: 'A hospitalized person on a strict diet of 600 calories a day can normally be expected to lose about 20 pounds a month ... in short the population of China is starving. The starvation is methodical and rationed but it is not even very slow starvation.'[6]

Greene dismissed this as 'a medical absurdity' but Alsop was correct in blaming Mao and his mad rush into establishing communes for the catastrophe, instead of the alleged natural disasters. Mao, he argued, was trying to follow a pattern of industrialization set by Stalin, but the Russians had got away with it because their standard of living was higher. Even if living standards fell by 50 per cent the Soviets had still had a sufficient safety margin to protect them from complete disaster. But China, he insisted, had no safety margin at all. Alsop repeatedly posed the question of whether mass starvation might lead to an uprising. Such concerns were given very serious consideration by the US State Department which was aware of the deep split between Liu Shaoqi and Mao. In the summer of 1962, Alsop wrote in the academic journal *China Quarterly* that no Western nation in modern times had experienced the 'nadir of wretchedness' seen in China:

> The most reliable data obtainable in Hong Kong this spring, derived from great numbers of refugee interrogations and collected and analysed with extreme care, showed an average food intake for mainland China of 1,300 to 1,600 calories per person a day, according to the individual's labour category. These figures are squarely based on the best first hand evidence that exists; and they are therefore unchangeable except by those experts who

think they know more about the Chinese diet than the people who have recently been eating it.[7]

The trouble was that it was all too easy to challenge refugee accounts. As an editorial in *The Times* pointed out: 'Most of the dispute over how much food the Chinese have been eating in the past three years centres on the evidence of refugees who cross the border into Hong Kong ... Many of the experts question this evidence, arguing that the refugee is sometimes biased, rarely accurate, usually interested in painting an adverse picture.'[8] This prejudice reflected an earlier opinion of *The Times* that 'the sufferings of the ordinary peasant from war, disorder, and famine have been immeasurably less in the last decade than in any other decade in the century'.[9]

Amidst this debate, no Americans were allowed into China to see for themselves, partly because of the obstacles erected by Beijing but above all because of Washington's own restrictions. The United States did not recognize the Communist Party as the legitimate government of China and McCarthyism's influence ensured that a very tough line was taken to prevent American citizens from going there. The only American journalist who found a way round these impediments was Edgar Snow. Snow had met Mao and other Communist leaders in Yanan in 1936, just after they had escaped encirclement by the Nationalist armies. His subsequent account of the Communists, *Red Star over China*, was a great scoop and even now still ranks as one of the best sources of information on the early history of the Chinese Communists. In 1960 Snow somehow managed to get into China and for five months was taken around the country. In *The Other Side of the River: Red China Today*, he later wrote an exhaustive account of his visits to communes, factories and schools, his talks with senior leaders and his travels to disparate parts of the country, from Inner Mongolia to Chongqing in Sichuan province. He concluded that the famine did not exist:

Throughout 1959–62 many Western press editorials and headlines referred to 'mass starvation' in China and continued to cite no supporting facts. As far as I know, no report by any non-communist visitor to China provided an authenticated instance of starvation during this period.

I assert that I saw no starving people in China, nothing that
looked like old-time famine (and only one beggar, among flood
refugees in Shenyang) and that the best Western intelligence on
China was well aware of this. Isolated instances of starvation due
to neglect or failure of the rationing system were possible. Considerable malnutrition undoubtedly existed. Mass starvation? No.

With no other American visitors to hoodwink, the Chinese
made use of other Westerners, especially the British. Sir Cyril
Hinshelwood, President of the Royal Society, returned from a
visit saying, 'There is much that is tremendously impressive and
admirable in new China . . . it is quite likely that many of them
are now freer in some ways than they have ever been.' The
distinguished poet and art critic Sir Herbert Read visited China
in 1959 and praised the communes: 'It does not matter what
the system is called . . . what counts more than statistics is the
happiness and contentment of the peasants.'[10]
Generally, the Chinese preferred to invite people who knew
as little about China as possible, such as the war hero Field
Marshal Montgomery, who in 1961 was given an audience with
Mao and afterwards reported that China's population had not
fallen, rather it had increased.[11] Even those who should have
known better were duped. Lord Boyd-Orr, an agricultural
expert and former head of the UN's Food and Agriculture
Organization, came back from China in May 1959 full of praise.
He concluded that China had indeed increased food production by up to 100 per cent and believed that 'modern farming methods had increased Chinese yields to levels comparable
with those of Britain and had ended the traditional Chinese
famine cycle . . . China has one quarter of the world's population but seems capable of feeding it well.'[12] The distinguished
scientist and sinologist Dr Joseph Needham thought it was nonsense even to think that the peasants might be oppressed, claiming that the collective kitchens were 'a matter of pride in China
today, not of compulsion or regimentation'.[13]
The British were not alone. A Swiss economist, Gilbert
Etienne, wrote with great confidence in *Le Monde* in December
1961 that 'It may be said at the outset – and it is one of the
rare points on which we can claim to be categorical – that it is
false to speak of "general famine". The grievous times of the

Kuomintang, when millions of human lives were eliminated for want of minimum subsistence, have not reappeared.'

At the height of the famine in 1960, only two writers other than Edgar Snow were allowed to enter China. One was Felix Greene. After his Potemkin-like tour he asserted that 'death by hunger has ceased in China. Food shortages and severe ones there may have been, but no starvation . . . The indisputable fact is that the famines that in one area or another constantly ravaged the farmlands of China and the fear of starvation, which for so long haunted the lives of Chinese peasants, are today things of the past.'

The third visitor in 1960 was the part-Chinese writer Han Suyin, who also saw no famine. Although her hosts pointedly ran a film for her about the Soviet famine in the 1920–1 period of War Communism, she missed the hint. Even in Sichuan she found no famine and concluded that 'despite the errors of the Leap [and] the shortages owing to agricultural disasters, the Leap did achieve its main goal which was accelerated industrial development'.[14]

She was followed by other admirers such as Che Guevara from Cuba and the Swedish writer Gunnar Myrdal who in 1962 was even allowed to spend time in a Chinese village. None of them came back with anything but praise for China. The most outspoken defender of Mao was the French socialist politician, François Mitterrand, who later became France's President. He spent three weeks touring China and was granted a two-hour interview with Mao which he reported in *L'Express* on 23 February 1961. Mitterrand was certain that 'Mao is not a dictator . . . the mastery which he exercises is conferred on him by a power over his people which is not produced by the demagogic fanaticism backed by a strong police state of Hitler in Germany, nor the cynical energy of Mussolini in Italy . . .' Unlike such right-wing dictators, Mao was a 'humanist' and 'a new type of man' in whom, Mitterrand said, doctrinal rigour was allied 'with a vigilant realism'. As such, Mao had to be speaking the truth when he said that 'the people of China have never been near famine . . . I repeat in order to be clearly understood: there is no famine in China.' In his meeting with Mitterrand, Mao boasted that Western newspapers had been unable to find proof of famine:

Oh, I know your Western newspapers have printed headlines about what they call the famine in China. Their propaganda needs a large helping of deaths. What they are looking for is proof that we have failed. Above all it is our people's communes which annoy them. They already see the rebels, the millions of peasants marching against our regime . . . but I want to make this point – we do not care about this campaign of lies which is nothing more than a new form of imperialist aggression . . . We are used to this. Honest and serious people will understand us in the end. All we care about is their verdict.

Among these 'honest and serious people' were the Western 'foreign experts' actually living in China at the time, such as the New Zealand poet Rewi Alley, the British left-wing journalist Wilfred Burchett and Isobel and David Crook, who in 1959 wrote *Revolution in a Chinese Village – Ten-mile Inn.* Such people at best remained silent but some went further, undermining reports of a famine by publishing books that showered praise on the Great Leap Forward and Maoist farming.

The worst apologist was probably Anna Louise Strong. A journalist and propagandist in the Communist cause in both China and the Soviet Union, she should have known better. She had been in the Soviet Union during collectivization and the subsequent famine. In their 1930s' paean to Stalinism, *The Soviet Union: A New Civilization,* the British socialists Beatrice and Sidney Webb quoted her as denying that there was any brutality or even force used to expel the *kulaks.* On the contrary, she said, 'the meetings I personally attended were more seriously judicial, more balanced in their discussion, than any court trial I have attended in America'. In 1962 Strong was in Beijing writing propaganda booklets for the Chinese that eulogized the communes. In *China's Fight for Grain,* published in 1963, she repeated Mao's line that China was suffering from the worst natural disasters in a century. The drought was apparently so serious that in 1960 a child could wade across the Yellow River. In this crisis, she claimed, the communes actually saved China from famine: 'The lives of the people and the lives of the communities were cherished. The nationwide slogan became: "No one shall starve!" . . . there was no pulverising of communities, no scattering of starving people to beg and die along the roads. All communities even when hungry stood, fought and were given aid.'

It is impossible to say whether such people really knew what was going on and told deliberate lies, whether they deluded themselves, or whether they had no way of finding out the truth, but not all of the 300–400 foreigners then living in Beijing can be accused of bias. One example was the resident correspondent for the Reuters newsagency, Clare McDermott.[15] The Chinese Foreign Ministry insisted that Reuters could only send journalists who did not speak Chinese and had no prior knowledge of the country. McDermott therefore relied heavily on his interpreter who was given careful instructions as to what he could tell the foreigner. One interpreter who confided too much disappeared. Not surprisingly, McDermott, though suspecting that there were acute food shortages, was unable to obtain much evidence or even grasp what the thinly disguised attacks on Mao in the press were alluding to. The significance of Deng Tuo's articles or Wu Han's work on Hai Rui, all too obvious to the Chinese, were also missed by more expert analysts in embassies. One of McDermott's translators, who went back to his home in Wutaishan, Shanxi province, in 1962 and found that his family was reduced to eating tomato leaves, returned to Beijing shaken, but McDermott could not make much of this. Felix Greene was thus able to claim that 'Reuters from their bureau in Peking, reported the food shortages, but never described them in terms of "famine" conditions.'

In stark contrast to the Ukrainian famine when some diplomats and journalists did find out what was happening and reported what they saw and heard, none of the foreigners in Beijing between 1958 and 1962 seem to have had any idea that millions were starving to death. The Chinese authorities were far more successful at keeping foreigners in the dark than had been the Soviet authorities. From 1960 to 1963 they restricted the movements of resident journalists and diplomats to the main cities and halted the circulation of provincial papers outside the country.

In such circumstances, the British press tended to assume that China was telling the truth about the natural disasters. *The Times* earnestly reported the theory of Lu Wo, the Deputy

Director of the Central Meteorological Bureau, that China's climate was changing. Lu Wo said that there were so many floods and droughts because China had entered a different cycle of weather. The weather story was largely accepted even though meteorologists in neighbouring countries such as Japan noticed nothing unusual.[16] Other papers gave wide coverage to Chinese claims that the food shortages were caused by deliveries to the Soviet Union. The Hong Kong-based magazine *Far Eastern Economic Review* gave little credence to the horror stories related by refugees who had crossed the border into Hong Kong. After all, in 1958 and 1959 China had stepped up its food exports to the colony. One of the *Review*'s contributors, Colin Garratt, commented: 'It is clear that many millions of Chinese are very, very short of food. Unlike some of their neighbours in South Korea, very few of them, if any, seem actually to be starving to death.'[17]

Refugee interviews formed the basis of academic research by Americans such as Richard Walker and Ivan and Miriam London who tried to raise the alarm.[18] Their reports became more credible when in early 1961 the Chinese government reversed itself and began to admit grave food shortages. As a result, offers of aid came pouring in. The Kuomintang in Taiwan said they were ready to give 100,000 tonnes of grain. Japan, too, offered help. All sorts of luminaries, among them the philosopher Bertrand Russell, signed letters demanding that something should be done, and the British Prime Minister Harold Macmillan spoke of the crisis in the House of Commons. Left-wing papers such as the *New Statesman* and the *Guardian* urged the United States to send food aid.[19] The Labour politician Michael Foot said that Washington with its overflowing granaries should not allow ideological differences to prevent it from delivering aid and US senators such as Hubert Humphrey took up the cause.[20]

From the start, China ruled out accepting aid from America. In February 1961, the Foreign Minister Chen Yi told Japanese visitors that China would never 'stoop to beg for food from the US'.[21] Later, President Kennedy also rejected the possibility, saying: 'The Chinese Communist regime is extremely hostile to us in their propaganda and so on. There are no indications they want the food, and they have never asked for it.'[22] The debate on food relief continued in 1962. One British MP compared the situation to the Soviet Union in 1926 and argued that if the West had done more to end the famine there, then the Russian Communists would have lost power and the course of history would have been changed. Western politicians had other motives for wanting to help.[23] Unrest and even civil war in China were greatly feared, particularly by the British government, which was alarmed by the flood of refugees arriving in Hong Kong in 1962. Some speculated that the refugees might be a Trojan horse to enable Beijing to overthrow British rule. The Hong Kong police started to send the refugees back to China on trains and even Taiwan began to refuse to accept them.

Whatever people outside China said or did, there was nevertheless little that the West could do. China rebuffed all offers of assistance, even those by neutral international bodies such as the League of Red Cross Societies. The Chinese Red Cross Society sent a cable to Geneva saying that although 'our rural areas have suffered from serious natural calamities in the past two years there has never been famine'. It went on to say that the nation was 'fully capable of overcoming temporary difficulties caused by these calamities'.[24]

China would not stoop to accepting charity from foreigners but she did begin to buy millions of tonnes of grain from Australia, Canada and other countries, and imports peaked in 1964 at 6.4 million tonnes. Beijing also appealed to overseas Chinese to send food parcels and donations to buy chemical fertilizer.[25] The Hong Kong press reported that China had offered to give a banquet to any of her citizens who persuaded their relatives in the colony to make a foreign exchange donation to a mainland bank. Hong Kong Chinese queued for hours to send food parcels and in the first half of 1962 alone sent packages worth £2.5 million.[26]

However, as the food shortages eased and the flood of refugees diminished, the world's interest in what had happened in China faded. China's agricultural crisis became an issue restricted to the narrow circles of the China-watchers and the grain traders.

Even now in the West the famine is still not accepted as a historical event. Sufficient doubt was cast on the allegations of

Alsop and others at the time for those who later wrote books on China to feel confident in dismissing the famine in a few lines; and this applied both to those sympathetic to Beijing and those mistrustful of the Communists. In his 1966 biography of Mao, the British academic Stuart Schram devoted little more than a sentence to the famine: 'The winter of 1960–61 was a bitter one in China. An extremely efficient system of rationing spread the hunger equally over the entire population but in order to attenuate the famine it was necessary to make large grain purchases from Canada and Australia.' In 1972, a much more critical and hostile work by the American journalist Stanley Karnow, *Mao and China: Inside China's Cultural Revolution*, took a similar line: 'Through their strong, pervasive control network, however, the Communists were able to equalize the food shortages by maintaining a strict rationing system. Widespread famine, which had so often afflicted China in the past, when the death toll during lean years ran into millions, did not occur.' Those who, like Karnow, tried to comprehend the Cultural Revolution were handicapped by this failure to accept the enormous scale of the famine. In fact it was the key to the puzzle.

Political analysts were not alone in making this mistake. An authority on Chinese agriculture, Dwight H. Perkins, wrote in *Agricultural Development in China 1368–1969* (1969) that the Communists' centralized control over the grain harvest had enabled them to cope with natural disasters:

> The impact of this change was clearly demonstrated in the poor harvests of 1959 through 1961. The 15 to 20 per cent drop in grain production which probably occurred in the entire country would have meant in years past many millions of deaths in the areas most severely affected. Tight control, particularly an effective system of rationing, together with the past development of the railroads meant that few if any starved outright. Instead the nutritional levels of the whole country were maintained, perhaps not with precise equality, but with a close approximation to it. As a result, the regime averted a major disaster.

A belief in the achievements of Maoist agriculture extended to the doyen of American China-watchers, John K. Fairbank, who in *China Perceived* (1974) stated that, 'valued in the Chinese peasant's terms, the revolution has been a magnificent achievement, a victory not only for Mao Zedong, but for several hundreds of millions of Chinese people'. Another even more influential American pundit, the liberal economist J. K. Galbraith, became convinced after a visit to China that the country's agriculture worked well. As he wrote in *A China Passage* (1973), 'There can now be no serious doubt that China is devising a highly effective economic system. Frank Coe and Sol Adler [who travelled with him] . . . guess that the rate of expansion in Chinese industrial and agricultural output is now between 10 and 11 percent annually. This does not seem to me implausible.'

Ignorant of the millions who had been sacrificed on the altar of Mao's vanity, academics and pundits now held up China as a development model, and Mao's policies began to cast a terrible and destructive shadow on the rest of the Third World. With unconscious irony, the *Far Eastern Economic Review* set the tone in an editorial published at the height of the famine in 1960: 'We believe that what is happening in China is of momentous importance because if the authorities succeed in their social, economic and political ambitions they will offer to the world a new champion of the non-European majority, a new model for human society and a new method of overcoming poverty.'

In *China Comes of Age*, published in 1969, the French writer Jean-Pierre Brulé took this a step further and declared that 'Peking's unique experiment thus presents the hungry masses of Asia and Africa with a compelling example, as they struggle to find some way out of their own underdevelopment . . .' A few years later, the China-watcher Leo Goodstadt wrote in *Mao Tse Tung – the Search for Plenty* that 'when it came to agriculture, Mao was well ahead of other Asian leaders, and his ideas tally with the sort of thinking found among non-Marxist economists . . .'

One of those economists was the Deputy Director of the World Food Council and a former senior official at the UN's Food and Agriculture Organization, Sartaj Aziz. In 1978 he devoted a whole book to praising the communes.[27] His book and his message were promoted by another important influence on development thinking, Barbara Ward, the co-author of works such as *Only One Earth – the Care and Maintenance of a Small Planet,* a report by seventy international development consultants. In the introduction to Aziz's book she wrote that 'The Chinese have found solutions to virtually all the major problems posed by the first stages of modernization . . . The Chinese achievement was contrived by ignoring the accepted beliefs of western development experts and the most sober tenets of orthodox Marxism.'

Most extraordinary of all, such books specifically credited Mao with having ended China's famines. Brulé, for instance, says that 'the fact that the regime survived the three black years in which natural conditions damaged harvests to an unprecedented degree proved to the Chinese that heaven had not withdrawn its mandate [from Mao] . . . there were no more of the horrible famines such as that in 1920–21 when half a million died and ten million were left destitute . . . Mao had fought the dragons and won.'

Others lavished praise on the great achievements of Maoist science. A team of Americans shown around Dazhai and other propaganda showpieces returned to publish *China: Science Walks on Two Legs – A Report from Science for the People.* This uncritical acceptance of Mao's success passed into university textbooks such as *Economics of Change in Less Developed Countries* by David Coleman and Frederick Nixson (1978) which asserted that

> China's scientific and technological capabilities have been developed so as to improve the living standards of the mass of the population, increase agricultural and industrial production and modernize Chinese society . . . great stress is placed on national self-reliance in technological progress and the policy of 'walking on two legs' is aimed at avoiding the sectoral, geographical and social class divisions and inequalities characteristic of the majority of LDCs [Less Developed Countries].

China's alleged egalitarianism was much admired, especially when compared with India. Egalitarianism was a key goal in development thinking in the 1970s and enshrined in several UN resolutions. In practice, this meant that policies which allowed some peasants to get richer than others were discouraged in UN-sponsored development projects. Indirectly, this approach endorsed the political persecution of rich peasants by Mao and earlier by Stalin. An Open University textbook by Gavin Kitching entitled *Development and Underdevelopment in Historical Perspective* declares, for example, that 'A total loss of individual peasant autonomy (in the use of land and labour power) has been the price of a continual rise in living standards and of greater equality both among peasants and between peasants and others.' He goes on to claim that Maoist China was a success because it fed its people and 'cut urban-rural migration to zero and indeed sent tens of millions of people out of urban areas into the countryside'.

It is perhaps unfair to criticize such books in the light of later knowledge, but many of these judgements were based on little evidence. After the Great Leap Forward, China published few statistics and those figures that were made available merely consisted of percentages, none of which could be verified, let alone measured, against independent research. China was an intensely secretive, tightly controlled society, as even her admirers conceded. Too many scholars readily accepted propaganda as fact, and even though more details of the famine emerged in the 1980s, there has still been a deep reluctance to reconsider the question. Gavin Kitching's book came out in 1989, several years after American demographers had announced that 30 million had died during the famine, and school textbooks such as *Modern China* by C. K. Macdonald also continued to promote the idea that the famine had nothing to do with the Great Leap Forward: 'Between 1960–1962 famine hit China. This was due mainly to the bad weather. In some parts of China there were floods, in other parts drought . . . It is difficult to judge how many people died in the famine. But one thing is certain; the big improvements made in farming in the 1950s saved millions more Chinese people [from] starving to death.'[28] Another children's book, by Gladys Hickman, *Introducing the New China* published in 1983, ignored the famine altogether and lauded the communes even as they were being disbanded: 'China has managed to do something almost no other developing country in the world has done: give everyone a better chance of a "good life". The communes are the key

to this success. It is through the communes that rural life in
China is being transformed.'[29]

Writers with a far deeper knowledge of China have also hesitated to face up to the famine. In 1990 Oxford University Press
published a history of China, *Rebellions and Revolutions* by Jack
Gray, which still avers that the famine was not man-made.

> It has been suggested in China that twenty million people died as
> a result of the agricultural disasters of these three bad years. If
> that is so, it was one of the greatest recorded famines in history.
> The figure is the result of indirect inferences drawn from the
> movement of China's population figures and cannot be taken
> literally. But there is no doubt that the number of deaths from
> famine and the results of malnutrition were at least of the order
> associated with the great famines of the past.

Gray even argues that Mao was the first leader to recognize the
existence of the famine and to issue orders to rectify the crisis.

Another textbook published two years later, *Chinese Communism* by Dick Wilson and Matthew Grenier, further minimizes
what happened: 'The bad harvest of 1959 following so closely
after the fragmentation and disorganisation of the peasant
economy, resulted in three years of the worst famine since the
Communists came to power.' And a recent biography of Mao
by the Australian scholar Ross Terrill which was reissued in
1993 devotes only a few lines to the famine and stresses the
positive side of the Great Leap Forward: 'As therapy the Leap
was not without benefit, each generation must find its own
excitement, and 1958 provided some for millions of young
farmers. Local initiative was sparked, communal spirit grew.
The ordinary person felt anew his Chineseness and a new
framework of rural government – fusing work life and civic life
– came into existence.'

Only one book devoted to the famine has been published in
English – *Famine in China, 1959–61* by Penny Kane, a British
academic. Though strong on demographics, elsewhere the
author appears to sympathize with Mao. She argues that Peng
Dehuai was wrong to challenge Mao in 1959 because this turned
the crisis into a leadership battle and she goes on to support
China's decision to reject outside help and to praise the ration-

ing system: 'Even in 1959–61, it seemed probable that co-ordinated group activity and the sharing of any available resources helped to protect the most vulnerable from suffering disproportionately.' She is also inclined to see the benefits of Mao's policies: 'Among the positive outcomes of the period of the Great Leap, now often overlooked, was that it was highly educational. Large numbers of agricultural scientists and technicians spent time in the rural areas instead of in laboratories and many experiments aimed at improving existing agricultural practices were attempted.'

Given these entrenched perceptions in the world of academia, it is not surprising that Third World students working abroad became enthusiastic about Mao's China. Many studied in China itself or visited it, including those men who would later play a leading role in Angola, Mozambique and Ethiopia. In Somalia, Tanzania, Guinea and Ethiopia, revolutionary leaders tried to copy the agricultural ideas of Mao and Stalin. Traditional agricultural practices were abandoned, large-scale irrigation schemes were launched, the small peasant farmer was made a social outcast and various types of collectives and communes were attempted. As in China, the goal was the mechanization of agriculture but the tractors rarely materialized. Instead many of these governments found themselves grappling with a hostile peasantry, famine and civil war.

China's close ally, President Julius Nyerere of Tanzania, for example, explicitly talked of creating a 'Great Leap Forward' when he resettled between four and six million of his subjects in collective villages and spoke of the need to prevent the growth of a '*kulak* class'. In Ethiopia, the revolutionaries who took power after overthrowing Emperor Haile Selassie were divided, some supporting Mao, others Stalin. Their debate over rural policy became so fierce that the different factions waged pitched battles in Addis Ababa during a period known as the 'Red Terror'. The Maoists lost but Colonel Mengistu later moved the peasants into semi-voluntary co-operatives and then launched a three-year forced collectivization programme. As the programme was stepped up, Mengistu attacked the rampant 'individualism' of rich peasants, and the private plots allowed to peasants were reduced from a fifth to a tenth of a hectare.

It was not just in sub-Saharan Africa that Mao's communes were admired and imitated. Iran, Iraq, Sudan, Algeria and Libya all tried various forms of collective agriculture. Some writers have argued that in Iran the Shah lost the support of the peasantry when he began forcing them out of their villages into 'agro-business units'. However, Chinese influence was most evident in North Vietnam and Cambodia. The Khmer Rouge leader Pol Pot was taken to Dazhai and when he won power he set out to imitate China's perceived success. Determined to restore Khmer pride, he tried to outdo Mao in his zeal to establish collective agriculture. The entire population was sent to the countryside and forced to labour night and day on massive irrigation schemes which the Party promised would create huge wealth. The canals and dams were built without expertise or learning, which the Khmer Rouge held in contempt, and, as in China, they soon collapsed. Haing Ngor, the Cambodian doctor who won an Oscar for playing Dith Pran in the film *The Killing Fields*, writes in his autobiography:

> Except for their dark skins, everything about the Khmer Rouge was alien, from China. They had borrowed their ideology from Mao . . . like the concept of the Great Leap Forward. Sending the intellectuals to the countryside to learn from the peasants was an idea of the Chinese Cultural Revolution. Their AK-47s and their olive green caps and their trucks were Chinese. Even the music they played from the loudspeakers was Chinese, with Khmer words.

As Haing Ngor points out, it was ignorance of what had really happened in China which gave Pol Pot the overweening confidence to think he could take a war-torn, bankrupt agricultural country and turn it into an industrial power. He believed that Mao had exploited the latent energies of the people by freeing them from cooking meals or raising children and channelling them into backbreaking manual labour.

> Unfortunately Pol Pot the maker of policy was the same Saloth Sar the mediocre student. He did not realise that Mao's Cultural Revolution was already a disaster and that Stalin's attempts had set the Soviet economy back by decades. He did not examine the

idea to see if it was practical. It was senseless to build huge canal systems and dams without using engineers, but then Pol Pot was like that. He tried to make reality fit politics instead of the other way round.[30]

Pol Pot's guilt for the terrible disaster which overtook Cambodia, where one in eight may have died in the space of four years, is beyond doubt. Yet some responsibility must also be apportioned to those in the West who shared his belief that politics could change reality.

Afterword

This book has tried to establish what happened during a famine but it also describes what happens when a country and its leader descend into total madness. China was gripped by what Carl Jung once termed a 'psychic epidemic', when all rational behaviour is abandoned. The absolute power which Mao achieved engendered a collective escape into a world of utter delusion. All that mattered to the millions in the Party was to pander to the fantasies of its leader. Many knew they were telling lies and that the truth was that the country was starving. Even Mao, at the apex of these lies, was not deluded. As his doctor Li Zhisui recounts, 'Mao knew the peasants were dying by the million. He did not care.' What Mao wanted from his followers, argues Dr Li, was proof of absolute and undivided loyalty: 'Mao was the centre around which everyone else revolved. His will reigned supreme. Loyalty, rather than principle, was the paramount virtue.'

In *Grass Soup*, one of the fellow prisoners of Zhang Xianliang is a Muslim, Ma Weixiao, who suggests that Mao intentionally used the famine to enforce the absolute and unquestioning servitude that he craved: 'Even the illiterate have to eat. Only by making the people endure hunger can you make them submit to you, to worship you. So you see, don't let Chinese people have full stomachs – keep them hungry and in a few years not just people, even dogs, will be reformed. Every one of them will be as obedient as can be: whatever Chairman Mao says will be right. Not one will dare refuse to prostrate himself before Chairman Mao.'

Yet Mao had won power by espousing a philosophy based on rationalism and modern Western thought. In place of the millennia of feudal emperor-worship, he promised democratic and scientific Marxism-Leninism. He was genuinely convinced that scientific farming and collectivization could transform both Chinese agriculture, the basis of the country's economy, and the lives of the vast majority of Chinese. After all, in the Soviet Union Lenin and Stalin had used the same methods and had created a superpower which had defeated Nazi Germany, built the nuclear bomb and, in the 1950s, launched the first satellite into space. It was strong and disciplined, modern and scientific: China could be the same. Even if Mao and his colleagues knew the terrible cost in human lives which Lenin and Stalin had paid, they might have considered this a sacrifice worth making. Yet Mao not only deluded himself about the supposed success of collectivization in the Soviet Union, he also refused to accept the evidence that these ideas were creating a catastrophe in China.

Listening to accounts from all over the country about the failure of the Great Leap Forward, it sometimes seemed to me as if the extreme violence it unleashed may have derived from this fundamental lack of comprehension of and frustration with an alien way of thought. Much in the same way that a child might vent his rage and smash a toy because he cannot get it to work, Mao could not accept that his peasants would not behave as he thought they ought to if the country was to jettison its legacy of feudal habits and beliefs. Mao wanted to modernize China but could not grasp the basis of modern thought, the scientific method: that the way in which the natural universe behaves can be proved or disproved by objective tests, independent of ideology or individual will. So instead of becoming 'new men', Mao and his followers lapsed into a pattern of behaviour established 2,000 years earlier by the first Emperor Qinshihuangdi, perhaps the greatest tyrant in Chinese history.

Yet if one accepts this as an explanation for Mao's behaviour, it still does not explain why so many others were willing to torture large numbers to death to deliver grain which they did not and could not have possessed. This deliberate and senseless cruelty has few parallels in history. These peasants were, after all, not the conquered slaves of some alien power but supposedly the beneficiaries of the revolution.

Perhaps the answer lies in the early history of the Chinese Communist Party. At least some of its members, such as Kang Sheng, had endorsed the use of unqualified violence against the peasants right from the beginning. Not only was no mercy shown to landlords, but rich and middle peasants, a much larger group, were treated with equal brutality. Those labelled as the enemy were beyond redemption. By the beginning of the Great Leap Forward officials are recorded in Party documents as saying that the peasants must be regarded as the enemy since they stand in the way of progress. This readiness to strip villagers of all their rights was allied to a general contempt for the peasants which may date back still further, to Confucius. He had described them as 'inferior beings' who, since they cannot be educated, must be exploited.

But during the Great Leap Forward local officials, often peasants themselves, saw their own kith and kin starve to death before their very eyes. Why did the peasants not rise up in mass revolt?

When the dissident Wei Jingsheng spent time in the countryside of Anhui and heard stories of the famine, he began to ponder this question, concluding that it was just because of class warfare that Mao retained his power: 'Mao used class struggle to divide people into imaginary interest groups, rendering them incapable of discerning their true interests. Thus, he was able to incite people to engage in mutual killing or goals that were, in fact, detrimental to their own interests. It was precisely through this technique that he fooled and oppressed millions and manipulated them into supporting him. It was precisely for this reason that he was able to conceal his real face and masquerade as the people's leader.'

Many interviewees also claimed that the peasants had developed such a deep trust in the Party that they were reluctant to act. In the opera *Huang Huo* by Du Xi, one of the characters, Zhang Sun, the Party Secretary of a production brigade, says: 'Even though the grain has been taken away, let us wait and see. The Communist Party will not let people starve to death . . . If the sky falls it will strike us all. Is it only our village which is starving? Let us wait a while and we will see more clearly. After all, the Communist Party would never let the masses starve to death.'

At first, the peasants also did not believe that they would starve because after all the grain was there, it existed. With cunning they might get it back from the state. In the opera the central character, Li Baisuo, resorts to one such subterfuge.

He offers to 'launch a sputnik' and, by promising to close-plant 330 lbs of seeds per *mu*, ten times the normal amount, hopes to get enough seed grain to feed the village through the winter. When an inspection team arrives, he organizes the villagers into staging a charade of sowing the grain which succeeds in convincing the inspectors. The stratagem only fails because the brigade chief, Zhang Sun, is too honest and loyal to the Party. He feels compelled to reveal the truth and so Li is arrested and struggled as a 'right opportunist' and then beaten and paraded around the villages wearing a cloth bearing the character 'right'.

Many interviewees also blamed the honesty of the peasants – in the Henan countryside people took pride in saying 'It is better to starve to death than beg or steal.' At the climax of Du Xi's opera, when all is lost, the villagers debate whether they should attack the state granary but some protest: 'Even though we are starving to death, we cannot take that road! . . . Without the government's permission, we cannot touch a single grain from the state granary.'

Many also retained a belief that Mao would save them. In some places I was told that peasants dragged themselves to the top of the nearest mountain, faced the direction of Beijing and called out aloud for Mao to help them. At the end of *Huang Huo*, the hero, Li, decides on a desperate course of action. He will go to Beijing and petition Chairman Mao. He declares that Mao will support him and prevent cruel local officials from oppressing the peasantry, and adds: 'This is not the same as [the] 1942 [famine]. For generation after generation, the years were poor, the harvests thin. This time there is only a temporary shortage of food.' After this speech, the brigade chief Zhang drags him off to be punished at the Party headquarters but Zhang's wife shows her anger at this by committing suicide. Zhang repents, confesses he has let the Party down, and allows Li to escape and, in the final scene, board a train to Beijing.

On the other hand, starving peasants had risen in revolt before in Chinese history: indeed much of China's dynastic history appears to have been propelled by such uprisings, not least that led by Mao himself. Yet never before had China been governed by such a ruthless and efficient police state. There was simply nowhere to go to escape the grip of Mao's control.

In the opera, the villagers consider fleeing to beg for food elsewhere but abandon the plan because they realize they would soon be caught by the militia and sent back. Throughout China, millions of others reached the same conclusion. Unable to leave their villages, they had little chance of organizing themselves in sufficient numbers to challenge the army or even the militia unless they too were starving. And in many cases, by the time the peasants had realized that the state would not save them, they were usually already half dead with hunger and too weak to take any effective action.

Many Chinese have blamed the tragedy of the famine not so much on Mao as on Chinese culture, claiming that both subjects and ruler were powerless to break patterns of behaviour enforced over 5,000 years. China is the world's oldest continuous civilization and the Chinese still use the same hieroglyphic characters as their distant ancestors and speak recognizably the same language. In the late 1950s, it was as if the slaves of the Pharaohs had somehow stumbled into the twentieth century. The peasants' way of life, their huts and tools, were little different from those of their forebears in the Shang dynasty. In the famine their moral code was still ordered by the injunction of the first Han Emperor who 2,200 years earlier had authorized them to eat their children if there was no other choice. Perhaps, too, they felt as powerless before the arbitrary will of the Emperor as had their ancestors. As the Shang dynasty inscription puts it: 'Why are there disasters? It is because the Emperor wants to punish mankind.'

Blaming the past for the Great Leap Forward may partly explain the psychology of both Mao and the peasants but it seems to ignore the singularity of what occurred. Mao could not be brought down because he had created a world in which all beliefs and judgements were suspended. No one dared move or act according to what he knew to be true. Instead, even the highest-ranking officials moved in a secretive society paralysed by an all-pervasive network of informers and spies. In a world of distorting mirrors, it became hard to grasp that such senseless cruelty could really be taking place. The grotesque efforts that some officials made to deceive leaders such as Liu Shaoqi almost defies imagination. Who could believe that Party officials would plaster and paint trees stripped of their bark by starving peasants to hide a famine from the country's President?

The bizarre nature of so much of what happened inspires a feeling of deep shame which still makes many Chinese reluctant to discuss the circumstances of the famine. For the absurdly triumphant claims of miracle harvests and the mass starvation that followed reflect badly not just on the Communist Party but on the entire nation. But what if Liu and others had conspired to overthrow Mao during the famine or afterwards? Mao had threatened to start a civil war and could indeed have led his followers to the hills and there held out as guerrillas. China might then have ended up like Cambodia, only on a far greater scale. Other powers, the Soviet Union, the United States and Taiwan, would soon have been sucked into backing different factions. Perhaps an intractable civil war with tens of millions of refugees might have been still worse than simply waiting and trying to persuade Mao to come to his senses.

All this is only speculation, though, for we are unlikely ever to know what passed through the minds of the leadership during this darkest period. The files may never be opened as they were in Cambodia after the Vietnamese invasion. There will be no museums devoted to the victims of the famine. The dead seem destined to remain hungry ghosts unplacated by any memorial or apology, and it is almost too late to charge those responsible with crimes against humanity. In China, Mao's reputation, tarnished though it is, cannot be completely destroyed without calling into question the whole edifice of Communist rule in China. And yet, if the Chinese are kept in ignorance of what happened, that would be another kind of tragedy. If the famine remains a secret, the country will draw no lessons from its past nor learn that only in a secretive society could so many have starved to death.

Appendix:
Biographical Sketches

CHEN BODA (1904–89): from a rich landlord's family, Chen was born in Fujian and attended Moscow's Sun Yat-sen University in 1927. One of Mao's personal secretaries and the editor of *Red Flag*, he held extreme left-wing views and was very influential during the Great Leap Forward and the Cultural Revolution. He fell from power in 1970 and subsequently spent years in prison.

CHEN YUN (1905–95): joined the CCP in 1925. In the 1950s Chen was one of the top seven leaders of the country and designed the first five-year plans. He opposed the Great Leap Forward and helped restore the economy in 1961–2 but afterwards withdrew from power. After 1979 he was one of the main architects of reform and a rival to Deng Xiaoping.

CHIANG KAI-SHEK (1887–1975): born in Zhejiang province, Chiang took over the leadership of the KMT after 1924. He lost the civil war and in 1949 retreated to Taiwan.

DENG TUO (1912–66): born in Fujian, Deng joined the CCP in 1930, became editor of a CCP newspaper in 1937 and after 1949 rose to be chief editor of the *People's Daily* and secretary of the Beijing Party committee secretariat. He wrote a history of famine in 1937, and in 1961 strongly attacked Mao. Deng was one of the first victims of the Cultural Revolution.

DENG XIAOPING (1904–): born in Guang'an, Sichuan, Deng studied in France and Moscow and joined the CCP in 1924. As General Secretary of the CCP he led the anti-rightist campaign and was a leading light in the Great Leap Forward. At the end of 1960, he withdrew his support for Mao's policies and favoured the dismantling of the communes. After 1978, he instigated the contract responsibility system.

GAO FENG (1914–76): born in Shaanxi, Gao joined the CCP in 1933. After 1949, he became Party Secretary of the Xinjiang autonomous region and then moved to Qinghai where he was also political commissar of the Qinghai military zone. As Party Secretary of Qinghai, he was responsible for 900,000 deaths. After 1961, he was dismissed and sent to Jilin as deputy director of the local Chinese People's Political Consultative Committee.

HU YAOBANG (1915–89): the son of a Hunanese rich peasant, Hu joined the Communists as a 'red devil' or child soldier and later rose to the leadership of the Party's Youth League. He supported Mao during the famine and was rewarded with senior posts in Hunan. Subsequently he became a protégé of Deng Xiaoping. After 1979, Deng made him General Secretary of the CCP. He was responsible for the liberalization of the rural economy but was toppled after student demonstrations in 1987 for being too liberal on ideological issues. His death in 1989 triggered the Tiananmen pro-democracy movement.

HUA GUOFENG (1921–): born in Shaanxi, Hua joined the CCP in 1940 and became Party Secretary of Xiangtan prefecture, Hunan, where Mao's home village is located. He solidly backed Mao during the Great Leap Forward by denying that a famine was taking place. He became Party Secretary of Hunan in 1970. In 1976 he succeeded Mao and became Prime Minister but was brought down in 1979. Mao had appointed him as his successor with a note saying 'With you in charge my heart is at ease'.

KANG SHENG (1899–1975): born in Shandong, Kang joined the CCP in 1925 and organized the first major purge in Yanan in 1942. He was a member of the ultra-left faction that promoted the Great Leap Forward and was in charge of Cultural Revolution purges. He died of bladder cancer.

KE QINGSHI (1900–65): born in Anhui, Ke spent time in Russia in 1922. An ultra-leftist, he later became Party Secretary of Shanghai and the East China Bureau. He died a natural death.

LI JINGQUAN (1909–89): born in Jiangxi, Li joined the Party Youth League in 1927 and became a member of the CCP in 1930 after which he took part in the Long March. As First Secretary of Sichuan and the South-west China Bureau during the Great Leap Forward he was responsible for 7–9 million deaths. He died in honourable retirement in Beijing.

LIN BIAO (1907–71): born in Hubei, Lin joined the CCP in 1925. He replaced Peng Dehuai in 1959 as Defence Minister and supported Mao in his hour of need in 1962. He was designated as Mao's successor in 1969 but died in a plane crash supposedly after a failed coup attempt.

LIU SHAOQI (1898–1969): born in Ningxiang, Hunan, Liu joined the CCP in 1921 and studied in Moscow's University of the Toilers of the East. He was second in rank to Mao from 1942 and actively promoted Mao Zedong Thought, but he opposed the rush into collectivization in the 1950s and resisted Mao's efforts to return to Great Leap Forward policies after 1961. He was the chief target of the Cultural Revolution, dubbed the number one capitalist roader and China's Khrushchev. He died in prison in 1969 after violent persecution. He was married to Wang Guangmei.

MAO ZEDONG (1893–1976): born in Shaoshan village, Xiangtan prefecture, Hunan, Mao was a founding member of the CCP in 1921 and leader of the CCP from 1935 until his death.

PANCHEN LAMA (1938–89): born in Qinghai province he was recognized as the tenth reincarnation of Tibet's second highest religious figure. He stayed in China after the Dalai Lama fled but described the horrors of the Great Leap Forward in a 90,000-word report to Mao. He was kept under house arrest or in prison between 1963 and 1977, and was only formally rehabilitated in 1988.

PENG DEHUAI (1900–74): born in Xiangtan, Hunan, Peng joined the CCP in 1928, one of the few leaders to come from a poor peasant family. He was one of China's ten marshals who later led Chinese forces in the Korean War. He criticized the Great Leap Forward at the Lushan summit and Mao dismissed him. Imprisoned in 1966, he spent years in prison suffering torture and physical humiliation.

WU HAN (1909–69): born in Zhejiang, Wu became a teacher at Qinghua University and a member of the China Democratic Alliance. He rose to become Dean of the History Department at Qinghua University and a member of the National Culture and Education Committee. An expert on Ming history he was Deputy Mayor of Beijing during the Great Leap Forward. During the famine he attacked Mao through the play *Hai Rui Dismissed from Office*. Persecuted in 1965, he died during the Cultural Revolution. He was rehabilitated in 1979.

WU ZHIFU (1906–67): born in Henan in Qi Xian county, Wu joined the CCP in 1925 and became a pupil of Mao's at the Peasant Movement Training Institute. During the civil war he ran a guerrilla branch of the New Fourth Army and orchestrated a campaign of terror against landlords. During the Great Leap Forward he was Party Secretary of Henan and was responsible for up to 8 million deaths. He died in October 1967 in Guangzhou.

ZENG XISHENG (1904–68): born in Hunan not far from Mao's home county, Zeng attended the Whampoa Military Academy, met Mao in 1923 and joined the Party in 1927. He was Mao's bodyguard during the Long March and then was in charge of military intelligence. He later became the political commissar of the Fourth Route Army. After 1949, he was appointed Party Secretary of northern Anhui before taking charge of the whole province. As Party Secretary of the whole of Anhui during the Great Leap Forward, he was responsible for the deaths of up to 8 million people, as well as a similar number in Shandong. He introduced agricultural reforms in 1961 but Mao dismissed him in 1962. He was tortured and killed during the Cultural Revolution.

ZHANG WENTIAN (1900–76): born in Jiangsu, Zhang joined the CCP in 1925 and studied at Moscow's Sun Yat-sen University. After 1949, he was posted as ambassador to the Soviet Union and then returned to serve as deputy foreign minister. He opposed Mao at the Lushan summit and was demoted to the level of researcher at the Chinese Academy of Sciences where he studied 'the theory of socialist economic construction'. He survived persecution during the Cultural Revolution and was rehabilitated in 1979.

ZHANG ZHONGLIANG (1907–83): born in Shaanxi, Zhang joined the CCP in 1931 and led a peasant uprising in 1933. After 1949, he was initially Party Secretary of Qinghai before moving to Gansu. There he was responsible for over a million deaths during the famine. He was dismissed in 1961 and sent to Jiangsu as chief secretary of the provincial Party secretariat. Though persecuted during the Cultural Revolution he died peacefully in retirement in Nanjing.

ZHAO ZIYANG (1919–): in charge of agriculture in Guangdong and a keen promoter of the Great Leap Forward under the provincial leader Tao Zhu. Zhao's report triggered off the first round of forced grain seizures. However, he was attacked during the Cultural Revolution for advocating private farming. In the late 1970s, he was brought back and, as Party Secretary in Sichuan, initiated rural reforms and ordered the first dismantling of a commune. Deng made him Premier after 1979 and later General Secretary. He was dismissed in 1989 for supporting democracy protests and is still under house arrest.

ZHOU ENLAI (1899–1976): born in Jiangsu, Zhou studied in France and then joined the CCP in 1922. Though he opposed collectivization in 1956 he later made a self-criticism and thereafter supported the Great Leap Forward. He did not challenge Mao after 1962 and served him throughout the Cultural Revolution.

Notes

Chapter 1: China: Land of Famine

1. Research by the Student Agricultural Society of the University of Nanjing under Professor John Lossing Buck, Professor of Agricultural Economy at the university.
2. Deng Tuo, *China's History of Disaster Relief*, p. 286.
3. Kay Ray Chong, *Cannibalism in China*, p. 110.
4. He Bochuan, *China on the Edge*, p. 6.
5. Graham Peck, *Two Kinds of Time*, p. 202.
6. Andrew James Nathan, *History of the China International Famine Relief Commission*, p. 6.
7. Annual report of the China International Famine Relief Commission, 1925.
8. Edgar Snow, *Red Star over China*, pp. 214–215.
9. Annual report of the China International Famine Relief Commission, 1927.
10. Quoted in Walter H. Mallory, *China, Land of Famine*, p. 2.
11. John Ridley in the *Daily Telegraph*, 29 May 1946.
12. A. K. Norton, *China and the Powers*, pp. 173–174.
13. Report by the South Manchurian Railway quoted in *Cambridge History of China*, vol. 12, p. 318.
14. Theodore H. White, *In Search of History*, pp. 147–149.
15. Theodore H. White, *In Search of History*, pp. 97–98.
16. *Daily Telegraph*, 29 May 1946.

Chapter 2: Arise, Ye Prisoners of Starvation

1. Jonathan Spence, *The Search for Modern China*, p. 175.
2. Quoted in *Far Eastern Economic Review*, 11 August 1960.
3. *Report on an Investigation of the Peasant Movement in Hunan*, pp. 23–24.
4. Much of this section is drawn from Robert Conquest's *Harvest of Sorrow* and Alec Nove's *An Economic History of the U.S.S.R.* The quotations of Soviet writers come from these sources.
5. R. H. Tawney, *China: Agriculture and Industry*.
6. Herman Graf von Keyserling, *The Travel Diary of a Philosopher* (trans. J. Holroyd Reece). London: Jonathan Cape, 1927, p. 401.
7. Fei Xiaotong, *Peasant Life in China*, p. 181.
8. Randolph Barker and Radha Sinha with Beth Rose (eds.), *The Chinese Agricultural Economy*, pp. 37–38.
9. Edward Friedman, Paul G. Pickowicz and Mark Selden, *Chinese Village, Socialist State*, pp. 80–86.
10. This material is taken from 'Historical Change of Land Reform of the CCP' published by the Research Group of Rural Institutes of China in *Rural Institutions*

and Development, No. 3, p. 48. See also Luo Fu, *The First Soviet in China,* p. 68; Zhao Xiaomin (comp.) *History of Land Reform in China, 1921–1949,* p. 85; and Ton Yingming (comp.), *Land Revolution Report, 1927–1937.*

11. John Byron and Robert Pack, *The Claws of the Dragon: Kang Sheng,* p. 193.
12. John Byron and Robert Pack, *The Claws of the Dragon: Kang Sheng,* p. 196.
13. Claire Hollingworth, *Mao and the Men Against Him,* pp. 82–83.

Chapter 3: The Soviet Famines

1. This chapter draws on Robert Conquest, *Harvest of Sorrow;* Alec Nove, *An Economic History of the U.S.S.R.; Khrushchev Remembers: The Last Testament;* and the 1988 US Congressional Commission's investigation into the Ukrainian famine, 1932–1933.
2. Michael Ellman, 'A Note on the Number of 1933 Famine Victims', *Soviet Studies,* 1989.

Chapter 4: The First Collectivization, 1949–1958

1. Edward Friedman, Paul G. Pickowicz and Mark Selden, *Chinese Village, Socialist State,* pp. 140–142.
2. Han Suyin, *Wind in the Tower,* p. 41.
3. Han Suyin, *Wind in the Tower,* p. 43.
4. Edward Friedman, Paul G. Pickowicz and Mark Selden, *Chinese Village, Socialist State,* p. 122.
5. Interview with officials in Sichuan.
6. Mao Zedong, *Selected Works 1954.*
7. Interview with Frank Kouvenhoven and Dr. Antionet Schimmelpennick, musicologists at Leiden University.
8. Edward Friedman, Paul G. Pickowicz and Mark Selden, *Chinese Village, Socialist State,* p. 189.
9. Edward Friedman, Paul G. Pickowicz and Mark Selden, *Chinese Village, Socialist State,* p. xxiii.
10. Edward Friedman, Paul G. Pickowicz and Mark Selden, *Chinese Village, Socialist State,* p. 203.
11. John Lossing Buck, *Food and Agriculture in Communist China,* pp. 18–20.
12. Li Rui, *A True Account of the Lushan Meeting,* p. 45.
13. See *Thirty Years in the Countryside—True Records of the Economic and Social Development in the Fengyang Agricultural Region,* p. 162.
14. Alec Nove, *An Economic History of the U.S.S.R.,* Chapter 12.
15. Frederick C. Teiwes, *Politics and Purges in China,* pp. 276–277, 286.
16. Unpublished biography of Zeng Xisheng, due to be published in 1996.
17. *Khrushchev Remembers,* pp. 272, 275.
18. *Far Eastern Economic Review,* 4 December 1958.
19. Li Zhisui, *The Private Life of Chairman Mao,* pp. 281–282.

Chapter 5: False Science, False Promises

1. Edward Friedman, Paul G. Pickowicz and Mark Selden, *Chinese Village, Socialist State,* pp. 216–217.

2. Quoted in Klaus Mehnert, *Peking and Moscow*, p. 356. Mehnert also describes how during the Great Leap Forward, Shanghai writers undertook to produce 3,000 literary works in two years. Soon they had far exceeded their plan: one single evening three thousand Shanghai workers and soldiers 'produced' 3,000 poems and 360 songs. One the poems awarded a special prize was 'Ode to the Red Sun':

> 'When Chairman Mao comes forth,
> The East shines Red.
> All living things prosper,
> The Earth is "red".
> Six hundred million, peony bright:
> Each one is "red".
> For all our beautiful hills and streams,
> Eternal time is "red".'

3. Quoted from a Red Guard magazine in Roderick MacFarquhar, *The Origins of the Cultural Revolution*, p. 84.
4. Dawa Norbu, *Red Star over Tibet*, p. 129.
5. Zhou Libo, *Great Changes in a Mountain Village*, was translated by Derek Bryan and published by the Foreign Languages Press in 1961. Quoted in *A Chinese View of China* by John Gittings, p. 139.
6. John Byron and Robert Pack, *The Claws of the Dragon: Kang Sheng*, p. 234.
7. John Byron and Robert Pack, *The Claws of the Dragon: Kang Sheng*, p. 234.
8. Li Rui, *A True Account of the Lushan Meeting*, p. 8.
9. Mikhail Klochko, *Soviet Scientist in China*, pp. 139–140.
10. *People's Daily*, 1958.
11. *They Are Creating Miracles*, Foreign Languages Press, 1960. The Chinese edition appeared earlier.
12. For a detailed account of Lysenko see Zhores A. Medvedev, *The Rise and Fall of T. D. Lysenko*, translated by I. Michael Wermner, Columbia University Press, 1969; and David Joravsky, *The Lysenko Affair*, University of Chicago Press, 1970.
13. Nikita Khrushchev, *Khrushchev Remembers*, p. 13.
14. Roderick MacFarquhar, Timothy Cheek and Eugene Wu (eds.), *The Secret Speeches of Chairman Mao*, p. 450.
15. Denis Fred Simon and Merle Goldman (eds.), *Science and Technology in Post-Mao China*, p. 48.
16. Denis Fred Simon and Merle Goldman (eds.), *Science and Technology in Post-Mao China*, p. 53.
17. Interview with the author.
18. British United Press, printed in the *Guardian*, 24 March 1960.
19. Reported in the *Sunday Times* by Richard Hughes, June 1960.
20. Alfred L. Chan, 'The Campaign for Agricultural Development in the Great Leap Forward: A Study of Policy-making and Implementation in Liaoning', *China Quarterly*, No. 129 (March 1992), pp. 68–69.
21. Bo Yibo, *Retrospective of Several Big Decisions and Incidents*, Central Party School, 1993.
22. Interview with Chen Yizi.
23. *China Pictorial*, 1959.
24. *Far Eastern Economic Review*, February 1959.
25. *Far Eastern Economic Review*, 10 December 1958.
26. Roderick MacFarquhar, *The Origins of the Cultural Revolution*.
27. Reuters, 7 April 1960.
28. Interview with the author.

29. Vaclav Smil, *The Bad Earth: Environmental Degradation in China*.
30. *Human Rights Watch Asia Report*, February 1995, pp. 37–44.
31. Dai Qing (ed.), *Changjiang Yimin (Population Transfer on the Yangzi River)*, a documentary anthology.
32. Richard Hughes, *The Chinese Communes*, p. 69.
33. Interview with the author.
34. Jung Chang, *Wild Swans*, p. 226.
35. Roderick MacFarquhar, *The Origins of the Cultural Revolution*, p. 121.
36. Interview with author.
37. Roderick MacFarquhar, *The Origins of the Cultural Revolution*, p. 139.
38. Jack Potter and Sulamith Heins Potter, *China's Peasants—The Anthropology of a Revolution*, p. 73.
39. William Hinton, *Shenfan*, p. 218.
40. Denis Twitchett and John K. Fairbank (eds.), *Cambridge History of China*, vol. 14, pp. 378–386.
41. *Far Eastern Economic Review*, 11 August 1960.

Chapter 6: Mao Ignores the Famine

1. From *Red Flag*, quoted in Richard Hughes, *The Chinese Communes*, p. 48.
2. I have not been able to discover who first proposed the name. Some claim it was Wu Zhifu's idea but it is more likely that it was the brainchild of Chen Boda and was a reference to the Paris Commune. Later, when Mao was trying to minimize his responsibility for the Great Leap Forward, he claimed he was misquoted by a local journalist.
3. Stanley Karnow in *Mao and China* writes that at a Central Committee meeting held in Wuchang at the end of 1958, it was decided to halt the Great Leap Forward and reverse some of its measures (pp. 111–112). At the same meeting Mao resigned as President and this was taken to mean that he had suffered a political setback. As with much of what happened (and still happens) inside the highest levels of the Communist Party, the full story is confusing and murky. However, it is important to remember that Mao rarely paid attention to what the Party organization planned or did, nor did his followers who regarded his utterances as imperial decrees.
4. Bo Yibo, *Restrospective of Several Big Decisions and Incidents*, Central Party School, 1993, p. 714.
5. David Shambaugh, *The Making of a Premier: Zhao Ziyang's Provincial Career*, Westview replica edition, 1984, p. 21.
6. Jurgen Domes, *Peng Dehuai: The Man and His Image*.
7. Sources based on Party documents.
8. Roderick MacFarquhar, *The Origins of the Cultural Revolution*, pp. 195–196.
9. Jurgen Domes, *Peng Dehuai: The Man and His Image*, has a different translation (p. 93): 'Grain scattered on the ground, / Potato leaves withered, / Strong young people have left to make steel, / Only my children and old women reap the crops. / How can they pass the coming year? / Allow me to raise my voice for the people!'
10. Jurgen Domes, *Peng Dehuai: The Man and his Image*, p. 113.
11. Li Rui, *A True Account of the Lushan Meeting*, p. 104.
12. The quotes from these exchanges appear in various books, notably Stanley Karnow, *Mao and China*, and Li Rui, *A True Account of the Lushan Meeting*.
13. Han Suyin, *Eldest Son: Zhou Enlai and the Making of Modern China, 1898–1976*, pp. 268–275.
14. Li Zhisui, *The Private Life of Chairman Mao*, p. 296.

15. In 1961 another opera was written, intended as a bitter and unmistakable allegory, in which Hai Rui is Peng Dehuai scolding the foolish Emperor. This was criticized by a future member of the Gang of Four, Yao Wenyuan, a protégé of the Shanghai Party boss Ke Qingshi. In 1966, the Cultural Revolution began with a further attack on the opera.
16. Roderick MacFarquhar, *The Origins of the Cultural Revolution*, p. 152.
17. David M. Bachman, 'Chen Yun and the Chinese Political System', China Research Monograph, Institute of East Asian Studies, University of California, Berkeley, 1985, pp. 71–74.
18. Roderick MacFarquhar, *The Origins of the Cultural Revolution*, pp. 293–294.
19. *Far Eastern Review*, 26 September 1959.
20. Ding Shu, *Ren Huo*.
21. Li Zhisui, *The Private Life of Chairman Mao*, p. 339.
22. Ding Shu, *Ren Huo*.

Chapter 7: An Overview of the Famine

1. Judith Banister in *China's Changing Population* (pp. 312–318) notes that there were also rebellions among the Yi, Dong and Miao minorities in south-west China and that a sizeable group of Dai people from Yunnan fled to Burma, Laos and Thailand. In 1962, 70,000 fled Xinjiang for the Soviet Union and another 60,000 the following year.
2. Unpublished Chinese sources.
3. Interviewees said that a member of each household had to report each week on the activities of neighbours. In addition, there was a curfew and a blackout during the famine. No buildings above one storey could be built and many other precautions were taken.
4. Pu Ning, *Red in Tooth and Claw*, pp. 184–185.
5. Resolution of 10 December 1958.
6. Interviews with the author.
7. *Thirty Years in the Countryside*, p. 170.
8. *China Youth Journal*, 27 September 1958.
9. *Thirty Years in the Countryside*, p. 170.
10. Liu Binyan, *A Higher Kind of Loyalty*, p. 98.
11. *Thirty Years in the Countryside*, p. 170.
12. Bo Yibo, *Restrospective of Several Big Decisions and Incidents*, p. 754.
13. Quoted from Mark Elvin, 'The Technology of Farming in Late Traditional China', in Rudolph Barker and Radha Sinha with Beth Rose (eds.), *The Chinese Agricultural Economy*, p. 14. Elvin cites 'Par les missionaires de Pékin', *Mémoires concernant les Chinois* (Paris and Lyon, 1776–1814), 14 vols.

Chapter 8: Henan: A Catastrophe of Lies

1. Some sources claim this took place in May when twenty-seven co-operatives were merged.
2. Instructions given by the Central Party Committee following the Xinyang Prefectural Party Committee Report on 'The Movement of Work Style Rectification, Commune Reconstruction and the Organization of Production and Disaster Relief', unpublished.
3. Figures from confidential sources.

4. Su Luozheng, *July Storm—The Inside Story of the Lushan Conference*, p. 360.
5. Su Luozheng, *July Storm—The Inside Story of the Lushan Conference*, p. 359.
6. Su Xiaokang, *July Storm—The Inside Story of the Lushan Conference*, p. 359.
7. Confidential sources based on internal Party documents.
8. The detailed descriptions of tortures which follow come from confidential sources but are discussed in less detail in books published in China.
9. Unpublished Party document.
10. Instructions given by the Central Party Committee following the Xinyang Prefectural Party Committee Report on 'The Movement of Work Style Rectification, Commune Reconstruction and the Organization of Production and Disaster Relief', unpublished.
11. Su Luozheng, *July Storm—The Inside Story of the Lushan Conference*, p. 360.
12. These figures appear in Su Luozheng's *July Storm*, Su Xiaokang's *Utopia* and Ding Shu's *Ren Huo*.
13. Confidential documents.
14. 'Bai Hua Speaks His Mind in Hong Kong', *Dongzhang*, No. 45/46, December 1987 and January 1988.
15. Interviews with the author.
16. Interviews with the author.
17. Confidential sources.
18. Jack Gray, *Rebellions and Revolutions*, p. 290.
19. Frederick Teiwes, *Politics and Purges in China*, p. 276.
20. See also Su Luozheng, *July Storm—The Inside Story of the Lushan Conference*, p. 358.
21. Interviews with the author.
22. Interviews with the author.
23. Su Luozheng, *July Storm—The Inside Story of the Lushan Conference*, p. 358.
24. Su Luozheng in *July Storm* claims that Wu also attacked the 'conditions only theory', the 'pessimism theory' and the 'mythology theory' (p. 359).
25. Su Luozheng, *July Storm—The Inside Story of the Lushan, Conference*, p. 359.
26. Su Luozheng in *July Storm* claims that people had starved to death even in November 1958. By the spring of 1959 many in eastern Henan were suffering from oedema and the number of deaths was increasing (p. 358).
27. Unpublished Party documents.
28. Unpublished Party documents.
29. *Daily Telegraph*, 6 August 1963.
30. Interviews with the author.

Chatper 9: Anhui: Let's Talk about Fengyang

1. A flower drum, or *huagu*, was used by travelling beggars to call for alms.
2. Wang Lixin, *Agricultural Reforms of Anhui—A True Record*, p. 269.
3. Interview with retired Anhui official.
4. Wang Lixin in *Agricultural Reforms of Anhui—A True Record* includes the story of how a team of oxen ploughed 36 *mu* in one evening (p. 270). He also points out that at the end of the Great Leap Forward 38 per cent of the arable land had been ruined and 36 per cent of the draught animals had died.
5. Wang Lixin in *Agricultural Reforms of Anhui—A True Record* claims that 97 per cent of the population ate at the county's 2,641 canteens and that often they served only half a pound of grain per person per day (p. 270).
6. *Thirty Years in the Countryside* contains this passage (p. 194): 'Some villages had to hand in their mouth food [daily consumption grain] and seed grains . . . some

brigades had no grains to cook but county Party Secretary Zhao still ordered the digging up of possible grain stocks. Zhao convened a big meeting of all county cadres to get more grain by struggle. In the struggles some cadres were physically beaten. After the meeting, similar struggle meetings took place all over the county. Special grain-hiding investigation teams were set up in many brigades, and teams were sent to search every household. The masses were strung up and beaten. People's mouth grains and grains grown on the private plots were taken away. Even the leaves of sweet potatoes, eggs, etc. were confiscated in the name of "anti-bourgeois" struggle.

7. The interviewee insisted that her name and that of her village remain confidential.
8. These figures and quotations are taken from *Thirty Years in the Countryside* (p. 195), but also surface in a number of books published in mainland China, including *The Later Years and Months of Mao,* and Wang Lixin, *Agricultural Reforms of Anhui—A True Record.*
9. Wang Lixin, *Agricultural Reforms in Anhui—A True Record,* p. 275. I was unable to discover the fate of Zhang Shaobao.
10. *Thirty Years in the Countryside,* p. 196.
11. A book of photographs published by the Party to commemorate the forty-fifth anniversary of the founding of the People's Republic of China contains a picture of a hastily scribbled note by Zhou Enlai. The accompanying caption reads: 'The errors of the "Great Leap Forward" and "Anti-Right Opportunist movement" caused serious difficulties to China's national economy and vital damage to the state and people. Early in 1960, there was a famine and disaster in He and Wuwei counties. Also, it was a fact that people starved to death, so immediately Zhou Enlai wrote to Zeng requesting him to investigate the situation and report back:

Comrade Xisheng,

I am writing this letter to request you to send people to Shancun [words indistinct] to conduct an investigation, after you read this letter, to find out if there is such a matter. Perhaps this has been exaggerated. This sort of individual case happened in every province especially in those provinces where there were disasters last year. It is worthwhile paying attention to what Chairman Mao said in the document of the 6th-level cadres meeting in Shandong province. He stressed that we should take this seriously. Please when you make everything clear, send a reply.

Best regards, Zhou Enlai
29 March 1960'

12. Wang Lixin, *Agricultural Reforms in Anhui—A True Record; Thirty Years in the Countryside,* p. 275; and interviews with the author.
13. One source claimed that 100,000 left Wuwei.
14. Interviews with the author in Anhui, 1994.
15. Interview with a former senior Party official, Chen Yizi.
16. *Thirty Years in the Countryside,* p. 275.
17. In Wudian 14,285 people died out of a population of 53,759. In the Guangming production brigade, 832 out of a population of 1,638 died and in the Banjing production brigade 1,627 out of a population of 4,100 died.

Chapter 10: The Other Provinces

1. Interview with the author.
2. Interview with the author.
3. Zhou Yueli, Zeng Xisheng's former secretary.

4. Peng Xizhe, 'Demographic Consequences of the Great Leap Forward in China's Provinces', *Population and Development Review*, Vol. 3, No. 4, December 1987, pp. 645, 663.

5. Peng Xizhe, 'Demographic Consequences of the Great Leap Forward in China's Provinces', *Population and Development Review*, Vol. 3, No. 4, December 1987, p. 663.

6. Stuart and Roma Gelder, *The Timely Rain—Travels in New Tibet*, pp. 106–111.

7. Judith Banister, *China's Changing Population*. On p. 304, Banister writes: 'During the period 1953–57 interprovincial movement appears to have been relatively great. Recipients of net in-migration during those years were Beijing and Tianjin municipalities and the northern provinces of Nei Mongol, Liaoning, Heilongjiang, Qinghai, and Xinjiang, judging from their high annual growth rates.' She also points out that 'Figures on provincial populations at the beginning and end of this period may mask enormous temporary migrations in the interim' and that 'many other provinces recorded a population gain from 1957 to 1964, but the annual rate of growth was so low that there must have been enormous loss of life plus a net out-migration. Shandong was severely affected, as were Guizhou and Hunan.'

8. Peng Xizhe, 'Demographic Consequences of the Great Leap Forward in China's Provinces', *Population and Development Review*, Vol. 3, No. 4, December 1987, pp. 662–663.

9. Interview with the author.

10. Edward Friedman, Paul G. Pickowicz and Mark Selden, *Chinese Village, Socialist State*, p. 241.

11. Interview with the author.

12. Edward Friedman, Paul G. Pickowicz and Mark Selden, *Chinese Village, Socialist State*, p. 241.

13. Interview with the author.

14. Interview with the author.

15. Interview with the author.

16. Edward Friedman, Paul G. Pickowicz and Mark Selden, *Chinese Village, Socialist State*, p. 241.

17. Ding Shu, *Ren Huo*.

18. Edward Friedman, Paul G. Pickowicz and Mark Selden, *Chinese Village, Socialist State*, p. 243.

19. Interview with the author.

20. Letter to the author.

21. *Great War Literary Magazine*, published in Henan province.

22. Zhao died in Taiyuan in his home province of Shanxi in September 1970. He was noted for his many books about the local peasants and for his accounts of land reform. He had joined the Party in 1937, becoming editor of the Eighth Route Army newspaper, and was highly regarded within the Party.

23. After 1949, the provincial capital, Lanzhou, was transformed into a major industrial centre. During the Great Leap Forward, huge numbers of peasants were dispatched to construct the massive Tao River scheme. Rain is irregular in Gansu so the Soviet-inspired planners designed a reservoir, a dam and hydro-electric plant, and a giant canal 120 feet wide as well as a network of irrigation canals.

24. Frederick Teiwes, *Politics and Purges*, pp. 273–289.

25. *October*, No. 5, 1988.

26. Peng Xizhe, 'Demographic Consequences of the Great Leap Forward in China's Provinces', *Population and Development Review*, Vol. 3, No. 4, December 1987, pp. 650–661.

27. Interviews with the author.

28. Interviews with the author.
29. Quoted in Ding Shu, *Ren Huo.*
30. Yi Shu, 'One Thousand Li Hunger', *Kaifang,* August 1994.
31. The dissident and democracy activist Wei Jingsheng has recalled that during his travels as a Red Guard he took a train along the Gansu Corridor around 1967. He was shocked to see starving and naked women and children begging for food in every railway station. His companion in the train, a cadre, told him that such sights were very common in these parts and said that they were former landlords and rich peasants, or just lazy, and that it did them good to be hungry. Wei refused to believe this and when he gave some of the beggars his food, they fought over it. A full account of what Wei saw is not available in a collection of writings by and about him which his sister made public in Germany in 1995.
32. Ding Shu, *Ren Huo.*
33. Interviews with the author.
34. Jung Chang, *Wild Swans,* pp. 230–231.
35. Judith Banister in *China's Changing Population* (pp. 303–305) provides the following statistics: Sichuan's population fell by 0.91 per cent from a population of 72.16 million at the end of 1957 to 69.01 million in mid-1964.
36. One former production leader told me: 'We were like slaves then. A man's life was worth nothing. People crawled around on their hands and knees dying of hunger.'

Chapter 11: The Panchen Lama's Letter

1. Interview with local official.
2. Interview with local official.
3. Another group of eastern Tibetans is also found in Yunnan province.
4. Identified as Xiao Cheng in western Sichuan.
5. Interview with former inmate.
6. Rewi Alley and Wilfred Burchett, *China: The Quality of Life,* p. 43.
7. Interview with former official. Another source claims the population fell by one-third.
8. Interview with former official.
9. Cited by former officials based on the Panchen Lama's findings.
10. Interview with survivor.
11. See also John F. Avedon, *In Exile from the Land of Snows.*
12. Information provided by the International Campaign for Tibet.
13. Jamphel Gyatso, *The Great Master Panchen.* The book was published in 1989 but was later withdrawn from circulation.
14. Jamphel Gyatso, *The Great Master Panchen.* A copy of the Chinese text of the Panchen Lama's report is in circulation outside China and confirms the magnitude of his anger at the severity of the crisis.
15. Jamphel Gyatso, *The Great Master Panchen.*
16. Dawa Norbu, *Red Star over Tibet,* p. 210.
17. Dawa Norbu, *Red Star over Tibet,* p. 208.
18. John F. Avedon, *In Exile from the Land of Snows,* p. 237.
19. The size of the garrison in the TAR also increased because of China's border war with India.
20. John F. Avedon, *In Exile from the Land of Snows.*
21. *Tibet under Chinese Communist Rule. A Compilation of Refugee Statements, 1958–1975,* published by the Information Office of the Dalai Lama, p. 56. The nuns, from Michungri monastery in the suburbs of Lhasa, arrived in Sikkim on 2 March 1961.

22. Tsering Dorje Gashi, *New Tibet: The Memoirs of a Graduate of the Peking Institute of National Minorities*, p. 105.
23. Dawa Norbu, *Red Star over Tibet*, p. 208.
24. Interviews with the author.
25. It is not certain whether the Nationalist Commission includes the TAR population in its figures and, in the absence of census figures, has used an estimate. Inner Tibet was counted separately until 1965 when the TAR was formally inaugurated. It is frequently said that it had 1 million residents, or 40 per cent of all Tibetans within China's borders. If the Nationalities Commission figures *do* exclude the TAR population, then altogether there would have been about 4 million Tibetans before the famine, the figure claimed by a number of Tibetan sources. This would imply a still higher death toll.
26. Press conference given by TAR officials at the National People's Congress in April 1955.

Chapter 12: In the Prison Camps

1. Some were arrested for warning of the dangers of Mao's agricultural policies. In Guangzhou, Zhang Naiqi was labelled as a rightist for writing letters drawing attention to the growing hunger among the peasants. One interviewee recalled that this was also why her father was sent to prison: 'In 1956 my father heard our maid tell him about the hardship of the peasants. She came from Shunyi, a county outside Beijing. They earned so little grain per work point—20 fen a day—that there was nothing to eat. This maid said everyone in her village was dying from hunger so my father decided to go and see for himself. I remember he brought back the food they were eating—cakes of mixed leaves, weeds and cornmeal. At the Ministry of Culture he told a meeting that the peasants shouldn't be suffering like this. People applauded him and shook his hand and said he showed the right concern for the peasants. Then, a few months later, he was accused of spreading anti-government stories and sent to a labour camp in the far North.'
2. A further 10 million were imprisoned for other crimes, bringing the overall total to at least 50 million. Harry Wu, *Laogai: The Chinese Gulag*, p. 17.
3. Interview, *South China Morning Post*, 5 May 1993, after he left China.
4. *Thirty Years in the Countryside*, p. 183.
5. Interview, *South China Morning Post*, 5 May 1993.
6. John F. Avedon, *In Exile from the Land of Snows*, p. 263.
7. In Qinghai, Han Weitian recalled that often his fellows were alive at night but would be dead by dawn. He, too, saw corpses piled up and said that every day more than 30 corpses were taken away by cart from each production team.
8. Interview with the author in Hong Kong.
9. John F. Avedon, *In Exile from the Land of Snows*, p. 262.
10. Dr Benjamin Lee has written an unpublished account of his experiences and his medical observations.
11. David Patt, *A Strange Liberation: Tibetan Lives in Chinese Hands*, pp. 184–185.
12. John F. Avedon, *In Exile from the Land of Snows*, p. 252.
13. Harry Wu, *Bitter Winds*, p. 109.
14. Harry Wu, *Bitter Winds*, p. 112.
15. Zhang Xianliang, *Grass Soup*, p. 205.
16. John F. Avedon, *In Exile from the Land of Snows*, p. 262.
17. David Patt, *A Strange Liberation: Tibetan Lives in Chinese Hands*, p. 82.
18. Interview with the author.

Chapter 13: The Anatomy of Hunger

1. *Encyclopaedia Britannica.*
2. *Thirty Years in the Countryside.*
3. Liang Heng and Judith Shapiro, *Son of the Revolution*, pp. 17–18.
4. Interviews with the author.
5. Emmanuel John Hevi, *An African Student in China*, p. 41.
6. Dr Lee's paper has not been published at the time of writing. It was rejected by a number of academic journals whose editors were unwilling to believe what he reported. For example, Dr. William J. Visek of the *Journal of Nutrition*, published by the American Institute of Nutrition, replied, saying 'there is a lack of verification and quantitative information that can be tested and which satisfies the policy of the *Journal* to provide new information about the science of nutrition in any species. On page 4 your manuscript states that two men would carry 200 kg of muddy earth on their shoulders with a shoulder pole up a slippery slope 100 times per day. This is equal to 440 lbs per trip. That seems unreasonable under any set of conditions.' However Dr. Lee's account is borne out by many other eyewitnesses and is undoubtedly accurate.
7. I interviewed Dr Choedak in 1995 but have taken this from the account of his time in prison reported in John F. Avedon, *In Exile from the Land of Snows*, p. 252.
8. Harry Wu, *Bitter Winds*, p. 102.
9. In fact, Wu Ningkun met Dr Lee in the camps and recalls his first conversation: 'Lucky dog. We had to be brought to this wilderness because Qinghe was packed to bursting. Well, you'd better get back to your labour now. Come see me at the clinic in the evening before the roll call, Professor. My name is Benjamin Lee, but just Lee here, for a Christian name will land you in more trouble.'
10. Zhang Xianliang, *Grass Soup*, p. 82.
11. David Patt, *Strange Liberation: Tibetan Lives in Chinese Hands*, p. 184.
12. John F. Avedon, *In Exile from the Land of Snows*, p. 253.
13. Interview with the author.
14. Interview with the author.
15. Liang Heng and Judith Shapiro, *Son of the Revolution*, p. 17.
16. Steven Mosher, *A Mother's Ordeal*, p. 37.
17. Interviews with the author.
18. Interview with the author.

Chapter 14: Cannibalism

1. Literally, it means 'swop child, make food'.
2. Steven Mosher, *A Mother's Ordeal*, p. 39.
3. The details and quotations in this chapter are taken from Kay Ray Chong, *Cannibalism in China*, unless otherwise stated.
4. There references are taken from the report of the US Congress Commission on the Ukrainian Famine held in Washington and issued in 1988.
5. This was an internal communication but it appears that while the authorities allowed millions to starve to death, they also publicly tried to dissuade people from resorting to cannibalism. Harry Lang, a Western traveller in the Ukraine at the time, noted: 'In the office of a Soviet functionary I saw a poster on the wall which struck my attention. It showed the picture of a mother in distress, with a swollen child at her feet, and over the picture was the inscription: "Eating of Dead Children is Barbarism". The Soviet official explained to me: "We distributed such

posters in hundreds of villages, especially in the Ukraine. We had to."' See Robert Conquest, *Harvest of Sorrow.*
6. The report of the US Congress Commission on the Ukrainian Famine held in Washington and issued in 1988. This extract is from 19 July 1933.
7. Reported by Nicholas D. Kristof in *The New York Times,* January 1993.

Chapter 15: Life in the Cities

1. Interviews with the author.
2. Interviews with the author.
3. Peng Xizhe, 'Demographic Consequences of the Great Leap Forward in China's Provinces', *Population and Development Review,* Vol. 3, No. 4, December 1987, p. 655.
4. Steven Mosher, *A Mother's Ordeal,* p. 32.
5. Tsering Dorje Gashi, *Memoirs of a Graduate of the Peking Institute of National Minorities,* p. 71.
6. Wang Lixin, *The Agricultural Reforms of Anhui—A True Record,* p. 271.
7. Interview with the author.
8. Interview with the author.
9. Interview with the author.
10. Interview with the author.
11. Interviews with the author.
12. Interviews with the author.
13. Nien Cheng is the author of *Life and Death in Shanghai,* the story of her arrest and detention during the Cultural Revolution. This incident, however, comes from an interview.
14. Tsering Dorje Gashi, *Memoirs of a Graduate of the Peking Institute of National Minorities,* p. 76.
15. Steven Mosher, *A Mother's Ordeal,* p. 37.
16. *Far Eastern Economic Review,* 10 November 1960 and 4 December 1962.
17. Interview with the author. Yuan Mu became a senior official and achieved considerable notoriety as the government's spokesman during the Tiananmen demonstrations in 1989.

Chapter 16: Liu Shaoqi Saves the Peasants

1. Ross Terrill, *Mao: A Biography,* p. 292.
2. Liang Heng, *Son of the Revolution,* p. 18.
3. Ding Shu, *Ren Huo.*
4. Interview with the author.
5. Ding Shu, *Ren Huo.*
6. One former senior official told me that Mao was pleased with what he heard and then sent Hu to investigate the famine in Anhui and report on the reforms taking place there. Hu returned with a report which accused Zeng of abandoning Communism. Mao liked this and circulated it, rewarding Hu by promoting him to a senior position in charge of the Party organization in southern Hunan. A biography of Hu claims that Hu's attitudes changed in 1961, after he was sent to supervise agricultural policy changes in Tang county, Hebei province. Furthermore, the Hong Kong magazine *Ming Bao* later carried a story with a more positive view of

his activities in Anhui: 'Twice inspection teams arrived in Anhui to look at the disaster but both times they were turned away. The investigators were confined to local guesthouses and not allowed to meet lower cadres or the masses. Deng and Liu both believed that without firsthand information it would be impossible to deal with Zeng Xisheng so they sent Hu Yaobang at the head of the third team.'

7. Wang Lixin, *Agricultural Reforms of Anhui—A True Record*, p. 279.

8. Li Zhisui, *The Private Life of Chairman Mao*, pp. 377–378.

9. Li Zhisui, *The Private Life of Chairman Mao*, p. 378.

10. Interview.

11. Denis Fred Simon and Merle Goldman (eds.), *Science and Technology in Post Mao China;* Lawrence Schneider, *Learning from Russia: Lysenkoism and the Fate of Genetics in China, 1950–1968;* and Merle Goldman, *China's Intellectuals: Advise and Dissent.*

12. Wu Ningkun, *A Single Tear*, p. 180.

13. Merle Goldman, *China's Intellectuals: Advise and Dissent;* and T. Cheek, Merle Goldman and Carol Lee Hanom, *China's Intellectuals and the State: In Search of a New Relationship.*

14. Wang Lixin, *The Agricultural Reforms of Anhui—A True Record*, p. 280.

15. Li Zhisui, *The Private Life of Chairman Mao*, p. 388.

16. Li Zhisui, *The Private Life of Chairman Mao*, p. 386.

17. Stanley Karnow, *Mao and China*, p. 106.

18. *Far Eastern Economic Review*, various reports in 1962.

19. Uli Frantz, *Deng Xiaoping*, p. 160.

20. Frederick W. Crook (ed.), *Agricultural Statistics of the People's Republic of China, 1949–86.*

21. Richard Baum, *Prelude to Revolution Mao, the Party and the Peasant Question, 1962–66*, pp. 112–113.

22. Interviews.

23. *The Struggle between the Two Roads in China's Countryside.*

24. John Byron and Robert Pack, *The Claws of the Dragon: Kang Sheng*, p. 366.

Chapter 17: Mao's Failure and His Legacy

1. Judith Banister, *China's Changing Population*, quotes this from Liu Guoguang and Wang Xianming, 'An Exploration into the Problems of the Rate and Balance of China's National Economic Development', *Social Sciences*, No. 4, 1980, pp. 254–255.

2. *China: Agriculture to the Year 2000*, p. 18.

3. Vaclav Smil, *The Bad Earth: Environmental Degradation in China*, p. 44.

4. Dan Connell and Dan Gover (eds.), *China: Science Walks on Two Legs*, pp. 45–54.

5. Liu Binyan, *A Higher Kind of Loyalty*, p. 99.

6. Wang Lixin, *The Agricultural Reforms in Anhui—A True Record*, p. 351.

7. When Wan Li returned from the meeting, he allowed some communes to contract out land to production teams but not households. This was first tried in Feixi county, not far from the provincial capital, Hefei, and here each team farmed the land collectively, so that in a village of 150 people, land would be split between four teams. Once the harvest was in, the state's grain would be handed over and the rest divided among the members. One brigade did try the household responsibility system but dropped it after the *People's Daily* published a letter attacking it. The letter caused widespread panic, prompting provincial leaders to summon emergency meetings to reassure the peasants.

8. *China: Agriculture to the Year 2000*, p. 128.

Chapter 18: How Many Died?

1. Judith Banister, *China's Changing Population,* p. 13.
2. Judith Banister, *China's Changing Population,* pp. 2–26.
3. Interview with Chinese officials. The worst fear for droughts and floods was 1954 according to tables produced by the Chinese Central Meteorological Centre. Both 1960 and 1961 had fewer floods and droughts than 1958 which was publicly hailed as an outstanding year.
4. Peng Xizhe, 'Demographic Consequences of the Great Leap Forward in China's Provinces', *Population and Development Review,* Vol. 3, No. 4, December 1987, p. 641.
5. Banister (p. 85) draws on work on Chinese population figures by John S. Aird, Ansley J. Coale and other authorities in the United States.
6. Wang Weizhi, *Contemporary Chinese Population,* edited by Xu Dixin, p. 9.
7. Cong Jin, *China, 1949–1989: The Zig-zag Development Era,* p. 272.
8. Wen Yu, *Disasters of Leftism in China,* p. 280.
9. See also Nicholas R. Lardy, 'The Chinese Economy under Stress, 1958–1965' in *The Cambridge History of China,* Vol. 14, which looks at mortality and compares China's famine with that in the Soviet Union.
10. Daniel Southerland in *Washington Post,* 18 July 1994. Chen Yizi is now President of the Center for Modern China at Princeton University.

Chapter 19: How to Record the Annals of a Place?

1. Yang Jiang, *A Cadre School Life: Six Chapters,* translated by Geremie Barmé.
2. *New York Review of Books,* 27 September 1990.
3. Anne Thurston, *A Chinese Odyssey: The Life and Times of a Chinese Dissident,* pp. 94–95.
4. *The New York Times,* 1980. Wei's autobiographical notes were smuggled out of China and translated by Lee Ta-ling. Reported in *South China Morning Post,* 8 March 1981.
5. Interview.
6. Interview.
7. Interview.
8. Steven Mosher, *A Mother's Ordeal,* p. 84.
9. Steven Mosher, *A Mother's Ordeal,* pp. 34–35.
10. Interview.
11. Loe Goodstadt, *Mao Tse Tung—The Search for Plenty,* p. 121. Here he cites a broadcast on Guangdong Radio of 22 April 1971.
12. Central Committee of the Chinese Communist Party, 'Resolution on Communist Party History, 1949–81.'
13. Zheng Zhengxi (ed.), *How to Record the Annals of a Place.*
14. Zhi Liang, *Hungry Mountain Village.*

Chapter 20: The Western Failure

1. *Starving in Silence: A Report on Famine and Censorship,* p. 3. See also Amartya Sen, *Poverty and Famines,* published in 1981.
2. *The New York Times,* 14 October 1962.
3. *New York World Telegram and Sun,* 25 June 1959.
4. *Time,* 22 August 1960.

5. Harry Schwartz, *The New York Times*, 22 April 1962.
6. *New York Herald Tribune*, 13 September 1961.
7. *China Quarterly*, July–September 1962, quoted in Basil Ashton, Kenneth Hill, Alan Piazza and Robin Zeitz, 'Famine in China, 1958–61', *Population and Development Review*, Vol. 10, No. 4, December 1984, pp. 631–632.
8. *The Times*, 1 January 1963.
9. *The Times*, 18 April 1962.
10. Quoted in Dennis Bloodworth, *Messiah and Mandarins*, p. 154.
11. *Far Eastern Economic Review*, 2 November 1961.
12. Quoted in Basil Ashton, Kenneth Hill, Alan Piazza and Robin Zeitz, 'Famine in China, 1958–61', *Population and Development Review*, Vol. 10, No. 4, December 1984, p. 630.
13. Quoted in Dennis Bloodworth, *The Messiah and the Mandarins*, pp. 154–155.
14. Han Suyin, *My House Has Two Doors*.
15. Interviewed in 1994.
16. *The Times*, 7 March 1961.
17. *Far Eastern Economic Review*, 27 June 1961.
18. See Basil Ashton, Kenneth Hill, Alan Piazza and Robin Zeitz, 'Famine in China, 1958–61', *Population and Development Review*, Vol. 10, No. 4, December 1984; and Richard Walker, *China under Communism — The First Five Years*.
19. *Weekly Post*, 21 January 1961.
20. *Daily Herald*, 22 May 1962.
21. *Daily Telegraph*, 12 February 1961.
22. *The Times*, 15 June 1962.
23. *The Times*, 2 June 1962. The MP was Philip Noel-Baker.
24. *Daily Telegraph*, 10 February 1961.
25. *The Times*, January 1961.
26. *Far Eastern Economic Review*—various reports in 1962.
27. Sartaj Aziz, *Rural Development—Learning from China*.
28. C. K. MacDonald, *Modern China*, p. 45.
29. Gladys Hickman, *Introducing the New China*, p. 21.
30. Haing S. Ngor with Roger Warner, *Surviving the Killing Fields*, p. 401.

Bibliography

Aird, John S., and Coale, Ansley, 'An Analysis of Recent Data on the Population of China', *Population and Development Review*, Vol. 10, No. 5, June 1984.

Alley, Rewi, *China's Hinterland in the Great Leap Forward*, Beijing, New World Press, 1961.

Alley, Rewi, and Burchett, Wilfred, *China: The Quality of Life*, Harmondsworth, Pelican, 1976.

Annual Report of the China International Famine Relief Commission 1925, Beijing, 1926.

Ashton, Basil, Hill, Kenneth, Piazza, Alan and Zeitz, Robin, 'Famine in China, 1958–61', *Population and Development Review*, Vol. 10, No. 4, December 1984.

Avedon, John F., *In Exile from the Land of Snows*, New York, Alfred Knopf, 1979.

Aziz, Sartaj, *Rural Development – Learning from China*, London, Macmillan, 1978.

Bachman, David M., 'Chen Yun and the Chinese Political System', Ph.D. thesis, Institute of East Asian Studies, Berkeley, Ca., 1985.

Banister, Judith, 'An Analysis of Recent Data on the Population of China', *Population and Development Review*, Vol. 10, No. 2, June 1984.

—— *China's Changing Population*, Berkeley, Ca., Stanford University, 1987.

Barker, Randolph, Sinha, Radha, and Rose, Beth (eds.), *The Chinese Agricultural Economy*, Colorado, Westview Press, 1982.

Baum, Richard, *Prelude to Revolution: Mao, the Party and the Peasant Question, 1962–66*, New York, Columbia University Press, 1975.

Bland, J. O. P., *China: The Pity of It*, London, Heinemann, 1932.

Bloodworth, Dennis, *The Messiah and the Mandarins*, London, Weidenfeld and Nicolson, 1982.

Bo Yibo, *Retrospective of Several Big Decisions and Incidents*, Beijing, Central Party School, 1993.

Bonavia, David, *Deng*, Hong Kong, Longman, 1989.

Brown, Lester R., *Who Will Feed China: Wake Up Call for a Small Planet. Worldwatch Environmental Alert*, New York, Norton & Co, 1995.

Brulé, Jean-Pierre, *China Comes of Age*, Harmondsworth, Pelican, 1969.

Buck, John Lossing, *Food and Agriculture in Communist China*, Stanford, Ca., Hoover Institution Publications, 1966.

—— *Land Utilisation in China*, Nanking, Nanking University, 1937.

Buck, Pearl S., *The Good Earth*, London, Methuen, 1931.

Byron, John, and Pack, Robert, *The Claws of the Dragon: Kang Sheng*, New York, Simon & Schuster, 1992.

The Cambridge History of China, Cambridge, Cambridge University Press.

Chailand, Gerard, *The Peasants of North Vietnam*, Harmondsworth, Pelican, 1968.

Chan, Alfred L., 'The Campaign for Agricultural Development in the Great Leap Forward: A Study of Policy-making and Implementation in Liaoning', *China Quarterly*, March 1992.

Chang Jung, *Wild Swans,* New York, Simon & Schuster, 1991.

Cheek, T., Goldman, Merle, and Hanom, Carol Lee, *China's Intellectuals and the State: In Search of a New Relationship,* Harvard, Council on East Asian Studies, Harvard University Press, 1987.

Chen Boda, *A Study of Land Rent in Pre-liberation China,* republished in 1958.

Cheng Min, *Lu Shan Tempest,* Beijing, Unity Publishing House, 1993.

China: Agriculture to the Year 2000, World Bank Country Study, September 1985.

Choedon, D., *Life in the Red Flag People's Commune,* Dharamsala, Information Office of His Holiness the Dalai Lama, 1978.

Chong, Kay Ray, *Cannibalism in China,* Wakefield, NH, Longwood Academic, 1990.

Coleman, David, and Nixson, Frederick, *Economics of Change in Less Developed Countries,* Manchester, University of Manchester Press, 1978.

Cong Jin, *China, 1949–1989: The Zig-zag Development Era,* Henan, Henan People's Publishing House, 1992.

Connell, Dan and Gover, Dan (eds.), *China: Science Walks on Two Legs. A Report from Science for the People,* Avon, Discus Books, 1974.

Conquest, Robert, *Harvest of Sorrow,* Oxford, Oxford University Press, 1986.

Crook, Isobel and David, *Revolution in a Chinese Village – Ten Mile Inn,* London, Routledge and Paul, 1959.

Crook, Frederick W. (ed.), *Agricultural Statistics of the PRC 1949–86,* US Department of Agriculture Economic Research Department.

Dai Qing (ed.), *Changjiang Yimin (Population Transfer on the Yangzi River),* a documentary anthology.

Deng Tuo, *China's History of Disaster Relief,* Shanghai, Commercial Press, 1937.

Denis, Fred Simon, and Goldman, Merle, *Science and Technology in Post-Mao China,* Harvard, Council on East Asian Studies, Harvard University Press, 1989.

Ding Shu, *Ren Huo,* Hong Kong, Nineties Magazine, 1993.

Domes, Jurgen, *Peng Dehuai: The Man and his Image,* Berkeley, Ca., Stanford University Press, 1985.

Ellman, Michael, 'A Note on the Number of 1933 Famine Victims', *Soviet Studies,* 1989.

Fairbank, John K., *China Perceived,* New York, Knopf, 1974.

Fei Xiaotong, *Peasant Life in China. Study of Country Life in the Yangtze Valley,* London, Kegan Paul, 1939.

Forty Years of Work on Nationalities, edited by the Policy Research Office and Economic Affairs Department of the National Minorities Affairs Commission, Beijing, Nationalities House, 1989.

Franz, Uli, *Deng Xiaoping,* trans. Tom Artin, New York, Harcourt Brace Jovanovich, 1988.

Friedman, Edward, Pickowicz, Paul G., and Selden, Mark, *Chinese Village, Socialist State,* New Haven & London, Yale University Press, 1991.

Galbraith, J. K., *A China Passage,* London, André Deutsch, 1973.

Gashi, Tsering Dorje, *New Tibet: The Memoirs of a Graduate of the Peking Institute of National Minorities.* A copy of the unpublished book was made available in Dharamsala, India.

Gelder, Stuart and Roma, *The Timely Rain – Travels in New Tibet,* New York, Monthly Press Review, 1964.

Gittings, John, *A Chinese View of China,* London, BBC Books, 1993.

Goldman, Merle, *China's Intellectuals: Advise and Dissent,* Harvard, Harvard University Press, 1981.

Goodstadt, Leo, *Mao Tse Tung: The Search for Plenty,* London, Longman, 1972.

Gray, Jack, *Rebellions and Revolutions,* Oxford, Oxford University Press, 1990.

Greene, Felix, *A Curtain of Ignorance*, London, Jonathan Cape, 1965.

Grunfeld, Tom, *The Making of Modern Tibet*, White Plains, NY, M. E. Sharpe, 1987.

Gyatso, Jamphel, *The Great Master Panchen*, Beijing, China Popular Literature, 1989.

Haing S. Ngor with Roger Warner, *Surviving the Killing Fields*, London, Chatto & Windus, 1988.

Han Suyin, *Eldest Son. Zhou Enlai and the Making of Modern China, 1898–1976*, London, Jonathan Cape, 1994.

—— *Morning Deluge*, London, Jonathan Cape, 1972.

—— *My House Has Two Doors*, London, Grafton Books, 1960.

—— *Wind in the Tower. Mao Tse Tung and the Chinese Revolution, 1949–76*, London, Jonathan Cape, 1976.

He Bochuan, *China on the Edge*, Berkeley, Ca., Pacific View Press, 1991.

Hevi, Emmanuel John, *An African Student in China*, New York, Praeger, 1963.

Hickman, Gladys, *Introducing the New China*, London, Hodder & Stoughton Education, 1983.

Hinton, William, *Fanshen: A Documentary of Revolution in a Chinese Village*, New York, Monthly Review Press, 1966.

—— *Shenfan*, London, Picador, 1984.

'Historical Change of Land Reform of the CCP', *Rural Institutions and Development*, No. 3, Research Group on Rural Institutions of China.

Hollingworth, Clare, *Mao and the Men Against Him*, London, Jonathan Cape, 1985.

Hsu, Robert C., *Food for 1 Billion: China's Agriculture since 1949*, Colorado, Westview Press, 1982.

Hughes, Richard, *The Chinese Communes*, London, Bodley Head, 1960.

Ingram, Paul, *Tibet: The Facts*, London, The Scientific Buddhist Association, 1990.

Investigation of the Ukrainian Famine 1932–1933. US Congressional Commission on the Ukrainian Famine, Washington, 1988.

Joravsky, David, *The Lysenko Affair*, Ann Arbor, Mi., University of Chicago Press, 1970.

Kane, Penny, *Famine in China, 1959–61. Demographic and Social Implications*, Basingstoke, Macmillan, 1988.

Karnow, Stanley, *Mao and China – Inside China's Cultural Revolution*, London, Macmillan, 1973.

Khrushchev, Nikita Sergeevich, *Khrushchev Remembers: The Last Testament*, trans. and ed. Strobe Talbott, London, André Deutsch, 1974.

Kitching, Gavin, *Development and Underdevelopment in Historical Perspective*, London, Open University Press, 1989.

Klochko, Mikhail, *Soviet Scientist in China*, London, Hollis & Carter, 1964.

Ladany, Laszlo, *The Communist Party of China and Marxism, 1921–1985: A Self-Portrait*, London, C. Hurst Co., 1988.

Li Rui, *A True Account of the Lushan Meeting*, Henan, Henan People's Publishing House, 1994.

Li Zhisui, *The Private Life of Chairman Mao. The Memoirs of Mao's Personal Physician*, trans. Professor Tai Hung-chao with the editorial assistance of Anne F. Thurston, New York, Random House, 1994.

Liang Heng and Shapiro, Judith, *Son of the Revolution*, London, Chatto & Windus, 1983.

Lindquist, Sven, *China in Crisis*, trans. Sylvia Clayton, London, Faber & Faber, 1963.

Liu Binyan, *A Higher Kind of Loyalty*, New York, Pantheon Books, 1990.

Luo Fu, *The First Soviet in China*.

McDonald, C. K., *Modern China*, Oxford, Basil Blackwell, 1988.

MacFarquhar, Roderick, *The Origins of the Cultural Revolution. The Great Leap Forward, 1958–60*, Oxford, Oxford University Press, 1983.

MacFarquhar, Roderick, Cheek, Timothy, and Wu, Eugene (eds.), *The Secret Speeches of Chairman Mao. From the 100 Flowers to the Great Leap Forward*, Harvard, Harvard University Press, 1987.

Mallory, Walter H., *China Land of Famine*, New York, American Geographical Society, 1926.

Mao Zedong, *Report of an Investigation of the Peasant Movement in Hunan*, 1927.

Medvedev, Zhores A., *The Rise and Fall of T. D. Lysenko*, trans. Michael Wermner, New York, Columbia University Press, 1969.

Mehnert, Klaus, *Peking and Moscow*, London, Weidenfeld and Nicolson, 1963.

Mosher, Steven, *China Misperceived. American Illusions and Chinese Reality*, New York, Basic Books, 1990.

—— *A Mother's Ordeal. One Woman's Fight Against China's One-child Policy. The story of Chi An*, Boston, Little, Brown, 1994.

Myrdal, Jan, and Hessle, Gun, *China: The Revolution Continues*, trans. P. B. Austin, New York, Pantheon, 1970.

Nathan, Andrew James, *A History of the China International Famine Relief Commission*, Harvard, Harvest East Asia monographs, Harvard University Press, 1965.

Ni Jianzhong and Xin Xiangyang, *South and North History: Will China Fall Apart?* People's China Press, 1993.

Nien Cheng, *Life and Death in Shanghai*, London, Grafton Books, 1986.

Norbu, Dawa, *Red Star over Tibet*, Oxford, Oxford Oriental Press, 1987.

Norton, A. K., *China and the Powers*.

Nove, Alex, *An Economic History of the U.S.S.R.*, Harmondsworth, Pelican, 1980.

Nuclear Weapons and Nuclear Waste on the Tibetan Plateau, a report by the International Campaign for Tibet, April 1993.

Pacific Viewpoint, Vol. 3, No. 2, September 1962.

Patt, David, *A Strange Liberation: Tibetan Lives in Chinese Hands*, Ithaca, New York, Snow Lion Publications, 1992.

Peck, Graham, *Two Kinds of Time*, Boston, Houghton Mifflin, 1967.

Peng Xizhe, 'Demographic Consequences of the Great Leap Forward in China's Provinces', *Population and Development Review*, Vol. 3, No. 4, December 1987.

Perkins, Dwight H., *Agricultural Development in China, 1368–1969*, Chicago, Aldine, 1969.

Petition addressed to the CCP Central Secretariat, the National People's Congress, and the State Council from Tibetan cadres in Gannan Tibetan Autonomous District. Unpublished.

Piazza, Alan, *Westview Special Studies in China. Food Consumption and Nutritional Status in the PRC*, Berkeley, Ca., Stanford University Press, 1986.

Potter, Jack and Sulamith Heins, *China's Peasants – The Anthropology of a Revolution*, Cambridge, Cambridge University Press, 1990.

Pu Ning, *Red in Tooth and Claw: 26 Years in Communist Chinese Prisons*, New York, Grove Press, 1994.

Report of China International Famine Relief Commission, American Geographical Society, 1926.

Report of the Peking United International Famine Relief Committee, Beijing, 1922.

Schneider, Lawrence, *Learning from Russia: Lysenkoism and the Fate of Genetics in China, 1950–1986*, White Plains, NY, M. E. Sharpe, 1987.

Schram, Stuart, *Mao*, Harmondsworth, Pelican, 1966.

Shambaugh, David, *The Making of a Premier: Zhao Ziyang's Provincial Career*, Colorado, Westview Press, 1984.

Shen Shi (ed.), *Hundred Years of Glory – Memoirs of Major Events of the PRC*.

Simon, Denis Fred, and Goldman, Merle (eds.), *Science and Technology in Post-Mao China*, Harvard, Harvard University Press, 1989.

Smil, Vaclav, *The Bad Earth: Environmental Degradation in China*, London, Zed Press, 1983.

Snow, Edgar, *The Other Side of the River: Red China Today*, New York, Random House, 1961.

——— *Red Star over China*, London, Gollancz, 1937.

Spence, Jonathan D., *The Search for Modern China*, London, Hutchinson, 1990.

Starving in Silence: A Report on Famine and Censorship, London, Article 19, 1990.

Strong, Anna Louise, *China's Fight for Grain*, Beijing, New World Press, 1963.

The Struggle between the Two Roads in China's Countryside, Beijing, Foreign Languages Press, 23 November 1967.

Su Luozheng, *July Storm – The Inside Story of the Lushan Conference*, Hainan Island, Hainan Photographic and Art Publishing House, 1994.

Su Xiaokang, *Utopia*, Hong Kong, Shanghai Book Co., 1989.

Tawney, R. H., *Chinese Agriculture and Industry*, London, Allen & Unwin, 1929.

——— *Land and Labour in China*, London, George Allen & Unwin, 1932.

Teiwes, Frederick C., *Politics and Purges in China. Rectification and the Decline of Party Norms, 1950–1965*, White Plains, NY, M. E. Sharpe, 1979.

Terrill, Ross, *Mao: A Biography*, New York, Simon & Schuster, 1980.

They Are Creating Miracles, Beijing, Foreign Languages Press, 1960.

Thirty Years in the Countryside – True Records of the Economic and Social Development in the Fengyang Agricultural Region, Research Centre for Rural Development.

'The Three Gorges Dam in China', *Human Rights Watch/Asia*, Vol. 7, No. 2, February 1995.

Thurston, Anne, *A Chinese Odyssey: The Life and Times of a Chinese Dissident*, New York, Charles Scribner & Sons, 1991.

Tibet under Chinese Communist Rule. A Compilation of Refugee Statements 1958–1975, Dharamsala, Information Office of the Dalai Lama, 1976.

Tong Yongming (comp.), *Land Revolution Report, 1927–1937*, 1982.

Wang Lixin, *Agricultural Reforms of Anhui – A True Record*, Beijing, Unity Publishing House, 1993.

Wang Weizhi, *Contemporary Chinese Population*, edited by Xu Dixin, Beijing, China Social Sciences Publishing House, 1988.

Wen Yu, *Disasters of Leftism in China*, Jiaohua Publishing House, 1993.

White, Theodore H., *In Search of History*, New York, Harper & Row, 1978.

Wilson, Dick, and Grenier, Matthew, *Chinese Communism*, London, Paladin, 1992.

Winfield, G. E., *China: The Land and the People*, New York, Sloane, 1950.

Wu, Harry Hongda, *Laogai: The Chinese Gulag*, Colorado, Westview Press, 1992.

Wu, Harry Hongda and Wakeman, Carolyn, *Bitter Winds. A Memoir of My Years in China's Gulag*, New York, John Wiley, 1994.

Wu Ningkun, *A Single Tear*, New York, Atlantic Monthly Press, 1993.

Xu Yi, *Huang Huo*, 1979 (unpublished).

Yang Jiang, *A Cadre School Life: Six Chapters*, trans. Geremie Barmé, Hong Kong, Joint Publishing Co., 1982.

Yang Zhongmei, *Hu Yaobang*, White Plains, NY, M. E. Sharpe, 1988.

Yi Shu, '1,000 Li Hunger', *Kaifang*, August 1994.

Zhang Xianliang, *Grass Soup*, trans. Martha Avery, London, Secker & Warburg, 1994.

Zhang Yigong, *The Story of Criminal Li Tongzhong*, Zhengzhou, Zhongyuan Peasant Publishing House, 1986.

Zhao Xiaomin (comp.), *History of Land Reform in China, 1921–1949*, Beijing, People's Publishing House, 1990.

Zheng Zhengxi (ed.), *How to Record the Annals of a Place.* One of a series of books called *Fanzhi Wenku (Collections of Annals),* first edition published by Guangxi People's Publishing House, December 1989.

Zhi Liang, *Hungry Mountain Village,* Guangxi, Li Jiang House, 1994.

Zhou Libo, *Great Changes in a Mountain Village.*, trans. Derek Bryan, Foreign Languages Press, Beijing, 1961.

Zhou Yueli, *Zeng Xisheng Biography,* unpublished.

Index